CONTENTS

COPYRIGHT ACKNOWLEDGEMENTS

alternative paradigm', which first appeared in J. C. Watson, R. N. Goldman and M. S. Warner (eds), *Client-centered and Experiential Psychotherapy in the Twenty-first Century: Advances in Theory, Research, and Practice*, Ross-on-Wye: PCCS Books, 2002, pp. 258–77. Reprinted with the kind permission of PCCS Books and Professor Arthur C. Bohart.

Chapter 20 is a much-extended version of ' "Psy" research beyond late-modernity: towards praxis-congruent research', *Psychotherapy and Politics International*, 8 (1), 2010, pp. 13–20.

Chapter 21 is previously unpublished, although written in 1996. Two other lengthy essays I wrote on Groddeck, drawing on similar background material, appeared as House 1997b; and as 'Precursor of postmodernity: the phenomenon of Georg Groddeck' (Chapter 9) in my *Therapy Beyond Modernity*, London: Karnac Books, 2003, pp. 175–98.

Chapter 22 first appeared in *Self and Society*, 25 (2), 1997, pp. 31–5. Original copyright.

Chapter 23 first appeared in *Ipnosis* magazine, 4, 2001, pp. 4–6. Original copyright.

Chapter 24 is an extended piece that first appeared *in Self and Society*, 36 (2), 2008, pp. 44–50. Original copyright.

THE SAFE DEEP BLACK HOLE

I am trapped in a hole, a deep black hole.
It was the safest place for me, you understand?
In the dark forest of all monsters,
in all directions I would go,
I would meet with a monster, and another,
and another.
How did I learn to fight some of them?
My feet and hands are experts in the matter.
But the last one I met was just too big for me.
I did not even try to fight him.
I jumped in a hole too small for the monster,
But now too high to climb out of.
I am trapped in the black hole.
I have no hope, no food, but it is safe.

Absolutely Safe

Sylvie Hétu

FOREWORD

Denis Postle

This book explores some of the political, psychological and spiritual territory of working with the human condition. The passion and intensity of the lived experience that shapes it might suggest that this is an heroic, even grandiose endeavour. Not so. It amounts to an overview, but one driven by insider experience. Again and again the author, a long-standing inhabitant of the UK psy world, plunges us into the intestinal nether regions of counselling and psychotherapy. What he finds reveals more often and more extensively than might be expected from such a field, collusion and damaging contradiction. Vested interests – convinced that clients must be protected – but failing to notice that the protection is from them as practitioners and the students they teach; year by year as courses get longer – the walled gardens of professionalised therapy expertise get higher, designed to exclude the 'unqualified'; and as the most determined of the proprietors of these gated communities now cosy up to the UK Health Professions Council, membership of them seems likely to become a form of imprisonment.

In a variety of ways Richard House unpicks, unravels, deconstructs and confronts this social architecture of the counselling and psychotherapy fields. He shows that the ethical engineering on which these edifices are often built looks to be the outcome of intense tribal rivalries and loyalty to fiefdoms concerned with market share and status. Not a finding that reflects well on therapies that purport to have the intricate nuances of client welfare at their heart. Perhaps we do need to be protected from them.

And yet ways of working with the human condition that do not display such an avid embrace of, and belief in, the value of hierarchical dominance are possible. A chapter on the Independent Practitioners Network (IPN), a long-standing example of peer-to-peer civic accountability free of coercive participation, demonstrates the relevance to the field of aggregations of individual practitioners based on shared commons of principles and procedures. And critically, where dominance, coercion and duress are challenged.

Threaded through Richard House's texts is the notion that the 'Empire' of bullying and duress is as much within us as out there. And yet proponents of the academicisation and bureaucratisation of psychotherapy, counselling and psychoanalysis continue to be eager to integrate such human condition work with what amounts to a 'warfare state' of control and surveillance. As chapter after chapter here shows, this seems to indicate denial or ignorance of a political gestalt which, unless diligently confronted, knits our work with clients into the power relations of the day.

This book collects together a series of devastating layers of critique examining these topics and other events and deficiencies of the psy field. It is with some pleasure that I imagine these accounts may have one or two of the more avid professionalisers hopping about.

We are a poem that cannot be read.
                    Hölderlin

INTRODUCTION

Mapping a Journey Towards
a 'Post-Therapy Era'

In compiling this book my aim has been several-fold: first, to describe a unique path of personal and professional development on my healthily idiosyncratic journey to becoming a therapy practitioner, or a 'worker with the human condition' (as I may soon legally have to call myself); secondly, to show how the modern institution of counselling and psychotherapy is just one of the sites in modern culture playing host to a veritable 'paradigm war' that is taking place between the conservative forces of a materialistic modernity on the one hand, and a radical trans- or postmodernity, on the other; and thirdly, how the professionalisation of the therapy world is a process full of tensions, contradictions – and multiple and compelling *contra*indications.

My five part-titles summarise succinctly the unfolding path that the reader who reads sequentially will be taking – namely:

I. Intimations of disquiet about 'professionalised' therapy
II. Emergent postmodern and 'new paradigm' perspectives
III. Direct challenges to the professionalisation of therapy and counselling
IV. Radical 'trans-modern' perspectives on training and research
V. Making what we want: towards practitionership in a post-therapy era

As will be clear from this listing, a number of key themes are threaded throughout the book – including: the prevailing paradigm of 'modernity', and its trans- or postmodern critique; the close epistemological examination of the nature of relational therapeutic work; the question of professionalisation, and whether it is appropriate in the psy field; the internal 'politics' of the field; questions of training and research in critical trans-modern perspective; and last but not least, an engagement with the *realpolitik* of the (possibly pending) Health Professions Council regulation of Britain's psy field, and the impact such regulation might well have upon the configuration of the field as a whole.

The book is a rather gargantuan 140,000 words long; and I fully expect (and perhaps even recommend) that the book is very much treated as a 'reader' rather than necessarily a sequential cover-to-cover read (thought it has certainly been compiled in such a way as to make the latter at least possible). In order to assist the reader on what might at times be a rather bumpy reading journey, I introduce each chapter with a footnoted contextualising commentary on the chapter that follows. The material in the book also covers writings from the period 1995 to 2010, so there is inevitably some unevenness in the text – though I have carefully gone through the whole book and rendered the style as consistent as possible, within the constraints of retaining the integrity of the individual pieces as originally published.

One novel feature of the book is its use of the extended and discursive *review essay* as a means of engaging in an alive and interesting way with key issues in the field. Ever since I started writing in the field in the early 1990s, I have been drawn to the review-essay form; and at the last count I have probably written between 20 and 25 since 1995. I leave the reader to decide whether the review-essay form works in a book of this kind, as there are seven (out of 24 chapters) in the book. For similar reasons, there are also two extensive review *commentaries*, in which I was invited to write a commentary on the papers in a journal special issue; and again, I hope this works well as an engaging medium for encouraging critical reflection.

I hope that the book's title doesn't suggest that this is yet another crude 'anti-therapy' book, for nothing could be further from the truth. On the contrary, it is precisely because I care so passionately for the cultural and individual importance of healing work (and I do see therapy as a form of healing) that I am attempting to retrieve what is best in such work from what I see as the pernicious and ultimately deadening forces of institutional professionalisation; credentialism and careerism; audit-culture obsessions with 'evidence-based practice'; and psychopathologising practices more generally that are uncritically caught up in what, some quarter-century ago, Rob Woolfolk and Frank Richardson called 'the ideology of modernity'.

In some cases I have taken the opportunity in the book to publish far more lengthy chapters than were able to be published in the original journal versions (my first drafts of commissioned papers are nearly always much longer than the required length, so that sometimes [err – very often] quite drastic pruning and discarding of text was needed for many of the originally published pieces). Where this is the case, it is mentioned clearly in the Copyright Acknowledgements.

The book has also given me the opportunity to make available to a wider readership previously published writings that have appeared in somewhat obscure places, and yet which are, in my view, of a standard comparable to those chapters that originally appeared in peer-reviewed journals.

There is inevitably some repetition and possibly unnevenness in the book, although I have striven to keep this to an absolute minimum. But in terms of the way the book will likely be read, as a 'reader' to be dipped into rather than as a text that must be read as an indissolubly sequential whole, such occasional repetition is perhaps far less of a problem than would be the case, were this a different kind of book.

By way of acknowledgement, I would first like to thank my remarkable wife Sylvie for her extraordinary forebearance as this book took over a major chunk of our all-too-rare summer holiday together. I would also like to thank my many colleagues and friends in the Independent Practitioners Network and in the Alliance for Counselling and Psychotherapy Against State Regulation for their colleagueship and multiple sources of inspiration. Several of my long-standing peer colleagues in the IPN deserve a special mention – Grace Lindsay Cook, Tony Donaghy, Irene Galant, Guy Gladsone, Jill Hall, Juliet Lamont, Arthur Musgrave, Denis Postle and Maggie Taraz.

More specifically still, I would like to thank my friend and peer IPN colleague of over 15 years' standing, Denis Postle, who, through his extraordinary websites, articles and several books, has probably done more than any other individual on the planet to bring the many vicissitudes of the professionalising mentality in the psychological therapies to public notice. I am truly honoured that he has written the foreword to the book. I would also like to thank both Denis and Art Bohart for allowing me to reproduce chapters which they originally co-wrote with me.

The director of the Research Centre for Therapeutic Education at Roehampton University (where I work), Professor Del Loewenthal, deserves a very special mention for the way in which he has created a learning-community milieu in the Academy where the kinds of critical ideas in this book can be openly discussed and explored.

I would also like to thank my most eminent dust-jacket endorsers – the Chair of the UKCP, Andrew Samuels, Professors Del Loewenthal, Ian Parker and Brian Thorne, and John Heron and Simona Revelli. I am again truly honoured that people in our field of such stature, and whose work I admire so much, have felt able to put their name to favourable comments about the book.

And last but by no means least: Heart-felt thanks to Pete Sanders and Maggie Taylor-Sanders, who simply *are* PCCS Books ... and in particular for the way in which they leave their writers free in an enabling, high-trust environment, rather than getting into the over-controlling and over-fussy ways that at least some mainstream publishers indulge in. They are a huge credit to independent publishing, and long may high-quality counselling and therapy books with a critical bent continue to cascade from their presses. And with that, you, the reader, are about to find out whether the present book warrants such a favourable descriptor. I hope you enjoy it, and are suitably and productively provoked by it; for as the great William Blake wrote, 'Without contraries is no progression'!

I dedicate this book, first, to my daughter Shanice, who inadvertently teaches all those around her about fully engaging with life; and to Richard Mowbray, whose extraordinary book *The Case Against Psychotherapy Registration* (1995) has done so much to seed the kinds of radical counter-cultural ideas about therapy practitionership and professionalisation that are at the heart of this book.

PART I

Intimations of Disquiet about 'Professionalised' Therapy

CHAPTER 1

The Be-coming of a Therapist: Experiential learning, self-education and the personal/professional nexus

THE 'STATE OF PRACTITIONER DEVELOPMENT WE'RE IN'

Let us search... for an epistemology of practice implicit in the artistic, intuitive processes which some practitioners do bring to situations of uncertainty, instability, uniqueness, and value conflict.
(Schön 1983: 49)

In this first chapter I present discursive retrospective reflections on my own particular 'journey' as a developing counselling practitioner, as a vehicle for generating some more general propositions about the future of practitioner development in what I maintain is an emerging 'trans-' or 'postmodern' future for our field (e.g. House 2003a). As I have discussed at length elsewhere (ibid.: 277–80; 305–7), recent trends towards the institutional professionalisation of the therapy field are fraught with difficulty and contradiction, and for a whole host of complex interrelated reasons. Not least, 'modernist' accountability structures which claim (or pretend) somehow to guarantee quality of therapy practice are shot through with internal contradictions, to such an extent that they can routinely bring about the very opposite of their professed intention (e.g. House 2009).

To take just one highly prescient example, in tandem with the inexorable rise of Cognitive Behaviour Therapy within the National Health Service (House and Loewenthal 2008a, b; Loewenthal and House 2010), we are now seeing the ascendancy of the notion of (allegedly articulatable) 'competencies', as a vehicle for 'delivering' the regulation of therapy in the UK (see Denis Postle's 'Ipnosis' website at http://ipnosis.postle.net/) – the assumption being that it is somehow possible to specify in a measurable, assessable form what

---

This first version of this chapter was written in 1999 as Chapter 1 of my book that was to become *Therapy Beyond Modernity* (2003a). However, in the event the chapter hit the cutting-room floor as the book came out many thousands of words over the word limit. I later updated it for the *British Journal of Guidance and Counselling*, where it was published in 2008. This is a very slightly edited version of the latter paper.

the main requisite competencies are that define the practice of psychotherapy and counselling. Such an assumption implicitly (or sometimes not so implicitly) treats therapy as *commodity* – that is, as a positivistic, utilitarian enterprise that is formulaicly measurable, capturable and definable (without remainder) by sense-data and experience, able to be rationally planned and controllable: in other words, a therapeutic *technology* that becomes a means for controlling and manipulating subjectivity, rather one that is enabling of human and spiritual potential development. Yet what if that which is most important in, and the central defining feature of, successful therapy is crucially and intrinsically beyond positivistic specification, beyond the rationalising instinct of the modernist mentality? – as the likes of Bion, (the later) Rogers, Winnicott, Jung, (Jerome) Frank, (Robert) Sardello and whole host of other giants of therapy's history would argue?

What I am proposing here is a case for practitioner development which is consistent with a view of therapy that is what I term 'trans-modern' – in the sense that it incorporates, yet moves crucially beyond, the ideology of Late Modernity and all that goes with it. Such a case will, first, need to challenge head on the so-called 'surveillance and audit culture' and its poisonous side-kick, the regime of 'New Public Management' (e.g. Power 1997; Cooper 2001; *Parallax* 2004; House 2007a) that is arguably doing such untold damage in modern culture in general, and in the therapy and education worlds in particular (witness, for example, the burgeoning hegemony of so-called 'evidence-based' and 'empirically validated' practice – e.g. Bryceland and Stam 2005; Bohart and House 2008; House and Bohart 2008; King and Moutsou 2010). Second, it will need to show just how it is essential, for the preservation of the therapy 'baby' from the professionalising 'bathwater', that paths to practitioner development are kept open, pluralistic and innovative rather than controlled, specified and 'officially' accredited and certified (possibly even by the state, if the crude version of Health Professions Council regulation is eventually imposed in Britain). In the course of this discussion I will show how the British Independent Practitioners Network is an early prototype of the kind of practitioner development that is apposite in a postmodern, 'post-professional' world in which the need for 'New Paradigm' thinking and being is becoming increasingly urgent, as the cultural and environmental degeneracy of Late Modernity threatens to engulf us all.

First I will present a personal description of my own particular path to practitionership, in the course of which I will illustrate the core themes of 'professionalisation and its discontents' about which I have written at length elsewhere (House and Totton 1997/2011; Bates and House 2003; House 2003a). The recounting of this vocational story within a personal and a

cultural context is important, not least, because 'journeys' like this one have
been becoming increasingly rare as our field becomes 'sown up' by the mono-
culturally inclined professional bodies and bureaucracies which aspire to
controlling the richly fertile heritage which is Britain's admirable therapeutic
legacy (Gladstone 1997; Postle 1997). Gladstone's trenchant warnings of
over a decade ago regarding the harm being done to the field's levels of
creativity and innovative spirit are, if anything, even more relevant today.
He presciently wrote:

> [B]ecoming a practitioner is an idiosyncratic process that escapes
> the marker-driven logic and production lines of the institutionalised
> therapy training industry now emerging.... [T]he route to
> competence as a therapist passes through vagaries and vicissitudes
> than can not be legislated for.... We can now look forward to the
> next generation of counsellors..., hatched at carefully conserved
> factory farms from which they will appear bagged BAC/UKCP/
> BPC/BPS. This will be the kiss of death for the evolution of creative
> praxis.... Bureaucratic, academic and commercial structures are
> variously antagonistic to the making of a therapist and will jointly
> further the corruption of the training market.
>   (Gladstone 1997: 171, 173−4, 185)

This chapter also affords the welcome opportunity to write up in detail the
fascinating history of the British human potential movement's reputable
and principled struggle through the 1990s and early twenty-first century
against didactic regulation, from the standpoint of someone who has been
centrally involved in that oppositional process.

A PERSONAL JOURNEY TOWARDS PRACTITIONERSHIP

> What is needed... is a broader notion of inquiry than the pursuit of
> knowledge of preexistent reality... including room for the basic idea
> that inquiry need not follow existing ideas of what it means to engage
> in inquiry.
>   (Roger P. Mourad 1997: 88, 89)

I locate my own practitioner development as part of a lineage that is traceable
back to a series of early radical anti-regulation/pro-pluralism literature
contributions, appearing predominantly in the humanistic journal *Self and
Society* (Heron's brilliant 1990 article is seminal); through the two National

Conferences on the Dynamics of Accreditation in the early 1990s, in which I was an active participant, and the Norwich Group Process Group originally led by Robin Shohet; to the founding of the Independent Therapists Network (now the Independent Practitioners Network) in 1994; and thence to the publication of Richard Mowbray's scholarly and seminal work, *The Case Against Psychotherapy Registration* in 1995 (see Chapter 13, this volume), and of the widely acclaimed anthologies *Implausible Professions* (House and Totton 1997/2011) and *Ethically Challenged Professions* (Bates and House 2003). (Full documentation of this substantial literature can be found in House 2003a.)

Beginnings: Open 'encounter' in 'pre-professional' days

I had always had a strong lay interest in psychology, and had by the mid-1980s amassed quite a collection of psychology books. Around that time I noticed a course on 'Post-Freudian and Post-Jungian Psychology' being advertised at the local adult education centre, and so I booked up. The course leader was Tony Storey, who was later to become my first counselling trainer on the Cambridge University Board of Extra-Mural Studies three-year course in Counselling and Groupwork.

Around that time I was told about a weekend 'encounter' group, which I was strongly encouraged to try, which I duly did – and which act proved to be the start of an extraordinary experiential learning process which was to last for the next 4–5 years, and the effects of which will always remain with me, both personally and professionally. I quite quickly settled into the 'rhythm' of the encounter-group experience, and attended some 35 full-weekend groups between 1986 and 1991.

If I am ever asked what has made the greatest contribution to whatever abilities I might possess as a practitioner, my reply is always instant and unambiguous: 'Jill and Tony's weekends' (though I also have sympathy with the view that effective therapists are far more born than made – House 1996a). A good number of the participants in these groups went on to become practising therapists themselves: all entered upòn a profound self-development journey, out of which, almost *as a by-product of the experience*, we 'found our way into' working with clients. This is a centrally humanistic, experiential approach to training which has almost become extinct in these assessment-obsessed days of didactic professionalisation, where, seemingly, people decide that they want to be 'career' therapists and only *then* train to be one, rather than their practitionerhood emerging organically from a personal development path. Gladstone (1995: 15) has similarly written about what he terms the 'apprenticeship model' of practitioner development, in which 'becoming a therapist is a personally transmitted craft for which no amount of academic course work can substitute' (see also Gladstone 1997, quoted earlier).

The Halls' encounter groups were open, freeing experiences, and I have an abiding sense of a strong 'community' dimension that the weekends succeeded in creating and nurturing. Of course there were 'transferences' towards the group leaders, but Jill and Tony Hall worked very openly and demystifyingly with these processes, which for me was an excellent model of practice from which I learnt a great deal about simply and *ordinarily* (Lomas 1981) being with others with 'presence', and relating from a place of relative openness and mutual respect.

In terms of professionalisation, the question of credentials never even crossed my mind for one moment. I had been fortunate enough to find an enormously valuable therapeutic experience right on my doorstep, and it clearly did not matter to me whether Jill and Tony had formal 'credentials' for what they were doing. I realise now that, without being aware of the process at the time, I was simply trusting my own discernment about whether this was a therapeutic experience in which I wanted to partake. Indeed, had the ideology of 'credentialisation' been paramount in the therapy culture at that time, I think it would have greatly complicated and interfered with my own authentic decision-making process and capacity for discernment – 'There is absolutely no evidence that emotional distress necessarily implies incompetence or an inability to judge what is helping or hurting in an attempt to alleviate that distress' (Dawes, quoted in Mowbray 1997: 33).

Questions (and some uncomfortable answers) about training

I referred earlier to my first training in counselling under the tutorship of Tony Storey. Tony was quite a maverick, independent-minded character – and often quite inspirational; and the so-called 'skin' model of carefully designed and explicitly contracted 'here-and-now' groupwork, which constituted the core of his training practice, was again an extremely rewarding personal development experience, as well as an excellent preparation for the often raw immediacy of the therapeutic encounter. I also did a four-year training (1991–5) in body-oriented psychotherapy with the then Midsummer Training in Cambridge, with Margaret Dyson as principal trainer. It was during this training that I was to begin to get a taste of things to come, in terms of the increasingly obsessional preoccupation with accreditation, stringent regulations about personal 'training' therapy, and so on.

The therapy field was changing from the open, 'pre-professional' milieu in which I was 'schooled', towards a predominantly (fear-driven?) preoccupation with meeting externally imposed 'standards' of training –

with most of my training colleagues seeming to exhibit a creeping but anaesthetising apathy, which in turn fostered a sense of unchallengeable inevitability about the whole credentialisation process. This was one aspect of a far wider cultural process that really took root in the early 1990s – 'the audit society' (Power 1997; Cooper 2001; House 2005b, 2007) and its accompanying accoutrements of the so-called 'New Public Management', with its quite unparalleled obsession with accountability, evidence and 'performance'.

Meanwhile, my own disquiet was being deepened through my involvement with the Norwich Group Process Group and the two National Conferences on the Dynamics of Accreditation (1991–2), which the Group organised. Yet colleagues were inhabiting a close-to-intolerable position, as the professionalising bandwagon gained momentum: for if we ignored the seeming inexorability of regulation, then ('grandparent' clauses excepted), it might be literally illegal for us to practise; yet by acquiescing in the face of these cultural pressures, we would have done ourselves a kind of inauthentic 'soul violence'.

The Norwich Group Process Group and the Dynamics of Accreditation, 1990–2

The Group Process Group was an experiential group that met regularly to explore the dynamics of the accreditation process. Initially, the Group met every month or so, for a day at a time, and we engaged Robin Shohet to facilitate the group. Before long, Robin became a peer member of the group, in which a prominent role was taken by Jill Hall. The original intention was to devise an alternative, specifically *humanistic* accreditation model for group facilitation and therapeutic practice which could in some sense be recognised or validated by the Norwich Collective (a self-directing and mutually-supporting group of therapists in Norwich that met for many years on a regular basis).

After meeting for well over a year, the group eventually decided to organise a national conference on the dynamics of accreditation. Two conferences were held in which (now Emeritus Professor) Brian Thorne and group consultant David Wasdell played a leading design and facilitation role. A hundred practitioners from all over Britain attended both events combined, and within a few years, at least some of those faces were to become familiar colleagues, with the inauguration of the Independent Therapists Network in 1994 (see below). These were certainly exciting, heady times for all of us.

On my psychotherapy training, my challenges to the didactic accreditation process were usually listened to politely and patiently by my trainers – but there wasn't much energy in my training group for looking deeply into the dynamics of accreditation, or for challenging the fundamental rationale for statutory regulation. The institutional 'madness' seemed to be infecting everyone in the therapy world: not least, the trainers, who seemed to be continually changing the requirements and boundaries of their trainings in mid-stream – much to the understandable chagrin of their long-suffering trainees.

One major conflict in my training came about over the question of my personal 'training' therapy. I had been working with an accredited body psychotherapist for 75-minute sessions fortnightly for three years, when my trainers said that I must do one year's twice-weekly therapy to obtain the training's diploma – thus bringing the dynamics around accreditation into clear and uncomfortable focus. My then therapist took exception to the implication that the quality of the work we were doing was somehow inferior, and an exchange of difficult correspondence ensued between him and my trainers. Despite outlining the arguments and research challenging the view that therapy should be of a certain frequency to be effective, I eventually gave up my (much-valued) therapy with my existing therapist (who lived 150 miles away), and entered twice-weekly psychoanalytic therapy for two more years. I now wish I had been sufficiently strong to put my own therapy experience before my fear of missing out on a course credential. Since that time, I have heard of a number of cases where gifted, experienced practitioners, non-accredited on principle, have lost clients, often in distressing circumstances for all concerned, because the latters' training organisations insisted that the client must work with an institutionally registered practitioner. Those responsible for perpetrating such abuse in the name of 'standards' surely have a great deal to answer for.

I had begun working as a counsellor in a voluntary agency in 1990, and before long I was well established in several local doctors' surgeries as a GP counsellor, and with the luxury of doing sometimes long-term therapeutic work in that setting. From a vocational viewpoint, I had been very fortunate to become established just before the accreditation 'stampede' got into full swing. I was therefore able to establish myself in the field without having to engage in the credentialised 'hoop-jumping' which those who followed me into the field soon afterwards had to endure. Latterly I did a great deal of one-to-one supervision, founded a private practice, became group supervisor for a Westminster Pastoral Foundation affiliate, co-facilitated many men's and mixed experiential groups, tutored on university counselling courses – and spent a lot of time writing papers and letters for therapy journals.

The founding and growth of the Independent Therapists (later, Practitioners) Network (IPN), 1994

When, in early 1994, I read an interesting letter in *Self and Society* (Totton 1994), I had no intimation that this tentative proposal for a 'Self- and Peer-Accredited Therapists Network' would, within a few years, have given birth to a pluralistic nationwide network of therapy practitioners. About sixty practitioners attended the ITN's inaugural conference at the Open Centre, London, on the 19 November 1994; and since then I have been a member of the 'Leonard Piper' IPN practitioner group, with seven therapists who meet for a day every 4–5 weeks to witness, validate, support and challenge each others' work. We have implemented a rigorous self and peer assessment (SAPA) process (see Lamont and Spencer 1997), through which we have all 'graduated', but not without some considerable difficulty for several of us – which in turn gives the lie to the view that such self and peer monitoring procedures are necessarily collusive, and therefore inferior or procedurally invalid. I discuss the IPN in more detail later in the book (e.g. see below, and Chapter 16, this volume).

The publication of Richard Mowbray's seminal *Case Against Psychotherapy Registration*, 1995

Hot on the heels of the first ITN conference 'gathering' (as our regular weekend meetings soon came to be called), and after a number of false dawns, Richard Mowbray's long-trailored book, *The Case Against Psychotherapy Registration*, proved to be well worth the wait when it appeared in 1995. *The Case* very quickly became the 'bible' for practitioners in the field who had severe doubts about the whole direction that the rapidly professionalising therapy field was taking.

I remember with great clarity the effect *The Case* had on me – like one of those profoundly integrating '*a-ha*' experiences where previously disparate ideas and feelings suddenly cohere into an integral whole. Here, for the first time, was an immaculately documented and thoroughly compelling rationale for all of the unease I had felt since I first encountered the professionalisation/ accreditation issue five years earlier. I immediately composed a verbatim summary of *The Case*, drawing on Mowbray's own text, typing it up and sending it to Richard Mowbray (reproduced as Chapter 13, this volume). The summary met with an enthusiastic response, and later become a 16-page booklet entitled 'Mowbray distilled', which was circulated both within the Independent Therapists Network and further afield (and since formally published; see House 1996/2004). Certainly, for anyone wishing to acquaint themselves with the history and advisability of therapy regulation, Mowbray's *Case* is still surely the indispensable starting-point.

The publication of *Implausible Professions*, 1997, *Ethically Challenged Professions*, 2003 and *Therapy Beyond Modernity*, 2003

The first edition of the book *Implausible Professions*, co-edited with my IPN colleague Nick Totton, was published in 1997 (second edition, 2011). Eighteen months on from the appearance of Mowbray's *Case*, not only had his book met with a largely deafening silence from those favouring regulation, but there had as yet been no real focus for the disparate voices of concern and principled protest (including some very respected figures in the field) who felt uneasy about the institutional rush into accreditation and regulation which was gathering momentum – and which process, we feared, might before long become quite unstoppable. *Implausible Professions* sought to give a coherent form to those previously disparate voices.

In our editorial introduction, Nick Totton and I recounted the extraordinary process of finding a publisher for the book (1997: 7–8). Through this difficult process we were beginning to understand just what a brave step it would have been for a major mainstream publishing house to publish our book. And ironically, it was the very refusal of major publishers to take on the book that provided the strongest possible rationale for its publication! Our experience merely confirmed that the professionalisation process is shot through with a combination of acted-out fear, insecurity and material vested interests (both personal and institutional) that have, at best, only a very tenuous connection with the values of honesty and integrity which should surely be the hallmarks of therapeutic practice and organisation. By 2000 there had been at least 14 published reviews of the book in the literature, all of which had been pretty much unreservedly positive – in stark contrast to the wodge of rejection letters which we received from the major publishing houses specialising in therapy literature.

Implausible Professions contains a wealth of high-quality articles on almost every conceivable aspect of the professionalisation process. Above all, however, it was not only about critique, but about *refoundation*; about showing that there do exist viable, practicable alternatives to didactic regulation which privilege values that are far more in tune with the core values of therapeutic practice than are those of the dominator-hierarchical institutionalised structures that the therapy bureaucracies at their worst embody (Postle 2003).

Then, in 2002 I approached the co-editor of *Ipnosis* magazine, Yvonne Bates, with a view to keeping the 'pluralistic flame' alive with another edited anthology, as the various arguments had not only not gone away, but there were signs that the therapy institutions were still pushing for statutory regulation, notwithstanding the wealth of cautionary arguments that had been piling up, unanswered, since the early 1990s. And so was born the anthology

Ethically Challenged Profession (Bates and House 2003), which took the arguments expounded in *Implausible Professions* to a deeper level, and included contributions from major practitioner-writers from around the world.

From the mid-1990s onwards, I had found myself becoming increasingly critical of the whole basis of therapy – of its very legitimacy as a healing practice in Late Modernity. This disquiet became manifest as I felt increasingly uncomfortable when actually doing counselling work, and also as my interest in so-called 'New Paradigm' thinking and 'the spiritual' grew. Around this time I enthusiastically joined the Scientific and Medical Network, and found there a fertile environment for challenging the assumptions of modernity, and its associated positivistic, materialist, and increasingly discredited world-view (e.g. Lorimer 1999). I also discovered the (until recently) neglected 'holistic' scientific studies of Goethe, and the associated works of the much neglected Austrian philosopher-scientist-mystic, Rudolf Steiner (I was also soon to train as a Steiner Waldorf class and Kindergarten teacher). And within the therapy world I stumbled across the criminally neglected writings of the inspired analyst-cum-healer and contemporary of Freud, Georg Groddeck (see House 1997b, 2003a; see Chapter 21, this volume).

In 1998 I wrote a paper for a special issue of the *British Journal of Guidance and Counselling* on Critiques of Therapy (House 1999a; see Chapter 6, this volume) – which, almost before I'd realised it, had turned into a 25,000-word critique of various aspects of what I then termed 'the Professionalised Therapy Form' and (borrowing a term from Nikolas Rose's work – e.g. Rose 1989) therapy's 'regime of truth' (House 2003a: Chapter 2). Once I had put together a book proposal it was only a short time before the proposal was accepted by a major therapy publisher. *Therapy Beyond Modernity* duly appeared in 2003, and one of its most notable features was the considerable space given to three major client commentaries on, and critiques of, their therapy experiences. And so was born the 'Client-Voice Movement' (House 2006; see Chapter 5, this volume), which has since been taken up and developed by Yvonne Bates both in *Ipnosis* magazine and also in her book, *Shouldn't I be Feeling Better by Now?* (Bates 2006).

Be-coming a practitioner: The 'post-professional' praxis of the Independent Practitioners Network (IPN)

[T]he independence, integrity and future evolution of practitioners will depend in large part on whether collegial/associations such as IPN, that are independent of training organisations, can maintain an alternative centre of gravity, counterbalancing the monopolistic hegemonies formed by members of the trainer's club, and acting as a space for counter-cultural values.

(Gladstone 1997: 184)

Since its founding in 1995, the IPN had been taking its first steps towards an accountability process far more in tune with the most progressive of 'New Paradigm' organisational thinking, striving in its organisational ethos and praxis to be congruent with the spirit of empowering therapy work at its best. The IPN attempts to respond openly and creatively to many of the shortcomings of a 'modernist' institutional approach to training and regulation – a new model of 'post-professional' accountability that aspires to the status of a self-regulating or '*self-generating*' practitioner community (Heron 1997).

The Network has no hierarchical power structure, and no 'executive' making centralised decisions about what qualifications are necessary or acceptable for effective practitionership. Administration is facilitated in an open, participative way at meetings which anyone can attend. Relatedly, no individual can speak for the Network, as there exists no power structure that could confer such authority on any one individual. The Network thus has a group, *communitarian* ideology, rather than a 'privatised', individualising focus. As of 2007, the Network's collectively written brochure stated that the IPN

> makes no distinction between more or less qualified, or 'registered' members, as we recognise that there are many routes to being a good practitioner.... We specifically favour a richly pluralistic and multi-skilled ecology [of therapeutic practice].... We are committed to defending freedom of practice and creating a culture of openness and challenge. The Network grows out of the belief that no organisation has the right or the ability to decide who should practise therapy, facilitation or equivalent skills.

The Network is therefore a form of 'self-generating practitioner community' in which responsibility-taking *participatory ethics* (House 1997a) are privileged over didactic, responsibility-eschewing institutional Codes of Ethics (ibid.; House 2003a: 82–90).

The only unit of Network membership is a *practitioner group* of at least five members, all of whom stand by each others' work through regular face-to-face engagement in ongoing peer-group experience via self and peer assessment (SAPA) and accreditation. The 'standing-by' process means that each and every practitioner has an intrinsic interest in the quality of their colleagues' therapeutic work. The Network's self-regulating participative process of accountability has indeed been quite explicitly fashioned so as to be consistent with the core values of pluralistic, empowering therapeutic practice.

To become a full 'member-group', each practitioner group must establish links with two other groups, such that the two link groups feel able to 'stand by' their work. There has been a great deal of discussion within the Network as to the precise meaning and procedural implications of 'standing by' – a debate which will no doubt continue to unfold and deepen as the Network matures. The overall Network structure is therefore horizontal rather than vertical or hierarchical – rendering it in tune with recent progressive thinking in 'post-structuralist' organisational development theory (e.g. Jackson and Carter 2006; Morgan 2006).

The Network stands for an approach to difficulties or complaints which encourages the willingness to own 'mistakes' in an atmosphere of non-defensive openness (Totton 1997a), and thereby seeks to transcend the regressive 'victimhood', blaming dynamics (Hall 1993) that dominate conventional punitive, shame-inducing and victimhood-reinforcing complaints procedures.

There are regular weekend National Gatherings (two or three a year), open to anyone to attend, together with occasional Regional Gatherings. Overall, the IPN is founded in the values of creative pluralism (Samuels 1997) and the celebration of growth and human potential development, rather than in those of infantilising hoop-jumping, 'power-over' hierarchy, ambition-infused institutional intrigue and a preoccupation with so-called 'psychopathology'.

It would be wrong to imply that the Network's strugglings with the intricate and subtle dialectic between radical individualism and communitarian values has not been variously challenging, frustrating, and sometimes exhausting. Yet these 'birth pangs' are arguably a necessary and unavoidable process with which any human grouping struggling towards a mature, operational *social community ethic and praxis* must contend. The extraordinary subtlety and complexity of what is at stake is beautifully captured by Rudolf Steiner in his 'Motto of the Social Ethic', given to Edith Maryon in 1920 (and cited in Lipsker 1990: 60): 'The healthy social life is found when in the mirror of each human soul the whole community finds its reflection, and when in the community the virtue of each one is living.'

There are many interesting philosophical and procedural commonalities yet to be explored between the IPN, on the one hand, and on the other, both the Quaker movement and the worldwide Steiner (Waldorf) educational and Camphill Community movements, founded as they are in Rudolf Steiner's work.

CONCLUSIONS: BEYOND 'COMPETENCIES', TOWARDS BEING

> Generalizable knowledge about teaching and learning will never fully
> reflect or be reflected in the individual cognitive framework of
> practitioners.
>   (Atkinson and Claxton 2000a: 4)

Over a decade ago, Ernesto Spinelli provocatively wrote that '[T]here exists precious little about therapy that we can say with any certainty... therapists really don't know what they're doing – even if they insist upon pretending ... they are "experts"'(Spinelli 1996: 56, 59). I strongly concur with this view, which paradoxically further entails that the more we are able to admit to our 'ignorance' – albeit it in a 'disciplined' way, perhaps (Tony Storey, personal communication) – then the more likely it will be that we will discover the requisite abilities and capacities really to help our clients sensitively and effectively.

A 'trans-modern' world-view (House 2008a; see Chapter 17, this volume) necessitates that we move far beyond therapy as *technology* and a medical-model 'diagnosis-and-treatment' model of care, and embrace instead the often uncomfortable reality that therapy as a healing practice entails many practitioner qualities that are *in principle* beyond rational 'modernist' specification (cf. Chapter 19, this volume) – as a number of writers in diverse fields well beyond therapy have argued (cf. Michael Polanyi's notion of 'tacit knowledge' and Donald Schön's 'reflective practitioner', for example). As Jerome Frank put it, '[P]sychotherapy transpires in the realm of meaning.... [I]n contrast to facts, meanings cannot be confirmed or disconfirmed by the objective criteria of the scientific method' (Frank 1989a: 144).

In their excellent anthology *The Intuitive Practitioner*, we find Terry Atkinson and Guy Claxton (2000b) arguing that there is a great value in 'not always knowing what one is doing', and that *intuition* (and, following Rudolf Steiner, possibly imagination and inspiration too) are often the key to effective and successful practitionership in the human caring vocations. Such radical counter-cultural perspectives on therapy in the twenty-first century clearly have major implications for the be-coming of therapy practitioners and the kinds of training experiences that might be most effective and enabling – and I hope that this somewhat indulgent autobiographical chapter might help readers to think about practitioner be-coming in quite new and innovative ways.

CHAPTER 2

The Unmasking of the Pathologising Mentality:
A review essay

The book *Deconstructing Psychopathology* (Parker and others, 1995) challenges in a quite fundamental way the scientific pretensions of the psychiatry profession by means of the deconstructive approach associated among others with the work of Michel Foucault. For the authors, deconstruction 'looks at things askew, seeing things that do not at first glance seem to be there..., and it breaks the rules to show that what is usually treated as normal is itself really rather odd' (p. 3). Typically, deconstruction is concerned with the analysis of language and discourses, where the latter are defined as 'sets of statements about an object which allows people to define and speak about things.... Discourses always entail relations of power' (p. 41).

Thus, the way in which (scientific) knowledge gains its privileged status, far from being taken for granted or being seen as the result of rational scientific progress, is understood as a fundamentally ideological, socially constructed and culturally relative process, indissolubly infused with issues of power. For, following Foucault, 'knowledge, theoretical and scientific, does not describe a pre-existing reality but constructs realities' (p. 131), and in this book the authors deny what they term 'the myth of scientific progress' (p. 132). Within this framework, Ian Parker and his co-authors pose the question, 'how did our ideas of psychological distress become current and what are their implicit assumptions and implications?' (p. 47).

Ian Parker and his colleagues' book *Deconstructing Psychopathology* was one of my first encounters with critical postmodern thinking. This book made a profound impact on me when I read it in the mid-1990s, articulating in a quite new way the concerns I had always held about the medical model and its underpinning epistemology and ontology, and chiming resoundingly with my Laingian anti-psychiatry interests that reached back to the 1970s. This is one of several extended reviews I wrote of the book, with a shorter review also appearing in *Self and Society*, 25 (1), 1997, p. 58.

CONTENTS SUMMARY

Chapter 1 sets out a historical review of the development of the concept of 'psychopathology' as the study of mental 'disorder', with an account of Foucault's work and of the practice of 'deconstruction', and a description of how the theory and practices of 'abnormal psychology' can be deconstructively challenged. Chapter 2 then reviews a number of different approaches to the notion of psychopathology, including psychoanalysis, anti-psychiatry (Laing, Szasz and Lacan), family therapy and cognitive approaches.

Chapter 3 focuses on symptomatology, describing the ways in which the diagnostic systems of DSM and ICD are used to categorise individuals as 'abnormal'. There is an examination of the 'demarcation dispute' between clinical psychology and psychiatry over the approach to mental distress, with a description of the effects of this dispute on other professionals.

Chapter 4 then looks at cultural representations of psychopathology, focusing in particular on the ways in which (following Foucault) language structures common cultural conceptions of 'illness' and 'abnormality'. 'Madness' is viewed, therefore, as a cultural representation; traditional conceptions of 'madness' are seen as fundamentally flawed, and the taken-for-granted distinction between professional and lay knowledge is fundamentally questioned. It is shown how clinical categories can be deconstructed by transforming conventional oppositions (e.g. between reason and unreason, illness and health, and so on); and the way in which shared structures of language influence professional judgements about different forms of distress are explored.

Chapter 5 looks at the construction of identity in relation to the categories of psychopathology, focusing in particular on identity construction around the diagnostic label 'psychopathy'. Specifically, the evolution of the category of psychopathy as it developed in the UK is examined, with an account of how contradictory forms of psychopathic identity are secured within the Special Hospital. The deconstruction of 'psychopathy' illustrates the more general proposition that 'language is significant in determining the individual's position and passageway through the mental health network', and that 'psychiatric... institutions provoke and contain abnormal identities' (p. 72).

In Chapter 6 the authors then examine research on language, challenging the tautological circularity of traditional psychiatry's approach to and labelling of 'psychosis'. Some alternative theoretical approaches – pragmatic, psychoanalytic and narrative-therapeutic – are explored, together with the implications of these different approaches for the interpretation of 'abnormal' speech. Chapter 7 then looks at the development of alternative mental health movements. After discussing how alternative histories are written and lived, Parker and colleagues go on to describe radical experiments in Trieste (Clotho), Germany (Lechesis), the USA, and the UK Hearing Voices Network. Important implications emerge from these case studies in terms of the context and politics of radical deconstructive alternatives to traditional psychiatry.

The final chapter attempts pre-emptively to field and respond to the various anticipated criticisms that Parker et al. imagine their deconstructive enterprise will provoke. In addition, the authors usefully list and describe some of the available practical radical resources that currently exist to challenge the hegemony of conventional psychiatric practices.

COMMENTARY

This is undoubtedly an extremely important book. Although written in the broad spirit of anti-psychiatry, *Deconstructing Psychopathology* fills out and extends the anti-psychiatry critique to provide a formidable challenge to the ideological assumptions and practices of traditional psychiatry (and by extension, much of clinical psychology and medical-model psychotherapy). It makes a series of major contributions. First, the interface between language and power (pp. 15–17) as it manifests in psychiatric practices is highlighted, with language being 'organised around different systems of meaning [or discourses] which offer positions of power to certain categories of people and disempower others' (p. 10). For Parker et al., the organisation of language is central to understanding mental 'illness': 'language does not only organize reason but it also structures what we imagine to lie outside reason' (p. 14), and structures of language are inevitably embodied in clinical/psychiatric institutions. This in turn has momentous implications for the way in which the identity of users ('patients') is constituted.

What this means, therefore, is that 'professionals could be said to bring forth or construct psychopathology by recourse to a language with which to point to disorder' (p. 66). Some kind of perverse alchemy seems to occur whereby the ordinary everyday difficulties of living and existence are surreptitiously transformed into a mechanistic professionalised lexicon of quasi-medical terminology that legitimises a professional ideology that, in turn, self-fulfillingly becomes the guarantee of its own existence. In short, *Deconstructing Psychopathology* fundamentally challenges the medical-model approach to emotional difficulties and distress.

The authors' critique takes a number of forms. They show how the conventional oppositions between sanity and madness, normality and abnormality, health and illness, are ideological and socially constructed rather than being the objective scientific categories that traditional psychiatry claims them to be. Thus, in the case of 'abnormal' speech, 'from the moment that "normal" speech is defined, the polarity between "normal" and "abnormal" is bound to be reproduced'. It follows that 'The very idea of "normality" is founded upon the idea of "abnormality", of that which lies outside the definition of the norm' (p. 104).

Perhaps the notion of 'abnormality' is more profitably viewed as a fear-induced, socio-emotionally produced linguistic category whose unacknowledged function is to reduce anxiety in the face of others' radical difference, rather than as some objective description of an independently existing reality: 'for those who diagnose others as pathological a position of normality is secured' (p. 61); and 'Only if the polarity between normality and abnormality ceases to exist can non-pathologizing ways of looking at difference be employed' (p. 104).

It follows quite naturally from this that the diagnostic 'mentality' of traditional psychiatric and pathologising practices comes in for quite devastating criticism (Chapters 3 and 4). Thus, 'diagnostic criteria could be said to be justificatory arguments rather than objective signs' (p. 66); and the authors brilliantly expose the self-fulfilling, tautological nature of psychiatric diagnostic practices. Thus, they show how, in the case of so-called 'psychotic thought and speech disorders',

> psychiatric research... actively constructs a version of both normal and abnormal speech, which is then applied to individuals who end up being classified as normal or abnormal.... Research draws on existing clinical categories and... its results are fed back into the diagnostic systems.... Psychiatric language, embedded in research and clincial practices, constitutes the very 'pathological phenomena' it seeks to explain.
> (pp. 92–3)

Thus, 'a vicious circle is created where diagnosis and research encourage one another leaving their assumptions unquestioned, while maintaining the same practices' (p. 97). Parker et al. show quite convincingly that '"Normal" everyday speech... cannot be clearly distinguished from or opposed to "psychotic" speech... [and] the opposition between "normal" and "psychotic" cannot be sustained any longer' (p. 110).

It is crucial to emphasise that this is by no means mere academic point-scoring or semantics – for the real practices of traditional psychiatry and clinical psychology are shot through with, and informed by, these fundamentally ideological conceptualisations. In particular, if Rom Harré is right in arguing that personal identity 'amounts to the assimilation of socially available theories and templates' (quoted on p. 89), and if 'How we reflect upon and define ourselves is determined and constrained by the structures of knowing available to us' (p. 88), then 'psychiatric patients, through the course of repeated assessments, come increasingly to define their experiences in accordance with a professional definition of "psychiatric illness"' (p. 89). In short, 'clinical discourses impact upon individual autobiography thereby influencing both the types of subjectivity and identity that are brought into being' (p. 73). Professional elites are seen as constructing peoples' realites through language, and 'the ubiquity of particular types of discourse makes it impossible for their subjects to "think" or even imagine an "elsewhere"' (p. 75). Further, patients are exposed to the objectifying diagnostic clinical gaze of the psychiatrist 'which supposedly records symptoms and compares them with diagnostic criteria' (p. 66).

In sum, rather than discovering a supposed objectively existing identity of the diagnosed, the clinician actively *constitutes* the identity of his/her 'patients' through tautological, ideological linguistic practices which are, in turn, indissolubly implicated in the power-infused discourse of traditional psychiatric practices. 'Discourses always entail relations of power' (p. 41), and

> we are caught in a historical process that positions psychiatrists... and other mental health professionals in relations of power over 'users' of services, and the best we can do is to identify the fault lines in that power, to open up new spaces of resistance for those working in and against the clinical apparatus.
>
> (p. 16)

Note that Parker and colleagues are careful to eschew any suggestion of a conspiracy theory here, for 'psychiatry itself is not the originating cause but an *effect* of regimes of power' (ibid., their emphasis).

These fundamental arguments are part of a wider meta-theoretical, postmodern view on what precisely constitutes valid science. For the authors of *Deconstructing Psychopathology*, 'Facts do not necessarily correspond to an external reality. Facts are constructed by associations between groups of professionals and institutions, by practices that bring them into existence and maintain them' (p. 101). The deconstructive mentality throws 'spanners in the works of the clinical truth machine', and leads us to 'give up the obsession with fixed truth that drives traditional research' (p. 102). The authors are quite explicit that their work 'is not based on the positivist paradigm of science, according to which the accumulation of scientific research will eventually provide the correct understanding of what lies out there, in reality' (p. 132). And the link between 'scientific' knowledge and power is both crucial and decisively influential on the form and content of 'scientific' knowledge: 'The persuasion of scientific knowledge does not rely on the power of its argument or on its correspondence with some kind of external reality, but on its involvement in powerful institutions' (p. 135).

It follows quite naturally from these arguments that the conventional distinction between professional and lay knowledge is highly problematic: thus, 'it is impossible to separate different realms of knowledge since all are thoroughly embedded in cultural practices of one kind or another' (p. 57), and 'there is no real distinction between professional and lay knowledge... professional knowledge too is deeply embedded in wider cultural stories' (p. 63). Clearly, the implications of these arguments for clinical practices can hardly be overemphasised. And if Parker et al.'s analysis is anything like right, then a wholesale Kuhnian paradigm shift in the theory and practices of 'mental health treatment' is surely indicated – sooner or later....

Paradoxically, it is perhaps only when we really face up to the reality that, as the great analyst-cum-healer Georg Groddeck put it earlier this century, 'everything important happens outside our knowledge and control.... It is absurd to suppose that one can ever understand life' (Groddeck 1951: 84), that we will be in the position of humility from which way-of-being, true, embodied 'knowledge' will quite naturally become available to us. Following the psychoanalyst Wilfred Bion and counsellor/writer Tony Storey, it might well be that the most effective counsellors/clinicians/healers are precisely those who do not (need to) take preconceived beliefs and defensive 'clinical gazes' into their work with clients, but rather, are able to enter into their relations with clients in a relatively undefended way that privileges the healing power of intimacy and the immediacy of the real I–Thou encounter (House, 1996b), as opposed to the objectifying, alienating and distancing manoeuvres that the diagnostic ideology of traditional psychiatry typically embraces. In the true spirit of the Trickster, Parker et al. mischievously write that the rigid discourses of psychiatry could themselves be termed 'psychotic' (p. 126), with its proponents perhaps suffering from the condition of 'Professional Thought Disorder'! (Lowson 1994: 29–30); and in similar vein I would hazard the view that what lies at the emotional root of the defensive clinical practices of psychiatry, clinical psychology and 'medical model' psychotherapy is a fear of intimacy (I develop this argument more fully in House 1996b: 21–6).

CONCLUDING COMMENTS

It is part of the conventional practice of writing a book review to save up some authoritative-sounding (often throw-away) criticisms for the closing paragraphs. However, I will dispense with this tradition here, as in my view *Deconstructing Psychopathology* is surely one of the most thoroughly argued and convincing critiques of the (psycho)pathologising mentality currently in print in the English language. It should be essential reading for all practitioners and trainees working in the 'mental health' field – from counsellors to psychiatrists, and all practitioners in between. Its message is fundamentally *humanistic* in tenor and implication (though the authors probably won't thank me for using such an adjective!), with its devastating critique of the dehumanisation of existing mechanistic clinical practices, and its proposing of a less alienating and more empowering approach to emotional distress and 'the necessary pain of living' (Peck 1993). Furthermore, the arguments developed in *Deconstructing Psychopathology* have massive implications for the professionalisation process currently gathering such steam in the fields of counselling and psychotherapy – a process which would surely take a very different form and direction if the arguments laid out in this book were taken on board by a critical mass of practitioners.

My only slight reservation is that the book is very much one for practitioners and theoreticians: users or clients might find it heavy-going in places, and I hope this review has succeeded in conveying the essence of *Deconstructing Psychopathology* in reasonably clear and understandable terms. Certainly, it would be a tragedy if the truly revolutionary message of this book were confined to the rarefied confines of Academia.

Once the central message of *Deconstructing Psychopathology* has been culturally assimilated and integrated, 'mental health' practices can surely never be the same again, and that will be cause for no little rejoicing and celebration in many quarters – not least those users and clients who are routinely exposed to the clinical practices that Parker and his colleagues so convincingly criticise and condemn.

CHAPTER 3

The Place of Psychotherapy and Counselling in a Healthy European Social Order: A commentary on Tantam and van Deurzen

You cannot make men moral by Act of Parliament.
(Waterman 1946: 281)

INTRODUCTION

...[W]e are addicted to institutions... [they] will never stop what is happening in the world... no organization is going to solve your sorrow... organization in the psychological world is destructive.
(J. Krishnamurti 1981, 1984; quoted in Tankha 1992: 381–2)

Tantam and van Deurzen's paper seems to this reader to be written from a position that assumes, or asserts by definitional fiat, the unambiguous beneficence of what Philip Rieff called 'the triumph of the therapeutic' (Rieff 1966). In this response, while some attention will be paid to socio-cultural aspects of the increasingly pervasive phenomenon of 'therapy' (for recent detailed analyses of this issue, see, for example, Cushman 1995; Rose 1996; Smail 1996; Cloud 1998), in what follows the main approach will be to work through the authors' paper, deconstructively highlighting in the process those points at which their argument threatens to lapse into assertion, assumptive invalidity or professional self-interest. The reader can assess whether the following commentary raises enough difficulties and doubts to undermine the main substance of their argument.

This is a much extended version of an invited response to a paper by Digby Tantam and Emmy van Deurzen, 'The European citizen's right to ethical and competent psychotherapeutic care', published in the *European Journal of Psychotherapy, Counselling and Health*, 2 (2), 1999, pp. 228-35. Written in the late 1990s, it touches on many of the issues around professionalisation and credentialisation which were then being aggressively promulgated by certain key figures in the field, and which, as you'll see below, elicited an equally robust response. Around this time, I was also having major concerns about the very project of psychotherapy itself (cf. Chapter 6, this volume).

The analysis offered here is very much informed by postmodern and 'New Paradigm' thinking, a world-view which is very different from the modernist one that seems to underpin Tantam and van Deurzen's paper – differences which will become clear below.

DISCUSSION

In what follows, five statements from the authors' paper will be extracted and explored at some length – statements which collectively illustrate the yawning gulf that separates the New Paradigm thinking informing this commentary from the conventional professionalising world-view consistently advocated by Tantam and van Deurzen over recent years (e.g. van Deurzen-Smith 1996, 1997; Tantam and van Deurzen 1998a, b).

First: 'The suffering of a child, born in a broken or disturbed family, is not of his or her own making. The suffering of the adult who has experienced such a childhood may be equally involuntary.' (p. 229)

In the light of the authors' subsequent line of argument, it feels important to highlight this statement as an assertion, and one that is by no means self-evidently true. The dynamics of 'victimhood' are exceedingly complex, perhaps even archetypal (Hall 1993); and not only does the uncritical assumption of 'involuntariness' skirt dangerously close to the ideology of victimhood, but it also ignores the possibility that other plausible world-views would give a very different account of human suffering (for example, the Buddhist distinction between pain and suffering, or Hillman's recent 'acorn theory' of human experience – Hillman 1997).

For current purposes, what is crucial is that the body of Tantam and van Deurzen's argument (based as it is around 'the right to relief from involuntary emotional suffering' – p. 229) relies centrally on the assumption of the involuntary nature of emotional suffering; and if that assumption were indeed to be erroneous – which at least some recent commentators (amongst others, Hall and Hillman) believe it to be – then the rest of their argument essentially collapses. For Tantam and van Deurzen would then have to make the (more difficult) case for 'societal' protection from suffering that was in some sense not wholly and unambiguously involuntary. Furthermore, if what Hillman calls 'the psychological fallacy' (1997: 87) of involuntariness were decisively undermined, then the very role of therapy within society becomes deeply problematic – for 'Psychotherapy compounds [this fallacy]. Its theory of developmental damage owing to the family actually turns the patient away from everything else that might give comfort or instruction' (ibid.: 88). It is clear, therefore, that one effect that the assumption of involuntariness does have is the legitimation of therapy as a cultural phemomenon. (This important issue will be explored later.)

It is worth noting, finally, that later in their paper, the authors state that 'People... do not want to be... treated as passive victims' (p. 231) – which is surely precisely what the assumption of involuntariness is in grave danger of doing. Henceforth, and for the purpose of this commentary, it will be assumed that the authors' assumption of the involuntariness of suffering is a valid one – though as will be clear from the foregoing, it is by no mean free of difficulties.

Second: 'European member states do have a duty to prevent or relieve involuntary emotional suffering whenever possible.... [T]he ethical basis of the state's authority derives from its ability to create opportunities for its citizens to thrive.' (p. 229)

The authors' 'Theory of the State' entails major assumptions which are completely glossed over in their discussion. No justification is given for the assumption that it is appropriate that the polity provide protection from suffering, and actively create opportunities to thrive. It seems to this writer that we are currently living in profoundly disquieting times [this written in 1999 – RH] when uncritical government 'control-freakery' is running rampant, virtually unchecked, throughout our culture – from massive state control of educational provision to (at the time of writing) the extraordinary spectacle of the British government intervening in a football club's participation in the FA Cup! The use of the term 'culture' here is crucial, for it is being quite deliberately used in the sense advocated by Rudolf Steiner in his specification of what he called the 'three-fold social order' (see below), born out of his understanding of the wreckage that was Europe in the aftermath of the First World War (Steiner 1972/1919) – a social order which Steiner saw as 'struggling confusedly into existence' (Waterman 1946: 10). For Steiner, 'The whole trend of the evolutionary force of modern mankind is in the direction of this threefolding of the social organism' – 1972/1919: 36 (see also Large 2010).

In Steiner's view, the three-fold social order framework was made up of the spiritual-cultural sphere, the economic sphere and the political sphere; and the 'social organism' as a whole worked best when the three spheres operate mutually respectfully with, *and relatively autonomously from*, each other. Thus, for Steiner it was a grave error for the polity to become embroiled in trying to influence or control activities of the cultural-spiritual sphere. Positing arguments which are as compelling today as they were nearly a century ago (see Large, 2010), Steiner argued passionately against state involvement in education (e.g. 1972: xiv–xv; cf. Waterman 1946: Ch. 23;

House 2007a); and he would have certainly argued equally forcefully against any undue state regulation of, or interference in, the field of psychotherapy or healing practices. (Interestingly, some commentators – e.g. Heron 1997, Totton 1997b and West 1998 – see psychotherapy and counselling as fundamentally a *spiritual* practice. Such a world-view seems very different from that of the authors, who later, revealingly invoking the language of 'psychopathology (cf. Chapter 2, this volume), refer to 'the treatment of emotional disorders' (p. 230), and also explicitly sanction the 'scientification' of such 'treatments' – on which, see below.)

For Steiner, then, 'the nation-state is unable to deal with spiritual matters' (Lissau 1996: 29): it has 'absorbed the spiritual life', with the result that 'no ground at all is left where grown-up men and women can feel fully equal to one another' (Steiner 1928/1921: 226); and 'free spiritual life can only [stand in its own separate essence] when it is actually there as a reality – self-administered and free' (ibid.). Elsewhere Steiner writes of how the insidious infiltration of state influence into the spiritual-cultural realm has become so routine that we scarcely notice it, such that in general, people 'neither see nor feel how... the state is bringing all spiritual life into a dependence on state requirements' (1972/1919: 32). (It is important to emphasise, incidentally, that Steiner was very far from being a pro-capitalist right-wing ideologue – for he was very critical of capitalism and its materialistic underpinnings.) We are surely seeing a classic example of such a process in the increasingly prevalent, insidious – and in this writer's view, wholly inappropriate – interpenetration of psychotherapy and counselling with formal legal frameworks and practices (e.g. Bird 1998; Palmer Barnes 1998; Bell-Boule 1999). In a recent issue of *Counselling* magazine, for example, we read that there are currently (in 1997/8) no less than 10,000 lawsuits pending against psychotherapists in the USA (Bird 1998: 235), and that in the UK, litigation in the field is on the increase (ibid.). Elsewhere, we read that in the USA, 'To date, damages in legal cases have totalled millions of dollars', and that US 'litigation mindedness' is inexorably spreading to the UK (Bell-Boule 1999: 193).

Now the anxiety-driven knee-jerk reaction of the aspiring 'profession' to this incursion of legality into the therapeutic healing domain is fairly predictable: 'counselling and psychotherapy must acquire a thorough knowledge of the law as part of their training', we are implored (ibid.: 201) – that is, we are urged to professionalise all the more assiduously, and to insure ourselves all the more comprehensively, for 'Without it [practitioners] are acting recklessly', we are unambiguously told (Palmer Barnes 1998: 67). And so the new profession unquestioningly colludes with the incursion of the polity into therapeutic healing work, rather than taking an informed, principled stand against such contamination, and daring to proffer an alternative approach to conflict in therapeutic work, based on a world-view that is congruent with, rather than a betrayal of, the foundational values of therapeutic healing work (House 1997a; Totton 1997c).

Moreover, an old paradigm, 'control-freak' response to litigation mindedness can only encourage and reinforce the regressive victimhood dynamics of our 'blaming' culture, referred to elsewhere in this commentary, and which therapy at its best should surely be seeking to transcend. Laura Brown, a feminist therapist, has written that

> [O]ur present ethical and legal *zeitgeist*, which is a concrete, literal-minded and legalistic one, is destructive to the human, relational qualities of psychotherapy.... These perspectives will *increase* the likelihood of violations; they encourage therapists to objectify, rather than encounter, the people with whom they work.
> (Brown 1994: 280, original emphasis; cf. Mowbray 1995)

There are also interesting parallels in all this with Ivan Illich's (1977a) observations about the 'disabling' professions and their tendency to engender infantilising helplessness, and Mowbray's argument that formal state regulation of therapy 'based on unconfirmed criteria *begets* vulnerability' (1995: 131, original emphasis), rather than protecting against it.

Third: 'The increasing salience of quality of life in the European health agenda is tacit recognition that European citizens consider that they have *a right* to be free of involuntary emotional suffering.' (my emphasis) (p. 229)

This is surely a woefully underdetermined non sequitur: just how the authors deduce the latter speculation from the former observation is pretty much unfathomable. More generally, it provides an illustration of a recurring impression gained throughout the paper – namely, that it was written 'from conclusion to premiss', rather than the other way around. That is, the authors appear to have set out with a view that the polity should regulate the therapy field, and then proceeded to fish around for plausible-sounding, *post hoc* rationalisations that, they believe, justify their preferred conclusion. Such an analysis is consistent with what is, for this writer, the underdetermined nature of much of the argument. And even if we assume they are correct in asserting that European citizens believe they have a right to be free of (involuntary) suffering, there seems to be no consideration or awareness of what world-view such a belief is (emotionally?) rooted in, nor of whether it is either realistic or appropriate to hold such a belief.

More generally still, Tantam and van Deurzen's paper is littered with the (politically fashionable) rhetoric of 'rights' (e.g. 'Human beings have a right to be helped when they are in emotional need.... [They] have a right to be given access to the knowledge that may help them live better lives' – p. 233), with the authors' arguments relying substantially upon the assumption that relief from emotional suffering is a human right (e.g. 'The existence of an appropriate remedy is important if a right to the relief of emotional suffering is accepted' – p. 230). The great danger of a rights-obsessed society and polity is that it can all too easily collude with, and even actively encourage, a non-participative, responsibility-eschewing, 'experts'-dominated set of values, beliefs and ways of living which are the very antithesis of the values which healthily responsible, so-called 'democratic' societies are alleged to represent and support.

We are already exposed in modern culture to the deeply distasteful, victim-creating spectacle of legal companies touting the small-ad columns for litigation business; and before long there will no doubt be uncomfortably parallel developments within the New Profession of psychotherapy, actively propagating its own particular 'regime of truth' (Rose 1996; House 1999a and Chapter 6, this volume). For example, we are told that 'We need to begin educating the public about the ways in which the profession can make a difference to our evolving world'..., and 'we have to engage in a public relations exercise to let people know about our profession' (van Deurzen-Smith 1996: 19, 20) – one aspect of which, no doubt, will be educating them about their 'right' to be free of involuntary emotional suffering. At which point, no doubt, forward will step the credentialed psychotherapist, ready to respond to what is in danger of becoming an increasingly self-interested, profession-created need for her or his services.... And in the light of all this, to this reader the following statement verges on the chilling: 'We [meaning whom? – RH] are fortunate indeed that the methods of psychotherapeutic intervention have been developed over the past century [at the last count, all 450-odd of them! – RH] in readiness to be applied more widely' (p. 233).

For this writer there is a mounting sense of uneasiness, even alarm, at the attempts of (often self-appointed) professionals to control life (and in this case, others' lives) – be it GM food, genetic engineering – or the emotional suffering of others (cf. Smail 1996). Certainly, Totton's sobering and highly prescient warning, that 'Trying to control "what therapy is" may end up preventing it from being anything worth having' (1997b: 336), is one which the didactic professionalisers would surely do well to contemplate long and hard. For do we really want psychotherapy professionals (whether well-intentioned, self-interested, or both) running around setting themselves up, via state-sanctioned institutions, as the arbiters of our emotional well-being? Indeed, it seems to be an extraordinarily presumptuous, even arrogant position to take up – to annex to oneself the right to be the arbiter of society's levels of emotional well-being; and worse, then to professionalise, institutionalise and state-regulate it! (Note, incidentally, that it is also far from unambiguously clear that the most appropriate response to the existence of emotional suffering, at either individual or social levels, is to 'eradicate' it: 'the client may need to face suffering rather than escape from it' – Rowan 1999: 51; cf. Peck 1993 and the earlier discussion.)

The overweening, internationalising grandiosity of organisations like the European Association for Psychotherapy, with its professionalising pretensions in the realms of emotional suffering, may well prove to be the high watermark of the obsessive control-freakery that is symptomatic of the death throes of modernity (Barratt 1993). 'Grandiosity' and 'presumptuous arrogance' are indeed strong terms; yet how else would one describe the stated aim that therapy be appropriately characterised as 'the professionalisation of motherhood'; or that psychotherapy 'move to a position where our new knowledge is applied to an increasingly necessary reorganisation of the world' (van Deurzen-Smith 1996: 17, 19); or that psychotherapy 'will be indispensable to a healthy and well functioning society in the 21st century.... Psychotherapists may need to become the gatekeepers of the quality of life' (pp. 234, 233)? This indeed sounds for all the world like 'The New Social Engineering' – and will no doubt go the same way as all previous institutional attempts at social engineering. And after Europe? – why, *the world*, of course!... 'Extending our networking through the World Council for Psychotherapy is the logical step onwards' (van Deurzen-Smith 1996: 21).

There is also no little degree of self-interest in all this; for the establishment of a legitimate right to relief from emotional suffering (underwritten and legitimised by the state) is clearly highly consistent with the setting up of a state-regulated institutional profession to 'treat' those so suffering. And in several places, indeed, the authors have let this particular self-interested cat out of the bag: for example: 'the European Association for Psychotherapy... is now lobbying Brussels to protect the profession' (van Deurzen-Smith 1997: 5); 'The EAP is concerned to protect *the interest of this profession* and the public it serves' (Tantam and van Deurzen 1998a: 127) (emphasis added). The double-think around the crucial issue of 'interests' is highly revealing, and is reminiscent of the amusing spectacle of British politicians not knowing whether to refer to other European states as 'our partners' or 'our competitors'!

Apologists for professionalisation typically speak with forked tongues over whether professionalisation is needed to protect the public, or the newly annointed professionals – with the respective interests of those two groups being uncritically assumed, albeit implicitly, to coincide one with the other. There are parallels here with the sociologically naïve and ultimately vacuous way in which the notion of the 'public' or 'national' interest is sometimes used in popular (and even some academic) discourse (e.g. 'it is in the public interest that we professionalise and create registers' – van Deurzen-Smith 1996: 15; 'the Independent Practitioners Network... is neither effective, nor is it in the public interest' – Pokorny 1998: 265). In reality, of course, the issue of interests is highly complex, and unavoidably infused with questions of power (struggle), hegemony and conflict (Postle 1998); and as has been argued elsewhere, the interests of professional therapists and their clientele are typically far from being coincident (House 1999a and Chapter 6, this volume). The onus is surely on proponents of institutional professionalisation to demonstrate the essentially unproblematic commonality of client and professional interests, rather than merely asserting or assuming it. For as Wilensky wrote many years ago, 'a client- or consumer-orientation is incompatible with a professional orientation' (1964: 146).

In sum, while the EAP's aspirations might arguably be in tune with the Blairite control-freakery of modern British culture [this written in 1999 – RH], they are most certainly way out of line with leading-edge developments in postmodern epistemology (House 2003a), participatory 'institutional' ethics (Lievegoed 1991; van den Brink 1996; Heron 1997; House 1997a), co-operative inquiry (Heron 1996 and Chapter 18, this volume) and New Paradigm thinking more generally (Lorimer 1998; Lorimer et al. 1999). Certainly, the successful development of the Independent Practitioners Network since 1994 (Totton 1997c and Chapter 16, this volume) has emphatically laid to rest the old-paradigm myth that in the course of therapy's move towards greater accountability, '*Inevitably* there has been a tendency for a hierarchy to form' (van Deurzen Smith and Jones 1995: 41, emphasis added). And if the present analysis is anything like right, then before long, initiatives like that of the EAP will, it is submitted, become little more than minor footnotes in the history of human evolution.

Fourth: 'In one survey 85 per cent of people in the UK thought that talking treatments were appropriate for depressed people.... There is an understanding that psychotherapy, counselling, and other relationship orientated treatments deal directly with the roots of emotional suffering, in relationship problems.' (p. 229)

Our old friend 'LDLS' ('Lies, Damned Lies and Statistics') is certainly alive and kicking in the first quotation. First, it seems very doubtful whether those surveyed were given the option of choosing 'no formal "treatment"', but rather, were asked 'what kind of treatment...?' – with the research frame thereby imposing a tacit, taken-for-granted therapy-centred 'regime of truth' (House 1999a and Chapter 6, this volume) right from the outset, whereby the necessity for 'treatment' is an assumed given, and only its nature is a permitted variable.

Second, it is very revealing if we remove the word 'treatment' from the first statement, for immediately we find that perhaps 'depressed people' would benefit from talking *per se*, which by no means necessarily implies *professionalised* talking. Indeed, recent research suggests that talking itself increases blood flow through that part of the brain associated with depression (Steiner 1999) – and though in terms of the Philosophy of Mind we need to be very careful in how we make sense of such materialistic neuroscientific information, this finding certainly coheres with the repeated research finding that paraprofessionals seem to obtain at least as successful therapy outcomes as highly trained professionals (Bohart and Tallman 1996, also in Bates and House 2003; House 2003a). (Tantam and van Deurzen are either ignorant of, or in disagreement with, such research: they write, 'It is actually a rather complex business to sort out emotional and relational problems, not to mention moral and spiritual ones. *It requires thorough training...* before a professional can do justice to the task.... [S]kilful therapists have better outcomes' – pp. 231), emphasis added.)

In common with Smail (1996), Riikonen and Vataja (1999) have strongly challenged what they see as the inflated, self-interested and ultimately inappropriate over-professionalisation of healing talk: 'many of these activities can hardly be separated from what people do continuously in their everyday lives.... [H]ealing... seems to mostly happen in everyday contexts and situations which most therapists would have difficulty in recognising as relevant at all' (p. 176). Yet in order to sustain their professionalising position, however, Tantam and van Deurzen must of course deny either the efficacy, or else the very possibility, of just plain (non-professional) talking for emotional troubles, if they are to retain a professionalised mystique around therapy's regime of truth. And sure enough, a bit later we read that 'The fact is that ordinary people's lives are too cluttered to pay such attention to self and other. Friends have enough problems of their own without having to resolve each other's' (p. 231). Well, therapists determined to create a professionalised reality where 'psychotherapists may need to become the gatekeepers of the quality of life' (p. 233) *would* say that, wouldn't they! And even if there were any substance to this assertion, is it really the most healthy and appropriate cultural response simply to set up institutionalised professional mechanisms for dealing with life's problems and people's difficulties of living? Might it not be preferable to seek out and pioneer alternative cultural forms for supporting people experiencing such difficulties? (Smail 1996; House 1999b). (There might not be nearly so much money to be made from the latter, of course.)

As for the assertion (quoted above) that 'There is an understanding' that therapy 'deals directly with the roots of emotional suffering' (p. 230), just whose understanding (or whose regime of truth) are we talking about here?; and just which of the 450-odd therapy 'understandings' do the authors have in mind? Therapists often claim a spurious scientificity for their work (House 1999a) – otherwise, how on earth could they justify their claims to constitute a plausible 'profession'? Riikonen and Vataja (1999: 180) sum it up well:

> For many different reasons, many of them economic, it is useful for a person of authority in the field of psychotherapy to make claims of knowing what his or her method is,... of its modernity, of its academic credibility, and so on. It is better to have a clearly defined, respectable package which can be sold.

Moreover, the state of theoretical disarray in which the (thankfully increasingly postmodernist) therapy world finds itself (Erwin 1997) seems to be far more accurately described by Spinelli than by Tantam and van Deurzen, when he bravely writes, 'There exists precious little about therapy that we can say with any certainty... therapists really don't know what they're doing – even if they insist upon pretending... they are "experts"' (1996: 56, 59). And in similar vein Riikonen and Vataja refer to 'the sheer impossibility of non-ambiguous descriptions of any human interaction and the healing elements it contains... there is no reason to think that we know *what psychotherapy really is*' (1999: 176, 177, original emphasis). (The issue of expertise will be returned to below.)

Fifth and finally: 'The scientific view of mankind is incomplete without an understanding of what makes for a well lived life.... For people need to base their lives and their overcoming of their problems on what... is proven to work.' (p. 231)

This all sounds very similar to the EAP's Strasbourg Declaration, which states that 'Psychotherapy is an independent scientific discipline.... Training in psychotherapy takes place at an advanced, qualified and scientific level.' Elsewhere, van Deurzen has written that 'We can no longer rely on prescriptive notions of faith, on beliefs or intuitive convictions: those were part of our heritage... in a pre-scientific era' (van Deurzen-Smith 1996: 18); and 'We have to transform what used to be a craft or an art based on moral and religious principles into a scientifically based accountable professional expertise' (1996: 17).

Quite apart from the latter statement's unholistic and artificial dichotomising of craft and art, on the one hand, and science, on the other, what seems crucial is that these authors are putting their faith in a modern (empiricist, objectivist) scientific world-view as a means of helping people with their difficulties of living; and that their model of science seems to be woefully ignorant of the devastating epistemological and political critiques of modern technocratic science that have been coming out of a burgeoning postmodern, New Paradigm, feminist and radical-left literature for a number of years (to give just a few examples – Keat and Urry 1975; Berman 1981; Harding 1986, 1991; Chubin et al. 1989; Polkinghorne 1990; Best 1991; Rose 1994; Bortoft 1996; Lorimer 1998; Lorimer et al. 1999). Elsewhere, the authors have written: 'we tend to wonder why the term "scientific" sparks such fascinated attention.... Science for many psychotherapists is merely a tool to improve practice....' (Tantam and van Deurzen 1998b: 504). Even a cursory acquaintance with the above-cited literature would indicate the untenability and foundational incoherence of the kind of pragmatically instrumentalist view of science apparently advocated by Tantam, van Deurzen and the EAP; and it seems ironic that the naïve myth of a value-free, non-ideological, power-neutral science is apparently still alive and kicking in the field of psychotherapy – where we would perhaps most expect it to be problematised and challenged.

Riikonen and Vataja have recently pointed out that a human potential (as opposed to a remedial psychopathologising) focus is indeed fundamentally antithetical to the project of modernist science:

> sources of joy and meaningfulness... will lead outside the domain of psychological theories, as we know them. These kinds of experiences have a relationship with... something which is directly in contradiction with science which aims at uniform knowledge and universal concepts.
>
> (1999: 181)

To this writer it conjures up a truly grotesque vision of a Brave New World of ultra-modernity when self-appointed professionals (or 'experts' on how to live?) exploit the ideology of science to buttress their credentials for showing others what 'makes for a good life' – and claiming in the process that scientific expertise should be invoked in this way rather than leaving people free to make those decisions and discoveries for themselves. The media is dominated by an unremitting stream of so-called 'scientific research findings' telling us what is or isn't good for us (advice which, incidentally, often seems about as robust and enduring as a chameleon in a discoteque). And of course, the part of us that easily and transferentially depowers ourselves in the face of an anxiety-relieving expertise will often tend to grab at such superficial reassurance. Yet the history of professional expertise displays a litany of professional vested self-interest and expert-created disasters (e.g. Hogan 1979; Friedson 1984; Martin 1996); and Illich (quoted earlier) is surely right in pointing out how a reliance on professional expertise necessarily infantilises us (cf. Mair 1997).

Finally, if Tantam and van Deurzen are correct in their view that people 'do not want to be... treated as passive victims' (p. 231), which perhaps we all sincerely hope they don't, then their position on the role of the scientific application of psychotherapeutic expertise in showing people what makes for a good life surely sits at best very uneasily with such a statement.

CONCLUSION

> Are we democratic psychotherapy organizations destined... to end up as mere bureaucracies...? Is the current catchword slogan of 'professionalization' a mere mask for anti-constitutional, anti-democratic, centralism and autocracy?
> (Wilkinson 1999: 118)

Tantam and van Deurzen's paper seems to me to offer a clear example of the way in which an overblown grandiosity can so easily consume a field which starts to believe its own propaganda about its indispensability to society. The sociologist Harold Wilensky warned us many years ago about the inappropriateness of professionalising occupations like that of psychotherapy:

> All occupations in the human-relations field have only tenuous claims to exclusive competence. This results... from... the embryonic state of the social and psychological sciences on which they draw [cf. Spinelli's quotation, earlier – RH] [and] from the fact that the types of problems dealt with are part of everyday living. The lay public cannot recognize the need for special competence in an area where everyone is 'expert'.
> (1964: 145; cf. Smail 1996)

No wonder, then, that Tantam and van Deurzen feel the need to educate the public about the need for a 'profession' of psychotherapy! In contrast to the above quotation, Tantam and van Deurzen believe that psychotherapists 'are uniquely qualified and experienced in the understanding of what people need for a satisfactory life' (p. 233). Following Wilensky, and Mair (1997), for example, perhaps professional therapists certainly seem to be uniquely qualified at self-interestedly propagating the myth that only they possess such 'expertise' – with 'the continuous overvaluation of the expert's actions typical of many psychotherapeutic theories and a corresponding devaluation of the well-being generated by everyday interaction' (Riikonen and Varaja 1999: 176).

In their paper Tantam and van Deurzen offer various comments about the place of psychotherapy within the wider society – and while the importance of so doing can hardly be gainsaid, the analysis offered here reaches very different conclusions from their own. Rudolf Steiner spoke and wrote in evolutionary terms of our being in what he called the Age of Consciousness Soul: as our consciousness soul develops, people tend to become increasingly anti-social: 'man's [sic] life has entered on a phase in which something that starts by being a social institution turns again and again into something anti-social, and has in turn to be reconstructed' (Steiner 1972/1919: xvi). And as van den Brink (1996: 11, 20) has it,

> We as people are no longer naturally bound to each other, and... all the ancient forms of society,... based on man [sic] as a groupbeing, are falling apart.... We become increasingly imprisoned in ourselves, living only for our own development, our own needs, desires and ideas. In the end it is possible to lose all meaningful contact with the world around us.

In response to this state of affairs, Steiner himself advocated that we quite self-consciously create new 'external' socio-cultural forms which will make a social, community life possible today, and which he saw as being essential for the very survival of sociality... for 'we are already sowing the seeds for the next cultural period, which has been called the "social age"' (ibid.: 20), and which will involve what he called 'communal wisdom'. As he so famously said, 'The healthy social life is found when in the mirror of each human soul the whole community finds its reflection, and when in the community the virtue of each one is living' (quoted in Lipsker 1990: 60).

Far from its being an appropriate antidote to the least healthy anti-social features of the age, the cultural surge in individualised therapy, and the associated privatisation of emotional distress, can be seen as just one more manifestation of this anti-social tendency. The great danger, then, is that individualised professionalised therapy – what Lowenthal (1998: 347) terms 'the egocentric "I Did It My Way" school of counselling and psychotherapy' – might actually be colluding with and reinforcing modernist anti-social tendencies that are at work in human culture more generally (e.g. Lasch 1979; Wallach and Wallach 1983; Bellah et al. 1985; Cushman 1992; Hermans et al. 1992; Rose 1996). And surely even the possibility that this might be so points to the importance of therapists and therapy's professionalisers having an openness to critically locating their theoretical ideologies and clinical practices within the wider evolution of human consciousness and culture.

There is a surely a great danger, then, that the kind of cultural ossification that an institutionalised 'professionalised' therapy, with its officially sanctioned regime of truth, will no doubt bring in its wake may be fundamentally antithetical to developing the kinds of socio-cultural forms that might actually successfully counter the individualising anti-social tendencies operating in modern culture. And if an ongoingly and processually deconstructive approach to therapy as 'profession', clinical practice and cultural form is indeed the most appropriate and healthy future path for psychotherapy (as advocated, for example, by House 1999a and Parker 1999b, or even a kind of 'post-deconstructionism – Riikonen and Vataja 1999), then one sure way to limit the field's capacity for open reflexive deconstruction is to build the kind of hierarchical, legally sanctioned organisational structures advocated by Tantam, van Deurzen and their EAP colleagues. More generally, as Riikonen and Vataja have written, 'the project of various schools and groups of therapists to claim and safeguard forms of interaction and call them "therapy" – in opposition to other forms of interaction thought to be less beneficial – is counterproductive and even dangerous' (1999: 176–7).

In his important book *Developing Communities*, Lievegoed sets out the kinds of procedures and processes that are necessary in developing what he calls a 'Consciousness Soul organisation'; and for him 'very much will depend, especially towards the end of the century, upon whether small groups succeed in creating real, true communities in this new style, and working further with them' (1991: 20). Similarly, Evans (1996: xv) has recently written that

> In the struggle to awaken the community we are trying to heal the separation and isolation which is the result of increasing individualism.... If the world is not to fall apart then groups will need to arise where people can really find each other and themselves.

It seems to this writer that the Independent Practitioners Network (Totton 1997c; Chapters 1 and 16, this volume) is far closer to such a New Paradigm organisational philosophy – of real face-to-face intersubjective encounter, relationship and co-operative inquiry and mutual growth – than are any of the old-paradigm hierarchical 'psycho-bureaucracies' whose stated aim is systematically to colonise and control the rich pluralistic field of therapy and counselling in Britain and beyond. Certainly, Totton's sobering warning, that 'Trying to control "what therapy is" may end up preventing it from being anything worth having' (1997b: 336), is one which the didactic professionalisers would surely do well to contemplate long and hard.

CHAPTER 4

Therapy on the Couch? – A client scrutinises the therapy phenomenon: A review essay

INTRODUCTION

What about therapy's shadow?.... Who needs who in psychotherapy?.... [B]eing the sole focus of someone else's interest is a double-edged sword.
                    (Sands, p. 112, 121)

As psychotherapy and counselling become progressively institutionalised as clinical practices and psychosocial cultural phenomena, it arguably becomes increasingly important for the health of therapy that there be a diversity of voices prepared to interrogate, emperor's clothes-like, the tacit assumptions that underlie and drive the therapy phenomenon (hereafter capitalised as 'Therapy'), lest its customs, practices and legitimising ideology lapse into self-serving expediency and/or self-fulfilling complacency. There have, of course, been a number of distinguished and varyingly cogent *practitioner*-critiques of the therapy phenomenon in recent years – by among others, John Heron, James Hillman, Alex Howard, John Kaye, Glenn Larner, Peter Lomas, Betty McLellan, Jeffrey Masson, Raj Persaud, David Pilgrim, Eero Riikonen, Robert Sardello, David Smail, Ernesto Spinelli, Brian Thorne... – together with an increasing number of more academically inspired critiques: George Albee, Dana Cloud, Frederick Crews, Philip Cushman,

This is a greatly extended review article of Anna Sands' (a pseudonym) enthralling book *Falling for Therapy: Psychotherapy from a Client's Point of View* (Basingstoke: Macmillan, 2000). At the time of writing some decade ago now, there was very little literature written by therapists commenting critically upon client testimonies of their experiences of therapy. At the time I entered substantial correspondence with 'Rosie Alexander', 'Anna Sands' and 'Natalie Simpson', all of whom were pioneers in what has subsequently become known as the Client Voice Movement (see Chapter 5, this volume); and three substantial chapters of my book *Therapy Beyond Modernity* are devoted to detailed and appreciative analyses of book–length client testimonies by Alexander, Sands and the late Ann France. The depth of insight into the therapeutic experience that Sands' book gives us is difficult to overestimate.

Robyn Dawes, Tana Dineen, William Epstein, Edward Erwin, Frank Furedi, Martin Gross, Nicky Hart, David Ingleby, Roger Lowe, Richard Ofshe, Ian Parker, Thomas Szasz, Ethan Watters, Bernie Zilbergeld.... Each of these critics has, in their own way, offered cautionary commentary on modern culture's tendency to embrace Therapy as a major, if not *the* major, solution to modern difficulties of living.

Alas, and in stark contrast to these lengthy lists of distinguished 'professional' critics, the number of therapy (ex-)*clients/patients* who have found the courage to challenge Therapy from a position of confidence and authority has been minimal – 'Rosie Alexander', 'Ann France', 'Natalie Simpson' (all, revealingly, pseudonymous critics) – and disquietingly less than would surely have been good for the field. I contend that Therapy would benefit greatly from such client perspectives; for no matter how much personal therapy/training analysis is done by trainee and practising therapists, the very fact that they *are* (trainee-) practitioners means that their client experience can rarely if ever be that of a client uncontaminated by what I call (following Foucault and Parker) Therapy's 'regime of truth' – whose motivation is simply that of seeking therapy for help with their difficulties (and very occasionally otherwise) of living. For as 'Anna Sands' points out in her formidably impressive new book *Falling for Therapy* (hereafter, *FfT*), 'Most of us [clients] stumble into therapy knowing little about it' (p. 3); and 'For many lay clients..., to go to a therapist means there is "something wrong with you"' (p. 5).

In short, we therapists and counsellors really need to know from the client's voice just what struggles are entailed in being a client, and the effects that our therapeutic regime of truth has upon client subjectivity and being-possibilities. For it is only with such knowledge that we might just have a sporting chance of creating a therapy culture which is truly humane, openly reflexive and enabling, rather than profession-centred and self-serving.

Ann France (in her 1988 book *Consuming Psychotherapy*) and Rosie Alexander (in her *Folie à Deux*, FaB, 1995) began the process of clients *talking back* to Therapy, and this important but suggestively sparse tradition has been greatly enriched by Sands' book. For in this engagingly intelligent, highly readable and timely book, she takes the client-critique of Therapy to new levels of sophistication. My own reading of *FfT* is very much informed by my own struggles with deconstructing Therapy's regime of truth (House 2003a), albeit from the limited perspective of the practitioner with considerable 'training' experience of Therapy as a client; and the themes which I will highlight and develop will draw heavily on the fruits of those struggles – in the process illustrating how I found many parallels with my own critical understandings of Therapy in this admirable book.

One of the key questions that recurred for me throughout the book was whether there is something intrinsic to therapy *qua* therapy that inevitably and necessarily leads to many of the difficulties she highlights, or whether her critique is more properly located with poor therapeutic practice, or one particular approach which did not suit her particular needs or personality. In what follows I will attempt to address this complex but critically important question – indeed, the answer to this question may ultimately determine whether Therapy is to fulfil its promise and pretension to being a truly emancipatory and sustainable healing practice.

SCENE-SETTING

The 'therapeutic' relationship can harm and hurt as well as help and heal.

   (p. 5)

In Chapter 1 Sands wastes no time in getting down to pinpointing some highly uncomfortable questions for *any* practitioner – and particularly, perhaps, psychodynamic ones. Thus, she asks, 'Are problems more likely to arise in therapy when a propensity on both sides to perceive a hidden agenda is a driving force of the work?'; 'Is there a sense in which "analysis" can pathologise our humanness?'; 'What happens… when dealing with feelings becomes a profession?'; '[D]o therapists, at times, help to create new problems – problems which stem primarily from the nature of some psychotherapeutic practice?'; 'What part do the system and the environment of therapy play, and what part is played by the individual psyches of those who create that environment?'. And all this in the first two pages – oouucchh! Clearly this book was to be no easy read for therapists wedded to any degree of taken-for-granted, profession-centred complacency about either their own particular practice, or the wider legitimacy of Therapy as a helping 'profession'.

For the record, and to facilitate understanding of what follows, I will just say at this point that Sands had two extensive experiences of therapy: the first being analytically inclined with a male therapist-analyst, and which Sands believed to have precipitated a major breakdown; and a second, humanistically/transpersonally inclined therapy with a female practitioner, which in general Sands found to be a healing and empowering experience.

PSYCHODYNAMICS AND TRANSFERENCE

[T]he concept of the unconscious means that nothing is irrefutable....
Once someone suggests that something is unconscious, anything –
in theory – is possible. This gives the therapist tremendous power....
[U]nder the gaze of the analyst, I felt at times like a laboratory
specimen laid out on a bench to be dissected.

> (pp. 136–7, 63, 76)

[T]he analyst can get off scot-free by... ascribing the destruction of
the involvement [in therapy] to the magic word 'transference'.

> (James Hillman, quoted on p. 171)

Throughout *FfT*, there are recurrent references to psychoanalysis, and the
ways in which a psychodynamic therapeutic approach can 'tie us up in
knots rather than straighten us out' (p. 7) (cf. the section on 'Material
generation', below). Not least is the way in which an analytic approach can
fetishise thinking and analysis, and, concomitantly, serve to distance both
therapist and client from direct emotional experiencing:

> If the therapist is expected to think about his feelings rather than
> allow them expression..., he might encourage the client only to
> interpret and analyse, to think about her feelings rather than
> experience them. This could, in practice, actually stifle her
> emotions....
>
> (p. 20)

Sands therefore echoes the humanistic view that it is *holistic experiencing*
that is necessary for an authentic experience of realness and participative
aliveness – while in her experience 'a psychoanalytic approach can weaken
our sense of connection with the world and our faith in the validity of all
our judgements and perceptions' (p. 34); for Sands, 'We cannot truly find
ourselves in a technical relationship with a technician of the mind' (p. 77).

In this discussion Sands echoes Indian philosopher Jiddu Krishnamurti's
devastating critique of the analytic attitude, whereby 'The analyser becomes
the censor... [and] must examine every thought' (quoted on p. 60) –
'latch[ing] on to the negative, pok[ing] holes in legitimate strategies for
living, using a stick of predetermined psychodynamic formulations' (ibid.).
For Krishnamurti, *the very act* of analysing oneself, or of being analysed by
another, actively *creates* division and conflict, and the associated artificial
splitting of subject and object, rather than enabling one to discover conflict

that already somehow exists (cf. p. 80): thus, 'If feedback is too clinical, the client can feel she has become... a kind of object' (p. 135). Sure enough, Sands' first therapeutic experience did lead to her reality becoming 'less, rather than more, sharply defined...' (p. 87); and at its worst, analysing can become a defensive substitute for engaged compassion for the client's suffering: '[W]e need to be seen in our wholeness *before* we are fragmented into analysable chunks' (p. 189, my emphasis).

The dangers of an over-reliance on a theoretical model (p. 91) should be self-evident: for the therapist can so easily be emotionally or spiritually unavailable to the client, 'having retreated into a theory about how we think and behave rather than staying with what feels real' (p. 41).

Sands devotes a full chapter to the question of transference – her Chapter 7 is entitled 'Transference – cure or catch-22?'. One danger of the transference is that its dramatic re-enactment can lead to reinforcement rather than reintegration (p. 64) – and there is also the poignant question of just 'who is trying to recreate what' in any re-enactment that might occur within a therapeutic relationship (p. 124). As will be discussed later, psychodynamic therapy commonly tends to accentuate and fetishise the negative aspects of the past, making it 'doubly hard for [the client] to free herself from their effect' (p. 65). As Ernesto Spinelli among others has shown, it is in fact pure surmise (and *deterministic* surmise at that) that the past *causally* influences or determines the present; and if indeed such a worldview is erroneous, then an approach which deliberately seeks to activate 'transference issues' 'can actually mitigate against those issues being properly worked through' (ibid.) by privileging what amounts to a causal-deterministic wild goose chase.

It's not just that 'transference allows therapists to distance themselves' (p. 72, quoting Spinelli); it is by no means necessarily the case that strong emotions aroused within therapy are transference-related (ibid.), and overall, the accurate distinguishing between 'inappropriate transference from the past' and a valid response to the current relationship 'is a minefield' (p. 71). There are surely, moreover, profound and well rehearsed ethical question-marks accompanying any therapeutic approach in which 'transference is artificially [and deliberately – RH] provoked' (p. 118) by the therapist's behaviour.

Sands also turns the psychodynamic approach back upon itself, with potentially devastating effect. Thus, she asks,

> What if... the client... soaks up what the therapist is unable to deal with in himself?.... If the work is coloured by the therapist's unresolved issues, and this is not clarified, then *the nature of the problems and their exact location get lost.*
>
> (p. 140, my emphasis)

And who can *ever* claim to have worked through all of their own 'material'? – as the work of Robert Young and Jeffrey Masson, among others, has conclusively shown, some of the most 'neurotic acting-out' behaviour imaginable is routinely perpetrated by psychoanalytic organisations run by practitioners who have been psychoanalysed or 'therapised' many times weekly for years on end!

In any case, the very idea of 'having fully worked through' one's 'issues' (the resolution of which is the prime *raison d'être* given for so-called 'training analysis' or therapy) is a peculiarly modernist, linear and individualised view of the psyche – one which is becoming increasingly untenable as postmodern, 'new paradigm', more spiritually informed perspectives on 'self' and 'identity' gain increasing prominence. In the light of all this, it is hardly surprising that, as Sands writes, 'The therapist will not always be able to follow where the client is going' (p. 142); and that 'the problems that arise in psychotherapy... might... also be caused by the confused nature of the relationship' (p. 25) as much as by the client's alleged 'psychopathology' or 're-enactments'.

If this analysis is anything like right, then Sands' assertion that therapists in general are 'playing with fire' in their work (p. 143) – not least because of sheer (and unavoidable) ignorance about what they're actually doing – is uncomfortably close to the mark. For she is surely right in asserting that we do not (yet?) possess 'a sufficiently clear and common understanding of what we mean by mental and emotional health...' (p. 158) – and in referring to 'the unfathomability of the human mind and, therefore, of what therapy is about' (p. 183). Yet this is in stark contrast to a 'profession' which includes 'those who believe that they know what other people really think and feel' (p. 190).

In sum, the dangers of a psychodynamic approach are that 'We become mesmerised by conjecture and hypothesis about what things mean, disappear up blind alleys and lose sight of the target' (p. 60); 'A therapist who tries to attribute everything to the client's experience outside therapy [e.g. to their past], or to what he sees as the symbolic nature of the relationship... implies that he is not prepared to accept her perception of or feelings about present reality' (p. 74); and 'the psychodynamic approach actually encourages the therapist to reenact parts of the damaging aspects of the parent/child relationship' (p. 120). And can any therapist ever guarantee that re-traumatisation will not be the result of therapy? – for 'How confident can practitioners be that their clients will always work through, rather than simply relive, early emotions and experience?' (p. 131).

PATHOLOGISATION

Is there a sense in which 'analysis' can pathologise our humanness?....
If my problems are played back to me as an indelible consequence of
my particular and defective upbringing, as evidence of what is wrong
with me, I feel pathologised.
>   (pp. 2, 28)

Related to the analytic attitude is the question of pathologisation, which,
usually tacitly or unconsciously, invokes some notion of 'healthy normality'
which then becomes a normalising benchmark against which '*ab*normality'
or 'psychopathology' is relationally defined (see in particular Chapters 2
and 10, this volume). Such a worldview on human experience has all kinds
of e(a)ffects – not least of which is to create a legitimate 'object' for the
therapeutic enterprise to work upon, to define itself against – and to give it
its very *raison d'être*.

Sands homes in on the pathologising mentality at a number of points.
Thus, she found that what were for her basic 'givens' of ethical mores in
relationships were pathologised (p. 24); and that the wish for 'a supportive,
natural and open relationship where the client is treated as an equal can be
pathologised in therapy' (p. 37). In engaging with this issue, Sands challenges
the very foundations of a widespread therapeutic worldview that accentuates
the 'negative' and the 'abnormal' and, concomitantly, plays down (or
sometimes even pathologises) the healthy – a notable example being the
analytic notion of 'flight into health'. For perhaps 'we can become *too*
conscious of our feelings, thoughts and actions', thereby 'run[ning] the risk
of losing our energy and enthusiasm, and an essential spontaneity' (p. 200).
She found that 'being more aware of my insecurities has not always been
helpful.... My sister tells me: "You're not as much fun as you used to be
before you did psychotherapy"' (p. 199).

It certainly seems that Freud's essentially pessimistic view of 'human
nature' has surreptitiously influenced generations of analysts and therapists
in this regard – and continues to do so, notwithstanding the strong growth
of the humanistic and transpersonal therapies in recent decades. Thus,
'Therapy cannot feel healthy if the therapist fails to employ the language of
health.... Isn't it primarily the language of psychological disturbance which
informs the concepts framing the work?' (p. 43); and 'Are practitioners
inadvertently [or even 'advertently' – RH] encouraged to stick unhelpful
and unfitting labels on their clients, pathologising rather then improving
their self-image?' (p. 44). There is also the greatly neglected question of
whether and, if so, how the discourse of 'psychopathology' *actively creates*

what happens in therapy (cf. the section on 'Therapy's regime of truth', below, and Chapter 2, this volume). Thus, '[I]f concepts of psychological disturbance form the basis of an exchange between two people, how will that affect what emerges?', asks Sands (p. 188).

Worse still, the regime of truth constructed by the discourse of 'psychopathology' can even create *the very way that clients think about themselves* – 'it is incorrect to claim that the client is free to choose whether or not she is influenced by such terms' (p. 45); and 'I began to wonder if I was riddled with unusual psychological deformities which somehow set me apart. Was I in some undesirable way different from other people?' (p. 87). Moreover, if the client actively resists the language of psychopathology (and I have had this experience as a client myself), no doubt such resistance is often pathologised too! (cf. the section on 'Iatrogenic "mad"-making effects', below). And at its worst, Sands 'began to feel that whatever I said to my analyst would be taken as yet another illustration of what was wrong with me' – leading in turn to 'the loss of a sense of my own identity' (p. 90).

Sands even questions the *motivation* underpinning the diagnostic-pathologising mentality: for 'Diagnosing the other person is a favourite pastime for most of us when we feel ill at ease, and won't the psychotherapist feel he is doing his job successfully when he identifies the client's difficulties?' (p. 97)

In sum, for Sands 'Therapy may… overemphasise difficulties, giving them a significance which is disproportionate' (p. 54); whereas for her, therapy should be about experiencing oneself 'as a whole person and not… as a case, a patient' (p. 86).

IATROGENIC 'MAD'-MAKING EFFECTS

The potential for damage should always be borne in mind….Therapy can play havoc with one's equilibrium and sense of reality… a kind of game which can become a maddening experience, in both senses of the word…. For me it felt, for a short time, as if I had gone permanently crazy…. The internal chaos I was caught up in bore little identifiable or obvious resemblance to anything that had happened to me before…. For the first time in my life I experienced panic attacks, constant nights of sleepless confusion and an eerie loss of self-confidence.

(pp. 5, 82, 135, 142, 143)

Sands invokes a common criticism of psychoanalytic therapeutic approaches when she writes

> If a disagree with what my therapist says, he can infer that I am denying it, that it is something that I am unable or unwilling to look at. If this angers me, my anger can be taken as a further indication of my need to deny. I am being defensive, so what the therapist says must be true.
>
> (p. 55)

The imposed discourse of psychopathology, in tandem with the assumed expertise of the therapist, can easily destabilise one's sense of coherent identity, creating rather than alleviating the kind of 'madnesses' that therapy is alleged to 'treat'. Thus,

> If our perception of and way of dealing with reality seem constantly to be called into question, this undermines our sense of our own sanity. And if our ways of interacting with the world seem suddenly no longer valid, then our sense of being able to manage the world can begin to dissolve.
>
> (p. 38)

And perhaps most damning of all:

> Knowing whether or not my perceptions are correct is fundamental to my sense of my own sanity. Leaving the client in the dark in this respect can promote feelings of confusion and helplessness, whilst preserving the power that the practitioner's distance gives him. Therapy can become an irresponsible charade in which the client is unable to pursue the truth.
>
> (p. 93)

Moreover, as Hillman and Ventura have suggested, there is a danger that 'the very focus on oneself… is, *per se*, a depressive move' (quoted on p. 139).

The question of iatrogenic effects will recur in diverse ways throughout this chapter – and not least in the next section.

THERAPY'S 'REGIME OF TRUTH'

Whose truths do we investigate during therapy? The client's, or that of the therapist, or of the particular school of thought which the therapist follows?... If an adherence to a particular theory takes precedence over an adherence to truth, the client is oppressed, the practitioner loses his way and both are squeezed into a straightjacket.... Is analysis itself irrational in its dependence on theory?... Does it also confine and narrow down?
>   (pp. 51, 150, 153–4)

My reading of *FfT* to this point has on several occasions pointed towards the radical and disturbing idea that, at its worst, therapy can construct a 'regime of truth' which self-fulfillingly creates a framework serving to guarantee its own legitimacy, and outside of the confines of which it is often exceedingly difficult for clients *or* therapists to think. Throughout *FfT*, Sands repeatedly describes aspects of her own client experience which highlight the dangers of a therapeutic regime of truth being 'imposed upon them' (p. 15). Thus, she refers to therapy's *'way of thinking* to which the client will become particularly susceptible' (p. 3, my emphasis), and the way in which 'the characteristics of the [therapeutic] interaction will, in great measure, be defined by [the therapist's] professional training' (ibid.) – 'a training which will have changed the way [the therapist] sees and hears the people who become his clients' (p. 19). Sands further offers a devastating counterintuitive insight that, in 'training someone to respond in a certain way', this may paradoxically render that person *less* able to be (spontaneously) responsive (p. 151). Sands even speculates as to whether therapy training might 'sometimes make practitioners less rather than better able to communicate with their clients' (p. 42).

A major danger, then, is that 'the practitioner... cannot be free of the theoretical assumptions on which he works' (p. 20) – and at its self-fulfilling worst, 'Could [the therapist's] reality even help to *create* what his training has told him to look for?... And how does such [therapeutic] vocabulary influence the practitioner's view of himself?' (ibid., p. 45, my emphasis). Certainly, 'Attachment to a particular theory can restrict and restrain, engendering tunnel vision and a dangerous narrow-mindedness' (p. 128) – and with the attendant danger that conventional procedural guidelines may 'take precedence over the ground rules about decent human behaviour' (p. 25).

There might even be 'a sense in which both practitioner and client can become victims – victims of the circumstances they have created, *of the way in which the practitioner works'* (p. 148, my emphasis). Moreover, therapy's regime of truth can only be reinforced in a situation in which 'what procedures the therapist propounds, the patient is predisposed to accept' (quoting Mark Aveline, p. 30) – not least because 'I felt it was my responsibility to learn to deal with my analyst's particular approach, since it was the psychotherapy contract I had undertaken to fulfil' (p. 68). And in a neat table-turning exercise on analytic orthodoxy, Sands asks whether the client might sometimes enter therapy as 'a blank wall for *the therapist's* projections'! (p. 58, my emphasis) – for 'Therapists make their clients the object of their negative projections, as well as the other way around' (ibid.).

Certainly, the effects of a constraining regime of truth can be dramatic, as in 'when a therapist is reluctant to take on board things which do not… fit his particular framework', which can in turn be 'hampering and demoralising for the client' (p. 62). In her first therapy, Sands describes the experience of feeling that she had done something wrong 'because I was not doing what I thought analysands were "supposed to do"' (p. 96). And in some regimes of therapeutic truth, 'practitioners encourage us to see ourselves as tainted, defective, as victims rather than effective survivors' (p. 139) – another unfortunate (deterministic) legacy of Freud, perhaps.

Perhaps the most damning example of therapy's regime of truth occurs when, 'if you challenge [therapy's] value, it is [seen as] a sign that you need more therapy' (p. 144). (Rosie Alexander and Jeffrey Masson are particularly revealing on this phenomenon.)

In sum, then, an unproblematised regime of therapeutic truth can lead a therapist to 'unconsciously expect the client to encompass their reality' (p. 13), and inculcate 'a way of thinking…' (p. 3). Even the *apparently* innocent endeavour of trying to find 'underlying themes' can *itself* become an inflexible regime of truth, leading to connections being made by the therapist where none exists in the client's mind (p. 10). The implication of this, as I have written elsewhere (e.g. see Chapter 6, this volume), is that in order to avoid imposing a subjectivity-constructing straightjacket of therapeutic orthodoxy, therapy at its best should be *ongoingly and processually deconstructive* of its professional ideologies and clinical practices if the kinds of dangers so ably highlighted in *FfT* are to be as far as possible avoided.

'MATERIAL GENERATION'

In the end, I found my relationship with my analyst… more difficult than those I had gone there to talk about….Therapy… will also create a chemistry of its own…. [D]oesn't therapy sometimes reveal, sometimes replicate, and sometimes create the feelings and behaviour that arise there?... Perhaps we need more theories – about therapy's contribution to psychological disturbance.

(pp. 76, 132, 133, 155)

Closely related to the question of iatrogenic effects is what I have come to call 'material generation'(House 2003a: 64–8) – which refers to the disturbing insight that therapy can, *in and of itself,* create (as opposed to simply respond to pre-existing) difficulties – which then provide 'material' which in turn gives therapy much if not most of its *raison d'être.* Or put differently, therapy can quite surreptitiously and self-fulfillingly generate the difficulties to which it *then* offers a solution. There are many points in her narrative at which Sands alludes to this danger. First, it is by no means necessarily true that problems that arise in therapy can always be ascribed to what is being imported from 'outside' – e.g. from the client's past (p. 133); and therapy can 'reinforce fear and pain' when it 'recreates and amplifies... old problems' (p. 137). For 'so-called solutions... may even perpetuate the problem' (p. 144), with the emphasising of difficulties 'simply mak[ing] us feel more imprisoned by them' (p. 152).

Sands cites Jung's (possibly generalisable) view that free association can debilitatingly 'lead the client back into the complexes which already imprison her' (p. 140). In the course of her first therapy, Sands moved from a state of being reasonably happy with herself and her life, to one in which 'Everything seemed overwhelmingly significant but nothing seemed quite real. I felt wonderful and terrible, powerful and impotent, full of love and full of fear, all at the same time' (p. 141) – what she refers to as 'the hallucinogenic state I went into' (p. 142). And at one point she refers to feeling like 'a rabbit caught and frozen in the headlights' (p. 163), and quite unable to assess whether her therapy was 'working' or not (cf. the section on informed consent, below).

Therapists' widespread propensity to 'remain unknown and anonymous' (p. 18) can precipitate doubt, uncertainty, paranoia – and maybe worse. New clients typically enter a therapy relationship in a position of far inferior knowledge about what to expect, and in such circumstances, 'Therapy then becomes, in part, a process of learning how to deal with an environment which is... singular and unknown' (p. 29) – one which can itself become 'an additional source of disturbance' (ibid.), particularly if the therapist does not see it as her job to do all she can to help neutralise the informational and procedural imbalances and set the client at his ease.

Perhaps it is, again, the analytic approach that is the main object of Sands' concerns. There can be little doubt that the clichéd orthodox analytic 'blank

screen' stance *is* material-generating: thus, 'An absence of response can...
become, in itself, a diversion away from what the client is trying to sort out' (p.
86); and more damningly:

> Knowing whether or not my perceptions are correct is fundamental
> to my sense of my own sanity. Leaving the client in the dark in this
> respect can promote feelings of confusion and helplessness, *whilst*
> *preserving the power that the practitioner's distance gives him.* Therapy
> then becomes an irresponsible charade in which the client is unable
> to pursue the truth.
>
> (p. 93, my emphasis)

It could be countered that it is not therapy (or analytic therapy) *per se*, as a
generality, that is the prime causal factor in material generation, but (for
example) the (previously hidden or dormant?) 'issues' the client brings into
therapy, or the personality of the therapist, or the particular therapeutic
approach she follows. I return at length to this critical question in my
'Discussion' section, below. Sands does herself offer one clear argument for
therapy *qua therapy* being the culprit, when she writes that '*Because the focus*
is always on the client, the system becomes pernicious, feeding the problems
it highlights and leaving the client carrying the burden of responsibility' (p.
153, my emphasis). There might well be much mileage in this insight for
sorting out precisely how it can be that therapy *qua* therapy is, or can be, a
self-fulfilling material-generating enterprise.

Might it also be that there can all too easily be something very seductive
about Therapy – or what commonly happens within a therapeutic framework
– which can then very easily precipitate counter-therapeutic effects? Certainly,
Rosie Alexander (in her client testimonial book *Folie à Deux*) repeatedly
describes the kind of hypnotic, mesmerising thrall into which she felt drawn,
and from which, once in it, she found it quite impossible to withdraw (see
House 2003a: Chapter 6). Similarly, Sands revealingly writes that although
some of her first analyst's comments were

> irrelevant, far-fetched or illogical..., at the same time *I was seduced.* I
> had fallen for therapy and, as a result, my truth... often took a back
> seat. Instead of rejecting ideas that felt out of place, I tried to find
> meaning in them
>
> (p. 57, my emphasis)

– material generation *par excellence*. On reading this I was left reflecting on
whether we remotely begin to understand the attachment and the sometimes

erotic dynamics that an intense individualised therapeutic encounter can easily trigger. Nor should we find this in the least surprising, given that 'In therapy, a lifetime's desire, hope, confusion and distress are condensed' (p. 141). It might be important for an ethical, responsible psychotherapy to do all it can to minimise such influences, in order to neutralise the seemingly pernicious counter-therapeutic effects that can so easily be precipitated in such an interpersonally intense, rarefied and individualised framework.

I refer to some of these crucial questions in the 'Discussion' section, below. For the moment I leave the final word to Anna Sands:

> everything is called into question, everything is up for grabs. Our feelings are put under a magnifying glass. Our psychological and emotional complexities can be emphasised to a point where, if we are not careful, the head begins to swim. We collude in the construction of misleading and damaging reinventions of ourselves.
>
> (pp. 80–1)

If this description is anything like accurate, then we might well ask whether it's any wonder that therapy and its associated practices commonly generate at least as much 'material' as the client took into therapy to 'work on' in the first place.

THE THORNY PROBLEM OF INFORMED CONSENT

> [I]f we knew exactly what to ask and what answers we needed, we probably wouldn't be there in any case.... There are no guarantees in therapy.... How do I, the client – or how, in the end, can anyone – distinguish with any certainty between those things which are caused by the flaws of the system, or by therapist error, and those things which are caused by transference and which, with any persistence, might be resolved?
>
> (pp. 3, 75, 166)

I believe the issue of informed consent to be one of the most difficult and under-recognised problems of the whole therapy experience, and Sands is very eloquent about these difficulties from the client's viewpoint. Thus, although 'most of us assume it will be beneficial' (p. 3), 'I had no idea what I was letting myself in for' (p. 4) – or more graphically, '[Going for therapy] feels a bit like applying for a job of being oneself, but we're not sure what the qualifications are' (p. 5). Moreover, this is particularly difficult when the newly encountered practitioner is less than forthcoming about the therapeutic experience and the language of therapy: 'The client has to learn the rules of her particular therapist. I learnt them through a process of trial and error' (p. 6). Later, we read that 'no one tells the client the rules of the psychotherapy game' (p. 22); and that 'Going into any kind of potentially healing relationship is, inevitably, an act of faith' (p. 26). Certainly, *how to be* in a relationship that is 'a hazardous journey to an unknown destination in which we are each dependent on our travelling companion' (p. 48) is far from being an easy position for the client to be in.

If it is impossible for *practitioners* to give any guarantees that 'clients will always work through, rather than simply relive, early emotions and experience' (p. 131), to what extent can *a client* ever exercise informed consent at the beginning of a therapy experience? – though it is, of course, arguable that one *is* consenting to there being no way of knowing what will subsequently unfold in the therapy encounter! – except that the therapist will very often be working within the bounds of a published set of ethical guidelines. The difficulties are only compounded when 'doubts about a certain therapist or style of therapy may only become manifest when it is too late' (p. 144). And when it comes to trying to define harm or damage, 'it is difficult to define "damage" or to be sure of its cause' (p. 161). For unless mistakes along the way are very obvious, 'it is only when the work is finished that we can properly judge the outcome. At what point in therapy do we evaluate the outcome?… How long does one wait? How many times does one try?' (pp. 164, 165). One might also add, to what extent is a client in therapy able to make a relatively dispassionate assessment of her therapy when she is in the middle of the process? – especially if, as for Sands, 'at the time [during my first therapy], I did not know what was happening to me. I had no intellectual knowledge of the stages and processes of what was… called "therapy"' (p. 175).

Moreover, even if one's psychic equilibrium is relatively unaffected and uncompromised, the client is still left with the difficulty of being 'caught, poised in wait for the benefits to materialise…. Perhaps it's a bit like fruit machines – the more you put in, the greater can be the desire to keep on going until you get something back' (pp. 121, 122).

What possible solutions or responses might there be to the inevitable asymmetry of knowledge about what therapy entails when clients enter therapy? At the very least, says Sands, 'Professional practitioners cannot afford to play down the dangers involved in the potency of the cocktail they offer' (p. 90) – for 'How many clients are aware of the… huge emotional investment and upheaval therapy involves? Most of us are not' (p. 131). For Sands, it is crucial that 'The negotiating rights of the client within the therapeutic contract must be disentangled from the notion of transference' (p. 161) – certainly no easy task! Perhaps the place to begin is for practitioners to be open right from the outset, at contracting/initial meeting stage, that it is *in principle* impossible for either party to know what will happen in a particular therapy relationship (within the ethical boundaries of the work), and therefore impossible for the client to give informed consent to the *content* of their therapy experience. Yet how many practitioners would dare to be so honest at the outset, for fear of putting off at least some, and possibly many, potential new clients? – difficult questions indeed. Certainly, it seems to me that a significant amount of therapy is a very long way from embracing such openness.

As I was penning this section it struck me that it would be very interesting to conduct the following thought-experiment (a useful and highly sobering training exercise, perhaps!): Were one to attempt to devise a therapeutic approach that was deliberately designed to minimise the capacity of the client to possess the resources for clear perception and decision-making about their therapeutic experience, how might one design it? – and then to consider just how many actual characteristics of real (psychodynamic and other) therapies coincide with the framework one has dreamt up. Certainly, one pretty safe bet for such a procedure would be to make it difficult if not impossible meaningfully to question one's therapist or analyst 'if the consequence [were] always a response directed back at one's own difficulties' (p. 164).

In sum, it seems to me that it is every practitioner's solemn responsibility to be fully aware of the 'impossible' position in which client's routinely find themselves on entering therapy, and that they should take active steps to inform clients from the outset about what they might subsequently experience in therapy – or in other words, a conscious and deliberate attempt to *demystify* therapy and its associated regime of truth; and that *such an ongoing demystification process should be explicitly built in to the therapeutic process from beginning to end.* In this way, at least the therapist will be doing her level best to minimise the possibility that a mesmerising or self-fulfilling 'regime of truth' is being imposed upon her client.

QUESTIONS OF ACCOUNTABILITY

There are no diplomas in emotional literacy.... (p. 42). [P]sychotherapists... have shown a marked resistance to taking critical feedback from users seriously. (quoting David Pilgrim, p. 178).... [T]here is no other profession in which the practitioner is so well equipped to attribute a lack of success to the client's problems rather than his own. And there is no other situation in which the client would so easily allow herself to be dumfounded by this assertion.... We hear relatively little about the aftermath of unsuccessful cases. (pp. 160, 173)

Sands has a lot of revealing – and sobering – things to say about accountability and professionalism, particularly in her Chapter 16. She makes it absolutely clear, first, that she did *not* want to make any formal complaint against her first therapist (p. 175): all she wanted was for him 'to acknowledge that he was partly responsible for what had been a terrifying disintegration' (ibid.). But the confusion, shame and hurt she had experienced 'was never addressed either by my analyst or his colleagues' (ibid.). She observes that 'The issue of mishandling or incompetence... is not... covered in ethical codes' (p. 176), and she paints a revealing contrast between therapists' willingness within therapy to evaluate the effects of others' relationships 'unstintingly', and their extreme reticence when it comes to evaluating their fellow therapists' work (p. 177). And the reticence she discovered hardly inspired Sands' confidence in the 'profession' of psychotherapy: 'When things go wrong in therapy, and no one is prepared to talk about why, the general public is right to question the integrity of the profession' (p. 178). Overall, then, it seemed as if no one in the 'profession' wanted openly to acknowledge – for whatever reason – that her therapy experience had, for whatever reason, gone badly wrong.

For Sands, the field's reticence and unwillingness openly to engage with unsatisfactory therapy experiences can precipitate yet more traumatisation, with clients being left 'feeling alienated and further disempowered' (p. 180). A therapist's silence in the light of client difficulties 'can chip away at her sense of self, and her perception of her own sanity' (ibid.).

All this is very sobering, of course, for those who would professionalise psychotherapy and counselling along the lines of the conventional professions. For 'Some therapists have a tendency to conduct themselves as if they belong to a secret society' (p. 179): 'the relevant umbrella organisation' told Sands that her ex-analyst couldn't meet with her 'for insurance reasons', because she had made a complaint (p. 181) – despite Sands having emphasised that that she 'had no wish to take him to court and the last thing I wanted was money' (ibid.). Rather, all she required was 'some insights into why things had become so unmanageable. This they could not, or would not, do. No one mentioned the responsibility of the therapist; and Sands had to turn to the professional literature for confirmation that things can indeed "go wrong" in therapy (ibid.). But what hurt her most of all was that 'my analyst never expressed any regret' (ibid.).

One can only speculate about the motivations for such quasi-Kafka-esque secrecy – therapists' (understandable?) fear of costly and potentially humiliating litigation?; an unwillingness of therapists and their professional organisations even to consider (at least in public!) that it might just be Therapy's regime of truth that was the problem? (turkeys seldom if ever vote for Christmas when livelihoods depend on it); professional organisations' spin-driven desire to minimise bad publicity at a time when they are assiduously courting respectability and seeking statutory regulation of the field?…

In spite of what was clearly a highly traumatic therapy experience which, in some sense at least, Sands attributes to Therapy, in her book she is impressively and maturely non-litigious about the whole situation: for as she states, 'If accountability is reduced to the villains-and-victims mentality of the insurance broker, then therapy will not move forward. Legislation and formal contracts can undermine the very principles one is trying to safeguard – those of partnership and, ultimately, understanding and agreement' (pp. 185–6) – therapy bureaucracies please take note!… Sands' deep desire is for *a human rather than a legalised resolution of conflict* – 'When therapy has been the opposite of therapeutic, the client needs and deserves an apology, and informed and balanced feedback' (p. 184). Would-be HPC regulators of the psychological therapies, also please take note!

PRECEPTS FOR GOOD-ENOUGH THERAPY

> The way that some practitioners treat their clients – in the name of therapy – is nothing short of outrageous…. When I worked with [my second therapist], I did not feel unequal or less powerful. Two people can meet as equals in a relationship which is asymmetrical, if they meet first and foremost as two people.
>
> (pp. 196, 27)

It will be useful to consider the lessons Sands draws from her two highly contrasting therapy experiences. One theme that recurs at several points – and which interestingly parallels the views of writers like Peter Lomas and David Smail – is how unpretentious *ordinariness* can be a highly effective antidote to the rarefied preciousness or incongruous over-affectation that can perhaps characterise therapy at its worst – but only if such ordinariness is real and authentic, of course, rather than just one more adopted 'therapeutic strategy'. Thus, we read that 'In my experience, good therapy feels not unlike a normal conversation… "normal conversations" about everyday things…

can have an important role to play' (p. 10) – rather than always being interpreted as 'a defence' or 'resistance', as routinely occurs within many regimes of therapeutic truth. Moreover, 'The therapist has to behave like a real human being, not a professional interpreter. If he does, key issues of power and control will not necessarily work against the client' (p. 28). And later, Sands refers approvingly to 'a matter-of-fact atmosphere' (p. 95): 'In my second experience of therapy... it was an adult relationship with a real, receptive person' (p. 76) – in contrast to her first therapist, with whom she 'sometimes felt he did not speak to me as if I was a normal human being' (p. 33). For Sands, 'Behaving abnormally seems to be an odd way of trying to help someone towards a greater normality' (p. 37). Finally, 'When therapy distorts the ordinary, we risk losing sight of compassion, clarity and logic, and instead perpetuate a feeling of illegitimacy.... [I]t is necessary to cherish the ordinary enough to leave it alone' (pp. 187, 153).

Sands also alludes to the not unrelated question of *flexibility* – the presence of which, of course, is a natural counterweight to the dangers of a rigid, subjectivity-creating, material-generating regime of therapeutic truth (cf. earlier discussion). Thus, for example, in terms of appointments, 'It should be possible to strike a sensible balance between flexibility and consistency' (p. 15) – a principle which, some might argue, might also be far more widely applied. Her second therapist was certainly perfectly happy to go along with meeting at increasingly infrequent intervals (p. 16). Moreover, rather than the roles of 'therapist' and 'client' being immutably fixed and immobile within a 'modernist' regime of truth, Sands evokes a more fluid, postmodern approach to therapy when she refers to how a therapeutic journey of freedom 'involves the client being able to act both as a person and a client, and the therapist being able to act both as a person and a therapist' (p. 157).

Sands also wants a therapist who is willing to discuss the dangers of therapy (p. 175; cf. earlier discussion). She wants laughter and joy as well as pain (p. 202); a therapist who believes in mystery and enchantment rather than psychopathology (p. 197); a therapy which 'salvage[s] the sacred and honour[s] our sacredness' (p. 195). She wants a therapy where 'heart' is not dominated by an authoritarian 'head', and which recognises that 'we are more than a simple reductionist equation of cause and effect. If psychotherapy is to be an honourable profession, it must honour and nurture our essentialness..., the unanalysable what-you-are-made-of' (ibid.). Therapists practising in this way will need both courage and sincerity (p. 194) – with therapy being 'a celebration of the richness and dynamism of the psyche', recognising 'the greatest gift of all – our shared humanity' (pp. 194, 149).

In her passionate advocacy of a deeply human(e) and creative approach to therapy, Sands' description offers us – if we are able to hear it – an invaluable cautionary reminder about just what can happen when a practitioner- and Therapy-centred discourse and ideology threaten to obscure the source of what is truly healing within a genuinely helping encounter.

DISCUSSION

It's not like buying something in Marks and Spencers, trying it on and then taking it back if it isn't right.
(p. 167)

I can only scratch the surface of the critical issues that Sands' client perspective on Therapy stirred up for me in reading this important book. A quite crucial question is to what extent Sands' criticisms are primarily and relatively exclusively a criticism of psychodynamic therapeutic approaches: that is, to what extent are her criticisms generalisable to therapy *in general*? For her second therapeutic experience with a humanistically inclined practitioner certainly seems to have been a successful experience for her. Yet we are faced with insurmountable methodological difficulties here – as Sands herself points out – as it is ultimately impossible to know what might have happened had Sands gone to the second therapist first. Thus, for example, the first experience might have prepared her in some way for the second, such that the latter would not have been nearly so successful had she not had the first therapeutic experience.

Sands maintains that '*The context of therapy* can generate fear very easily' (p. 87, my emphasis); and she does refer to the problem that psychotherapy *qua psychotherapy* 'can promote a dissolving of the adult's boundary between fantasy and reality, and cause similar confusion and turmoil' (p. 81). However, to say that confusion and turmoil (for example) *can* occur within a psychotherapeutic framework is not *necessarily* the same as saying that it is 'psychotherapy' *in and of itself* that causes such experienced malaise. This is surely a critical – and highly complex – area of concern that requires far more urgent attention in the field than it has received to date. It might be, for example, that *certain approaches* to therapy are more likely than others to precipitate such an effect; or that a certain type of 'personality' (however one defines such a term, and whether it be client, therapist, or the way they meet) might, for whatever reason(s), precipitate it. But to sustain the view that psychotherapy as a generality *necessarily* generates such client difficulties needs far more research and reflection than can be offered either here or in *FfT*.

The *kind* of argument that would be required to sustain this radically disquieting view might look something like the following. Because therapy in general tends to focus on, and disproportionately accentuate, 'the negative' in human experience (cf. earlier discussion), this in turn can 'cause our existing fears [for example] to *appear* more rather than less substantial, and throw in a few extra ones for good measure' (p. 90, my emphasis). Or in other words, the subjective experience of clients in therapy may take on a distorted one-sidedness that matches the artificial bias towards the negative of the typical therapeutic regime of truth. And if, then, clients in therapy experience such distorted subjectivity as an intrinsic aspect of their 'true' identity rather than as, in some sense, a distorted artefact of the artificial therapy setting, this can easily *create* and precipitate (for example) crises of identity, and even sanity, that simply were not present or active before the client entered therapy. In such a case, it could very plausibly be claimed that it is therapy *qua therapy* that has (unnecessarily?) precipitated distress or disturbance that would not have otherwise been present.

These are issues, I repeat, which surely require urgent and sustained attention by a field which aspires to full 'profession' status; for if they are not fully and adequately addressed and dealt with, then severe and justifiable doubts will inevitably remain about whether Therapy can ever qualify as, and deserve the hallowed status of, a legitimate 'profession'.

Sands is very insightful about the many contradictions at the heart of the psychotherapeutic experience, which can themselves become highly destabilising. Thus, she found her first (analytic) therapist's refusal to call her by her name highly incongruous within what is 'a highly personal setting' (p. 12). Moreover, therapy is at once 'relatively formal' *and* 'unusually intimate' – and to Sands, 'the two seemed at times to be impossibly incompatible' (p. 21). And 'If the therapist is a blank screen we may function at the level of the personal but without the personal.... This ambivalence can cause one to feel adrift and "ungrounded"' (p. 86).

There can also be a profound contradiction in therapy to the extent that the ethical therapist's task is, in effect and when viewed from the level of individual therapy relationships, *to put herself out of a job* – i.e. to help clients (presumably as effectively *and efficiently* as possible) *not* to require further therapy. (Now at least some therapists would probably not agree with such a view of therapy – but I think that the majority of clients *would* do so; and at the risk of embracing an uncritical consumerism, it is surely the client who is buying the service who should be listened to most in defining just what the purpose of therapy is and should be – or else we would most certainly be open to the quite indefensible charge of being a practitioner-centred 'profession'.)

Put bluntly, then, therapists (at least those in private practice) commonly need their clients in order to pay the mortgage – and so in such a situation, we must surely ask: *Just what conscious or less-than-conscious forces might be surreptitiously feeding into our therapeutic approaches that might – albeit unwittingly – bring about situations in which therapy is grossly inefficient from the paying client's viewpoint, and self-serving from the practitioner's?* (Note that I am not needing to invoke some kind of conspiracy theory here, as the cruder critics of therapy often do; I am merely suggesting that therapists' collective survival needs may well have all kinds of scarcely visible and unintended side-effects in terms of their chosen institutionalised therapeutic practices – and indeed, given all we know about unconscious group processes, it would be very surprising if there *weren't* such effects.)

One such example might be that of endings – for as Sands observes, while in principle the client is responsible for determining when to end therapy, 'some practitioners seem reluctant to allow their clients to exercise fully that responsibility' (p. 164). Having had such an experience myself, where my own expressed intention to end my therapy (with many months' notice) was systematically pathologised, with all the self-doubt that this inevitably precipitated, the 'endings question' and how therapists routinely make such a precious, fetishised drama out of them, might well constitute one example of the way in which therapeutic practice is unwittingly colonised by the therapist's agenda rather than that of the client.

Sands does indeed directly address this thorny and (for the field) intensely uncomfortable question:

> the therapist is also dependent on the client. He needs the fee his clients pay him and is, in most cases, dependent on them for his income.... He is also dependent on [clients'] need for his help, the very thing which he works towards eliminating. Is there a temptation for the therapist to go on looking for problems in order to keep the client, and for the client to go on looking for problems in order to keep the therapist?
> (p. 123)

In other words, might therapy not typically be setting up *an institutionalised co-dependency relationship* from which, once established, it often becomes very difficult for either client *or therapist* to extricate themselves? – albeit for different dependency reasons, of course. These again are highly prescient and challenging questions that the nascent therapy 'profession' simply cannot sweep under the carpet and ignore.

Overall, *FfT* is certainly *not* a partisan or partial 'therapy-bashing' exercise (as a book such as this one could so easily have become) – and in this it continues the admirable tradition initiated by the late Ann France in her excellent book *Consuming Psychotherapy* (France 1988; see also House 2003a: Chapter 7). As mentioned earlier, Sands is quite explicit about never wanting revenge, or even to make a formal complaint: 'It is not my intention to dismiss the value of therapy which is genuinely therapeutic, but rather to draw attention to what might be counterproductive' (p. ix). Notwithstanding this commendable even-handedness, however, a strong advocate of the beneficence of Therapy might object that the analysis offered in *FfT*, and in this chapter, is heavily biased against therapy – and is perhaps, in the process, guilty of the very 'fixation on the negative' which Sands claims to be a defining feature of bad therapy.

Let me pre-emptively respond by emphasising that, in this chapter, I do not attempt, or pretend to have offered here, a balanced view of therapy; rather, I see it as providing *some kind of necessary counterweight to the heavy preponderance of largely uncritical therapist- and profession-centred literature that dominates the therapy field*. For as Sands herself correctly points out, 'the literature on therapy... often fails to demonstrate a consideration of the client's perspective' (p. 191). I want to state quite unambiguously, then, that I am convinced by the efficacy and beneficence of a great deal of therapy; but I am equally convinced by the importance of the arguments and challenges in *FfT*, and the urgent need for Therapy to face and respond to them fearlessly and without trimming, if therapeutic practice is to continue to mature rather than degenerate into a self-serving, self-perpetuating 'regime of professionalised truth'.

The book only very obliquely alludes to the possibility that *therapists* struggle too – and that there might be considerable personal costs involved in being a professional therapist. Certainly there is no overt mention of this – and yet why should there be, in a book offering a client perspective on Therapy? Perhaps both client *and* therapist are subject to therapy's constraining regime of truth – albeit in different ways, and clearly with different effects (see Chapter 6, this volume).

It seems to this writer that what is required is a sincere, whole-hearted attempt by *both* therapists *and* clients to place themselves in the shoes of the other (*Verstehen*) – and to carry an awareness of the *inherent impossibility* of the relational enterprise in which they are co-creatively engaged. Notice that what I provocatively call therapy's 'inherent impossibility' (following Freud and Janet Malcolm) does not necessarily entail that therapy can't work – indeed, *perhaps the undoubted benefits that can result from it derive specifically from each side's honourable struggle with this very impossibility*.

CONCLUSIONS

Sometimes therapy becomes part of the problem instead of offering some solutions.... Are practitioners sufficiently well-informed about or sensitive towards the possible destructiveness of their work...?
(pp. 171, 163)

In her Introduction Sands states that her book is 'about how it feels to be on the receiving end of therapy' (p. viii). My overriding impression of *Falling for Therapy* is that it is veritably overflowing with intelligent, 'dispassionately passionate' insight into the process of therapy from a client's viewpoint – together with a series of remarkably astute and sometimes uncomfortable insights into *the practitioner's* world too. In her poignantly titled chapter 'The compulsion to repeat – who needs what?', for example, Sands offers a whole list of questions that anyone aspiring to be a therapist should surely ask themselves – for example, 'Why do you spend all day being anonymous...?; Do you enjoy being in a position of power?... What about your need for control?... Why do you wish to have intense relationships, closeted behind a closed door, in return for money?... What makes you want to analyse another, to play the role of parent, to be of such importance to those who come your way?' (p. 112). In response I trust I can hear a collective 'oouucchh!' from 'the profession' – which would in my view be a very appropriate response to such crucial and uncomfortable questions.

Sands is surely right to highlight Carvalho's statement that 'the vocation for psychotherapeutic work is likely to come from at least some degree of disturbance and pathology, and from a need for repair in the analysts themselves' (quoted on p. 114). I contend that, far from being dismissive (which *will* no doubt happen if we are too defended and self-interested to hear what she has to say), we should be extremely grateful to 'Anna Sands' for having opened a revealing portal into this most challenging of areas for our constructed professional selves – and, in the process, showing we therapists that we have *at least* as much to learn from our clients as they have to learn from us.

In sum, *Falling for Therapy* could very profitably become mandatory reading on all therapy training courses – indeed, for all practising therapists, especially psychodynamic ones, and however experienced they may be. In my view, the extent to which this does or does not happen will strongly indicate whether psychotherapy and counselling are yet sufficiently open or mature to deserve their increasingly sought-after status of recognised, legitimate 'professions'.

I will leave the final word with 'Anna Sands':

Therapy, like life, is a paradox and the art lies in containing the paradox.... There are many contradictions in the ways of psychotherapy.... Good therapy is a high-wire act, a balancing trick, and the trick is to get the balance right.

(pp. 188, 201)

CHAPTER 5

Welcoming the Client-Voice Movement

[T]here exists precious little about therapy that we can say with
any certainty... therapists really don't know what they're doing –
even if they insist upon pretending... they are 'experts'.
> (Ernesto Spinelli)

The behaviour of 'the profession' is the next piece of resistance that
needs looking at.
> (David Kalisch)

It is a privilege to have been asked to contribute an Afterword to a book
that is actually looking to take our field down new vistas, rather than being
merely yet another deck-chair-rearranging example of what I (less than
flatteringly) like to refer to as the 'profession-centred' literature which tends
to dominate the therapy world. Yvonne Bates has done a splendid job in
taking forward a theme which she and I signalled in our 2003 anthology
(Bates and House 2003), and to which a number of brave and intrepid
client-writers have also recently contributed, and who are strongly
represented in *Shouldn't I Be Feeling Better by Now?* – not least, 'Rosie
Alexander', 'Anna Sands' and 'Natalie Simpson'.

In my book *Therapy Beyond Modernity* I developed the radical view, based
in part on the substantial client testimonies of 'Rosie Alexander', the late
'Ann France' and 'Anna Sands', that therapy can become a 'material generating
enterprise' in which the therapeutic milieu *itself* actively creates the 'material'
for which therapy then posits itself as the cure (see Chapter 4, this volume;
House 2003a: 64–8). Similarly, in her splendid book *Falling for Therapy* (see

---

In 2004 the then editor of *Ipnosis* magazine, Yvonne Bates, asked me if I would
contribute to her new book, *Shouldn't I Be Feeling Better by Now?*, which featured
client testimonies of challenging therapy experiences (Bates 2006). As well as
contributing a themed verbatim summary of Ann France's pioneering book
Consuming Psychotherapy, I also contributed the following chapter (abbreviated
for this book), in which I welcome the advent of the client voice in our work,
arguing that we therapists can learn things about our peculiar activity from
clients that we simply won't learn anywhere else.

Chapter 4, this volume), Anna Sands has posed the question, 'Doesn't therapy sometimes reveal, sometimes replicate, and sometimes *create* the feelings and behaviour that arise there?' (2000: 133, my emphasis). However, to say that confusion and turmoil (for example) *can* occur within a psychotherapeutic or counselling framework is not necessarily the same as saying that it is 'therapy' *in and of itself* that causes such experienced malaise. This is surely a critical – and highly complex – area of concern that requires far more urgent attention in our field than it has received to date. To sustain the view that therapy as a generality *necessarily* generates such client difficulties needs far more systematic research and undefensive reflection than it has received heretofore.

While I could take issue with at least some of Virginia Ironside's impassioned 'anti-therapy' assertions, I believe she is on to something very important in her reference to the benefits she has personally received from *short-term* therapeutic help (cf. House 1997c, 2004a) – as she graphically puts it, which is 'designed to get you back on your feet as quickly as possible'. Short-term therapy is clearly one solution to both the worst excesses of the 'material-generation' problem referred to earlier, and also to the transference-cum-dependency problems repeatedly problematised in *Shouldn't I Be Feeling Better by Now?* Indeed, and based on my own experience of working in a time-limited General Practice medical setting for over 15 years, it could be that (sometimes periodic) short-term interventions might well be adequate or appropriate for a clear majority of the clients/patients who ever seek therapeutic help (and by this I most emphatically do *not* mean lowest-common denominator IAPT-type, CBT-dominated interventions).

Amidst the manifold richness of the book's practitioner contributions, I was particularly struck by the commentaries by John Freestone, John Heron, Sylvia London and Scott Miller. In these refreshing statements, we see the beginnings of an emerging 'new paradigm' for therapy which is thorough-goingly *collaborative, demystifying, participative* and *co-creative* – a kind of therapy which lies crucially *beyond* 'modernity' and its professionalising pretensions (House 2003a), and which actively and quite deliberately embraces 'new paradigm' thinking in all its depth and challenge. That the client-voice movement must needs play a central role in these exciting, pioneering developments seems to me self-evident and unarguable – and *Shouldn't I Be Feeling Better by Now?* makes the case for this view more strongly than any other yet to appear in the literature.

It also requires that we are able to relax our profession-centred 'regimes of truth' for long enough to allow new forms and subtleties of understanding to make themselves manifest in our individual and collective awareness. I strongly agree with John Freestone's crucial and quintessentially postmodern insight that we should not be obsessed with fashioning necessarily clear, unambiguous answers to the manifold questions raised in this book – for, as he writes, 'Our society is obsessed with defining things…. The value of a question is not merely that it precipitates an answer…. Our sureness is much more dangerous than a lack of facts.' Just to *raise the questions* and to allow them to resonate, unhurried, in our souls may well yield evolutionary insights and that could scarcely be dreamt of from within the confines of our traditional therapeutic schools and orthodoxies.

It might be argued by some 'defenders of the faith' that the kind of client voices showcased in Bates' book present a highly selective and, therefore, biased view of the overall effectiveness and beneficence of therapy as a healing practice. That might well be so; but I view these testimonies as providing some kind of necessary, even *essential* counterweight to the heavy preponderance of largely uncritical therapist- and profession-centred literature that routinely dominates the therapy field. As a counselling practitioner I am convinced by the effectiveness of a great deal of therapy, but I am also convinced by the importance of the arguments and challenges developed in *Shouldn't I Be Feeling Better by Now?*, and the urgent need for our field to reflect upon and respond to them, if therapeutic practice is to continue to evolve and mature.

Far from being relatively passive consumers of the professionalism of the therapist, it is now becoming a commonplace view that the client/patient is a crucial *co-creator* of their own therapeutic experience (cf. Bohart and Tallman 1996) – and that the client's *active* input into this process is an indispensable aspect of the outcome of the therapeutic encounter. In this situation, in any attempt to specify what a human healing experience consists in, it is patently absurd to exclude from consideration the client/patient's actual experience of the therapy process; yet this is precisely what has effectively occurred, until quite recently, in the history of therapy and counselling. It would be very interesting to speculate as to the complex (often unconscious?) dynamics of this shameful neglect, which I believe to be one of the least auspicious features of therapy's (to date) century-long history. Any such analysis would need to consider, *inter alia*, issues of power, the 'victimhood' phenomenon (Hall 1993) and the associated deference to so-called 'expertise' (Illich et al. 1997a), the hegemony of the 'medical model' in healing relationships (e.g. House 1996c), and the dynamics of the professionalisation process and the vested interests involved in that process (House and Totton 1997/2011; Chapters 15 and 24, this volume).

Historically, the therapy world has arguably shown itself to be notably reluctant – or even resistant – to engaging with the substance of client commentaries on the therapy phenomenon, when those brave (ex-)clients who have dared to question their therapy experiences have earnestly attempted to articulate their concern within the public domain. I refer here to practitioner book reviews of Ann France's compelling client commentary, *Consuming Psychotherapy* (France 1988; distilled in Chapter 7 of *Shouldn't I Be Feeling Better by Now?*) – namely, those of Nini Herman (Herman 1991) and John Rowan (Rowan 1988). The tenor and content of these reviews are, for me, symptomatic of the routine professional resistance with which challenging client commentaries have been met in our field.

In a review which does at least attempt to face some of Ann France's challenges, Rowan does acknowledge that 'I think anyone reading this book and trying to decide whether to go for therapy would stay away, would run a mile if they had any sense' (1988: 276). What I find most fascinating, however, is that the book (writes Rowan) 'made me angry' (ibid.):

> [for all of her therapists] failed her in the end.... My own best guess is that none of them went far enough back into the origins of the depression... they did a bad job and did not succeed with this particular person... it seems crystal clear from this book that authenticity and genuineness are not enough... none of the people she consulted had enough knowledge to deal with her deep problems.
> (Rowan 1988: 276, 277; 1996: 12)

Thus, rather than problematising the very project of therapy itself (which France does herself several times in her book – barely mentioned in Rowan's review), the legitimacy of professional therapy is rescued by the argument that it was shortcomings of the thera*pists* rather than of thera*py per se* that was the problem.

But far more disturbing is the review article by Herman (1988), which goes into some detail about the circumstances of France's book, and quotes the reviewer's own initial response to it:

> Not in a million years should such a book have been let loose on the unsuspecting public without at least an introduction by a sane, containing voice. Is it not our duty who subscribe to the tenets of rigorous analysis to voice that we do not hold with the anarchic goings on in psychotherapy, which the author sets out before us with plangent ambivalence, claiming objectivity?... The whole book bristles with denials.
> (ibid.: 250)

Though Herman does admit that this, her first response to the book was fuelled by no little projection and personal distress, she goes on to 'analyse'

Ann France in the following nine pages of her article, without any reference to the substance of the book's discussions. Rather, France's 'psychopathology' is what is examined – for example, we read that

> the entire book is punctuated by... a plangent dialogue between an infant part of Ann which cannot stand the least frustration..., and an adult part of her..., expressing anger and regret that nobody trusted her adult to get to grips with her inner resources.
> (ibid.: 256)

Finally, in a classic reassertion of the sanctity of psychoanalytic orthodoxy, Herman writes: 'We all fail with certain patients, often with tragic consequences. But *is this not the more reason to stay on well trodden paths?*' (ibid.: 257, my emphasis).

This new 'client-voice' movement in our field, then, which is moving towards respectfully and non-patronisingly *listening to* and involving the client's perspective, has multiple potential for good – not least, in promising a way towards what I have called elsewhere a genuinely empowering *post-professional* ethos (House 2003a) that transcends the stultifying dynamics of institutional professionalisation (crucially different, of course, from professional*ism*), which has threatened to rip the heart from and deaden the innovative creativity that surely must lie at the core of therapy practice at its best (e.g. House and Totton 1997/2011; Bates and House 2003). As Ivan Illich inspiringly put it, 'The Post-Professional Ethos will hopefully result in a social panorama more colourful and diverse than all of the cultures of present and past taken together' (Illich 1977a: 39).

A recurrent theme in *Shouldn't I Be Feeling Better by Now?* has been client-writers' strong challenge to the very language of therapy, its often mystifying nature, and its concomitant neglect of the ordinary-yet-extraordinary virtues of real, intimate relating ('Anna Sands' is especially strong on this in her excellent contribution). Certainly, the client-voice movement makes it far more possible that therapy as praxis might begin to move away from its tendency towards *theory-centredness* (see Chapter 11, this volume) and the latter's toxic handmaiden, clinically-minded psychopathologisation (which trend has been strongly reinforced by the rampant and, arguably, inappropriate 'academicisation' of counselling and therapy training over the past decade – House 2001a; Parker 2001), and towards a more *being-centred*, transpersonal approach illuminated by, for example, existential-phenomenological, Person-Centred and transpersonal philosophies (cf. House 2003a: Chapter 12).

The focus on *listening to the client voice* that is the central theme of

Shouldn't I Be Feeling Better by Now? is not just one more ephemeral fashion that ambitious career-writers are opportunistically seeking to exploit; rather, it is in my view an evolutionarily essential development of a maturing psychotherapy and counselling field, whose arrival on the therapy scene should be welcomed and celebrated by any- and everyone who wishes to see therapy develop in a humanising, post-professional way, rather than in a narrowly conceived, professionalised direction that can only limit the enormous healing potential that this most human of practices is capable, at its best, of achieving.

Finally, I maintain that it is now incumbent on each and every training course in counselling and psychotherapy to include, as a major and essential module or component, a long, sober look at the broad swathe of challenging questions raised in this book. And to the extent that this does *not* happen in the near future, therapy will have shown itself not yet sufficiently mature to rise to the compelling ethical subtleties and contradictions to which these peculiarly 'impossible professions' inevitably give rise – and certainly not yet remotely ready to claim the authenticating label of legitimate 'professions' to which the therapy bureaucracies still assiduously, and less than modestly, aspire.

PART II

Emergent Postmodern and 'New Paradigm' Perspectives

CHAPTER 6

Limits to Counselling and Therapy: Deconstructing a professional ideology

> ... this historical period of therapy ... that [tries] to fix what we do
> not understand.
>> (Hillman 1997: 81)

INTRODUCTION

> [T]here exists precious little about therapy that we can say with
> any certainty ... therapists really don't know what they're doing –
> even if they insist upon pretending ... they are 'experts'.
>> (Spinelli 1996: 56, 59)

In 1977 Ivan Illich published a seminal book, *Limits to Medicine* (Illich 1977b), in which he made a radical counterintuitive case for the cultural institution of professional medicine being deleterious to societal health. In this chapter I will make the equally radical suggestion that the professionalised institution of 'Therapy' is also in danger of perpetrating net harm at the cultural level.

Despite decades of research that point to the unifying, so-called 'non-specific' or 'intangible' factors being what really matter in a therapeutic encounter (Frank and Frank 1991; Shepherd and Sartorius 1989), the all-too-common internecine warfare between different therapeutic approaches (e.g. Hugill 1998; King and Steiner 1990), and the commonly observed

---

This paper proved to be the precursor to my book *Therapy Beyond Modernity*, the first draft of which was written around 2000, and was eventually published in 2003. As well as critical–postmodern ideas beginning to influence my thinking, the Foucault-inspired and informed work of Nikolas Rose and Ian Parker had a major influence on my thinking in the late 1990s, as I found it to sit very conformably with my own independently developing views on the shortcomings of therapy as an increasingly professionalised form of talking help. This paper, reprinted here with minor updating, is still one of the fullest and most closely argued pieces that I've written to date on 'professionalised therapy' and its vicissitudes.

emphasis that specific approaches give to difference rather than to factors of commonality, suggest that such parochial preoccupations may have far more to do with practitioners' own insecurity-driven need to self-define and self-justify themselves as a 'professionals' than they do with any disinterested 'objective' perspective on what the therapeutic experience consists in. What if, we may justifiably ask, the 'non-specific' healing factors triggered within a therapeutic experience occur *despite* rather than because of any particular distinctive characteristics of the various therapeutic approaches? And what, furthermore, if there were no demonstrable, statistically significant difference in outcome between the therapeutic help offered by highly trained 'professionals' and that of very lightly trained 'para-professionals', as a significant amount of empirical research (well summarised in Bohart and Tallman 1996) seems to indicate? Perhaps these counterintuitive findings aren't so outlandish when seen in the context of Smail's view that 'we are all highly skilled and experienced psychologists who have spent a lifetime developing ways of living in a world which contains other people, observing the regularities of their conduct, and conducting ourselves in accordance with our observations' (1983: 18; cf. Parker 1998b). Of course, any 'professional' is likely defensively, even desperately, to resist such uncomfortable possibilities (House 1997d: 104), because their acceptance would throw into considerable doubt the legitimacy of therapy as a 'professional' practice. To be blunt, the whole edifice of 'professionalised' therapy would immediately be thrown into very severe question. As Kalisch (1996: 46) has challengingly put it, 'The behaviour of the "profession" is the next bit of resistance that needs looking at'.

In what follows, I hope to show that many of therapy's most taken-for-granted conventional 'wisdoms' have far more to do with the creation of a self-serving, self-justificatory (and typically self-deluding) ideology than they have to do with authenticity and 'truth' in the healing encounter. (These arguments are developed at greater length in House 2003a.) It must be emphasised that this chapter is largely confined to considering therapy at the level of its (predominantly) individualised practice and discourse. As a consequence, I have not addressed the political and cultural effects of the therapy phenomenon – which have been penetratingly detailed by a number of authors (e.g. Albee 1990; Cloud 1998; Cushman 1995; Pilgrim 1992, 1997; Smail 1996). One of the dangers, of course, is that in a therapy culture, 'there is an obsession with persons at the expense of social relations. Politics degenerates into the struggle for self-realisation not social change' (Kennard and Small 1997a: 214); and an accompanying tendency, perhaps, tacitly to sanction a normalising ideology which 'reinscribe[s] individuals into the very social relations that produced their "illnesses"' (Cloud 1998: xv). There is also the question of material self-interest in any professional field: for Cloud (ibid.: 20), for example, 'the therapeutic comprises a set of discourses which are linked ... to a particular historical moment and to the interests of those who benefit from the perpetuation of a therapeutic society' (cf. Nolan 1998; Furedi 2004). Certainly, this literature has made no little contribution to the arguments I develop below; and any thorough-going critique of therapy must take account of its possibly deleterious consequences at the level of culture – and not least, its increasingly pervasive institutionalisation within Western culture.

It has been argued that the price we are paying in the course of therapy's institutional professionalisation is the loss of therapy's soul (Edwards 1992); and if she is right, then some pretty swift 'New Paradigm' footwork (or rather, *heart*work) may well be required if the fundamentally beneficial impulse that surely underpins therapy is to be rescued from the deadening hand of self-serving professionalisation, and thereby preserved in some organically healthy and culturally enabling form. Such heartwork, however, is not the prime concern of this chapter (see the chapters in Part V, 'Making What We Want', this volume); rather, here I set myself the far more limited task of *using old-paradigm thinking against itself*: that is, I use the language and style of the old (modernist) paradigm to show how its own ideological discourse and associated therapeutic practices contain inherent self-contradictory elements which potentially render it self-refuting and in urgent need of transcendence (cf. House 2003a). Finally, my own project is not, of course, without its own inevitable tensions and contradictions, to which I return briefly at the end of the chapter.

THE IDEOLOGY OF PROFESSIONALISATION

It is fear that has, in my experience, characterised the response of psychotherapists to the whole political process of professionalisation. They fear loss of livelihood, loss of status and recognition, loss of legitimacy. And in this fear I detect a strong element of transference itself.
(Heron 1990: 18)

It is highly sobering to read a prominent therapist writing the following: 'perhaps too many therapists have as their *raison d'être* a need to see themselves as extraordinarily powerful, virtually omniscient healers. Consequently, *they have a penchant for infantilizing and overpathologizing their patients*, viewing them as extraordinarily fragile' (Lazarus 1994a: 301, my emphasis; see also

Lazarus 1994b; cf. Mowbray, 1997) – with consequences for therapeutic practice which, I will argue below, are in danger of being intrinsically abusive and unethical. That is, I make the strong claim that client/patient abuse may well be intrinsically inscribed into the very form increasingly taken by professionalised therapy.

A further effect of institutionalised professionalisation is the rigidification and rendering legitimate of what some might call the precious, often mystifying language and procedures of the therapy world-view. Nearly 20 years ago Hinshelwood described how different therapeutic schools 'protect themselves by arcane terminologies', with insecurity being dealt with 'by inculcating each other ... into a system of mutual confirmation of the grouping's theoretical ideas' (1985: 16). More recently, Hart (1998) cites Habermas's work on communicative distortion (1978, 1982) to make the point that power is often exercised through the manipulation or distortion of communication (cf. Hart 2003, and Parker's views on discourse and deconstruction, discussed below), and that therapy has become a dominant cultural discourse which threatens to 'direct communication towards the achievement of [therapists'] own ends'. Below I will outline some concrete examples of how power is arguably being abused through the intrinsic nature of what I will call the 'Professionalised Therapy Form' (hereafter, the PTF). This is a convenient short-hand term to connote the increasingly commodified and professionally boundaried form which psychoanalysis, and the so-called 'new professions' of psychotherapy and counselling, have been taking in recent years, as professionalisation gathers steam.

Perhaps it is possible to trace the flawed project of professionalised commodified psychotherapy right back to the very origins of psychoanalysis itself. For as Frosh points out, Freud was

> far less interested in psychoanalysis as a therapeutic system than as an instrument of knowledge [about individual and society]. Freud's project was ... to develop a system of ideas that could make sense of people ... psychotherapy was a secondary project, *undertaken to make a living.*
>
> (Frosh 1987: 211, my emphasis)

In his highly revealing clinical diary, Ferenczi is even more blunt in recounting how, for Freud, 'patients are only riffraff. The only thing patients were good for is to help the analyst make a living and provide material for theory' (quoted in Rowe 1990: 19; see also Dupont 1995: 93). Kurtz (1989) has similarly pointed to the less than auspicious historical origins of the therapeutic/analytic form: he painstakingly shows how 'The narcissistic and psychotic ... layers of Freud's personality entered profoundly into his creation of the psychoanalytic situation and its manifestation in space ... *[E]very analyst to some degree recreates that office in the Berggasse*' (ibid.: 28–9, my emphasis).

If the very framework in which therapy is 'delivered' is in principle antithetical to what really matters in a therapeutic experience, then the professionalised, commodified direction which therapy is increasingly taking may well be doing a kind of violence to the foundational values from which the healthy and fundamentally good therapeutic impulse no doubt springs (cf. Bracken and Thomas 1998).

THE DUBIOUS ETHICS OF PSYCHOTHERAPY AND COUNSELLING

...a setting which, infused with ambiguity, encourages the development of an insatiable love in both therapist... and patient... Once attained, these affective states... then become the prime focus for the psychoanalytic process of government....
(Kendall and Crossley 1996: 192)

Heron (1990) has referred accusingly to therapy's exploitation and abuse of the transference: 'psychoanalysts in particular were hypocritical in wanting to protect the public from transference abuse [in their professionalisation strategies], when their own therapy was riddled with this very phenomenon'! (ibid.: 17, describing the behaviourists' response to the 1972 Foster Report). Perhaps the very way in which therapy as a PTF is structured (rather than the particular features of psychoanalysis *per se*) may actually encourage, if not *actively produce* client infantilisation and dependency through the unconscious(?) dynamics triggered by the PTF, and often buttressed by the assumptive framework typically embraced by the professional therapist (cf. McDougall 1995). As one of the ex-clients in Alexander's book *Folie à Deux* remarks, 'it doesn't seem to matter whether the therapist encourages [dependence] or discourages it. It's just there, like the weather' (Alexander 1995: 145). On this view, then, the PTF may be self-fulfillingly constructing a framework which then guarantees the conditions of its own existence.

Hinshelwood (1997), a leading psychoanalyst, has bravely outlined some profound ethical dilemmas encountered by the analytic project. Chief among these is 'the prior-agreement argument' (ibid.: 101-2), an unavoidable ethical aspect of which is that:

The patient does not have the capacity to conceive, at the outset, what will befall him [in analysis].... The unconscious cannot be explained to the patient to any useful degree. The nature of the [analytic] process... cannot really be understood prior to treatment at all. We cannot rely on the patient consciously to understand what his unconscious will do.... [The consent to analysis] is not a fully informed consent.

(ibid.; cf. Pilgrim 1997: 117)

It follows from this that the analyst cannot but take up a paternalistic stance in relation to 'patients' who necessarily (it is assumed) cannot make informed decisions about entering analysis, and therefore need the analyst to take responsibility for knowing what is in their best interests.

But it gets worse still... for:

patients become immobilised, as if transfixed, upon the couch until the end of each session.... For periods, the patient in psychoanalysis may subjugate himself.... And this lasts until *these unconscious processes that deplete the patient's personality* have been adequately dealt with in the process of the treatment.

(ibid.: 103, my emphasis)

In other words, the PTF of psychoanalysis actively encourages a particular psychic state within patients, which then requires extensive 'treatment' to cure! The self-serving, ethically dubious nature of such an 'enterprise' (I use the term advisedly) should be relatively clear for all to see – except for the 'patient' in analysis, of course!

The tell-tale opposition to the politicisation of therapy by those 'who regard "the clinical" as an untouchable, privileged category, on the basis of its contribution to the alleviation of human suffering' (Samuels 1993: 6) is suggestive of a rationalised, therapist-centred professional self-interest. Yet of course, the 'individualising' of distress is in many ways necessary to legitimate psychoanalysis – and much of therapy – as forms of treatment (cf. Parker's arguments, below); and this in turn constitutes another dimension of the self-serving PTF ideology.

Hinshelwood's frank discussion surely throws a very long shadow over the ethical basis of not only psychoanalysis, but over any (and conceivably, every) therapeutic practice in which such relational dynamics are tacitly or explicitly encouraged, or can be triggered. As Kovel (1976: 82) argues, 'Transference wishes are stirred up willy-nilly, whether the therapist cultivates them or not'. Thus, I maintain that therapeutic approaches (like many humanistic and cognitive behaviour therapies) which claim to offer an open and unmystifying description of their procedures may be no less immune from these ethical difficulties than are the more purist versions of psychoanalysis and analytic therapy – and not least through the degree of practitioner self-delusion typically involved! (House 1998). Thus, therapists never really 'know what they're doing' in any comprehensive, 'objective' sense (Frank and Frank 1991; Spinelli 1996). And it could conceivably be that the boundaried PTF itself and the 'therapeutic frame' (relatively ubiquitous as it is across the generality of therapeutic approaches) *actively encourage* client infantilisation, dependency and associated processes through the deep ('unconscious') dynamics that are precipitated in the therapeutic encounter, *irrespective of theoretical approach*. In House (2003a: Chapter 3) I elaborate in detail on what I call the '"material"-generating nature' of the PTF (see also Chapter 4, this volume): as France put it, 'Psychotherapy... can merely be the replay of past traumata... which lead to nothing.... It creates an artificial situation... *which could lead to... the artificial creation of [problems]* (France 1988: 139, my emphasis). And Freud himself, arguably the 'father' of therapy, made no secret of his therapeutic intention: 'it remains the first aim of the treatment to attach [the patient] to [the treatment] and to the person of the doctor' (1913: 139).

The way in which culturally legitimated therapeutic discourse structures both client and therapist subjectivities is a major focus of the next section.

THEORY, TRUTH AND POWER

> Certain categories of experience can never occur unless elicited and
> maintained by the actions of another.
> (Daniel Stern, quoted in Arden 1998: 84)

Professions typically legitimate their existence by claiming privileged access to a body of expert (typically theoretical) knowledge or theory, which is seen as being indispensable to their professional practice. Here is David Smail (1996: 56):

> There is, of course, a constant struggle within society for certain
> professional groups to mystify and monopolise 'truth', but it is still
> perfectly possible to clarify the reasons for our unhappiness without
> recourse to a professional psychotherapist. In many respects, it may
> even be easier.

No-one involved in the field will have missed the extraordinary and intemperate stampede into the 'academicisation' of therapy training and practice which has accompanied professionalisation (House 2001a; Parker 2001). Clearly, if an activity is to become sedimented into a legitimate 'profession', then it must find a way of claiming that what it has to offer to clients is distinctive, 'specialistic' and broadly undeliverable in any other way – here is Smail again in his classic 1983 paper:

> When professional claims are made, expectations established among clients, and money changes hands..., it becomes important to establish a solid justification for psychotherapy as a discipline.... Ever since the beginnings of psychoanalysis, psychotherapists have been desperately anxious to establish the validity of their credentials... in order, no doubt, to justify their professional (fee-taking) status.
>   (1983: 7–8)

There is certainly no general agreement about what it is that therapists do (cf. Spinelli's epigraph at the start of this chapter), and the field has repeatedly been described as being in a state of (theoretical) disarray (e.g. Erwin 1997: 2). And more generally still, some commentators have been starting to challenge the epistemological relevance of theory (and its associated form of 'technical' knowledge) to the healing practice of therapy (Craib 1987; McDougall 1995: Riikonen and Smith 1997), as 'New Paradigm' epistemologies begin to challenge head on the ideology of 'modernity' and its arguably narcissistic preoccupation with ego, control, technocratic science and the material (cf. House 2003a).

As Burman points out, 'mainstream' psychotherapy is – or pretends to be – a quintessentially rational, modernist enterprise which 'rehearses the modern condition of western, split subjectivity wedded to singular truths and linear histories' (1997: 126). But what if, as Smail maintains, 'the technical rhetoric of psychotherapy has... more in common with magic than with a truly scientific spirit of enquiry' (1987: 34; cf. Frank and Frank 1991 and Chapter 11, this volume)? In the highly contrasting New Paradigm, postmodern world-view that encompasses Chaos, complementarity and participative consciousness (e.g. Skolimowski 1994), our very foundational notions of 'explanation', 'understanding' and 'truth' are 'up for grabs' – which situation, of course, has very profound implications indeed for the practice of any healing art.

There exist a number of modernity-transcending "'theories" [sic!] of truth' (e.g. the coherence theory, the participative theory and the congruence 'theory of truth' – e.g. Lacan 1965; Skolimowski 1994; Alcoff 1996; Heron

1996; see House 2003a: 190–1), which challenge quite fundamentally the aridity of the epistemologically dubious 'correspondence' theory that has tended to dominate Western analytic philosophy and the modernist world-view of positive technocratic science since Francis Bacon, Descartes and the Enlightenment (Tarnas 1991; cf. Burr and Butt 1999). Parker's important work on the 'discursive complex' (1996, 1997a, b, 1998a), discussed below, points to how notions of truth within therapeutic discourse can themselves actively structure subjectivity – with the implication that 'we must be attentive to the power of the therapist as a... part of the regime of truth that defines what subjectivity must be like' (Parker 1996: 459). And ultimately, 'the subject does not know what the truth is; nobody knows....' (ibid.).

Parker et al. (1995: 135) have written that '"theories" about distress masquerade as "Truth"... that truth is relentlessly forced upon people'. The question of 'theory as abuse' has also been courageously addressed by Ernesto Spinelli, who argues that therapist reliance on interpretations derived from theory can become

> ...more abusive than anything else ... Many of the assumptions we take for granted don't really have any basis to them ... we might hold [them] because at the very least they keep us employed, or they provide employment for our trainees.
> (Spinelli and Longman 1998: 181, 183)

All this, of course, ultimately leads quite naturally into questions of power. It is a sobering and highly revealing fact that, with a few notable exceptions (e.g. Guggenbühl-Craig 1971; Embleton Tudor and Tudor 1994; Hart 2003), the issue of power is scarcely discussed in the therapy field (Hart 1998). The real substance of power is never really fearlessly and fundamentally addressed. Perhaps we can all convince (delude?) ourselves into complacently thinking that we've dealt with therapy's thorny power issues by simply repeating the word a few times, like some sort of mantra. Yet as some commentators have either suggested or implied (e.g. Masson 1988; Hart 1998), 'power' probably constitutes one of therapy's most embarrassing can of worms.

Hart (ibid.) maintains that it is illusory to believe that clients are free to explore their inner worlds in therapy, for 'the boundaries and rules, like the vocabulary, are as fixed as they ever were in the psychiatric world of the fifties and sixties': all that has changed is that we now *pretend* that the client has power, and that we as therapists do not use a normalising and subtly impositional discourse. And 'Therapy can never be value free.... It happens within a context and someone has set the agenda' (ibid.).

In psychoanalysis (possibly generalisable to therapy in general), Hinshelwood (1997) does concede that the patient's 'lack of conscious knowledge of his unconscious does put him [*sic*] at some disadvantage. It makes him consciously helpless in the search for his knowledge' (ibid.: 167). Moreover, the extent to which patients operating within a therapeutic milieu (and all that goes with it in terms of both individual and cultural dynamics) are free to exercise full conscious consent may well be significantly compromised (ibid.; cf. House 2003a: 110–11, 232–3). All this can routinely lead to a kind of power-imbalanced Laingian 'knot' in which the therapist 'knows [or *thinks* s/he knows – RH] a great deal, but also *knows* that he [*sic*] knows a great deal and *knows* that his client does not know much' (Hinshelwood 1997: 168, original emphases). For Hinshelwood, this power imbalance can be carried through 'to a degree that distorts both identities. Professional relationships based on this redistribution of knowing will result in the expert enhancing the depletion of the personality of his more vulnerable clients' (ibid.).

It seems to me that abuses such as these are ones to which the 'professions' of therapy are by their very nature peculiarly and intrinsically susceptible. And in the light of this we would do well to follow family therapist Lynn Hoffman's injunction that 'therapists of all kinds must now investigate how relations of domination and submission are built into *the very assumptions* on which their practices are based' (quoted in Hart 1998, my emphasis). Below, I will propose that therapy must routinely and ongoingly embrace a radical deconstruction of its theories and practices (cf. Parker 1999a, b; Chapter 7, this volume), paradoxically entailing a continual undermining of its own conditions of existence, if it is to avoid the kinds of abuses which are, I believe, intrinsic to the PTF as currently practised and culturally legitimated.

THE DISCOURSE OF THERAPY AND ITS CRITICAL DECONSTRUCTION

[A]ny system of therapeutic talk conveys an enigma to the subject, and positions the subject in a regime of truth. Then it may not be good to talk.
(Parker 1996: 459)

[T]he therapeutic as a modern ideological, strategic discourse... has as its ultimate effects the privatization of social experience and the disciplining of private subjects into a regime of self-blame and personal responsibility.
(Cloud 1998: xxi)

The so-called discursive, deconstructionist approach to therapy typically views language and discourse, and the power relations intrinsic to them, as actively constituting notions of '(psycho)pathology' (Parker et al. 1995), aspects of psychic 'reality' and so on. By extension, moreover, our associated subjective experiences are themselves seen as being deeply structured through the culturally sanctioned discourse which is available to us. Thus, 'Language... is not a reflection of another world, but an implement of construction for the world we now occupy' (Gergen and McNamee 1997: viii). It follows that words are always far more than merely 'labels for objective things' (Riikonen and Smith 1997: 3). And such a perspective is so crucial to therapy and human relationship more generally because 'our conceptions of language and words have a close connection to the kinds of relationships which *can* exist between people' (ibid.: 7, original emphasis).

Critical psychologist and Lacanian analyst Ian Parker has made a very considerable contribution to the discursive deconstructionist line of thinking. He explores 'the way meaning is transformed and reproduced in culture, rather than trying to find the sources of meanings inside individuals alone' (1997a: 9). More specifically, Parker maintains that psychoanalytic concepts (particularly around intellectualisation, transference and trauma) have increasingly infiltrated cultural discourse such that it becomes difficult for people to think about their experience outside of this discourse (e.g. Parker 1997a, b).

On this view, then, Western culture is actively structured by psychoanalytic notions which 'saturate and support cultural phenomena' (1997a: 258); and '"regimes of truth"... make it difficult for participants to challenge the "realities" [a discourse] refers to... [and] govern what can be spoken about...' (ibid.: 7). Laplanche expresses a similar view: 'psychoanalysis *invades the cultural*, not only as a form of thought or a doctrine, but as a *mode of being*' (1989, quoted in Parker 1996: 449, original emphases). What Parker calls 'discursive complexes' structure subjectivity, 'so that when we speak within them they provoke certain types of emotional response, certain notions of what it is to be a self' (1996: 451). For current purposes, what is most relevant is the way in which specifically psychotherapeutic discourse actively 'structures the way a person, as therapist or patient, participates in the therapeutic enterprise' (Parker 1997a: 256; see also Parker, 1996: 458). Thus, for example, it is arguable that the very way in which the notion of 'transference' has surreptitiously penetrated cultural discourse makes it more likely that transference dynamics will be created within therapeutic relationships (particularly when the therapist is also expecting to find 'transference'! – cf. McDougall 1995: 234, 236).

All this clearly has very considerable implications for the ways in which the self-experienced identity of 'clients' and 'patients' is actively constructed by a psychotherapeutic discourse which is culturally sanctioned, and buttressed by a massively influential ideological framework of professionalisation. Thus, people with 'personal problems' will tend immediately to think of themselves as potential therapy 'clients' – thereby positioning themselves within therapeutic discourse – precisely because that discourse constitutes a dominating set of values and culturally legitimated practices that circulates within the culture and actively helps to constitute subjective experience (cf. Hook 2001, 2002).

In a very real sense, then, it can be argued that the psychotherapeutic world-view actively and self-servingly creates the cultural conditions that guarantee its own existence and perpetuation – erecting, as with any ideological apparatus, 'a system of defences and discursive operations which guarantee its place in a regime of truth' (Parker 1997b: 489). Pilgrim (1997: 141) agrees:

> The gaze of professionals constructs both normal and abnormal subjectivity and leaves little space for ordinary people to speak for themselves in ways which are unmediated by the inscriptions and conceptual filters of experts. Moreover, professionals control not only the language associated with the technologies of the self but also the style and even the occurrence of these representations.

This situation surely places a very considerable ethical imperative upon therapists continually to deconstruct their own therapeutic practice, such that therapy continually revolutionises its own theories and practices – actively subverting itself whenever there is any whiff of complacent self-satisfaction – rather than conservatively (like Ted Hughes' roosting hawk) 'keeping things like this' through overly rigid, self-serving and institutionalised 'professional' procedures which demonstrably have far more to do with therapist self-interest than with client well-being.

Parker seems to be saying something quite similar when he writes of 'a "deconstructing psychotherapy" as [being] a practice that is always *in process* rather then something fixed, a movement of reflexive critique rather than a stable set of techniques' (1999b: 2, original emphasis; see Chapter 7, this volume); and that 'We must be attentive to the power of the therapist as... part of a regime of truth that defines what subjectivity must be like' (1996: 458). Clearly, there are crucial issues of power and control at work here:

> The issue of control – on a grandiose, omnipotent scale – permeates the analytic situation. It is always the analyst... who establishes the

rules that govern behaviour in this primal space. However much these rules may be constructed to enable the patient's cure, the analyst is their maker and enforcer.

(Kurtz 1989: 27–8)

Nor are these features unique to psychoanalysis alone.

Is there anything special and distinctive about the healing properties of the PTF *qua* PTF, over and above its coercive ideological and discursive effects on clients/patients, and which could not be found elsewhere in other cultural forms, outside of the confines of the discrete commodified PTF? Following the kind of arguments outlined above, perhaps therapy might be 'no more than another ideological stance, an "as if" way of relating to the world which provides relief from confusion and personal emptiness because it happens to be relatively coherent' (Frosh 1987: 220).

Elsewhere (House 2003a: Chapters 3–4) I critically deconstruct what I see as some of the more pernicious self-serving categories and assumptions of therapeutic discourse – including 'resistance', 'the frame', 'boundaries', 'holding', and the infantilisation intrinsic to the PTF and its associated relational dynamics. In that work I reach the conclusion, unpalatable as it will be to many, that there may well be far more examples of routine client abuse *stemming directly from the Professionalised Therapy Form itself* than there are the kinds of overt abuse against which the therapy institutions so assiduously attempt to legislate.

FINAL REFLECTIONS

I merely wish to invite ethical reflection upon the nature of a society in which the provision of love becomes increasingly a matter for paid professionals.

(Smail 1987: 36)

Despite first appearances, this is not an anti-therapy chapter, but an anti-*profession-centred* therapy chapter. For although I do see therapy as an historically specific and ultimately transitory cultural phenomenon, it must necessarily be serving an important evolutionary function; and to this extent I think it crucial to rescue what is the essentially 'good baby' that exists in therapy from the professionalising bathwater, and its accompanying ideology of late modernity, that in my view threatens to engulf it. Needless to say, therefore, I do not agree with Craib's assertion that 'if we decide we want the baby, we *have to* swim in the dirty bathwater' (Craib 1992: 244, my emphasis).

Heron (1997) and Totton (1997d), among others, have both made a strong case for the activity of therapy being far more akin to *a spiritual practice* than to a medicalised 'treatment' for so-called 'psychopathology'. For Totton (ibid.: 138–9), for example, 'psychotherapy... functions as a deconstructive spiritual and political practice rather than as a form of medicine or social work'. Similarly, in a wise editorial in the former British Association for Counselling's *Counselling* magazine, the then-editor Judith Longman referred to 'knowing [being] false understanding, truth being beyond language, and the sensibility of the mystic or the poet perhaps being at least as effective as the practitioner-scientist' (1998: 82; see also House 1998: 175; and Chapter 11, this volume). Views such as these clearly have profound implications for the question of whether counselling and psychotherapy can, with validity, be viewed as 'professions' in anything approaching a conventional sense.

I hope I have shown in this chapter that as soon as we embrace the ideology of professionalisation (rigidifying institutionalisation, commodification, a technocratic 'treatment' mentality and so on), then we quite possibly do a terminal violence to those very intangible, 'non-specific' 'being'-qualities (Heron 1996; Chapter 19, this volume) that are surely what make at least some therapeutic experiences worth having. On this view, if our culture does continue to demand some form of help for those struggling with what Peck calls 'the necessary pain of living' (Peck 1993), then it behoves us bravely and fearlessly to embrace the full implications of Samuels' (1992: xi) statement that what we do 'cannot even be named', and perhaps to find a paradoxical '*anti*-form' of 'deconstructive therapy' which is foundationally and ongoingly deconstructive of its own appropriately precarious conditions of existence, such that we minimise the danger of its becoming a commodified, institutionalised, self-reproducing set form – a form that is necessarily reproductive of the modernist status quo, rather than a force for transcending it. As Smail so aptly puts it, 'the foremost obligation on power is to "deconstruct" itself' (quoted in Rowe 1990: 22).

If professionalised, individualised therapy as currently constituted is part of the problem rather than part of the solution to our malaise, then we surely need *cultural-level* transformations to support people in their 'difficulties of living' (cf. House 2003a), remembering in the process what the therapy 'profession' might well wish us to forget – that 'the process of healing can be brought about by other kinds of relationships than psychotherapy' (Arden 1998: 85). Such practices would presumably challenge the individualised commodified therapeutic practices which only tend to mimic the ideology of modernity, and which can therefore surely only exacerbate the spiritual malaise of modernity rather than ameliorating or transcending it (cf. Burr and Butt

1999). For Smail (1983: 16), many clients entering therapy 'have been mystified and crippled by the bludgeon of objectivity' (and modernity – RH) – which places an enormous moral and ethical responsibility on therapists not to reinforce and compound their 'bludgeoning' still further through dogmatic and ideological professional practices.

In a typically far-sighted paper written over two decades ago, Smail warned that 'through becoming unthinkingly over-extended, [psychotherapy] is in danger of being ethically misused or abused. In order to guard against such misuse, psychotherapists must beware of slipping into the role of established and technically sound professional expert' (1987: 43). And as if anticipating Smail's objections, describing the American situation in 1973, Carl Rogers wrote:

> If we did away with... the 'certified professional'..., we might open our profession to a breeze of fresh air, a surge of creativity, such as it has not known for years.... Can psychology find a new and a better way? Is there some more creative method for bringing together those who need help and those who are truly excellent in offering helping relationships?
> (Rogers 1990: 366; see Chapter 14, this volume)

Perhaps this latter is one of the most urgent – and most challenging – questions facing the therapy *Weltanschauung* as we enter a new millennium, and is one that will recur throughout this book.

CODA: PARADIGMS, PARADIGMS...

> ...any system of logic is unable to prove its own logical consistency.
> (Michael Guillen 1983)

If Guillen (and Gödel's famous 1931 theorem) are anything like right, then of course I am on very shaky ground if I pretend to claim any kind of universal truth-status for the ideas set out in this chapter. For I would certainly be comprehensively hoisting myself with my own petard if I tried to replace one 'regime of truth' with my own! And while it is arguably legitimate to demonstrate how the old paradigm's most cherished values and procedures are self-refuting from within its own discourse, we must always remain alert to the seductive strength of the old paradigm – how easy it is to delude ourselves that we've transcended it when we're still inextricably and unawarely still caught up in it (cf. House 1996d).

In their book *Re-Imagining Therapy*, Riikonen and Smith write, 'Will this book be a systematic, single-voiced text which argues against systematic single-voiced texts? Will it present yet another set of well ordered truths as it argues against well ordered truths?' (1997: 7). In the writing of their book the authors clearly realised that in order for their 're-imagining' of therapy to have credibility, it was crucial that they transformed and transcended the traditional language and style of conventional, modernist 'therapy' – which they achieved by

> speak[ing] differently, metaphorically, even strangely.... We have to use different styles.... We have to exaggerate and use wrong words (*and lose at least some of our academic respectability*). In addition to this, we have to disrupt the automatic and even flow of ideas.
>   (ibid.: my emphasis)

Alas, I have not been nearly as brave as this in this chapter: for I have simply challenged conventional therapy from within the (for me) safe terrain of academic rigour, a third-person (and relatively distanced) 'detachedness', and careful, intellectually dominated rationalist analysis. Such an approach seems very double-edged: on the one hand, it shows how the old paradigm can be used against itself, and that it contains within it the seeds of its own transcendence; but on the other, if my (albeit critical) use of old-paradigm procedures is valid, then the danger is that this self-refutingly undermines the veracity of my very challenge to that self-same paradigm.

These are very difficult philosophical issues (particularly around relativism) which I cannot pursue here; suffice to say that, first, I do not present these ideas as *the* Truth about therapy, or as being a better 'regime of truth' than the one it challenges – for I see the very ideology of 'Truth' as being even more problematic than whatever particular content a regime of truth contains. Over three decades ago, George Steiner graphically wrote of 'the drug of truth': 'The quality of the obsession is clear from the start. The search for truth is predatory. It is a literal hunt, a conquest' (1978: 42).

I agree with the Derridean view that it is a fundamental error of the (ironically named) 'Enlightenment' project to expect humanly built systems of Truth to lead to reliable, 'objective' accounts of 'reality' (Tarnas 1991; cf. Chapter 7, this volume). Rather, my own particular 'truth' is unavoidably 'local', based on my own unique experiences of therapy as client, trainee, practitioner, supervisor and trainer – and upon my best endeavours to interrogate the therapy phenomenon as openly and in as presuppositionless a way as I have been able. I further believe that views such as these are never anyone's personally 'owned' property or creation, but have in some mysterious sense been channelled through the writer from the culture; and in this particular case I happen to be the person who has channelled and expressed them. Whether what I have written proves to have any credence or mileage will depend upon whether it finds a resonance within the evolving culture of therapy, and not on whether it is in some sense 'objectively true' in any naïve 'Correspondence Theory of Truth' sense.

It might also be objected that there is some personal disappointment about therapy fuelling the arguments in this chapter. Kennard and Small (1997b: 161) write that 'It may be that many of psychotherapy's critics criticise... [because] they feel let down that it doesn't have all the answers' (David Kalisch has made a similar point to me in a personal communication). My response is that although there is some truth in this in my own case, it does not follow that critical arguments are therefore *ipso facto* invalid. That is, and as Masson (1992) has also implied, whether an argument is plausible or realistic is logically independent of its emotional rootedness or drivenness. Indeed, I believe that all of the positions we take and the belief systems to which we adhere – including polarizing 'pro' and 'anti' therapy positions – have crucial emotional roots; and this chapter will have more than served its purpose if it leads those with (emotionally rooted) pro-therapy views to examine more deeply their own particular belief systems, assumptions and clinical practices.

ACKNOWLEDGEMENT

I am very grateful to Jutta Gassner and David Kalisch for their (as always) detailed and incisive comments on an earlier version of this chapter, which helped me significantly to improve it.

CHAPTER 7

Deconstruction, Post-(?)-modernism and the Future of Psychotherapy: A review essay

Ian Parker has the enviable knack of producing leading-edge books which are significantly ahead of the therapy field in terms of their theoretical and practical prescience. In this regard perhaps it is a positive advantage not to be thoroughly and professionally immersed in the therapy world! (Parker's 'academic label' is that of a critical (social) psychologist, being Professor of Psychology and Director of the Discourse Unit at the UK's Bolton Institute). (Today, in 2010, he is Professor of Psychology at Manchester Metropolitan University and a practising Lacanian analyst.) Just as the multiply authored text *Deconstructing Psychopathology* (Parker et al. 1995; see Chapter 2, this volume) brilliantly challenged the incoherent ideological trappings and abusive professional practices surrounding the notions of '(ab)normality' and 'psychopathology' in the field of mental health and emotional distress, so this anthology offers us a truly cutting-edge introduction to some of the most exciting developments in the therapy field. As such, the book makes a thoroughly refreshing change from the unremitting diet of mainstream, profession-centred therapy literature that has poured forth from publishers' presses in recent years (and which, of course, itself constitutes a central aspect of the political economy of the burgeoning therapy 'profession', and its accompanying material interests).

It is central to the book's *raison d'être* that 'deconstructive therapy' (if such a phenomenon can even be meaningfully proposed, which at least some of the book's contributors would dispute) is emphatically not just one more school or type of therapy, to be added to the 450-odd other versions identified at the last count. Rather, the book offers a fundamentally different 'approach' to therapy – one that, not least, challenges the very notion of an 'approach' or 'position' (or 'an approach *which is not one*', one might say).

Ian Parker's edited text *Deconstructing Psychotherapy* (Sage, 1999) is still surely one of the key landmark texts in therapy's 'postmodern turn'. Over a decade since its publication, it still remains absolutely essential reading for anyone interested in leading–edge critical thinking about therapeutic practice, and for those dissatisfied with conventional therapeutic approaches. This extensive review article, written a decade ago, serves as a discursive introduction to this seminal text.

The term 'postmodernism' (or the 'P word', as Roger Lowe calls it – p. 73) is a rather malleable, loosley defined term which often triggers strong emotional reactions, and which can serve to obscure far more than it illuminates; and for this reason some have suggested that we replace the term with less emotive ones, like (for example) 'a generalized climate of problematization' (Lowe, ibid.). Philosopher Richard Rorty has gone as far as concluding that 'The term [postmodernism] has been so overused that it is causing more trouble than it is worth' (1991: 1).

Certainly, the 'postmodern turn' in therapy and psychology (Messer et al. 1988; Faulconer and Williams 1990; Kvale 1992; House 1999a) has been prompted by a profound epistemological and political disillusionment with their perceived modernity, and with their accompanying beliefs in a representational view of language; individual autonomy and rationality; scientific progress; the quest for unifying theories and replicable forms of knowing; and 'objective' knowledge and ideologies of professional expertise (Lowe, p. 75)

The book's title constitutes a highly pertinent *double entendre*, in that it conveys both the notion of 'a therapy which is deconstructive', while also conveying a deconstructive critique of the very notion or project of therapy as conventionally understood. As will become clear in what follows, the book does indeed address both of these important senses of the term 'deconstructing psychotherapy'. In addition, Parker further disaggregates the former into 'deconstruction in and as psychotherapy' (p. 11) – see below.

In what follows I set out a brief overview of the book, followed by a more detailed discussion of its central themes, with particular attention given to the central post-structuralist figures, Michel Foucault and Jacques Derrida, whose work is recurrently influential throughout the book.

CONTENT SUMMARY

Deconstructing Psychotherapy begins with a position chapter by the book's editor Ian Parker, in which he critically reviews the field in general, as well as offering contextualised summaries of the book's constituent chapters. Part I, 'Sources and Contexts for the Deconstructive Turn' (or what Parker calls 'Deconstruction in psychotherapy' – p. 11) is for this writer the core of the text, with five chapters that offer theoretical perspectives on deconstruction and postmodernism, and with some reference to institutional settings. More specifically, there are chapters on narrative therapy (John Kaye), Derrida (Glenn Larner), Foucault (Vincent Fish), postmodernism (Roger Lowe) and feminism (Nollaig O'Reilly Byrne and Imelda Colgan

McCarthy). The chapters by Kaye ('Toward a non-regulative praxis', Larner ('Derrida and the deconstruction of power as context and topic in therapy') and Lowe ('Between the "no longer" and the "not yet": Postmodernism as a context for critical therapeutic work') were found to be especially outstanding contributions.

Part II, 'Deconstruction in Practice' (or – Parker – 'Deconstruction as psychotherapy') contains four chapters which offer practice-orientated commentaries on how deconstructive approaches can transform power relations and discursive practices in relation to: a feminist-informed narrative therapy (Vanessa Swan), therapy with men (Ian Law), working with issues of (religious) faith (Wendy Drewery, with Wally McKenzie), and the stunting of identity stemming from an objectifying psychiatric framework (Stephen Madigan). Finally, Part III, 'Deconstructing Psychotherapeutic Discourse' (or 'Deconstruction of psychotherapy'), concludes with two chapters that, respectively, discuss how deconstruction can problematise conventional problem catagories (John Morss and Maria Nichterlein) and how it can lead to a fundamental questioning of the very foundations of psychotherapy (Eero Riikonen and Sara Vataja). Of the six chapters in Parts II and III, those by Madigan ('Inscription, description and deciphering chronic identities', and Riikonen and Vataja ('Can [and should] we know how, where and when psychotherapy takes place?'), made a particularly strong impression.

One interesting and notable feature of the book is its truly international authorship: for apart from Parker, no other contributor is from Britain, with authors from Australia and New Zealand, the USA and Canada, Ireland and Finland. Australasia is particularly strongly represented with no less than six contributors (out of sixteen), which is no doubt fitting given the important deconstructive-therapy movement which has thrived there for over a decade, centred on the pioneering work of Michael White and David Epston (White and Epston 1990; White 1991). The dearth of British contributors highlights the importance of the book's publication for British practitioners increasingly dissatisfied with the conventional modernist therapy paradigm, and who are looking for new radical directions for their theory and practice.

The central 'protagonists' in this text are the two great and controversial post-structuralist theorists Michel Foucault and Jacques Derrida. I will devote two major sections to their work and the way it is weaved into the text, before moving on to a more general discussion.

FOUCAULT AND POWER

Power is surely an issue which has received a woeful lack of attention in the therapy world, and in this book Michel Foucault's views on power, including what he called 'power/knowledge' (p. 55), are a central and recurring theme, with readers thereby being offered a highly illuminating viewpoint on this much neglected issue. For Foucault, accompanying the Enlightenment, 'reductive theoretical constructions of various aspects of human existence cohered with modern forms of social regulation; [and]... these regimes of power/knowledge continue to structure the field of human interactions while constituting the terms of individual experience' (Fish, p. 54). For Foucault, power/knowledge refers to 'the constant, ubiquitous effects of [the] conjunction of systematized knowledge and material arrangements upon both subjectivity and human interactions' (ibid., p. 55):

> Foucault described both the mutuality of knowledge and power and the extent to which all ways of knowing are exercises of power. This power is not reducible to interpersonal domination, but is constitutive of social life and culture generally.... Power is normalized, rendered into discipline, practised routinely by subjects upon themselves as they re-enact the premises of their culture.... We must... see [power] as a dynamic or network of non-centralized forces.... [T]hese forces... assume particular historical forms, within which certain groups and ideologies do have dominance... – sustained through multiple processes of different origin and location regulating the most intimate elements of the construction of space, time, and desire.
> (Madigan, pp. 156–7)

Moreover, there is no need whatsoever to invoke conspiracy or Milibandian theories of (state) power:

> power does not derive from a central authority, is non-conspiratorial, and indeed non-orchestrated.... Where power works from 'below', prevailing forms of selfhood and subjectivity are maintained through individual self-surveillance and self-correction of established norms.
> (ibid.)

Or as Foucault himself put it, the individual will be 'his own overseer, each individual thus exercising this surveillance over, and against, himself' (quoted on p. 157).

For Foucault, then, power is 'exercised rather than possessed' (quoted on p. 119), and power 'is not a possession of individuals or the central apparatuses of the State' (Byrne and McCarthy, p. 94). For Foucault there exists a dialectical relationship in which 'the individual constitutes power relations and is in turn constituted by them' (ibid.).

For Law, 'Power is the collection of discursive practices performed that serves to maintain the strategic position of a given discourse and those persons who have access to its privileges' (p. 119). In turn, discursive practices are defined as 'ways of talking, thinking, feeling and acting that, when enacted, serve to reinforce, reproduce or support a given discourse and at the same time deny, disqualify or silence that which does not fit with that discourse' (ibid.).

If one really embraces these radical views on power, then one cannot but conclude, with Fish (p. 55), that 'it is critical for psychotherapists to keep in mind the immediate, inescapable connection between, on the one hand, clients' and therapists' subjectivity and behaviour, and, on the other, historical, ongoing institutional and cultural processes'. Moreover and of equal import, it also becomes crucial to 'explore psychotherapy as an institution', and 'to further our understanding of the political, historical forces that have shaped, and continue to shape,... its discourses and practices' (ibid.).

It is worth noting that Foucault did not argue for what he would have seen as an untenable denial of expertise and knowledge, for he 'contradicts those... who suggest that therapists can and ought to mitigate the power inherent in their "expert" knowledge' (Fish, p. 67). For Foucault,

> power relations are not something that is [sic] bad in itself.... I do not think that a society can exist without power relations.... The problem, then,... is to acquire the rules of law, the management techniques, and also the morality... that will allow us to play these games of power with as little domination as possible.
> (quoted on p. 67)

This seems to be both an overly optimistic and overly pessimistic view of power, at the same time: over-optimistic in the (naïve?) faith it places in the capacity for 'rules of law' and 'management techniques' healthily to address issues of power (cf. House 1999b); and over-pessimistic in its view that power relations are necessarily an inevitable accompaniment of human relationship. It might be argued that Foucault's view is one that is still rooted in the discourse of modernity, from which position he could, of course, reach no other conclusion. A view of these same issues from a 'transmodern', new-paradigm 'position' might well yield very different perceptions. For some of us at least, then, it seems that Foucault may not be radical enough!.... Elsewhere, for example, Luepnitz has pointed out that, contrary to the practice in much narrative therapy, Foucault would never have concurred with a therapist being defined as 'non-expert'; and that nowhere does he propose 'liberation' from technologies (though some are certainly more oppressive than others) (1992: 281, 282).

Both Swan and Law (Chapters 7 and 8 respectively) draw heavily upon Foucault's perspectives on power, gender and discursive practices to outline the relevance of his work to a feminist-informed narrative therapy and a discursive approach to working with men, respectively. Law uses the notion of 'discursive practice' in a case study (pp. 120–7) in which the therapist 'explicate(s), situate(s) and trace(s) the history of the various discourses that are mediating the sense that [clients] are making of their experience' (ibid, p. 120); for in such an approach, 'Naming... may open space for the consideration of alternative practices or counter practices' (ibid.).

DERRIDA AND DECONSTRUCTION

In his introductory chapter, Parker offers us a useful first handle for grappling with what deconstruction might consist in: 'Deconstruction is... a processual activity that defies definition... [it] is not a thing, and cannot be summed up in a neat definition or be put to work as a discrete technique' (p. 11). What Parker (p. 2) terms 'deconstructive unravelling' is a kind of 'method which is not one', a looking for 'the ways in which our understanding and room for movement is limited by the "lines of force" operating in discourse' – or the role of power in defining problems, with the location of our own understanding of problems lying within discourse (ibid.). Parker defines deconstruction as

> a process of critical reading and unravelling of terms, loaded terms and tensions between terms that construct how we read our place in culture and in our families and in our relationships, and how we think about who we are and what it might be possible for us to be.
> (pp. 6–7)

While modern(ist) 'scientific' psychology seeks 'essential', universal laws and largely ignores difference, Derridean deconstruction maintains that 'the recognition of difference forces us to abandon any essentialism or foundationalism... since language constitutes meanings not in terms of the essence of a thing but in its difference from other things' (Madigan, p. 153). Deconstruction highlights the paradoxes, contradictions and double binds that inhere in discourses of power, with the intent of limiting the repression of the other's difference (Larner, p. 39).

Indeed, paradox and contradiction are central to the phenomenon of deconstruction – 'a postmodern quandary' in which 'the dilemma of power is how to take a position... when such positioning itself involves a "violence that founds or positions"' (ibid.: 40, quoting Derrida). For Derrida, deconstruction is actually defined in terms of the paradoxes of power and justice (ibid.: p. 44); the paradox of power cannot be grasped via reason and language, and must be lived with (ibid.); and deconstruction 'can never begin and is always beginning, as an impossible enquiry into the limits of power and knowledge' (p. 43).

Derrida himself has in fact never described his writings as 'deconstruction' (p. 42): for him, deconstruction constitutes 'a proliferation of genres, styles, voices... plurality that no concept of deconstruction could hope to totalise' (Gasche, quoted in ibid.). For Derrida, then, deconstruction should never be reduced to a 'fashion, a school of thought, an academic current, a theory or a method.... There is no such thing as a deconstructive enterprise – the idea of a project is incompatible with deconstruction' (Derrida, quoted on p. 43). Moreover, deconstruction embraces 'both–and' rather than 'either/or' logic, and 'thinks opposites – for example, meaning and non-meaning, power and non-power – together' (p. 45).

It is impossible, then, to *not* take a position, and it is an illusion to believe that we can step outside of power, foundations or the real: 'The deconstructionist has one foot inside and the other outside the deconstructed system' (ibid.). As the adopting of a postmodern position simply repeats a modernist violence, Larner advocates a 'para-modernism' which is at the same time both modern and postmodern – referring to 'a knowledge that is "not-knowing" as a stable instability, a groundless ground, an uncertain certainty and a position of power that is non-powerful' (ibid.). For 'All positions are grounded in "a kind of violent exclusion that must efface its other and eliminate difference to preserve its purity"' (Nealon, quoted by Larner, p. 50).

With specific reference to psychotherapy, a deconstructing psychotherapy expresses a tenacious double bind around power and knowledge (explored more fully below): 'To deconstruct psychotherapy in the spirit of Derrida is to purge the cultural idols of power, technology and mastery from therapy, while acknowledging that we can never quite leave them behind' (Larner, p. 40). There is clearly a strong link between Derrida's and Foucault's work around power: thus, for example, the way in which

Derrida does not renounce or argue for the dissolution of power, and advocates its humane and just exercise, is not dissimilar to Foucault's position (see earlier discussion). The influence of these two important thinkers recurs throughout the book – as will become clear in the remainder of this chapter.

GENERAL COMMENTARY

In his position chapter, editor Ian Parker offers a wide-ranging, contextualising perspective on deconstruction in/as/of psychotherapy. He begins by pointing how conventional approaches to therapy can all too easily be re-abusive rather than emancipatory: 'Forms of psychotherapy... whether these are behaviourist, cognitive or psychoanalytic..., take for granted descriptions of pathology which often oppress people as they pretend to help them' (p. 2; cf. Parker et al. 1995 and Chapter 2, this volume). In the practice of 'deconstructing psychotherapy', in contrast, people's difficulties are 'understood as narrative constructions rather than as properties of pathological personalities, and as embedded in discursive practices rather than flowing from developmental deficits' (p. 2).

Parker usefully outlines a number of key features of what he terms 'a deconstructing psychotherapy' (the '...ing' being important, as it conveys the idea of an ongoing process):

- it is 'always in process, rather than something fixed, a movement of reflexive critique rather than a stable set of techniques' (ibid.);
- it is 'profoundly respectful' (p. 3);
- it pays close attention to contradiction (ibid.);
- it is 'intensely critical...: [it] does not presuppose a self under the surface.... To be "critical"... means understanding how we come to stand where we are' (pp. 3–4).

In the world of deconstructing therapeutic practice 'We are always already embedded in a particular set of perspectives, operating from within certain positions when we try to understand ourselves and others' (p. 4); and 'the task of the deconstructing therapist... is to... comprehend the role of patterns of power in setting out positions for people which serve to reinforce the idea that they can do nothing about it themselves' (p. 3).

Parker goes on to examine two existing examples where deconstruction and therapy have already had a fruitful meeting – namely, in family therapy, and in critical psychology. In the former case, he points out à la Foucault, for example, the parallel between the double binds and 'knots' found within families, and 'the paralysing contradictory messages that traverse a culture and position individuals within various discourses and discursive practices' (p. 7; cf. the later discussion). The more radical deconstructive family therapy practices focus directly upon how discourses and power actually constitute 'problems' 'that position the client as helpless and as believing that the problem lies inside them' (p. 8). The adoption of a reflexive stance within family therapy leads practitioners to reflect upon the cultural assumptions underpinning the project of psychotherapy and to engage in a process of ongoing deconstruction of the communities of which they are a part (p. 8; cf. House 1999c).

Critical psychology (e.g. Fox and Prilleltensky 1997/2009; Sloan 2000) entails a strong critique of the conventional professional institutions of psychiatry and psychology, and their accompanying clinical practices which consist of ideologies which 'locate thinking and feeling inside individuals' (p. 9). Thus, for example, the narratives of institutional Psychology constitute through reification certain 'psychological states', and

> Psychologists are then able to recognize these states as being the things they can predict and control, and this then constitutes individuals as subjects of the wider apparatus of surveillance and regulation in Western culture that psychology feeds upon and operates within.
> (ibid.)

Parker concludes by warning us not to expect a book whose contributors speak with one single, non-contradictory voice – which, in an appropriately pluralistic universe in which deconstruction in psychotherapy takes different forms in different parts of the world (p. 14), is just as it should be.

The chapters in Part I of *Deconstructing Psychotherapy* collectively offer an authoritative and convincing overview of the postmodern, deconstructive turn in therapy. Larner's chapter, referred to in the earlier section on Derrida, provides an outstanding introduction to Jacques Derrida's work and its relevance to deconstructing/ive therapy. The deconstructing therapist is immediately faced with what Larner terms 'the postmodern quandary': 'how to think, act and know in the absense of transcendent grounds, reason, truth and foundations; how to critique an institution when no outside grounds or positions can be taken, and avoid one's position becoming institutionalized...' (p. 40). For the deconstructing therapist, the inherent paradox of deconstruction, referred to earlier, means that the deconstructing of power within therapy 'requires the action of a powerful therapist to "not know" and it requires a powerful knowing at another level, a "not knowing" knowing' (ibid.).

Thus, a deconstructing therapy is both powerful and non-powerful (p. 41); and in ongoingly deconstructing its own power and authority as an institution, it will hopefully 'remain innovative and open to its own possibilities, rather than being subject to closure under the regime and institution of theory' (ibid.), and 'prevent its institutionalization as yet another totalizing discourse of truth, a deconstructive orthodoxy which is potentially violent in closing off difference and otherness' (p. 43). The approach to theory is central here, for the other is related to as a 'strange' other, rather than in terms of *a theory* of the other (p. 48):

> The other is not merely the 'socially constructed' other, but other, with a different existence.... [T]o listen to, rather than assimilate the other as one's construction (in imagination or in theory), requires a hierarchy that is for or favours the other..., in which both therapist and client are powerful and non-powerful.... The position the deconstructing therapist takes is both inside and outside power simultaneously.
>
> (pp. 48, 49)

Thus, in taking up the question of the ethical aspect in therapy, Larner emphasises that the therapeutic relationship is 'intentionally asymmetrical or hierarchical' (p. 47); and although the therapist is unavoidably invested with the power of technology and expertise, the ethical stance of the therapist towards the other 'balances this hierarchy, tempering the violence' (ibid.; cf. Chapter 9, this volume). Such a stance necessarily involves the honest, and sometimes painful, interrogation of the therapist's own interests in the therapeutic encounter – including, for example, 'the need for therapists to be successful, to establish a career and reputation in the market place, a professional niche; personal needs for control and power; the demands of a particular approach or ideology' (p. 49).

In sum, then, a deconstructing psychotherapy is not a particular method, school or theoretical doctrine that can be labelled (p. 49), and the task of deconstruction is 'to expose the violence inherent in the notion of "therapy"' (p. 48).

Roger Lowe interestingly and provocatively locates postmodern deconstruction in the in-between transitional space between the modernity that is no longer viable, having essentially lost all epistemological credibility, and the kind of 'post-postmodern' therapy which we have not yet created. I liked Lowe's characterisation of postmodernism as 'a metaphorical transitional boundary', evoking 'a self-consciously transitional moment' (p. 72, quoting Patti Lather) – that is, postmodernism is in fact not an 'ism', a thing, but rather, a key transitional moment in the evolution of ideas and human consciousness, a moment denoting both an important disillusionment with the objectivist Enlightenment project of modernity, and a liminal space which presages a 'new' which is as yet undefined and unknown (and may, of course, remain intrinsically so, as 'knowing' and 'definition' themselves are increasingly problematised; cf. Chapter 11, this volume).

Lowe also highlights the critical question of how we can avoid a postmodern 'approach' simply becoming another modernist discourse under a different label:

> how can we avoid reinventing the modernist wheel?... how can we ensure that postmodernist ways of talking do not end up doing the same work as modernist ones?... The... danger is that of professional institutionalization and re-assimilation to a modernist conversational repertoire based on objectivist knowledge and instrumentalism.
> (pp. 77, 82)

Relatedly, he also makes the sobering point that postmodern critique is the easy part (p. 77); whereas the operationalising of a descriptive postmodern praxis is another matter altogether. This will be very familiar, of course, to those who embraced critical Marxian theory in the 1970s and 1980s, and found its devastating critique of capitalism to be far from matched by viable and sustainable implications for real-world political practice.

The modernist world-view is indeed still extraordinarily powerful (as Thomas Kuhn [1962] showed, paradigms that are on the verge of being transcended go to desperate lengths to re-assert themselves, even in their death throes); and it seems that for the foreseeable future, new-paradigm thinking must needs assert itself in a kind of 'ongoing revolution', while we are still routinely faced with a control-obsessed modernity saturating our culture and institutions. Lowe also raises the question that has concerned many a critical realist (e.g. New 1996) – namely, how is it possible to reject the foundationalism of modernity without necessarily lapsing (as he would see it) into an anti-realist stance? Swan (p. 106) offers a potentially fruitful answer to this when she writes that 'We cannot stand outside of discourse, but we can be selective about which discourses fit better with our values and have less harmful effects on the wider community'. Unfortunately, there is no overt representation in the book of the radical new-paradigm viewpoint which would even problematise '(critical) realism' as a legitimate and suatainable epistemological world-view (House 1999d).

Lowe also has some interesting things to say about the ideological 'regime of truth' which conventional therapy so commonly becomes:

many conventional therapy 'realities' such as the classification of disorders... [in] DSM-IV are no longer seen as actual states of being, but as historically situated ways of talking which have constitutive effects in the way clients and therapists are positioned in terms of identities, obligations and entitlement.

>   (p. 76)

And such a discomforting perspective is even more 'disruptive' when applied to the professionalised way in which the field institutionally constitutes itself (cf. House and Totton 1997/2011; House 1999a, b, c):

The modernist conversational repertoire tends to speak into existence a specialized sphere of activity which is the appropriate business of 'psychotherapy', and to demarcate this from the non-therapeutic sphere.... [T]he profession of psychotherapy can be seen as an institution which gate-keeps the discursive repertoire of cultural standards and desired ways of being.... [H]istorical emergence within a particular modernist discourse... has contributed to a distinctive individual and internal focus in the profession's conversational repertoire, rather than a cultural and relational focus.

>   (p. 76, 77)

In other words, postmodern deconstruction problematises not only the 'clinical' procedures of therapy, but also the professionalised institutional structure which it takes and the individualised, privatised self-focus which the 'Professionalised Therapy Form' (House 1999a; Chapter 6, this volume) actively creates. And for Lowe, all therapists have 'an ethical obligation... to actively participate in the deconstruction of their own texts, rather than complying with an external mandate' (p. 81).

Finally, I was strongly drawn to Lowe's notion of 'discursive health warnings'(pp. 81–3), whereby 'Perhaps all therapy discourses should contain built-in discursive health warnings, through which their role in rhetorically shaping the objects of which they speak is revealed rather than concealed' (p. 81). There is a major issue around informed consent (or, rather, the notable lack of it) within therapy (see Chapter 4, this volume); and it seems to me that there is a very considerable ethical imperative for therapists ongoingly to question the particular 'regimes of professional truth' with which they (self-interestedly?) expect their clients to comply (cf. ibid.).

In his chapter on narrative therapy, John Kaye starts out with the question as to whether therapy can be effective without at the same time becoming an instrument for social control and a reinforcer of dominant discourses (p. 19). His chapter presents a formidable and thorough-going critique of conventional therapy, as well as a useful articulation of what he calls 'discursive therapy'. For Kaye, 'The word "psychotherapy" unavoidably carries overtones of acting instrumentally on another in order to remedy some psychological defect or deficiency' (p. 34). Thus, conventional psychotherapy is seen as a 'normalizing practice' (pp. 20–2), which assumes 'an underlying cause or basis of pathology; the location of this cause within individuals and their relationships; the diagnosability of the problem; and treatability via a specifically designed set of techniques' (pp. 20–1). Lurking within such a top-down, instrumentalist formulation are implicit assumptions about ab/normality (cf. Parker et al. 1995 and Chapter 2, this volume), the objectively establishable 'true root cause', and the concept of the therapist as having privileged knowledge, a socially accredited expert who can both provide an authoritative true version of a problem and act according to a set of prescribed activities to correct it (p. 21). Moreover, conventional therapy typically 'instantiates the notion of people as rational autonomous individuals possessing a fixed identity, an essential self vested with agency and a consciousness which is the cause of their beliefs and actions' (p. 22).

Drewery and McKenzie (Chapter 9) offer an interesting and highly readable discussion of how a deconstructive narrative therapy approach might respectfully work with clients bringing strong religious convictions – their aim being to show 'how it is possible to both acknowledge external authority or power [e.g. God – RH] and invoke personal agency' (p. 135). In other words, the authors set themselves the delicate task of showing how a belief in God can be compatible with notions of personal volition and agency. For these practitioners, 'the overt respect of the therapist for this dominating discourse in his life is an integral part of this therapeutic encounter' (p. 143).

The authors interestingly refer to parallels between their approach to narrative deconstructive therapy and cognitive therapy (p. 144) – an impression I have also found myself thinking from time to time. Consider, for example, the following passage from Swan's chapter (p. 105), which is in some ways remarkably evocative of cognitive therapy:

> [T]he process by which wider societal discourse and the normative rules this constructs can be seen to operate and inform our sense of who we are in the world. By specifically looking in detail at how this happens, opportunities for change... can be highlighted and thereby made available.

It might make for a very useful 'compare and contrast' exercise for someone to articulate the extent and the limits of these parallels, lest narrative therapy be assimilated by a 'flavour of the moment' cognitive therapy (House and Loewenthal 2008) which in reality surely differs in quite fundamental ways from the narrative approach, notwithstanding some superficial similarities (but see Smeyers et al. 2007: Chapter 4).

I really liked Drewery and McKenzie's boldness in questioning quite fundamentally the highly problematic modernist assumption that therapists necessarily know what they're doing (cf. Spinelli 1996): 'we have to come to understand...every client to be, in some sense, a mystery' (p. 139, cf. Chapter 11, this volume). And such a view is echoed in the book's final chapter, in which Riikonen and Vataja write of 'the sheer impossibility of non-ambiguous descriptions of any human interaction and the healing elements it contains... there is no reason to think that we know what psychotherapy really is' (pp. 176, 177).

In what is another outstanding chapter, Stephen Madigan offers a thorough-going critique of the institutional discourses of psychiatry and psychology. The chapter positively teems with memorable quotations and incisive insights – for example, that as language constitutes meanings in terms of its differences from other things (following Derrida), then we are logically forced to abandon the foundationalist search for the essense of the real (p. 153); and that there is an important distinction between 'identity' and the self-contained individual of the western Enlightenment (pp. 153–4). I found particularly conducive Madigan's openly subversive challenge to what I have elsewhere called the 'Professionalised Therapy Form' (House 1999a, 2003a), where he refers to 'the rules of organized therapy', which include 'the ritualized dialogic structure of the interview..., a session's temporal organization, client billing and other relational politics *often left as unquestioned practices and performances of power*' (pp. 154–5, emphasis added).

More generally, Madigan's chapter is an exemplary model of how to do effective case study reporting, with actual transcriptions weaved into a wide-ranging discussion of the radical deconstructive therapeutic approach he was using, and its underlying philosophical rationale. I found delightful and deeply moving Madigan's description of so-called 'therapeutic letter writing campaigns' which help clients to reconnect with their lost and (often institutionally) damaged identities (pp. 158–61). Such campaigns are designed as counter practices to the dis-membering effects of problem lifestyles and the isolating effects that psychological discourses often create in people's lives. The letters form a dialogic context of preferred re-membering, re-remembering and meaning (p. 160).

Drawing on Foucault's perspective on power, that seek a balanced view that takes account of structural effects as well as the agency of individual actors, Madigan makes the important point that it is at the least misleading simply to impugn the personal predilections of those who wield institutional psychiatric and psychological power: for

> psychologists (viewed as persons) find themselves embedded and implicated in institutions and practices that they as individuals did not create and do not control – and they frequently feel tyrannized by it.... Psychologists are not the enemy, but they often have a higher stake in maintaining institutions within which they have historically occupied positions of dominance over their clients/subjects.
>
> (p. 161)

Finally, Madigan echoes a point that recurs throughout *Deconstructing Psychotherapy*, that a socio-political perspective within therapy is crucial if it is not to become an individualising, self-serving (and -perpetuating) regime of truth:

> Without a consideration of the cultural and socio-political context of any problem brought to therapy, therapy could be considered as merely reproductive of culture and its institutions and as such uncritical.... [T]he therapeutic questions we ask or don't ask,... the files we keep, the interpretations we make,... if left unknown, unwarranted, and unchecked, will act to help solidify traditions and techniques of psychology's power.
>
> (p. 162)

CRITICAL DISCUSSION

I was taken by surprise by the essentially pro-institutional professionalisation position taken in Chapter 4 by Fish, who advocates institutional regulation (p. 68), arguing that 'The legal and administrative governance of psychotherapy... require constant attention and improvement' (ibid.). Fish seems to accept this viewpoint as an unproblematic given. It is ironic that his views are no doubt influenced by his own location within the culture of the US therapy world and its massively state-regulated environment, and that he fails to submit that very context to deconstructive gaze. Even if we accept (with Foucault) that 'power relations are not something that is bad in itself [sic]... I do not think a society can exist without power relations' (quoted on p. 67), it surely by no means follows from this that 'The therapist's power should be... monitored... by others (such as supervisors, consultants, and institutional regulators' (pp. 67–8).

Perhaps it is naïve to think that all those who embrace a broadly deconstructionist, postmodern position in relation to therapeutic practice will necessarily generalise such views to the political, institutional organisation of the therapy field – particularly in the light of Foucault's surprisingly sanguine perspective on organisations, discussed earlier.

I am also not nearly as confident as Lowe (in Chapter 5) that 'psychotherapy will easily outlive the current interest in postmodernism' (p. 72) – no sense here, certainly, of psychotherapy as an historically specific and ultimately transitory moment in human evolution. Lowe's otherwise outstanding chapter contains a view of post-postmodernism that sits very uneasily with both his own chapter and the rest of the book. He offers what seems to me to be a quintessentially (not to mention ironic) modernist view of postmodernism! – i.e. assuming it to be some-thing that will become part of history (p. 71), rather than a way of being which may well be inherently processual and ongoing rather than just another 'position' which will be transcended in due course of time.

The only chapter I struggled with was that by Byrne and McCarthy (Chapter 6). Even allowing for the challenging style that deconstructionist/ feminist writing often takes, I found this chapter recurrently mystifying and stylistically obscure – e.g.:

> Therapeutic discourse specifies a multiplicity of practices which hold possibilities to bring into view the different contents of colonization that circumscribe autonomy and, hence, a derogation of the primacy of ethics as 'self-esteem' in an individual life;

and

> Within this approach therapeutic discourse becomes a vernacular exploration and dialogue, economized by the movement of ambivalence which narrativizes provisional and coherent identities from the force lines of multiple constituent discourses.
>
> (pp. 87 and 96, respectively)

Clearly this is a difficult and sensitive area, not least because it might be somewhat unfair selectively to quote the authors out of context in this way. I most certainly do not take the overly simplistic view that any worthwhile idea can necessarily be expressed in easily understood, everyday language.

But equally, I am not un-used to reading this literature, so my own struggle with this chapter suggests to me that the authors could have made more of an effort to make their ideas more accessible. The following chapter, by Swan, certainly showed that feminist writing in this broad field does not necessarily need to adopt an obscure style. Thankfully, given the postmodernist literature's tendency to lapse into an almost studied stylistic obscurity, this was certainly the only chapter that presented any serious difficulties of comprehension for this reader.

Less than one-sixth of the book's content is devoted to case material. This felt like a not unreasonable balance, given the relative newness of the 'approach-which-is-not-one' being presented, and the appropriateness of providing the reader with a thorough theoretical introduction to it. In future literature, though, it will certainly be important that the actual practice implications of 'deconstructive psychotherapy' be given far more attention. As Spears (1996: 4) has graphically written, 'Isolated critique, no matter how profound, cannot challenge an endless production of knowledge from the paper mills of positivism if this is not tied to new and impactful practices'.

Finally, there is no mention in *Deconstructing Psychotherapy* of so-called New Paradigm thinking (e.g. House 1997b, e) – a rapidly growing movement that embraces, and is progressively crystallising around, an epistemologically sophisticated, anti-reductionist and often spiritually informed 'holistic-scientific' world-view – well represented by the world-wide Scientific and Medical Network (Lorimer 1998; Lorimer et al. 1999), which not only questions an ontology based on exclusively materialistic assumptions, but is prepared to take seriously areas of 'ineffable' human experience which traditional empiricist science invariably dismisses as 'unscientific' (House 1999e). It may well be that anything that smacks of 'the spiritual' would be anathema to most of *Deconstructing Psychotherapy*'s contributors – which would be a great shame, as there is surely great potential for major progress to be made from a cross-fertilisation of the kind of views represented in *Deconstructing Psychotherapy* and the exciting strain of New Paradigm thinking that 'the New Science' is currently spawning (e.g. Clarke 1996; Laszlo 1996; Hitter 1997; Lorimer 1998; Wilber 1998).

CONCLUDING REFLECTIONS

[T]here is... the perpetual illusion that we have passed beyond the modern.

(Parker 1998c: 612)

> Could it be... that the most important contribution to postmodern psychotherapy might be to serve as a harbinger of the 'not yet' – the fashioning of therapy discourses which move, ironically, beyond the modern/postmodern distinction?
>
> (Lowe, p. 83–4)

The widely and uncritically embraced duality of modernism/postmodernism is perhaps not only unhelpful and overly simplistic, but itself actually creates a polarised either/or debate which ironically replicates the very world-view which postmodern thinking at its best has pretensions to transcending (cf. Goss and Mearns 1997). As Parker (1998c: 610) puts it, 'those who characterize themselves as "postmodern" are defining themselves against and within the terms of the debate laid down by the moderns'. On this view, any concept which is rooted in an emotionally driven process of reaction-formation (i.e. as a reactive, if understandable, counterweight to the excesses of modernity, distorting ego-dominated rationalism, technocratic positivism and the like) is itself very likely to be unbalanced (in this case, with an excess of 'emotionality', a-rationality and disorder). The secret, of course, then becomes to step out of the polarised modernity/postmodernity duality, and into a more pluralistic, both–and way of being which can respect and work with difference and the in-between (cf. Goss and Mearns 1997; Samuels 1997). For Parker (1998c: 612), 'There is a powerful discursive frame around our accounts of the modern and the postmodern, and we need to step outside that frame to be able to understand how it has gripped us'. And as Goss and Mearns (1997: 193) have it, 'Perhaps we need a new logic – one in which apparent "opposites" can co-exist within a pluralist perspective'.

Perhaps we might then seek an alternative term, like 'transmodern', which reflects 'an ongoing transcending movement beyond', rather than a polarised, adversary position. Smith (1994: 408), for example, has also argued for the term 'late modern' as less misleading. On this view, which recognises 'modernity' as a necessary (albeit immature) stage in the evolution of human consciousness, the transmodern will not reactively repudiate and condemn what went before as a 'mistake', but rather, will organically assimilate and build upon all that has gone before, but healthily transcend it into a more highly evolved level of consciousness (cf. Steiner 1966).

It should be noted in passing that I have not given any attention in this chapter to the thorny question of relativism in postmodernist and social constructionist approaches (for useful discussions see Spears 1996: 7–12; Parker 1998c: 617–19). Certainly, critical realists are typically strongly critical of relativism (e.g. New 1996; Parker 1998c) and its alleged politically paralysing effects. However, I find myself agreeing with Hare-Mustin at this point, when she writes that 'The notion that relativism is an evil to be avoided is itself a culturally embedded claim, shaped by political ends' (1994: 32).

Roger Lowe (p. 71) rhetorically asks whether, in the future, postmodernism will be looked back upon as 'a kind of watershed, that future generations will continue to look back to with pride as a major turning point in the betterment of therapy'. My own hunch is that the very rise of postmodernist, new-paradigm and deconstructionist thinking marks a crucial moment in the evolution of human consciousness, being an indication that we are, as a species, starting to approach a time when we will be mature enough to let go of the reassuring but hugely limiting (illusory) certainties of the ego-dominated, control-obsessed 'infant' of modernity, and into a 'transmodern' realm of experience of which we are as yet only dimly aware, still being so thoroughly caught up as we are in the death throes of modernity (Barratt 1993). The journey from modernity through 'transmodernity' to whatever lies beyond it will not be an easy or straightforward one; and if – not unreasonably – we can expect therapy to take an active part in these momentous developments, then books such as *Deconstructing Psychotherapy* will surely serve as leading-edge pioneering texts to help us through the transition.

Certainly, one message that comes over loud and clear in the book is that therapy simply cannot continue with its current conventional, predominantly modernist orientation: as Lowe has it,

> [S]taying within the modernist repertoire may render psychotherapy obsolete in the sense that its emphasis on cultural adjustment tends to preclude its potential to assist in the construction of new relational possibilities.
>
>   (p. 81)

With regard to postmodernism more generally, Lowe (p. 71) further points out that 'it can be bewilderingly difficult to gain a foothold, let alone a vantage point, for discussions of postmodernism'; and for Drewery and McKenzie (p. 148), 'there is a lot more work to be done investigating the application of post-structuralist ideas to therapeutic conversation'. *Deconstructing Psychotherapy* shows quite conclusively that the most exciting, leading-edge thinking in the therapy sphere of the future will be critical, radical and deconstructivist.

In my view this book offers us an excellent beginning on the journey of 'transmodernity' – a journey which I believe to be essential if the future development of therapy as a helping practice is to be a healthy and viable one in what will in the future become an increasingly 'transmodern' world.

CHAPTER 8

Therapy and Postmodernist Thought: Martin Heidegger's relevance to therapy and traumatic experience: A review essay

No event can be objectively described as traumatic.
  (Patrick Bracken)

...[In Heidegger's analysis], stress is not seen... as the physical response to a mental injury, but as the existential response to a demand of Being.... It is not a pathological event as such.
  (Hans W. Cohn)

Seldom if ever in the history of philosophy has a philosopher attracted such extreme assessments as has Martin Heidegger – from, on the one hand, being regarded by some commentators (e.g. Jacques Derrida and Richard Rorty) as perhaps the greatest philosopher of the last century to, at the other extreme, Oxford philosopher A.J. Ayer's (in)famously contemptuous dismissal of Heidegger as 'a charlatan'. Heidegger is certainly widely regarded as 'the most complex and obscure of all philosophers' (Watts 2001: xi); and this, added to his potentially revolutionary challenges to the very foundations of 'modernity' and conventional Western thought, perhaps explains why his work has not, to date, had nearly the influence upon the therapy world that it surely merits. This chapter hopes to make a contribution to setting right this noteworthy neglect.

There are fewer more controversial figures in the history of philosophy than Martin Heidegger, yet Heidegger has had an enormous influence upon many of the most important existential and postmodern thinkers, including the 'father' of phenomenology, Edmund Husserl. Influenced, no doubt, by the first and welcome appearance in English translation of the celebrated Zollikon Seminars in 2001 (on which, see below), several books soon began to appear that engaged quite explicitly with Heidegger's philosophy and its relevance to psychotherapy and counselling. The following review essay looks closely at two such books, Pat Bracken's *Trauma: Culture, Meaning and Philosophy* (Whurr, 2002) and the late Hans W. Cohn's *Heidegger and the Roots of Existential Therapy* (Continuum, 2002). It will soon become clear that, notwithstanding the political controversies and complexities that surround Heidegger's career and life, his post–Cartesian philosophy has a great deal of relevance to the practice of the psychological therapies.

For this reason alone, these two recently published books by Hans Cohn and Patrick Bracken are especially welcome. Not that Heidegger was completely untouched by the world of psychoanalysis and psychiatry – for in the post-war years, later on in his academic career, he became involved as a tutor and consultant to a project directed by the Swiss psychiatrist Medard Boss, which led to the establishment of one of the first schools of existential psychotherapy, *Daseinanalysis* – being the first attempt, according to Cohn (p. xviii), to develop a form of therapy with existential foundations. Much of this path-breaking work emerged in the vital but, until recently, little considered *Zollikon Seminars* (lasting from 1959–69), in which Heidegger lectured to trainee and professional psychotherapists on the implications of his own philosophy for therapy practice.

These key seminars had not been published in English translation before Cohn's and Bracken's books were written, though both authors do helpfully manage to quote the seminars in their respective books, and at some length. As well as being of direct relevance to the concerns of (existential) psychotherapy, these seminars are especially useful in rendering the sometimes near-impenetrable arguments of Heidegger's earlier magnum opus, *Being and Time* (1927), far more understandable and transparent to fellow philosopher and lay reader alike. The recent and greatly welcome publication (Heidegger 2001) of an English translation of Heidegger's Zollikon Seminars is of considerable importance in bringing Heidegger's post-Caretesian therapy-relevant thinking to the attention of an English-speaking readership.

HEIDEGGER AND THE ROOTS OF EXISTENTIAL THERAPY (COHN)

Hans Cohn explores the role of Heidegger's thought in providing an alternative, existential-phenomenological basis to the dominant psychodynamic, humanistic and cognitive approaches to therapy. In his Introduction, Cohn refers to how Heidegger's ideas have been 'strangely neglected' by the psychotherapy world – a lacuna which he aims to rectify with his book. In Chapter 1, Cohn is at pains to emphasise just how divergent Heidegger's philosophy is from mainstream Western thinking, just how easy it is to underestimate the extent of that divergence, and how his thinking has the potential to revolutionise therapy practice. Chapter 2, 'Heidegger's way to psychotherapy', usefully describes how Heidegger's central philosophical concepts (Being, Dasein, existence and 'existentials') have relevance for psychotherapy praxis, with some interesting biographical details about his differences with Ludwig Binswanger, and the way in which Medard Boss approached him prior to the historic Zollikon Seminars. These seminars covered a wide range of themes, including the body/mind question, Descartes and natural science, and the subject/object question (p. 15). We also read about Heidegger's highly controversial involvement with Nazism – his public silence about which, though 'very nearly intolerable' to such an intellectual luminary as George Steiner, is lightened somewhat by the revelation that Heidegger expressed profound shame about his Nazi involvement in private letters written to Karl Jaspers in 1950 (p. 21).

Each of the following ten chapters focuses on a central theme from Heidegger's *oeuvre* – namely, Being-in-the-World, Being-with, language, body-mind, 'attunement', temporality, the priority of phenomena, Being and beings, authenticity, and thrownness and choice; and at the end of each of these thematic chapters, Cohn has a very useful 'Therapeutic Relevance' section in which the practical therapeutic implications of Heidegger's ideas *vis-à-vis* the theme under consideration are clearly set out.

I will highlight just a few of the more interesting features that impressed me as I read the book. First, below I have compiled a list of fifteen of the more striking implications stemming from Heidegger's ideas in so far as they are relevant to the theory and practice of counselling and psychotherapy: namely,

• that the therapy relationship cannot be one of 'observer' and 'observed' (p. 31), but is rather a world that therapist and client share 'with each other' (p. 40);

• that therapy cannot have a 'secure frame' with rigid rules, but requires flexibility to take account of the uniqueness of each therapeutic context (p. 31);

• that the space for therapy is *the contextual world* inhabited by the client (ibid., 48), and which the client needs to create (p. 49);

• that therapists cannot justifiably impose explanatory expectations and interpretations, but rather should stay open to what the phenomena are telling them (p. 31);

• that the context is in constant flux, and the notion of a fixed 'internal' psychic structure is a therapist construction (p. 40);

• that what clients say is what they mean and not something else (p. 48);

• that body and mind are not separate – bodily and mental spheres are aspects of the same phenomenon, with so-called 'psychosomatic symptoms' being 'a total response to a total situation' (p. 56);

- that feelings cannot be 'split off' from the context in which they occur (p. 61);
- that there is no purely cognitive approach to problems, and rationality is not superior to other ways of being (p. 62);
- that phenomenologically speaking, the present contains at any moment the past and also points to the future (p. 67), and causal-explanatory mechanisms only serve to obscure and distance one from the interconnection between past and present (p. 68);
- that the future is crucial (but neglected) in therapy (ibid.);
- that *understanding* is privileged over explanation, and is an open, unending, never-completed process (p. 77);
- that some aspects of human Being are universal givens, or 'ontological' in nature (p.83 – with important implications for the extent of human freedom, pp. 122–3); that therapy is commonly concerned with individuals' 'ontic' responses to these universal givens (p. 83); and that therapists need to avoid making ontological interpretations of ontic events (p. 93);
- that a kind of 'pre-ontological' understanding in 'included' in 'every ontic understanding' (p. 83.); and finally,
- that (non-dualistically speaking) it cannot be 'false' to live 'inauthentically', and it cannot be more 'real' to live 'authentically', if both states are aspects of existence itself (p. 92).

Ten 'aspects of existential practice', as they 'flow from a Heideggerian view of the human experience of Being' (p. 115), are also usefully summarised by Cohn on pages 116–24.

This stimulating 15-point list gives a really good flavour of the wealth of therapeutic wisdom that Cohn derives from Heidegger's ideas. We also read, *inter alia*, about the formidable difficulty involved in translating Heidegger's terms into English (pp. 59, 85–6; see below); Cohn's convincing problematising of the Winnicottian 'true/false self' dichotomy (pp. 91–2); the key importance of *context*, and of maintaining a careful, subtle balance between person and world (pp. 110, 127); and about Cohn's principled reluctance to offer case-history material for fear of misleadingly wrenching the client's story from its unique living context (p. 126).

All in all, the radicalism and revolutionising potential of Heidegger's thought for therapy practice comes through loud and clear in Cohn's book – indeed, it can hardly be exaggerated: for as Howard has dramatically put it elsewhere, 'If Heidegger is right, then *the most basic common-sense assumptions within counselling – about self, world, interaction and communication – must be abandoned'* (Howard 2000: 327, emphasis added) – and the relevance of Heidegger's thought to therapy is 'overwhelming' (ibid.: 331). Cohn has certainly performed a vitally important service in beginning to articulate with admirable clarity and insight the nature of these revolutionising effects for the practice of therapy, and just what is at stake if we seriously and consistently dare to embrace Heideggerian thought.

TRAUMA: CULTURE, MEANING AND PHILOSOPHY (BRACKEN)

In *Trauma*, Patrick Bracken offers us a wonderfully impressive Heideggerian critique of conventional thinking about traumatic experience (which every- and anyone involved in its 'treatment' would greatly benefit from reading) – together with a healing alternative that posits a new socio-cultural framework for helping traumatised communities and individuals that is centred on, and deeply respectful of, local communities and their cultural specificity, as opposed to an approach which uncritically assumes the universality of what is a limited and *limiting* Eurocentric 'individualised' form of 'treatment'.

It is heartening indeed to find thinking such as this coming out of psychiatry (Bracken is a Foucault-influenced Consultant Psychiatrist based at Bradford University, who has written widely in the critical psychiatry literature, has established an inner-city home treatment service for the severely mentally disturbed and has pioneered new approaches to user/provider partnerships, as well as working with Ugandan victims of violence). For Bracken, Heidegger's thought affords a framework for a viable, more appropriate approach to trauma treatment, privileging as it does an interpersonal and socio-cultural rather than an intra-psychic and individual orientation. Along with his colleague Phil Thomas, Bracken has pioneered an exciting '*Post*psychiatry' which 'de-centres the tools of traditional psychiatry and instead foregrounds questions of values, social contexts and… personal meanings' (p. viii; see also pp. 223–7).

With specific regard to trauma, Bracken's own concerns are well summed up in a quotation from Kirby Farrell (cited on p. 3), who sees 'trauma' as 'a strategic fiction that a complex, stressful society is using to account for a world that seems threateningly out of control'. In other words, Bracken is concerned not only with individual instances of traumatic experience and their explanation and treatment, but with the rapid growth of the notion of 'trauma' within modern Western culture, its historical specificity and the function it serves within that culture, and the way in which the cultural legitimacy of the concept itself feeds into contemporary subjectivity. Unsurprisingly, Bracken is highly sceptical about an approach which simplistically medicalises and objectifies traumatic experience, and wants instead to strive for a far more subtle socio-cultural understanding which questions the uncritical assumption of the universal, trans-cultural validity of trauma discourse. This entails an explicit and humble recognition that different cultures have very different approaches to, *and subjective experiences of*, these phenomena. More specifically, in his work in Uganda, Bracken 'became increasingly dissatisfied with Western psychiatric models of distress and suffering…, being too individualistic and "mentalistic"…, [and paying] little attention to the importance of social context, economics and culture' (p. 5). Bracken's central target, then, is the Cartesianism and crass positivism of modernity (referred to elsewhere in this chapter and volume) in so far as they dominate the culturally ascendant 'trauma discourse' pervading Western clinical consciousness (and which many Western professionals have quite inappropriately attempted to export wholesale into non-Western cultural contexts).

It is quite impossible to do justice to this excellent book in a brief essay. Quite apart from the (to this reader) refreshing critical perspectives on modern conventional psychiatry and its associated 'medicalisation' of distress, there are a number of major chapters which explicitly embrace Heideggerian thinking in a way that seamlessly complements Hans Cohn's more general text, showing as it does the rich potential that exists for applying Heidegger's world-view to a specific clinical issue – namely, trauma discourse. Along the way, we see information-processing and cognitive understandings of trauma, along with the clinical category of so-called 'Post Traumatic Stress Disorder' (PTSD), subjected to a quite withering and, to me, wholly convincing critique of their manifold shortcomings (e.g. pp. 63–81).

Section II of the book consists of four 'Heideggerian' chapters under the collective title 'A phenomenological approach to meaning and loss' (80 pages in all), with chapters on Heidegger's account of human reality; a Heideggerian approach to psychology and psychotherapy; meaning, anxiety and ontology; and authenticity. Most if not all of the themes discussed in Cohn's book are also addressed by Bracken, but in an *applied* context which is quite invaluable, both in terms of opening up the issue of 'trauma' to a deeper understanding, and also in illustrating how, in principle, Heidegger's insights into Being and 'existence have a profound *practical* relevance that are easily translated into clinical-practice contexts more generally.

A central aspect of Bracken's discussion is the thorough and insightful way in which he systematically lays bare the erroneous assumptions of modernity and its cultural handmaidens, positivistic scientism and technologism (not least within conventional psychiatry). For example, he revealingly deconstructs the uncritically assumed causal mechanisms of 'PTSD', showing that far from traumatic events necessarily *causing* resultant symptoms, it is at least as plausible to reverse the causality and see the focus on the traumatic event in question as being *the result*, and not the cause, of other psychiatric symptoms like depression and anxiety (p. 205). The book brims over with thought-provoking deconstructive moves like this, making it a refreshingly invigorating read.

Bracken's lucid discussion of *postmodern ethics* is worth dwelling on for a moment (pp. 196–202 *passim*) – both to give the reader a flavour of Bracken's text, and also because his discussion has profound implications for the therapy industry's institutional pursuit of ethical behaviour via centralised (modernist) ethical codes (cf. Pattison 1999). For as he points out (following Zygmunt Bauman), 'the modernist search for codification, universality and foundations in the area of ethics was actually *destructive of* the moral impulse' (p. 197, emphasis added), with modernity being animated by the misguidedly naïve belief that non-contradictory, non-ambivalent ethical codes were not only possible but desirable. Indeed, Bracken maintains,

> the modernist and rationalist attempt to render our moral issues in simple dichotomies of good and bad, right and wrong has had disastrous consequences..., [and] the search for ever more efficient therapies and codes of behaviour is part of the problem and can be expected to generate new forms of oppression and suffering.
>
> (p. 202)

Modernist ethics, then, is driven by the 'impulse to order and control the world, to make it – and us – function more efficiently and predictably' (ibid.). Yet as Howard elsewhere so eloquently puts it (following Heidegger), 'The idea that we get more control over our affairs by consciously revisiting, discussing and analysing everything we do is absurd' (Howard 2000: 333) – control-freaks everywhere, please note!...

A rationalist modernity, then, simply cannot neatly *legislate away* 'the immense ambivalence at the heart of our ethical situation as human beings' (pp. 202–3), however hard it might try to do so. *Postmodern* ethics, on the other hand, does not prematurely shut down possibility or negate difference; and it creates a space wherein doing nothing, or holding back, can be the most morally appropriate of responses – an example of 'morality without ethics', as Bauman calls it. Postmodern ethics also involves, *inter alia*, 'facing the world without easy recourse to guiding codes or principles', and 'an acceptance of ambivalence and disorder [that] are here to stay, not just temporary difficulties that need to be overcome by further analysis, or the application of ever more structured ethical systems' (p. 203; cf. House 1997a). Steven White's notion of 'responsibility to otherness' is also usefully invoked by Bracken here – involving 'a concern *not* to impose order on the world but instead to allow the emergence of other voices and visions even when this involves increasing complexity and ambivalence' (p. 199). The relevance of such a perspective in helping to illuminate the nature of 'best moral practice' in relation to engaging with trauma in non-Western cultures should be clear (and would that this kind of thinking were having some purchase on the calamitous unfolding of events in Iraq – as written in 2004; RH).

To my mind Bracken has made a wholly convincing case for the profound relevance of Heideggerian hermeneutics to *everything* therapeutic – including his own chosen theme, the 'trauma industry'; and, taken together, these two books by Bracken and Cohn make a compelling case for a root-and-branch re-conceptualisation of the very nature of therapy praxis, which any progressively minded practitioner would be ill-advised to ignore.

COMMENTARY: HEIDEGGER AND THE EVOLUTION OF HUMAN CONSCIOUSNESS

For this writer, what is of overriding importance in all this is the relevance of Heidegger's thinking to *the evolution of human consciousness*. It is surely very revealing that the thinking of a number of key therapist-writers has tended to move increasingly towards a quasi-mystical, spiritual world-view in their later years – W.R Bion, Carl Jung, Ronnie Laing and Carl Rogers immediately come to mind. Certainly, Heidegger and other 'postmodern' thinkers have demonstrated – to my mind quite conclusively – the fundamental incoherence of the Cartesian dualism that still dominates Western 'modernity' (with its mind/body, reason/emotion, subject/object splitting), and the crass positivism of vast swathes of the modern scientific enterprise and its one-sidedly materialistic world-view (cf. Chapters 18–20, this volume).

As a number of commentators, including Heidegger, have pointed out, the Cartesian ontology has thorough-goingly infiltrated our everyday awareness, language and *very ways of thinking about ourselves* (which infiltration needs *itself* to be accounted for, of course). Commonly, for example, we often unwittingly *still* think and talk in a Cartesian way *at the very moment when* we are attempting to argue for *post*-Cartesianism! Here is Hans Cohn, for example: 'The very moment we ask a question about the relation between body and mind, we have already entered the dualistic trap'

(p. 51). On this view, then, we must begin by raising to conscious awareness just how thoroughly immersed we all are in dualistic Cartesianism (cf. House 1996d), before we can begin to know how to transcend it. What is surely required, then, is a decisive *evolutionary shift in Being* such that we, as a species, can transcend the limiting straight-jacket of Cartesianism and materialism and all that accompanies the world-view of modernity.

These are, of course, grand(iose) themes that, nonetheless, must needs be addressed if humankind is to mature through and beyond its current dire predicaments. A new post-Cartesian, post-materialistic way of experiencing and, therefore, thinking about human Being is arguably essential, therefore, and Heidegger's work makes a crucial, specifically philosophical contribution to preparing the ground for this urgent evolutionary shift to occur. As von Eckartsberg (1998: 11) has put it, we can begin to avoid the trap of Cartesian dualism

> if we conceive of our existence completely in relational and field theoretical terms as a field of openness into which things and the world appear and reveal themselves in a dynamic way.... Persons are not selves separated from [the world]...; rather, they are personal involvements in a complex totality network of interdependent ongoing relationships that demand... participation.

Heidegger's own philosophical style is actually designed to help break the pattern of thinking that leads us to take Being for granted, and to help us question the meaning of Being – which he did by constructing *a new way of thinking* about Being, not least because, for him, existing language was shorn of meaning and quite incapable of addressing existence in an adequate way (Watts 2001: 13). Heidegger also recognised that Being's essence is never fully sayable in language – and for him, poetry was the deepest revelation of what *is*, in its disclosing of the essence of ordinary things that usually go unnoticed (cf. Chapter 11, this volume). He therefore went on to develop *a language of metaphor* unique to him, attaching new meanings to simple everyday words (ibid.: 71–2). It is no surprise, then, that Heidegger is commonly regarded as having engaged more deeply than any other philosopher with the influence that language exerts on human thought.

A further possibility is provided by Heidegger's own Zen-like recommendation (cf. Watts 2001: Chapter 7) of a shift from what he calls the control and domination-orientated '*calculative reasoning*' mode of modernity and technologism, to a more *meditative*, reflective thinking mode, sometimes rendered as '*Gelassenheit*' – a 'letting-be', 'without why' kind of thinking which allows things to 'rise up out of concealment' (Caputo 1998: 229). Heidegger was deeply concerned that humankind is becoming so totally captivated and beguiled by technologism and means/ends rationality that, ultimately, calculative thinking 'will come to be accepted and practised as the only way of thinking' – and that meditative thinking can serve to rescue our loss of the sense of Being's mystery and enchantedness (see Chapter 11, this volume).

Such a movement away from control-fixated calculative thinking depends, in turn, on a resolute preparedness to face basic existential-ontological questions, not least *anxiety* in the face of our own mortality; and it necessitates a maturing beyond 'victimhood consciousness' (Hall 1993) and towards a full acknowledgement of one's self as illuminator and creator of one's world. Certainly, it is no coincidence that, through his anti-technologism, Heidegger 'demonstrated a remarkable ecological awareness' (Watts 2001: x) many years ahead of his time, which led him strongly to challenge the abuse of planetary resources and to predict the coming planetary-ecological crisis.

Any practitioner looking for a conducive, manageable way into the profound challenges of Heidegger's thought could do no better than to read these two excellent books. The celebrated philosopher of deconstruction and student of Heidegger, Jacques Derrida, wrote that 'Heidegger's texts harbour a future of meaning which will ensure that they are read and reread for centuries.' And in the specific context of counselling, we find Alex Howard (2000: 338) writing that 'Much of what he said deserves to be taken forward. He is not widely enough known. He will, I hope, reach way beyond the time of many brighter celebrities who will, much sooner, be forgotten.' Cohn and Bracken certainly make a major contribution to taking Heidegger's potent counter-cultural ideas out into a therapy world that is arguably in desperate need of new, radicalising thinking lest it be overtaken by a kind of self-satisfied profession-centred complacency. And these texts also open up the possibility that therapy itself could conceivably begin to take a key role in contributing towards, rather than being just one more Cartesian fetter upon, the urgently needed evolution of human consciousness.

POSTSCRIPT

When this review essay appeared in *Ipnosis* magazine in the autumn of 2004, it elicited a highly critical letter to the editor from Chris Willoughby, in which he strongly challenged the idea that we should pay any credence to the ideas of an apparently unapologetic ex-Nazi. I reproduce below my response to Willoughby's criticisms, which was published in *Ipnosis* magazine, 17 (Spring), 2005, p. 7.

Dear Editors,

I read Chris Willoughby's letter in the previous issue of *Ipnosis* with a mixture of surprise and sadness. *Surprise*, because I have been stimulated by his previous writings in the magazine and his generous quoting of my own work, which led me to think that we thought quite similarly on at least some of therapy's central concerns (though I also share many of the cogent challenges from John Freestone to Chris's apparent wholesale rejection of therapy – Letters, issue 16 – not least, John's admirable approach of 'holding his ideas lightly'). And *sadness*, because I was left wondering just where forgiveness figured – if at all – in Chris's world-view.

First, the issue of the location of distress in human experience. Of course it would be foolish to question the contention that a great deal of human suffering *in some sense* (I carefully emphasise) originates in social oppression and structures. I view the work of commentators like David Smail and Robert Sardello as seminal in this regard. But to admit this as fact does not *necessarily* entail that individualised therapy is therefore an irrelevance to such suffering. Thus, individual therapy at its best can help people to empower themselves and then effectively and responsibly to challenge those very sources of societal oppression that Chris rightly abhors – for 'the personal' and 'the political' are today surely just as much an indissoluble couple as they were argued to be at the heady heights of the feminist revolution in the 1960s and 1970s.

But to take the issue deeper, I am pretty much invariably suspicious of over-simple 'either–or' thinking – and it seems to me that Chris is in danger of such thinking in his wholesale rejection of therapy culture and in his determination to locate distress outside of the individual. For in the trans-modern world that I falteringly strive to inhabit myself, I believe that distress is both societal *and* individual *at the same time*, and in highly complex, co-constituting ways that we are as yet scarcely able to comprehend at this juncture in our evolution as a species. I have written at length elsewhere (House 2003b) about issues of karma and destiny in so far as they are relevant to therapy, and the implication of these controversial issues for human responsibility-taking and freedom. My emerging view is that any approach to personal development and change, and to human evolution more generally, that does not pay attention to 'the transpersonal' can only ever offer us an, at best, unsatisfactory and, at worst, wholly misleading understanding of human experience. Focusing, as Chris does, on injustice and societal oppression is a matter of great concern to any progressive thinker; but to assume that it is anything like the whole story – or even the most important part of it – is an assumption that I simply don't share with him.

I think that these latter comments will also throw some light on the status of Chris's criticisms of my review essay on Martin Heidegger's relevance to therapy (issue 15). I am accused by Chris of 'skating over' Martin Heidegger's Nazi involvement in my essay. It would have been all too easy and convenient for me simply not to mention this issue at all; and on reading about this difficult history, I spent some time investigating what had happened, and satisfied myself that Heidegger had indeed deeply regretted this aspect of his personal biography – albeit expressed in private letters to Karl Jaspers. But even if he hadn't expressed such contrition, in my view it would still be highly questionable to reject in a wholesale way the deep thinking of someone just because of their uncomfortable or (to most) unacceptable political views. The history of Nazism and its rise in Europe, and its place in German culture more generally, is an enormously complex issue, as is the multitude of effects that these fateful decades had on the individuals implicated in their unfolding. Unlike Chris, I am not about to make unqualified condemnations of individuals who were caught up in this appalling historical conjuncture – not least because none of us can say with any certainty just how we would ourselves have acted, had we had the equal misfortune to have been caught up in that history.

Similarly, that Heidegger was a flawed individual (witness, for example, his treatment of Husserl) is, in Chris's worldview, meant to lead us to reject his contribution to human thought in its entirety. I would submit to Chris that if we had meated out such treatment to every individual in the History of Ideas who possessed 'character flaws', then we'd still be living in the Dark Ages or in caves. I far prefer to embrace a model of forgiveness, as so movingly pioneered in post-Apartheid South Africa, in which *healing happens for all through the forgiveness of wrong-doing*, rather than the 'punish, name and shame' approach that will surely eventually end up in the dustbin of history, where it rightly belongs. And for what it's worth, when Heidegger said (as Chris quotes) 'He who thinks great thoughts often makes great errors', he was almost certainly talking, quite self-awarely, about himself.

Richard House

CHAPTER 9

Taking Therapy Beyond Modernity?
The promise and limitations of a
Levinasian understanding

INTRODUCTION

This chapter offers a 'non-expert' perspective on the 'Levinas and Psychotherapy' symposium of the *European Journal of Psychotherapy, Counselling and Health*, volume 7, nos 1–2, 2005, highlighting in particular Levinas's overarching focus on the constitutive primacy of the ethical obligation to the other, and its attendant implications for therapeutic work. In particular, the chapter examines the relevance of Levinas's radical thinking to questions of knowing and certainty in the Western psychology tradition, and to the culturally urgent challenges posed by individualism, other-centredness and intersubjectivity. It is argued that in the epoch of late modernity, Levinas's work makes an important contribution to 'new paradigm' thinking and to the evolution of human consciousness in which we are all caught up.

SOME CONTEXT

The name of Emmanuel Levinas (1905–95) has recently come up with increasing frequency in my own reading and conversations – reflecting, I can only assume, a strong and growing interest in his work in therapy circles. Until comparatively recently (House 2004b), however, I knew little about Levinas's philosophy. In my reading for a major review article on Levinas (ibid.), I learnt that he challenges the 'ontological' focus in mainstream

Like Heidegger, Emmanual Levinas is one of the most challenging of continental philosophers to understand in the original, so it was with some trepidation and no little foolhardiness that I agreed to a request in 2004 from the editor of the *European Journal of Psychotherapy, Counselling and Health*, Del Loewenthal, to write an 'invited commentary' on a special issue of the journal on the implications of Levinas's ideas for psychotherapy. My self-labelled 'non-expert' commentary is reproduced below, in large part because my discovery of Levinas through the Research Centre for Therapeutic Education at Roehampton University has only helped to confirm and reinforce my own particular journey through and beyond a 'modernist' conception of and approach to therapy praxis.

therapy thinking, with its emphasis on 'autonomy, ego-centricity, or notions of a bounded unitary self' (Loewenthal and Snell 2003: 151), by maintaining that ethical questions must always come before those of being – for 'phenomenologically, the face of the other is prior to ourselves' (ibid.). In the case of the culturally unquestioned notion of personal autonomy (certainly within humanism and modernity), for example, in Levinas we find the sobering argument that:

> [H]eteronomy must come first, autonomy second. Most of counselling and psychotherapy has wrongly chosen autonomy over heteronomy.... Thus the client/patient is in danger of becoming a bit player on the therapist's stage, with the further danger that as a result of therapy, everyone else becomes a bit player on the client/patient's stage.
> (Loewenthal and Snell 2003: 153; cf. Sayre's special issue paper, 2005)

Fred Alford has referred to 'the peculiar way in which Levinas writes about human relations', and to his 'remarkably subtle and complex understanding of human relations' (2002: 3, 35). While Alford is clearly appreciative of Levinas's work, referring, for example, to 'a rare and radical teaching' (ibid.: 4), he is also quite clear in the areas where he takes issue with Levinas, not least in the latter's thorough-going subjection of the self to the other. Alford presents Levinas as a critic of humanism and humanistic thinking – but on the grounds that humanism *isn't humanistic enough* (ibid.: 6), for Levinas is arguing for a quite new humanism that invariably puts the other first, 'making our responsibility to the other an impersonal obligation and divine command' (ibid.: 8) and thus deepening the capacity to give love more purely and non-narcissistically. Moreover, Levinas is arguing strongly against what he calls universalising 'totalisation' – or the tendency to reduce the other to the same, to a version of myself, and to the elimination of difference, positing, instead, *infinity* as the answer to 'the hegemony of universals' (ibid.). Alford is clearly unconvinced by Levinas's response to the problem of totalisation, and, as a viable alternative, explores at length the works of Winnicott, Murdoch and Adorno, who all share the basic assumption that *particularity* can overcome totalisation without the need to resort to 'the infinite' favoured by Levinas. I return to this question of self and other later.

Levinas's work is notoriously difficult for anyone unschooled in continental philosophy (in part, perhaps, because it brings a welcome spiritual impulse to philosophy). Few would argue that 'postmodern' thinking such as this can make for an extremely challenging read – and even sometimes an impenetrable one for those relatively unschooled in (continental) philosophical thinking. For some (Sokal and Bricmont 1998, for example), such thinking is entirely vacuous and lacking in anything useful to say in our ongoing struggles to understand human life, and illustrates postmodernist literature's alleged tendency to lapse into an almost studied stylistic obscurity. I certainly do not take the overly simplistic view that any worthwhile idea can necessarily be expressed in easily understood, everyday language. But, equally, I am not unused to reading this kind of literature, so my own struggle with several of the European Journal's symposium papers suggests the possibility that several of the contributors might have elected for greater accessibility. It is also worth noting that, according to Gantt, 'Levinas often uses highly metaphorical and symbolically charged terminology in making his arguments', with the 'often vividly hyperbolic nature of Levinas's rhetorical style' (2000: 24).

The problem that every one of us faces is this: when we read something that we do not immediately or easily understand, just how can we tell whether what we are reading is indeed the obscurantist, mystifying ramblings of one of Sokal and Bricmont's 'intellectual impostors' or a profoundly subtle contribution that has the potential to take us beyond our 'normal' awareness and towards new, previously un-thought levels of insight and understanding? Certainly, I have had both experiences: on the one hand, for example, I clearly remember understanding very little when I first came across Marxist geographer David Harvey in the early 1970s (later to become an authoritative commentator on postmodernism – Harvey 1989) and, in the mid-1970s, the work of Althusserians Barry Hindess and Paul Hirst; yet, after no little effort, I eventually found their radical countercultural writings very enlightening. Yet I have also encountered some postmodern writings, and listened to Lacanian analysts presenting conference papers, that have left me quite baffled, and wondering just where the responsibility lies for my lack of comprehension. Certainly, there were several of the contributions to this symposium which left me with little if anything to say – particularly those of Bloechl, Warren and Faulconer – either because I did not understand them sufficiently even to offer any kind of critical commentary or because, for me, they had no particular relevance to psychotherapy and counselling.

Before offering my critical commentary on the journal symposium, I should note that there are several key themes in this symposium which are obvious targets for discussion, yet which I will reluctantly pass over as I broadly agree with the thrust of the arguments being made. First, with regard to the ethical (relation), I broadly agree with the Levinasian position that the ethical is intrinsic to, constitutive of and *prior to* relationship, and that it is a grave error of modernity to treat the ethical as some kind of 'tacked-on' rationalist after-thought – with the latter being the typical approach to ethics observable in the modernist world of professionalised, technicised psychotherapy (cf. House 1997a, 2003a: 82–90). Richard Williams (2005: 8) sums it up well: '[Psychology's] discourse about ethical matters [is] immature and naïve … [P]sychology has not been able to come to grips with the ethical as fundamental to our nature…. We lose a crucial element of the ethical when we conflate the ethical with the rational.' What we are offered in Levinasian philosophy, then, is quite new ways of engaging with the ethical. Thus, it soon becomes clear that with Levinas, we are by no means merely talking of the ethical *codes* of the therapy institutions; rather, for him, ethical codes *themselves* can be seen as being unethical (cf. Pattison 1999), 'since, however well intentioned in their systematisation, they are putting the code rather than the other first' (Loewenthal and Snell 2003: 152; cf. House 1997a). It certainly seems to be in the realm of ethics and the therapist's complex interrelation with the other(ness) of the client/patient that Levinas's thought has a profound and telling contribution to make.

The other issue which I would highlight is the way in which Levinasian thought takes us beyond conventional 'technical' therapy as we commonly know it – a theme with which I have much sympathy; and the papers by Robert D. Walsh (2005) and George Sayre (2005) are seminal in this regard. In this sense, Levinas offers us the welcome opportunity to discover quite new understandings which fundamentally problematise therapy's core conventional assumptions. For Walsh, for example:

> It is not through the application of theoretically derived interventions by a certified technician… that… healing occurs…. Genuine therapy would thus be a kind of invisible therapy…. Levinas' ethical phenomenology looks forward to an overcoming of the modernist, commercial, and institutionalized model of contemporary psychotherapy.
>
> (2005: 31)

Amen to that. And here is Sayre:

> Individual therapy… is intentionally constructed to preclude the client from being confronted with the needs of an Other. Thus, from a Levinasian perspective, the 'client-centred' ethics of individual therapy as traditionally understood are fundamentally unethical for the client…. I propose the possibility of individual therapy as a process of de-centring, for both the therapist and the client.
>
> (2005: 37)

Amen again.

It will probably be clear by now that I do not pretend to be any kind of authority on Levinas's writings or philosophy; rather, apart from the symposium papers under current consideration, I have merely read a number of scholarly articles on his relevance to psychotherapy (e.g. Dueck and Parsons 2007; Gantt 2000; Robbins 2000). In mitigation, however, it is sometimes a positive advantage to inhabit such a presupposition-less position, rather than inhabiting a 'regime of truth' of the initiated – not least because the former position sometimes enables one to see in ways which the assumption-encumbered initiate finds it very hard to do.

It follows that I cannot pretend to offer a comprehensive critique of the symposium papers. Rather, I have selectively drawn out a couple of themes from the contributors which resonate with my own particular concerns and experience of the therapeutic, as practitioner, sometime-client and cultural critic, and on which I offer below a critical commentary. I therefore ask the reader to forgive the selective partiality of my particular contribution to this special theme issue.

SOME LEVINASIAN THEMES

Contra modernity: Undermining the dogmatisms of psychology and conventional Western approaches to knowing and certainty?

> Psychotherapy as an Enlightenment project construes religion in ways it can investigate and in the end the research hardly reflects the religious language of the client's original community. Within such a framework, attempts to relate religion to therapy tend to make spirituality secular and capitalist and to represent spirituality as essentialist, individualist, and foundationalist.
>
> (Dueck and Parsons 2007: 271–2)

Clegg and Slife (2005) forcefully argue that Levinas's philosophy presents a strong challenge to what they term the 'dogmatism of psychology' (ibid.: 65) – by which they mean the empiricist, positivist psychology of the mainstream scientific thinking of 'modernity'. Thus, they write of the methods of psychology reduc[ing] knowledge to prediction and control' and the enshrining of empiricism as 'the ideal research practice' (ibid.).

For Clegg and Slife, then, Levinas's philosophy 'denies the adequacy of all rational, thematic accounts of human beings and thus undermines psychology's dogmatic adherence to the methods, institutional procedures, and economic practices of empiricistic, positivistic psychology (ibid). Yet Levinas seemingly does this using a style that is rhetorical, highly metaphorical, symbolically charged (Gantt 2000) – which is likely to alienate anyone steeped in the academic, rationalist tradition of the academy; and for this reason there seems to be a significant danger of his work being ignored, save for the very radical fringes of the conventional academic disciplines. Moreover, the fact that Levinas's writings do not lend themselves to straightforward systemisation (Clegg and Slife) merely reinforces the likelihood of their being ignored or marginalised by the conventional academy.

Clearly, what is at stake here is the very basis of modern scientific psychological knowledge, and what might count as 'valid' knowledge – not least within the conventional academic framework of the 'modernist' academy, with the latter in turn being a reflection of the prevailing Enlightenment world-view which still holds sway in modern Western culture. There does, of course, exist a substantial lineage of explicitly and self-consciously *critical* perspectives in/on psychology (for a recent example, see Fox and Prilleltensky 1997/2009), with 'critical psychology' representing a very diverse field of critique emanating from a rich plurality of left-political, feminist, epistemological, deep-ecological and spiritual perspectives. There is certainly a question here about just how Levinas's writings might be effectively introduced into the conventional psychology discipline, given the latter's crass positivism, limiting rationalism and technocratic experimental ideal – especially when his kind of 'language and rhetorical style are not often found in journal articles dealing with psychological issues' (Gantt 2000: 24).

What this suggests is that, until such time as there is a major *paradigm shift* in human consciousness (cf. my concluding section, below), Levinas's ideas will be confined to a comparatively marginal role of critique (possible exceptions being the fields of Jewish theology and continental philosophy), rather than taking a mainstream place in the academy. These ideas certainly deserve to take their place in the 'paradigm war' that is raging in modern culture (Woodhouse 1996) between a one-sidedly materialistic modernity, on the one hand, and a trans-modern, so-called 'new paradigm' world-view (e.g. Lorimer 2001) on the other.

Just what is at stake in such a paradigm shift is illustrated by James E. Faulconer (2005: 50), when he writes that 'to understand the world we must cease thinking in terms of substance (metaphysics) and knowledge of substance (epistemology) and think instead in terms of the event (phenomenology)'. For Clegg and Slife (2005: 69), it is the primacy of the ethical which leads to the inevitable consequence that we abandon any 'dangerously comfortable illusion of objectivity'. On this view, *indissolubly ethical experience*, rather than propositional knowledge and abstract theorising, should be taken as the primary datum. There are clear affinities and commonalities here with hermeneutic, existential-phenomenological thinking (e.g. Spinelli 2005a), yet it is interesting and revealing that Spinelli's seminal text fails *even to mention* Levinas. In a book that claims – rightly in my view – to offer a viable 'new paradigm' for psychology, it is rather disconcerting for Levinasians that Levinas's work fails to feature in Spinelli's text, which, I speculate, might in turn be a function of the challenging, often rhetorical nature of Levinas's writings (Gantt 2000: 24).

Clegg and Slife also emphasise the necessary *uncertainty of knowing* – but also that such uncertainty 'does not undermine the possibility of knowledge' (2005: 69), as they are at pains to make clear that Levinas's philosophy is not a nihilistic one that entails 'a purely negative deconstruction of all knowledge or system' and that 'uncertainty should not be confused either with falsehood or with a lack of knowledge' (ibid.: 71). Further, knowledge has both an ethical and an intersubjective dimension, in that '[a]ll questions of epistemology, of science, follow in the wake of the ethical dimension [and] knowledge practices are essentially ethical in character' (ibid.), and (quoting Levinas) '[t]ruth is made possible by relation with the Other… because it is only *in relation* that the occasion for knowledge arises' (ibid.: 72, emphasis added). New-paradigm physicist Chris Clarke agrees: '[R]eality is to be found within relationships, not within concepts' (1996: 41). I have great sympathy with this understanding of what knowing and knowledge actually consist in, but, again, this approach essentially dissolves the subject–object splitting of conventional empiricist psychology; and until such time as there is a major paradigm shift in psychology in particular and in late-modern culture more generally, then it is difficult to see how such a hermeneutical phenomenological approach to psychological knowledge will hold any significant purchase within the discipline.

Self and other: Fundamentally challenging taken-for-granted Western notions of autonomy, freedom and self-hood?

> Dualistic ontologies based on the opposition of self and other generate two related views of the person and of ethics: the patriarchal and that of individualism.
>
> (Whitbeck, quoted in Schaef 1992: 207)

I referred earlier to Alford's critique of Levinas's relentless subjection of the self to the other, with Levinas arguing for a 'new, radical humanism' that places the other first, 'making our responsibility to the other an impersonal obligation and divine command' (2002: 8). This is a theme that is referred to in several of the symposium contributions. Thus, for example, we find George Sayre writing about Levinas 'plac[ing] our call to respond to the needs of the Other at the centre of human existence' (2005: 37), which stands in sharp contrast to conventional psychology's 'ego-ology'.

It is certainly arguable that, far from its being an appropriate antidote to the least healthy anti-social features of modern culture, the extensive and fashionable surge in individualised therapy, and the associated privatisation of emotional distress, can be seen as just one more manifestation of an anti-social tendency that seems to be on the ascendancy in Western culture. The great danger, then, is that an individualised professionalised therapy – what Loewenthal (1998: 347) terms 'the egocentric "I Did It My Way" school of counselling and psychotherapy' – might actually be colluding with and reinforcing modernist anti-social tendencies that are at work in human culture more generally (e.g. Bellah, Madsen, Sullivan, Swidler and Tipton 1985; Cushman 1992; Hermans, Kempen and van Loon 1992; Lasch 1979; Rose 1996; Wallach and Wallach 1983). And surely even the possibility that this might be so points to the importance of therapists and therapy's professionalisers having an openness to critically locating their theoretical ideologies and clinical practices within the wider evolution of human consciousness and cultural change (House 2003a), an issue to which I return below.

I tend to agree with Jeff Warren when he writes that 'Gadamer focuses on the understanding of the self, whereas Levinas focuses on the Other.... *I argue that these approaches are strengthened and clarified by the other*' (Warren 2005: 24, emphasis added). In other words, while Levinas's emphasis on the primacy of the Other is arguably a useful, and even a *culturally necessary* counterweight to humanism's and modernity's current and unbalanced obsession with selfhood, self-sufficiency and autonomy, it is also the case that his emphasis on the Other can easily be *at the expense of* the self, and is arguably just one more instance of 'either–or' dualistic thinking. This leads in turn to questions of *intersubjectivity*. In moving beyond the discrete Aristotelian logic of 'self' and 'other', then, new-paradigm perspectives on intersubjectivity illuminate profound possibilities for the future evolution of human consciousness. In the therapy field itself, it is also arguably in the realm of intersubjectivity that new-paradigm and spiritual perspectives have greatest relevance.

It is worth noting in passing that, as with all theoretical systems and cosmologies, we need to consider the cultural embeddedness and historical specificity of Levinas's other-centred viewpoint – not, by any means, necessarily to 'pathologise' it by claiming that it was somehow *determined* by culture or personal biographical history, but rather just to be aware that there is a history to these ideas that needs to be acknowledged and, as far as possible, understood. Dueck and Parsons are clear about this:

> [Levinas] was a Jew born in Lithuania whose family was slain in the Nazi death camps. When Martin Heidegger, his philosophical model, accepted a position with German National Socialism in 1933, Levinas was demoralized. Out of his response to this crisis emerged an anthropology that is profoundly Jewish, pacifist, relational, theological, and ethical. It has ramifications not only for psychological anthropology but also for psychotherapy and personal transformation.
> (Dueck and Parsons 2007: 273)

Returning to 'intersubjectivity' (Crossley 1996), it can be defined as the view that relationship is created by two or more interpenetrating subjectivities, and is crucially indissoluble into its component parts (i.e. *your* subjectivity and *my* subjectivity; transference and countertransference and so on), because the very act of analytical decomposition destroys the Gestalt of the relational whole, and that whole simply cannot be successfully apprehended and understood by artificially decomposing it into its constituent parts. Here is Crossley himself:

> intersubjectivity is the key to understanding human life... it is irreducible and *sui generis*, a generative principle of our identities.... And it is something we cannot step out of. No amount of methodological procedure... can negate this or even bracket it out. *We are inter-subjects.*
> (1996: 173, emphasis added)

Thus, relational intersubjectivity is intrinsically un-measurable, ineffable and beyond rational understanding from within the conventional world-view of technocratic science, which typically splits subject from object, observer from observed – and self from other. This situation in turn has profound implications for therapy research, for, apart from a quite limited number of phenomenologically informed 'process' studies, the vast corpus of therapy research is squarely trapped within the naïve causal realism of technocratic science, attempting as it does to explain the therapeutic process by decomposing, analysing, atomising, manipulating, predicting and controlling what is, I believe, an indissoluble intersubjective unity quite beyond first- and third-person ways of description and explanation (cf. Chapter 11, this volume).

With the exception of, perhaps, a limited number of therapeutic approaches which privilege existential-phenomenological ontologies (Spinelli 1994, 2005), it is quite clear that the very way in which we commonsensically think about therapy and the therapeutic process is essentially trapped within the constraints of an increasingly discredited old paradigm of technocratic science (see, for example, Best 1991; Clarke 1996; DiCarlo 1996; Griffin 1988a; Pylkkanen 1989; Schaef 1992; Skolimowski 1994; Woodhouse 1996). It is certainly no coincidence that new-paradigm writers commonly place spirituality at the centre of their world-view, for an explicitly spiritual dimension is arguably essential if we are to make sense of a world which the tired modernist paradigm is increasingly failing to describe or explain with any degree of adequacy.

In his co-operative inquiry procedure (see Chapter 18, this volume), John Heron (1996) has shown how the spiritual values of new-paradigm philosophy can be operationalised through a grounded, mature and enlightened participative methodology – so it is no longer adequate for the apologists for the old-paradigm *status quo* to shrug their shoulders and proclaim 'TINA!', or that 'There is no alternative' to conventional approaches to understanding the intersubjective therapeutic process.

Fundamental paradigm shifts require, *inter alia*, a relative undefendedness and openness to the new, to uncertainty, to the 'chaotic' (I use the term technically), and, concomitantly, it is of course fear of the unknown which tends to paralyse, fix and lead to professionalised retrenchment (Robert Walsh) in the face of a world where our very ontologies of what exists are suddenly being problematised in quite fundamental ways (Clarke 1997). We can respond openly and creatively to these developments or we can 'act out' from our fear of the unknown, desperately striving to buttress the conventional world-view of technocratic positivistic science.

At the risk of accusations of essentialist developmentalism (e.g. Morss 1996), I want to argue that perhaps the most central problem with both the (humanistic) autonomy and the (Levinasian) heteronomy positions is that they commonly fail to take into account any kind of historical-*developmental* perspective – whether of a psychoanalytic or a 'spiritual-scientific' (or anthroposophical) nature. On this view, for any approach to selfhood and otherhood to ignore the ways in which developmental stage (or, for that matter, biographical history) influences both individual orientations on the 'self–other focus' spectrum and also the development of human consciousness more generally is to leave out of account that which is perhaps most decisive of all.

In other words, it simply makes no sense to advocate ahistorical, contextless moral 'ground rules' about individualism or heteronomy and their respective ethical statuses, when such advocacy can amount to little more than idealistic assertion or wish-casting. Van den Brink (2004) offers a stimulating commentary on such a developmental approach, outlining the phases through which she believes that human relationships and groups pass. Referring to the developmental phase (number 5) of 'the spiritual Self', for example, she writes, 'you are still engrossed in your own personal and spiritual development. *It could not be otherwise*. In order to be able to build up new, i.e. free, relationships, *you first have to become self-sufficient spiritually* as well' (ibid.: 89, emphasis added). Then, only in phase 6, termed 'The new community', does the individual become central as 'the other members of the group put themselves at the disposal of that individual's development' (ibid.: 93) – this sounds very like Levinas's putting the other first – and in the final phase, that of 'differentiated unity':

> The more you develop your skills individually... and the better you [work] together, concerned about the other as a person and about their contribution, the more beautiful the result will be. You become inspired, lifted above your own individual limitations.... Here a unity is formed in cooperation, which is more than the sum of the component parts.... [E]veryone contributed with their specific skills to the realization of a new entity.
>
> (Van den Brink 2004: 99–100)

In such a realised spiritual community, individual potentials are maximised, but not in *either* an 'ethical individualistic' sense *or* in a selfless, other-focused way, but in an environment in which *both* occur *together*, in an emergent indissoluble mutuality. This process is well captured in Rudolf Steiner's motto of the social ethic: 'The healthy social life is found when in the mirror of each human soul the whole community finds its reflection, and when in the community the virtue of each one is living' (quoted in Lipsker 1990: 60).

Of course there are significant dangers of a creeping determinism in such a developmental approach, for such a 'phases' approach can only ever signify broad tendencies rather than fixed unfolding life paths; but in my view the difficulties in merely *asserting* moral injunctions about selfhood and otherhood, and what constitutes a healthy moral life, carry even greater dangers.

Finally, and related to the discussion in previous paragraphs, what is also urgently needed is a widely understood, overarching cosmology that attempts to account for the phenomena of consciousness that are observable at this juncture in the evolution of consciousness. The seer Rudolf Steiner (e.g. 1966) offers one highly promising framework which is most revealing about what he terms the age of 'consciousness soul' which humankind currently inhabits, the engagement with which leads to all manner of challenges, and the rising to which, in turn, can only help to enable and fuel our evolving human path (see Crook 1980; House 2003a; Steiner 1966). To the extent that our strugglings to understand and contextualise these massive historical epochs in the evolution of consciousness are successful, this in turn then offers us the possibility of a greater reflexivity and comprehension of the predicaments in which we currently find ourselves.

CONCLUDING THOUGHTS

Elsewhere I have claimed that 'therapy must routinely and ongoingly embrace a radical deconstruction of its theories and practices, paradoxically entailing a continual undermining of its own conditions of existence' (Chapter 6: 84, this volume), if it is to avoid the kinds of abuses which are arguably intrinsic to over-professionalised therapy as currently practised and culturally legitimated. The *European Journal*'s symposium papers I have highlighted in this commentary share this common theme, and one that could hardly be of greater import to modern therapy culture: that is, that therapy as currently understood and practised is very much a creature of (late?) modernity; and that as soon as we begin seriously to problematise the (routinely taken-for-granted) assumptions that underpin and legitimise modernist therapy practice, whether through Levinasian or 'postmodern' critique more generally (House 2003a), then the possibility of a very different kind of therapy practice begins to emerge – just a few of the implications of which have been discussed in this commentary. In this sense, and at the risk of grandiosity, these are indeed momentous discussions taking place at the level of historical paradigms of thought; and, if we are 'in' or 'passing through' what Barratt evocatively terms 'the death throes of the masterdiscourse of modernity' (1993: xii), then we can scarcely exaggerate the gravity of just what is at stake in these engagements.

Such considerations lead in turn not only to the question of paradigm incommensurability and change, and to the issue of just *how* meta-paradigms do or might change in the evolution of human consciousness (Kuhn 1962; Woodhouse 1996), but also to the question of how 'the spiritual' might weave into, and even be foundational to, this process – and Levinas clearly has a significant contribution to make to these debates. But we should not underestimate the enormous fear aroused by, and the trenchant resistance to, revolutionary ideas that lie outwith the taken-for-granted 'normality' of the *status quo*: as the great psychologist William James said, 'in admitting a new body of experience, we instinctively seek to disturb as little as possible the existing stock of ideas' (quoted by Clarke 1997).

Certainly, those adaptive therapy practitioners (Kirton 1994) content to ply their trade in a Kuhnian 'normal science' way, even in the face of the old paradigm's increasing philosophical incoherence, are open to the charge of being apologists for modernity, and (unwitting?) proponents of a kind of '*status quo* theory' (Harvey 1973) that merely reproduces what exists in modern(ist) culture, rather than offering the genuine prospect of transcending it.

I have read enough about Levinas now to possess a strong sense that his thinking has a major contribution to make to the evolving body of ideas which presage the transcendence of late modernity, with the stultifying fetters that this increasingly outmoded world-view is still stubbornly placing on the healthy evolution of human consciousness. And while we should certainly not ignore or minimise the historical-cultural location of Levinas's ideas and the impact that this conjuncture has had upon them, for those of us for whom therapy should be a genuinely innovative, subversive and revolutionising force in evolving thought, the work of Emmanuel Levinas offers us one highly fertile starting-point for our questings, to which the papers in this journal symposium make a timely if, at times, unavoidably uneven contribution.

CHAPTER 10

'Psychopathology', 'Psychosis' and the Kundalini: 'Postmodern' perspectives on unusual subjective experience

We should not try to 'get rid' of a neurosis [including psychosis], but rather to experience what it means, what it has to teach us, what its purpose is. We should even learn to be thankful for it, otherwise we... miss the opportunity of getting to know ourselves as we really are.... We do not cure it – *it cures us.*

C.G. Jung (interpolation and emphasis added)

INTRODUCTORY THEMES

The threatening ambiguity of mental disorder (Who is mad? Who is sane?) leads us to take our system of perceiving mental illness for granted when it is just that system which should be the object of study, since it defines our experience of mental illness.

(J.D. Blum)

Despite the existence of major philosophical objections to the conceptual coherence of the notions of '(ab)normality' (e.g. Freides 1960; Buck 1990, 1992a; Caplan 1995; Smail 1996: Chap. 3) and 'psychopathology' (e.g. Halling and Nill 1989; Parker et al. 1995; Chapter 2, this volume), their ubiquity in both popular and academic contexts suggests that there are emotionally rooted, anxiety-driven reasons for their longevity in discourses

---

In this chapter, which first appeared in 2001 in the first edition of the pioneering edited collection *Psychosis and Spirituality* (and which is only very slightly updated here), I attempted to bring together thinking from the fields of anti-psychiatry, critical psychology, existentialism, postmodernism and new-paradigm spirituality in order to show how what I deliberately call 'unusual subjective' (or 'psychotic') experience can be accounted for without recourse to the professionalised psychiatric discourse of 'abnormality' and 'psychopathology'. As will become clear, a coherent account is at least possible to achieve which draws upon these disparate realms of post-materialist thinking.

about human behaviour and experience. Starting from a critique of the concepts of psychopathology and (ab)normality, and the assumptions that underpin diagnosticism in the mental health field, I will argue that what is commonly called 'psychotic' experience may typically constitute:

- a struggle towards meaning-making (cf. Howarth-Williams 1977: 172; Bannister 1985; Barham 1993);

- a meaningful process (Lukoff and Everest 1985; Halling and Nill 1989; Jenner et al. 1993), typically operating at many levels, rather than some kind of 'abnormal malfunction' of the (physical) brain (as asserted by materialist 'theories of mind'); and rather more speculatively and controversially

- a harbinger, albeit often a highly distressing one, of qualitative advances in human consciousness which, as yet, the 'ordinary' Cartesian ego consciousness of modernity finds it difficult if not impossible either to contain or make sense of (e.g. Laing, 1967; Harvey, 1987).

I will draw extensively on the phenomenon of the so-called 'kundalini awakening experience' to illustrate these arguments. (The following paragraphs draw heavily on the discussion in Chapter 2, this volume.)

A constructivist, postmodern perspective on the notion of '(ab)normality' views it far more as a fear-induced, socio-emotionally rooted linguistic category whose unacknowledged function is to reduce anxiety in the face of the Other's radical difference, than as an objective description of an independent reality existing separately from our own emotionally driven 'construction' of it. This in turn leads into interesting philosophical questions about perception, objectivity and subjectivity, 'the real' and theories of truth – issues which will emerge from time to time in what follows. There are a number of (interrelated) factors holding the conventional psychiatric approach to abnormality and psychopathology in place, whose common theme is what I will call 'the ideology of modernity'. Not least of these factors is the way in which the medicalisation and pathologising of what I will call 'unusual subjective experience' (hereafter USE) conveniently locates it outside of the comfort-zone of what is familiar, predictable and 'normal' – in turn distancing mental health professionals from direct engagement with the challenging, often disturbing subjective experience of their 'patients'.

In this medicalisation of USE, then, a perverse alchemy seems to occur, whereby such experience is surreptitiously transformed into what is an essentially circular and self-fulfilling diagnostic system (Parker et al. 1995; Chapter 2, this volume) – a mechanistic lexicon of allegedly scientific terminology, legitimising an ideology whose spurious scientific authority, in turn, self-fulfillingly becomes the guarantee of its own existence within a professional 'regime of truth' (cf. House 1999a; Chapter 6, this volume). (Several mischievous commentators have comically dubbed such a process 'Pervasive Labelling Disorder' [Buck 1992b] and 'Professonal Thought Disorder' [Lowson 1994].) Mary Boyle's painstaking (and brilliant) unpicking of the evolutionary history of the concept of 'schizophrenia' (1990, 1996) is highly revealing in this regard. As William James dramatically put it,

> medical materialism finishes up St Paul by calling his vision... a discharging lesion of the occipital cortex.... It snuffs out St Theresa as a hysteric; St Francis of Assisi as a hereditary degenerate; George Fox with the sham of his age.
> (quoted in Goleman et al. 1985: 188)

An increasing number of commentators are indeed highlighting the blindness of the modernist scientific worldview to the spiritual, mystical, non-material dimension (e.g. Smith 1976; Berman 1981).

It follows from these arguments that the distinctions between 'psychotic', 'unusual' and 'mystical/transpersonal' experience are not only far from clear-cut, but might well be fundamentally misguided and philosophically unsustainable. The great Indian philosopher Jiddu Krishnamurti's life-long struggle with what he called his 'Process', together with a more general examination of the phenomenon of kundalini awakenings, will be envoked in this chapter to illustrate these challenging arguments. In the course of the discussion, I will have cause to weave into the argument: social constructionism and postmodern, so-called 'deconstructionist critiques' of positivist science (House, 1999e); critical perspectives on 'madness' and 'psychosis'; and the phenomenon of 'spiritual emergence/y'). Cross-cultural and historical perspectives in psychiatry are also very relevant to the arguments in this chapter (e.g. Benedict 1934; Kleinman 1988; Lipsedge 1995; Heinze 1999; Benatar 2006).

I maintain that a radical shift in world-view, from naïve technocratic scientism and towards a postmodern, more spiritually informed 'new paradigm' perspective opens up creative, liberating and potentially healing avenues for thinking about and understanding the widest spectrum of human subjective experience. And rather more speculatively, I will suggest that perhaps USEs' most important evolutionary feature may be their constituting an early, falteringing uncertain manifestation – albeit often a highly distressing and scarcely containable one, both individually and culturally – of qualitative advances in human consciousness which, as yet, the Cartesian consciousness of modernity either pathologises as 'irrational', or else finds it difficult if not impossible to contain and 'hold'.

Thus, subjective experiences like fear of difference, and the felt emotional need for security and predictability, can be seen as historically specific features of the human psyche at this point in the development of human consciousness; and perhaps those people who somehow allow themselves (or are in part a vehicle for some greater spiritual-evolutionary process?) to challenge and transcend our 'normal' consensual perceptual and experiential constraints (be they mystics, Krishnamurtis, or so-called 'schizophrenics' or 'psychotics'), far from being psychologically 'deficient', can plausibly be seen as the harbingers of qualitatively new paradigm-advances in the development of human consciousness. This is not to deny, of course, the suffering and traumatic biographical factors involved in (notice I am not saying 'caused by') at least some USEs (e.g. see Glass [1993] on so-called 'multiple personality disorder' and 'schizophrenia'), but to suggest that such suffering also has a wider, evolutionary or transpersonal function, which should not be ignored in our decisions about how to respond individually, professionally and culturally to such experiences.

It is argued, then, that the real practices of conventional mental health treatment are uncritically rooted in the ideological world-view of modernity with its attendant metaphysical assumptions. And if Rom Harré is right in arguing that personal identity 'amounts to the assimilation of socially available theories and templates' (quoted in Parker et al. 1995: 89), and if 'How we reflect upon and define ourselves is determined and constrained by the structures of knowing available to us' (ibid.: 88), then 'psychiatric patients, through the course of repeated assessments, come increasingly to define their experiences in accordance with a professional definition of "psychiatric illness"' (ibid.: 89). In short, 'clinical discourses impact upon individual autobiography, thereby influencing both the types of subjectivity and identity that are brought into being' (ibid.: 73). Professional elites and their 'regimes of (professional) truth' are seen as constructing people's realites through language, and 'the ubiquity of particular types of discourse makes it impossible for their subjects to "think" or even imagine an "elsewhere"' (ibid.: 75).

Finally, the 'treatment' implication of these arguments is that rather than USEs being routinely (psycho)pathologised, with brain-altering, psychotropic medication often being prescribed for those undergoing such experiences, it is far more fitting that attempts be made to understand with the person, in appropriately and sensitively containing environments if necessary, what their experience might be indicating, presaging or portending – in cultural-evolutionary perspective as well as in purely individual biographical terms. Such assistance bears some resemblance to the Grofs' important work on 'spiritual emergence' (1987, 1990), and will likely require qualities far more akin to the shaman or the 'spiritually realised person' than to the skills of the mental-health diagnostician.

For Levin (1987a), the 'cultural-evolutionary perspective' is crucial: for 'the diagnoses of clinical medicine are not scientific statements of fact referring to "real" disease entities; rather, they are theory-laden representations... products of culture; symbols of our time, constructs of the "rational" discourse we call "medicine"' (74–5). On this view, which unambiguously eschews a one-sidedly materialist world-view, all human maladies are reflections of, and commentaries on, our culture and the 'ego-logical' Self (Levin's term) which has produced it.

SOCIAL CONSTRUCTIONISM AND KRISHNAMURTI'S 'PROCESS'

> ...it is hard for us in the West to recognise that much of what we see 'out there' is our own work... – mental additions to what the senses actually record.
>
> (Mary Scott)

In making a bridge from the foregoing discussion to considering the kundalini awakening experience, (social) constructionist viewpoints on human experience become relevant. If we accept that in some sense, attitudes to unusual subjective experience – both our own and that of 'expert' professionals – can at the very least contribute to creating these experiential realities and the way they subsequently play out, then it is clear that the psychopathologising mentality of professionals within conventional psychiatry will very likely have a profound effect on those who are undergoing USEs. Thus, in the case of kundalini experiences, Sannella (1992: 111) writes that 'Disturbances must... not be viewed as pathological. They are, rather, therapeutic inasmuch as they lead to a removal of potentially pathological elements.' Sannella also reports the case of a writer whose spontaneous trances greatly disturbed him. He recounts how 'I had communicated to him the attitude that his trances were valid and meaningful. Because of my acceptance of his experience, he was able to accept it' (ibid.). And most importantly, 'The trances ceased to control him as soon as he gave up his resistance to them and their underlying forces' (ibid.) – not least, I would surmise, because in the very giving up of his resistance, there was less ego-presence left to experience being controlled by the trances, and concomitantly, more free space for whatever process needed to happen to unfold, unencumbered by fear-driven, ego-rooted resistance. In general, therefore, pain, tension and imbalance

> result not from the process itself but from conscious and subconscious interference with it. Helping a person to understand and accept what is happening to him or her may be the best we can do. Usually the process, when left alone, will find its own natural pace and balance.
> (ibid.)

I will return to the issue of ego-control below. It is worth noting in passing that, in embracing such a constructionist approach, we are concomitantly moving away from the materialist objectivist world-view, in which matter and mechanistic malfunction, rather than consciousness, are assumed to have causal primacy in creating our realities.

It can be argued, then, that people's experienced incapacity to contain or 'stay with' their own exceptional subjective experiences might itself be a significant function of our culture's socially constructed notion of 'normality', rather than being due to their own intrasubjectively authentic and appropriate response to their own experience. In my own work as a counsellor and psychotherapist I have been repeatedly struck over the years about the extent to which much of clients' anxiety seems to be rooted in their fear of 'not being normal'. The experience of Jiddu Krishnamurti (or K) is seminal in this regard. His life-long 'Process' (as he called it – Holroyd 1991), which at least one biographer (Michel 1995) has compared to a Kundalini experience, offers us a fascinating way into some of these issues.

The crucial point is that this experience was clearly extremely challenging and distressing for K: he was routinely, and for many decades of his life, in very considerable, scarcely bearable pain, had regular out-of-body experiences, and found it impossible (or, more precisely, inappropriate) to cast his experience into 'objective' analytical language. And had he not himself known that he must allow his 'Process' to take its natural course, and had he taken his 'symptoms' into the psychiatric system for treatment, then he would no doubt have been treated with a range of psychotropic medication, which may well in turn have done a great violence to K's experience, and its central importance for his own particular journey. It may also be that the individual's attitude towards their USE may itself significantly influence whether it manifests as a mystical-transformative or 'psychotic' experience: as Grof (1987: 476) writes,

While a 'mystic' keeps the process internalized and does not relate to the external world until the experiences are completed and well integrated, a psychotic resists the process, projects its elements on the external world, and confuses the inner and outer reality.

K lived into his 90s – so clearly his refusal to countenance any formal medical-psychiatric treatment for his 'condition' didn't seem unduly to foreshorten his earthly life. (Indeed, I would argue, his undefended facilitation of 'The Process' almost certainly greatly enhanced it.)

THE KUNDALINI AWAKENING EXPERIENCE (HEREAFTER, KAE)

[T]he dominant scientific paradigm is still intolerant of the realities encountered in the kundalini process and spirituality in general.... We must begin to look again... at much of what scientism has tried to debunk as meaningless and worthless fantasy. ...[W]e must embark on... the demythologizing of the myths of scientific materialism.   (Lee Sannella)

Psychiatrist and ophthalmologist Lee Sannella, M.D. (1992) has explored at some length the existing literature and evidence on the KAE, particularly with regard to its association with so-called 'psychosis' (a term the scientific validity of which, incidentally, Sannella seems to accept quite uncritically). He points out that KAEs, with all their 'psychotic'-like symptoms, 'seem pathological only because the symptoms are not understood in relation to outcome: a psychically transformed human being' (1992: 7). There are echoes here of Rosenberg's important argument (1984) that we only call behaviours 'psychotic' when we are unable to understand their logic or point of view – in which case we tend to jump to the conclusion that the limitation lies with the sanity of the other, rather than with our own limited framework of understanding.

Gopi Krishna's account of his own KAE (1971) provides copious evidence about the subjective aspects of a KAE. Krishna himself refers to how his 'thoughts were in a daze' (p. 14); to his disturbance, depression, fear and uncertainty (p. 15); and to how 'a condition of horror, on account of the inexplicable change, began to settle on me, from which... I could not make myself free by any effort of my will.... [T]henceforth for a long time I had to live suspended by a thread between... sanity and insanity' (pp. 16, 17). Much later, we read that 'a life and death struggle was going on inside me in which I, the owner of the body, was entirely powerless to take part' (p. 152).

Sannella refers to the effects of a KAE upon thinking:

> Thinking may be speeded up, slowed down, or altogether inhibited. Thoughts may seem off balance, strange, irrational. The person may feel on the brink of insanity... and generally confused.... The individual may feel that he or she is observing, from a distance, his or her own thoughts, feelings, and sensations.
>
> (1992: 98, 99)

Out-of-body experiences (OBEs) are also typical in a KAE; and in this case we can see all too clearly how the seemingly incompatible worldviews of modernist materialism and so-called 'new paradigm' thinking clash head on. Conventional psychiatry typically interprets OBEs as delusional and therefore fictional – for to accept them as in some sense ontologically 'real' would undermine the very foundations of our Western materialist understanding of the relationship between the brain and consciousness (ibid.: 102; cf. Fenwick 1999). In his appendix to MacIver's book (1983), in which she graphically describes her OBEs, Sannella wrote that 'her journeys into the hidden levels of reality had a positive, healing and revelatory effect on her life' (quoted in Sannella 1992: 102). Finally, psychic capacities are commonly reported by those undergoing KAEs, which, if authentic, would again require an explanation going far beyond our currently prevailing materialist neurophysiological framework.

Sannella comes close to endorsing the kind of critique of the modernist paradigm supported in this chapter, when he cites Jacques Lacan and Berman (1981) in emphasising the historical and evolutionary specificity of our notions of ego, self and rationality. For Sannella,

> The ego-bound rational consciousness is ultimately unfit for life.... [W]here [ego and reason] are made the principles by which life is lived, they become destructive.... [B]oth ego and reason are recent appearances in the history of consciousness. And both are destined to be surpassed by superior forms of existence.
>
> (pp. 19–20)

The issue of control is closely related to that of ego, and the approach to control in KAEs may have profound lessons for our response to USE more generally. In the era of modernity, the metaphor embraced by conventional medical-model psychiatry is that of cure, or 'fixing the malfunctioning machine', rather than trusting and facilitating the inherent wisdom of the person's healing or transformative process (cf. the work of legendary healer-cum-analyst Georg Groddeck – see Chapter 21, this volume). In making this claim I am of course assuming a qualitative continuity and commonality between KAEs and what are labelled 'psychotic' or 'schizophrenic' experiences more generally. Certainly, in the case of KAEs, it seems unarguable that attempts to control the process lead to more pain and distress rather than less (it was Krishnamurti who said that ego-driven attempts to control reality typically bring about the very opposite of their original intention). Thus, the female psychologist quoted by Sannella did try to control her KAE, and found that 'pain during the physio-kundalini cycle might be caused by conscious or subconscious resistance to the process' (1992: 97). And Sannella himself goes on to argue that resistance to the KAE can 'result in hysteria or a state akin to schizophrenia' (99; see also p. 109). This observation in turn suggests that it is perhaps not the symptoms that accompany USEs per se which are the problem, but rather, our ego-fixated attempt to resist and avoid pain, discomfort or suffering, which in turn disrupt and complicate what would otherwise be a transformative or healing process. And on this view, conventional psychiatric 'treatment' will tend to be routinely iatrogenic rather than healing and healthily restorative (cf. Breggin 1993). I return to this issue below in my discussion of what I call a 'spiritualised cognitive therapy'.

Thus, the state of dissociated detachment typically accompanying a KAE can become severely unbalanced 'when deep psychological resistances, fear, confusion, or social and other environmental pressures are present' (Sanella 1992: 99). Moreover, Sannella implies that the stirring up of 'the sediments of the unconscious' is an intrinsic aspect of the KAE, confronting a person with 'just those psychic materials he or she wishes to inspect least of all' (ibid.: 98–9). Thus, in depth-psychological terms, repressed or unresolved traumata seem very likely to erupt in the course of a KAE – which suggests that the KAE may be a multifaceted process that includes both the deeply personal and the transpersonal. Again, then, it is clear from this how the symptoms of a KAE could easily be (mis)diagnosed as 'psychopathology' with the underlying generative psychospiritual process being completely missed within a medical-model framework.

For Sannella, then, the KAE constitutes 'an aspect of psychospiritual unfolding' – 'part of an evolutionary mechanism, and... as such it must not be viewed as a pathological development' (ibid.: 9). And Gopi Krishna viewed the KAE as that which 'enable[s] human consciousness to transcend the normal limits..., to transcend the limits of the highest intellect... – the final phase of the present evolutionary impulse in man' (quoted in ibid.: 12; cf. Krishna 1974). For example, there is 'the ecstatic unification of subject and object' (p. 31), which transcends the dualistic split consciousness of the Cartesian ego, and which the epistemologies of the 'new science' are increasingly beginning to embrace (e.g. see Bortoft 1996; House 1999e). According to Sannella, once Gopi Krishna's active kundalini was stabilised, 'it formed the basis for the gradual development of extraordinary mental gifts, creativity and tranquillity – [and] to all kinds of mystical experiences' (1972: 51). Gopi Krishna himself goes as far as arguing that the KAE is, *inter alia*, 'the real cause of all so-called spiritual and psychic phenomena [and] the master key to the unsolved mystery of creation' (quoted on p. 20; Krishna 1974).

It is clear that in the course of a KAE, the sometimes profound emotional changes that occur are often mistaken for 'mental illness'. Thus, Sannella gives us the following female psychologist's description of her KAE:

> she felt, during meditation, as if she were two feet taller than her normal self and as if her eyes were looking out from above her head... [S]he was sure she knew what people were thinking.... At times she questioned the reality of her experiences, wondering if they were just a crazy episode.
>
> (p. 72)

We are further told that she was determined to avoid psychiatric help, being afraid she would be labelled and treated as insane (ibid.). Certainly, Sannella quotes many cases where those undergoing a KAE heard voices (pp. 79, 83, 85, 143) or had profound fears about their own sanity (pp. 60, 64, 72, 87, 88, 113, 115).

The fact that what Sannella refers to as 'the intellectual-emotional component of the transmutative experience' (p. 24) is very variable suggests that each person's unique personal history and way-of-being in the world puts a correspondingly unique 'spin' on the way the KAE manifests for every individual who undergoes the experience. Where there are 'inherent weaknesses' and 'negative environmental factors' present (ibid.: 153), it is in these cases where a KAE can so easily become conflated with 'psychosis'. Here is Sannella again: 'our Western culture cuts off the tender shoots of the delicate plant of feeling with the cold sharpness of mechanical insensitivity..., [and] in this way, the entire system is thrown out of balance, and harmonious development becomes impossible' (ibid.). There are echoes here of the many devastating critiques of biological psychiatric treatments of 'psychosis' – e.g. Johnstone 1989; Breggin 1993; Newnes et al. 1999. Certainly, regarding Swami Muktananda's KAE, 'it is easy to imagine the diagnosis if he had approached a psychiatrist instead of a guru for his help' (p. 50). Scott expresses a similar view when she states that 'evolutionary disorders' (her term) are best not treated medically: rather, the aim should be to 'discover what transfers of control are taking place within the personality..., with a view to assisting inner growth rather than removing symptoms by medical means' (1989: 180–1). She goes on to urge that science 'admit mind into physics, [and] psychics, sensitives and intuitives onto its advisory panels and into its laboratories' (ibid.: 181). For 'So thoroughly are we now embedded in matter that there can be no further development unless [man] can free himself from some of its dead weight' (p. 240).

It seems, then, that those undergoing a KAE who possess no previous theoretical framework for understanding it are very likely to fear for their own sanity (p. 34) – and certainly more so than those who do have the anchor of such a psychospiritual framework. Both Sannella (ibid.: 31) and Jung (quoted on p. 18) refer to the autonomous, self-directing nature of the KAE; and no wonder this can so easily lead to a self-experience of 'madness' in a (Western) evolutionary conjuncture which tends to fetishise ego-control, and creates an 'abnormalising', pathologising discourse around any experience which either lies outwith conscious ego-control (Gopi described being 'completely at its mercy' – p. 51), or contradicts the rationalist logic of the dominant materialist world-view.

GOPI KRISHNA'S KAE

> ...if an adept seems to 'act mad' it is just because people around him do not see what it is all about, as they are lacking the adept's frame of reference.
>
> A. Bharati (quoted by James Hillman)

Perhaps the most detailed personal report of a KAE at the time of writing (2000) was that laid out in Gopi Krishna's *Kundalini: The Evolutionary Energy in Man* (1971), referred to above. For current purposes this book is particularly useful because it contains an illuminating running commentary by maverick Jungian analyst James Hillman, which, not least, attempts to build a bridge between what often seem to be the incompatible world-views of Eastern mystical/transpersonal experience and Western (depth) psychology. Thus, Hillman refers to how

> we call those psychic events for which our theory is inadequate, 'alien', placing them in patho- or para-psychology, [while] we call radical theories (like those of Kundalini yoga) 'mystical speculation' when the poverty of our psychic life fails to produce the empirical data on which the psychological theories have been erected. (pp. 42–3)

In his introduction, Frederic Spiegelberg refers to how Krishna's account illustrates the 'acceptance of everything that happens inwardly' – including despair and 'depressions and dangers almost to the point of ruination' (1971: 7). Certainly, many of Krishna's experiences seemed to be phenomenologically indistinguishable from what are in Western psychiatry diagnosed as 'psychotic' symptoms. Thus, for example, Krishna's experience of 'immersion of the ego in [a] stream of light is a common theme of religious mysticism, and also of psychopathological derangement' (Hillman: 69); Hillman compares Krishna's reported experiences with 'states of psychological dissociation, in which consciousness appears to break up into multiples of itself' (p. 70); and other events occurred 'which we call in the language of psychopathology, "depersonalization", "disorientation", "alienation"' – and which are common to so-called 'paranoid', 'schizophrenic' and 'epileptoid' states (ibid.). Indeed, Hillman is convinced that had Krishna presented at a Western psychiatric clinic, he would have undoubtedly been diagnosed as having a 'psychotic' episode (and no doubt been 'treated' accordingly).

In an absolutely key passage of his commentary (pp. 70–2), Hillman points out that the world-view of Western psychiatric medicine has nothing other than its diagnostic categories for understanding these experiences, and that Krishna was fortunate to possess a non-pathological framework of understanding with which to make sense of what was happening to him. He makes a similar point later, when he states that it was 'the ideational context', 'the supporting frame which kept his experience from going wrong', and which enabled him to integrate what was happening to him (p. 94). Indeed, for Hillman 'it is conceivable that some of the experiences described in Western psychiatric interviews could also be viewed as the beginnings of enlightenment rather than as the beginnings of insanity (p. 71) (note that even Hillman seems to be assuming a valid qualitative distinction between 'mystical enlightenment' and 'insanity', to which I do not necessarily subscribe – though a bit later he does acknowledge 'How close the borderlines are!' – ibid.). But 'in the West, we are so lacking in an adequate context [for these experiences] that we do indeed go to pieces at the eruption of the unconscious, thereby justifying the psychiatric view' (p. 95). Though Hillman, being a Jungian depth psychologist, envokes the metaphor of 'the unconscious' as an explanatory principle at this point, other, more transpersonal explanatory factors could of course also be envoked. Certainly, it was clearly valuable for Krishna 'to feel that what he was going through... had... a universal meaning' – a 'transcendent purposefulness' (pp. 95, 96).

Echoing a view I strongly advocate in this chapter, Hillman states that, in Western diagnostic psychiatry, 'what a person *has*, his diagnosis, has become more important than who a person *is*' (p. 71, my emphasis); and for Krishna,

> He did not want to be treated; [and] to be 'cured' of what he had would have meant loss of both who he was and why he was.... [B]y avoiding professional help, and by staying within the guidelines of tradition he guaranteed his own sanity.
>   (ibid.)

For 'If [his experience] were... argued away, diagnosed as sick, a whole world would collapse' (p. 131). Moreover, Hillman points to the disempowering, infantilising dynamic intrinsic to the professional medical-model relationship, where 'All health is on one side, sickness on the other.... Gopi Krishna did not split the archetype of the healed one and the wounded one' (pp. 71–2).

In a passage which has strong commonalities with Krishnamurti's teachings, we are also told how Krishna managed to stay with his own ambivalences – 'believing and doubting, feeling himself lost and found at the same time. This ambivalence was his balance' (p. 72). And relatedly, in a later passage Hillman touches on a similar theme which leads into fundamental questions about modernity and human consciousness: 'The balance is delicate indeed: too little ego and there is no observer, no central point; too little consciousness apart from ego and there is too little objective field of awareness apart from subjectivity, too little impersonal sensitivity and compassion' (p. 156). Krishna clearly responded to his KAE in a way very similar to the way K embraced his 'process' (referred to earlier):

> He let the ego sleep in its world of dreams; he observed merely what was going on, trusting... and letting the process transform him. Rather than let his ego integrate the luminous other world, he let the luminous other world integrate him. *His approach... was just the reverse of what we assume in the West.*
>   (Hillman, pp. 176–7, my emphasis)

In considering the Jungian approach to the evolution of consciousness (e.g. Neumann, 1954), for current purposes the crucial point is that 'the ego only plays one of the roles, since the consciousness of other archetypal components... is also an aim of the work' (ibid.). In the current era of modernity, typified as it is by scientism, materialism, and a ego-control fixated narcissism (e.g. Lasch 1979; Levin, 1987c), it is arguable that human consciousness has become grossly unbalanced in the direction of ego (over)development. Such an insight not only accounts for why, at both individual-experiential and cultural levels, we find it scarcely possible to contain so-called 'psychosis' and its accompanying loss of ego (in the process pathologising and 'treating' it as an 'illness' to eradicate), but more generally, perhaps those who do experience such (often deeply distressing) ego-loss – for whatever reason and in whatever circumstances – are expressing a crucial species-wide evolutionary imperative from which we must be open to learning.

Perhaps until 'ego', along with all its accompanying ideological assumptions and practices, is prepared to reflect critically on its grandiose pre-eminence and hegemony in the human psyche (as is thankfully beginning to happen in much 'new-scientific', postmodern epistemology and transpersonal thinking), then 'unusual human experience' will continue to be pathologised, scientifically medicalised and subjected to the fear-driven bludgeon of normalisation of orthodox Western psychiatry. Perhaps this is the key insight towards which those who have been so critical of medical-model psychiatric practices – Foucault and other postmodern critics, Laing and Cooper and the anti-psychiatrists, Szasz, the *Asylum* magazine collective, Lucy Johnstone, the Grofs, the Breggins, Mary Boyle, Parker et al. (1995) and Newnes et al. (1999) (to name but a few) – have been struggling in recent decades. It is extremely difficult for those steeped in the ideology of modernity and scientism to accept that the KAE, or USEs more generally, might be in principle impossible to describe in language (Krishna, p. 13), or that 'the ego cannot grasp the totality of the event' (Hillman, p. 155) – or indeed that 'the ultimate development of the ego is its submission to, even immersion in, a field of wider psychic consciousness' (ibid.).

Certainly, I agree wholeheartedly with Hillman when he writes that for Western therapists/analysts/healers, 'the distinction between ego and consciousness means a re-thinking of our therapeutic aims' (ibid.) – which the deconstructive and transpersonal 'turns' within the psychology and psychotherapy worlds (if not yet psychiatry) are thankfully beginning to address, as the legitimacy of the old modernist paradigm is increasingly called into question (see, for example, Grof and Grof 1990; Kvale 1992; Schaef 1992; Nelson 1994; Anderson 1997; Parker 1999a, b; House 2003a, Chapters 6 and 7, this volume, and the global Scientific and Medical Network). For Levin (1987b: 13, following Kovel), 'our institutional channels for responding to schizophrenic suffering only render the mad doubly mad'. The approach to KAEs described in this chapter certainly suggests alternative possibilities for responding to USE which Western psychiatry could meaningfully pursue – approaches which have already been successfully tried and tested (e.g. Perry 1974; Lamb 1979; Soreff 1985; Grof and Grof 1990; Mosher 1996).

Concluding this discussion of the kundalini, it seems that the KAE is probably multiply determined or has multiple levels of meaning, being simultaneously a 'purificatory process' (Sannella 1992: 107), a process of healing deep unconscious psychic material, and a transmutative process into a higher, qualitatively new level of consciousness. On this view, all those USEs that are typically labelled 'psychotic' and treated biologically with psycho-active medication may well have a crucial transpersonal evolutionary aspect that conventional 'treatments', rooted in the old Cartesian paradigm, not only completely miss, but actually do a profound violence towards. However, the chances of alternative, supportive-facilitative modalities gaining ground are at present small, given the massively entrenched vested material and commercial interests in the modernist status quo, manifested by the burgeoning global pharmaceutical industry and its close relationship with the professional institution of Psychiatry (e.g. Breggin 1993; Jenner et al. 1993; Newnes et al. 1999). As Newnes and Holmes (1999: 274) bluntly assert, 'capitalism [as an instance of modernity? – RH] rather than altruism seems to be the dominant force in the shaping of modern psychiatry'.

Krishna himself was only too aware of 'the low, insistent voices of innumerable doubts that have to be satisfied... in the light of modern knowledge before... the possibility of development of a higher state of consciousness in a normal man can become acceptable to a strictly rational mind' (p. 240) – or that an evolutionary mechanism exists, 'ceaselessly active in developing the brain towards a pre-determined state of higher consciousness' (p. 245). Certainly, 'So many questions flood in – metaphysical, historical, religious' that it is little wonder that Western psychologists and psychiatrists are 'unable to cope' (Hillman, p. 251) from within their modernist world-view.

TOWARDS A 'SPIRITUALISED COGNITIVE THERAPY'?

[Spiritual change] involves a continuous process of seeing in new ways. In particular seeing suffering in new ways. The suffering that comes to us from outside is only suffering if we see it as such and fight it as something forced upon us against our will.... The conflict is... between our essential nature and the ego.... It is at mental levels that the disruptive influence comes in. The fault... is in... that part of [the mind] which gets caught up in ego-distortions, errors of judgment made by the conscious self about the nature of things.
(Mary Scott)

At this juncture an interesting link with cognitive therapy (CT) suggests itself. I have written at some length in the therapy literature about the often mechanistic and un-holistic nature of much technique-orientated cognitive therapy (e.g. House, 1996b; see also the papers/chapters in House and Loewenthal 2008a, b), with its tendency to privilege the 'cognitive' over the 'emotional' and the spiritual. While I still hold to the main substance of those criticisms, I also believe that there could be an important role for a type of 'spiritualised' cognitive therapy, which: (1) transcends CT's narrowly cast empirical-scientific world-view; (2) which is strongly informed by constructionist theory and postmodern deconstruction; and (3) which embraces some limited aspects of Albert Ellis's rational-emotive therapy (RET) approach. On this latter view, a central source of people's distress is their (culturally sanctioned) assumptions, attitudes and beliefs about what is '(ab)normal' – which they apply like a template to themselves, discover a mismatch between their belief(s) about 'normality' and their own self-experience, and then distress themselves further about the mismatch. On this view, such 'secondary' distress is, then, at the very least an active contributor towards their experienced symptoms of distress – and, at least sometimes, even the central factor. (There are clearly some important parallels in all this with K's teachings, Zen philosophy and spiritual-contemplative practices more generally.) On this view, then, it is people's anxiety-driven, normality-fixated, ego-bound response to their experience of themselves which becomes the problem (part of which may be related to death/annihilation anxiety), and not the experience *per se*. Grof (1987: 476) is saying something similar in suggesting that 'the difference [between psychosis and healthy mysticism] seems to be less in the nature and content of the experiences than in the attitude, experiential style, and ability to integrate these experiences'.

I am also tempted to argue that there may *always* be some kind of spiritual, transbiographical (but by no means random) dimension to any and every unusual/exceptional subjective experience, and that to ignore this (which medical-model diagnostic psychiatry routinely does) is to miss what is sometimes, perhaps, the most important aspect of those experiences, and – far worse – to do an untold violence to those people whose experiences are subjected to the blunt 'chemical cosh' of materialistic psycho-chemical treatment and objectifying regimes of professional 'truth'. This in turn suggests that a facilitator-therapist 'must be prepared to acknowledge and confront successively material from all these levels. This requires great flexibility and *freedom from conceptual orthodoxy*' (ibid.: 463, emphasis added).

CONCLUDING REFLECTIONS

We fall ill for our own development.
        (Rudolf Steiner)

It should be clear from the foregoing that there is a profound methodological danger in deducing causal, generative 'mechanisms' from observed symptomatologies – and particularly when one is unaware of the 'truth constructing' effects of one's tacitly held metaphysical world-view. In the specific case of the kundalini phenomenon, for example, if it were not for the existence of a well-testified transpersonal context of meaning for it, then in response to this 'condition' (as we have seen), Western materialist psychiatry would diagnose 'abnormality' and '(psycho)pathology', rooted in the 'malfunctioning machine' metaphor of conventional Western medicine, even more routinely than it does already. More generally, we should continually remind ourselves that the forms of explanations we embrace to account for unusual human experience will be, at the very least, significantly subject to the prevailing (modernist) *Zeitgeist* – which, in the case of modern Western science, is essentially positivistic, mechanistic and materialistic. Moreover, and contrary to the incoherent assertions of some apologists for mechanistic science, the latter inevitably entail foundational and irreducible metaphysical assumptions just as assuredly as do the most spiritual or transpersonal of worldviews (e.g. House 1997e; Chapter 21, this volume).

It should be noted that, contrary to popular anecdote, I am certainly not claiming that kundalini phenomena are a typical, ever-present aspect of what is commonly termed 'mental illness': for as Greyson (1993: 54) has shown, 'an unselected sample of psychiatric inpatients reported an incidence of physio-kundalini symptoms no different than a normal control sample'. However, just because the speculative assertions of some commentators, that large numbers of psychiatric in-patients suffer from misdiagnosed kundalini awakenings, may be unwarranted (ibid.), it by no means follows from this that 'psychiatric' suffering in general is not at some important level a kind of spiritual/transpersonal experience, that a narrow positivistic worldview inevitably misses. On this view, the psychiatric category of 'mental illness' may be highly questionable as a legitimate scientific concept (cf. Parker et al. 1995; Chapter 2, this volume) – a viewpoint which even writers sympathetic to a transpersonal worldview can so easily fall into. Thus, for example, Greyson writes of 'differentiating kundalini awakening from mental illness' – 1993: 56; and Lukoff writes that 'differentiating psychotic from spiritual experience is not easy' – 1985, cited in Krippner and Welch 1992: 213 – with both views clearly assuming a valid ontological distinction between 'psychosis' and 'kundalini/spiritual awakening'. It is all too easy for aspiring new-paradigm thinkers to delude themselves that they have transcended the modernist paradigm (e.g. House 1996d); and perhaps the visionary healer, Georg Groddeck (see Chapter 21, this volume), was pointing to something similar when he wrote that 'it is impossible to get human thought habits away from their beaten tracks' (1930, quoted in Schacht 1977: 11).

Some encouraging progress is being made towards the depathologisation of USE. First, the important work of the International Association of Spiritual Psychiatry (IASP) is of significant note, founded as it was in 1994 to promote the integration of the spiritual dimension into modern medicine, psychiatry and psychology (see, for example, O'Callaghan 1996; Smith 1996–7). Psychologist David Lukoff has also done some important work in proposing, and having accepted, a new diagnostic category for the DSM-IV (APA 1994: 685), 'psychoreligious or psychospiritual problem' (Lukoff et al. 1992; see also Lukoff 1985: 160–2). Yet of course, such a development courts the danger of colluding with, and thereby tacitly legitimising, the diagnostic ideology of conventional Western psychiatry, Thus, Harvey (1987) has convincingly demonstrated that, far from the DSM offering a 'standardized symptomalology and diagnostic system... based on "neutral" clinical observations and mere "descriptions", [the DSM] relies on an implicit but powerful prescriptive, normative, metaphysical foundation that is never examined' (pp. 324, 325; cf. Johnstone 1989; Farber 1993; Caplan 1995). And Harvey concludes that 'to embrace Western metaphysics and impose its standards of normality without awareness and without questioning is surely a form of blindess within a profession that takes pride in the emancipatory power of its insight' (p. 326). Finally, following the relatively fallow 'latency' period since Laing, there is again a steadily mounting and formidable literature quite fundamentally challenging to the foundational metaphysical assumptions of psychiatric diagnosis (e.g. Harvey 1987; Boyle 1990, 1996; Parker et al. 1995; see also Duncan Double's website at http://www.mentalhealth.freeuk.com/article.htm), and also a welcome renewed interest in Laing's path-breaking work (e.g. Burston 1996, 2000; Kotowicz 1997; Mullan 1999; Raschid 2005).

Within a truly postmodern approach to healing and transformation, it is paradoxically only when we really face up to the reality that, as the great precursor of postmodernity Georg Groddeck put it earlier this century, 'everything important happens outside our knowledge and control.... It is absurd to suppose that one can ever understand life' (Groddeck 1951: 84; see Chapter 21, this volume), that we will be in the position of humility, from which way-of-being true, grounded, embodied 'knowing' will quite naturally become available to us. Following the psychoanalyst and mystic

Wilfred Bion, it might well be that the most effective healers are precisely those who do not (need to) take preconceived beliefs and defensive 'clinical gazes' into their work with clients or 'patients', but rather, are able to enter into their professional healing relationships in a relatively undefended way, without memory or desire, that privileges the healing power of intimacy (House 1996b) and the immediacy of the I–Thou encounter, as opposed to the objectifying practices that the diagnostic procedures of conventional psychiatry typically entail.

In Trickster-esque spirit, Parker et al. mischievously write that the rigid discourses of psychiatry could themselves be termed 'psychotic' (1995: 126), with its proponents perhaps suffering from the condition of 'Professional Thought Disorder' (Lowson 1994). Certainly, in an increasingly post- or trans-modern age, our very taken-for-granted notions of what a healthy 'self' consists in are coming under formidable challenge (e.g. Gendlin 1987; Cushman 1995; Heinze 1999), and any progressive and enlightened approach to USE simply cannot afford to ignore these profound changes in our evolving subjectivities. As Levin (1987b: 12) has it, 'we continue to think of "the self" in ways that impose conformity and do not promote new forms of subjectivity'.

In this chapter, I have challenged what Walsh and Vaughan have called 'our arbitrary, culture-bound definitions of normality' (1993: 1), in a wide-ranging critique of our ideological constructions of 'ab/normality' which routinely masquerade as objective scientific fact under the prevailing *Zeitgeist* of modernity (Woodhouse 1996). I agree with the psychologist William James that 'most people live... in a very restricted circle of their potential being' (quoted in Walsh and Vaughan 1993) – and to such an extent that rather than what I have termed unusual subjective experience being embraced in our culture as an opportunity and an invitation to enlarge that circle of being, it is routinely psychopathologised, chemically suppressed and brutally categorised as 'abnormal', and in need of remedial 'treatment' by a mental health industry whose procedures and assumptive base express the anxiety-driven, security-fixated ideology of modernity which still holds sway at this juncture in the development of human consciousness.

Levin succinctly sums up the position taken in this chapter:

> [S]eemingly psychotic experiences are better understood as crises related to the person's efforts to break out of the standard ego-bounded identity: trials of the soul on its spiritual journey. The modern self is nearing the frontier of a historically new spiritual existence.... It is time for a real paradigm shift.
> (Levin 1987b; 16)

We could do far worse, finally, than to follow the wise words of Plotinus, who, in many ways presaging the recent upsurge in Goethean science (Bortoft, 1996), urged us to 'close our eyes and invoke a new manner of seeing... a wakefulness that is the birthright of us all, though few put it to use' (quoted in Walsh and Vaughan 1993: 1).

CHAPTER 11

Therapy's Modernist 'Regime of Truth': From scientistic 'theory-mindedness' towards the subtle and the mysterious

> Look within yourselves and you will find everything.... [W]e must investigate experience as it is concretely lived on all levels, including the dark, hidden recesses of the mind.
> (Goëthe, quoted in Askay and Farquar 2006: 72)

> The need to recoup the loss of depth and particularity is urgent if we are not to treat fellow human beings as abstract objects.
> (Marcia K. Moen 1991: 6)

INTRODUCTION

A ubiquitous assumption of the psychotherapy landscape is the axiom that theory is an indispensable accompaniment of psychotherapy praxis. Yet a range of leading philosophers and spiritual masters tell a very different story, which can give us incisive and productive purchase on some of the central lacunae of modern(ist) psychotherapy practice. At least some existentialist and kindred philosophers maintain that the embrace of theory and scientism necessarily constrains, and at worst determines, what we can perceive and experience of the world (which includes knowledge about ourselves). This chapter offers an account as to why a 'modernist' view of the role of theory is not only unsustainable, but also fundamentally antithetical to

At Roehampton University's Research Centre for Therapeutic Education where I lecture, the centre's Director, Professor Del Loewenthal, has been developing the notion of 'post-existentialism' (Loewenthal 2011), which attempts to take and weave together the complex insights of existentialism, phenomenology, psychoanalysis and postmodernism into a coherent-enough approach to therapy practice which stays true-enough to this multiplicity of influences. Several members of the centre recently contributed to a special theme issue on 'Post-existentialism' for the US journal *Philosophical Practice* (2008), and this chapter was my own contribution. It represents one of my most recent attempts to draw out in detail the practice implications of an approach to therapy that transcends the paradigmatic confines of modernity.

psychotherapy practice at its best. On this view, what is termed a 'post-existential' therapy praxis (Loewenthal 2011) is the very antithesis of the kind of scientism that still dominates much psychotherapeutic thinking. The chapter concludes with some speculatively sketchy comments about the place of what is (riskily) labelled 'the subtle' and 'the mysterious' in therapy work and in human experience more generally – comments which are couched within a 'trans-modern', New Paradigm cosmology, a theme to which I have been returning repeatedly in this book. As we pass through what are arguably the death throes of Late Modernity (Barratt 1993), such a 'post-theoretical' approach to therapy practice is tentatively labelled as 'post-existential', as while it shares many features in common with what is termed 'existential-phenomenological psychotherapy', at the same time it also moves crucially beyond the latter both in its due recognition of the importance of psychoanalytic and postmodern thinking in challenging a more naïve existential conception of human agency, and in its explicit openness to the trans-modern, the spiritual and the ineffable unknown.

This chapter will explore the view that theory and 'modernity' (Heidegger, Merleau-Ponty, Wittgenstein) or even thinking itself (Bohm, Krishnamurti) have so interfered with direct experience that human perception and experience are routinely occluded and obscured as a result. The implications of this issue for psychotherapy praxis will be discussed throughout what follows. In the author's book *Therapy Beyond Modernity* (2003a), the argument is made that modern professionalised therapy, with its accompanying credentialisation mentality, routinely entails an approach which, from the outset, creates a theory- and interest-driven assumptive base that self-fulfillingly (if often unwittingly) creates the very 'pathologies' that it then claims to 'cure' or heal. This chapter will develop just one strand of this argument in more depth – namely, the place and the effects of 'theory-mindedness' and its sequelae in psychotherapeutic attitudes and practices.

One of the great insights of phenomenology has been to challenge the relevance of theory in human experience, and to privilege description and hermeneutic understanding over causal explanation in the human realm. Although it is notoriously difficult to generalise about existential philosophy, it certainly seems true that some existentialist thinkers pay at least some kind of lip-service to theory. What is proposed in this chapter is that what we might call a 'post-existential' therapy (Loewenthal 2007, 2011) might be one which, whilst paying due consideration to core existential concerns or 'givens', at the same time strives both to move beyond theory and its unavoidable constraints, and find a way of embracing the imponderable and the mysterious in human experience (Cooper 2002) – much as Merleau-Ponty was striving to do in his work shortly before his tragically premature death (Merleau-Ponty 1968). A central aspect of this journey will be to weave in aspects of psychoanalytic, deconstructionist, postmodern thinking, not least because the latter is – as argued by Del Loewenthal elsewhere in this special issue (Loewenthal 2008) – a necessary counterweight to what can be seen as naïve and unrealistic existentialist views about freedom, agency and choice. An existential-phenomenological approach to psychotherapy tends to have a strong philosophical emphasis, which in turn can easily (and often unwittingly) slide into an emphasis on rational thinking, and thence even a reification of theory. On the view taken in this chapter, at best such an emphasis can be a fetter on effective therapy practice for reasons that I hope will become clear later. However, whilst fundamentally challenging the hegemony of, or over-emphasis on, rationality, thinking and theory, one can retain many if not most of the Heideggerian characteristics of existential psychotherapy, like its views:

- that the therapy relationship cannot be one of 'observer' and 'observed'
- that therapists cannot justifiably impose explanatory expectations and interpretations, but rather should stay open to what the phenomena are telling them
- that there is no purely cognitive approach to problems, and rationality is not superior to other ways of being
- that understanding is privileged over explanation, and is an open, unending, never-completed process; and
- that some aspects of human Being are universal givens, or 'ontological' in nature

  (For a fuller list, see House 2004: 23 and Chapter 8, this volume; drawn up from Cohn 2002.)

It is in this sense that the author wishes to ally the 'approach-*which-is-not-one*' outlined below to what this journal special issue terms 'post-existentialism', being an 'approach' to therapy which both retains some core existential concerns whilst building upon 'classic' existentialism by interweaving psychoanalytic, postmodern and 'New Paradigm' thinking around what will be termed 'the subtle' and 'the mysterious'.

TROUBLED PLACE OF THEORY AND SCIENTISM IN PRACTITIONER TRAINING AND EFFECTIVENESS

> Theories are not innocent, value-free constructs, but are often themselves defenses against, or attempts to get rid of, the very phenomena that is their subject matter.
>
> (Davis 1989: 274)

Freeman (2000: 77) has helpfully cited Heidegger's retrieval of the Greeks' notion of *theoria*, connoting (quoting Heidegger) 'the reverent paying heed to the unconcealement of what presences', which understanding both Heidegger and Freeman see as having been 'buried' by the modern(ist) rendition and appropriation of the term. For Heidegger, then, the modern 'project' of theory is one which 'entraps the real and secures it in its objectness' (quoted in ibid.). This is a key theme which will be elaborated in what follows.

From the perspective of 'post-existential' thinking, one strong claim is that empirical or positivist ways of knowing, rooted as they are in a naïvely untenable 'correspondence theory of truth' (House 1997b; Chapter 21, this volume), are inherently limited and limiting, and are being increasingly challenged by what are more holistic, participative, tacit-intuitive, and even spiritual-clairvoyant ways of knowing, as seen, for example, in the recent renewed interest in Goethean science (e.g. Bortoft 1996; Naydler 1996; Edelglass et al. 1997; see also Steiner 1988a).

One could argue that the psychodynamics, or existential-emotional drivenness, of theory within the therapy field (Craib 1987) is at least as important in therapy's preoccupation with theoretical models and rationales as is any pretension to 'objectivity' or 'scientificity'. In his little-known and appropriately discomforting paper, Craib maintains that:

> When I engage in theory, I am deploying a range of defences and projections.... I am bringing into play or even acting out a range of phantasies and displaced early experiences.... [The use of complicated languages] has to do with making the world safe and *bringing it under control*, a phantasized omnipotence.... Theory provides a means of establishing... an infantile omnipotence which protects itself by... *a denial of real complexities, ambiguities and contradictions*.... The quantitative increase in this type of theory over the past decades... can be seen as a symptom of a cultural malaise.
>
> (Craib ibid.: 35, 47, 52, emphases added)

In response to those who would suggest it to be a somewhat risky alliance to invoke psychoanalytic thinking in a paper on 'post-existentialism', Askay and Farquar (2006), for example, have made strenuous attempts to reconcile existential phenomenology with psychoanalysis – concluding, with Ricoeur and Merleau-Ponty, that psychoanalysis and existential-phenomenology can 'converge without merging' (ibid.: 343), and that all that prevents a complete merger is their 'irreconcilable difference' with regard to freedom – with the existential-phenomenological acknowledgement of humans' 'spontaneous, productive and creative capacity to make choices and to act in the world based on those choices' (ibid.: 344), in contrast to the arguably quasi-deterministic (and pessimistic) worldview of Freudian psychoanalysis. The main point here, perhaps, is that, as described by Loewenthal (2008) in the first paper in this special issue, a post-existential approach differs from an existential one in that, it is argued, human beings have some but not full agency, contra to the view of at least some existentialist philosophers; and that it is perhaps psychoanalysis and the postmodern that can help us to account for aspects of human experience where being 'subject to...' can prevail over autonomously free existential agency. These important questions recur in many different ways throughout the special issue (*Philosophical Practice* 2008) of which this essay forms a part.

HEIDEGGER AND WITTGENSTEIN ON THEORY, SCIENTISM AND TECHNOLOGISM

In their later philosophies, the two figures often regarded as the last century's greatest philosophers, Martin Heidegger and Ludwig Wittgenstein, reached very similar conclusions in writing about the related themes of science and technology. It is maintained here that a pre-occupation with theory and positivistic science and technology are interrelated instances of the modernist worldview that is challenged in this chapter and in much of this book. Thus, we find Heidegger (quoted in Cooper 2002: 344) writing that what is really 'messing up' modern thought is 'the dominance and primacy of the theoretical'; while even more dramatically, for Wittgenstein, 'it is by no means obvious' that the dominance of science and technology is not 'the beginning of the end of humanity', and the view or assumption that everything necessarily has to have an explanation is tantamount to superstition (Heaton 2000: 43). According to Heaton, and consistent with a core feature of existential-phenomenology, Wittgenstein 'replaced theory by *carefully describing* how we are initiated into language and how it is used..., resist[ing] the *compulsion* to penetrate phenomena to seek some ultimate cause' (ibid.: 44. italics added). Again parallel to Heidegger's view, everything already lies open to view – to which, in the spirit of this chapter, can be added the term *potentially* (open); and for Wittgenstein, to the extent that we are indeed unable to see, it is because of our over-familiarity with what is before our eyes. Here is Heidegger again: 'The simple hardly speaks to us any longer in its simplicity because the traditional scientific way of thinking has ruined our capacity to be astonished about what is supposedly and specifically selfevident' (quoted in Askay and Farquar 2006: 190).

Now at this point one must be careful before embracing Wittgenstein too closely, however, as his view that 'It is the idealising gaze that compels us to look for mysterious entities, whereas we need to see what actually is' (Heaton 2000: 44) is one that does not sit too easily with the approach to 'the mysterious' taken in this chapter. Yet it is fascinating that both Wittgenstein's and Heidegger's view on simplicity and 'seeing what is' seems very close if not identical to that of the great Indian sage J. Krishnamurti (discussed below). Yet as Cooper has it and as argued in this chapter, a central concern of both Heidegger and Wittgenstein is that *the privileging of theory occludes experience* (ibid.). For Heidegger, for example, 'By looking at the world theoretically, we have already dimmed it down to [a] uniformity', with the consequence that 'ways of revealing' our experience get 'driven out' (quoted in ibid.). And for Wittgenstein, writing about science, 'the cold grey ash' of scientific theory extinguishes 'the glowing embers' of life (Cooper 2002: 344).

Cooper shows at length just how much damage the hegemonic primacy of the theoretical in modernity has replaced what another important philosopher of psychology, the late Edward Reed, has termed (in his notable book of the same phrase) 'the necessity of experience' (Reed 1996) – with the occlusion of the experience of mystery being a particularly important casualty of the modernist hegemony of the theoretical. In common with Wittgenstein and Heidegger, Reed refers damningly to 'the Cartesian degradation of experience' (ibid.: 61); and in his section evocatively called 'The machining of the mind', he maintains that 'the scientific desire for certainty [has] led to the complete undermining of primary experience' (ibid.: 57).

THEORY BEYOND THEORY, AND THE POETICS OF THE OTHER

In an important and further corroborating paper sumptuously entitled 'Theory beyond theory', Freeman (2000) has also convincingly argued that there is a profound need for Psychology as a discipline to move beyond theory, if it is to respond adequately to Theoretical Psychology's growing impulse to transcend the Cartesian modernist *Zeitgeist*. For Freeman, much of theoretical psychology is still wedded to the Cartesian project of a technocratic modernity, and he draws upon the analysis of philosopher of science Stephen Toulmin in the latter's important book *Cosmopolis* (1990), in which Toulmin argues for the rehabilitation of the much-neglected humanist dimension of modernity, which is rooted in the ideas of Renaissance humanists like Michel Eyquem de Montaigne (1533–92). In brief, such a view advocates 'a reformed version [of Modernity] which redeems philosophy and science, by reconnecting them to the humanist half of Modernity' (ibid.: 72).

Freeman further quotes Toulmin in arguing for limiting 'the scope of even the best-framed theories, and fight[ing] the intellectual reductionism that became entrenched during the ascendancy of rationalism' (quoted in ibid.), and urging us 'to extricate ourselves from theory in its abstract rationalistic form' (ibid.: 73). He goes on to propose what he terms 'a poetics of the Other', citing Bakhtin, Buber, Heidegger and Levinas to foreground 'the desirability of opening up dimensions of thought and feeling that theoretical discourse… cannot readily accommodate' (ibid.: 75) – being 'a displacement of emphasis from the cogito to the Other', and thus calling forth phenomenological and ethical fidelity to the Other (ibid.: 76), in contrast to the objectifying 'thingification' and dehumanisation of the Other. Levinas takes a similar view – writing that 'Concrete reality is man always already in relation with the world…. *These relations cannot be reduced to theoretical representation*' (quoted in ibid., italics added). Freeman clearly has firmly in his sights the mechanistic positivism that dominates much of contemporary psychology: 'Theoretical work is oriented toward the theorizable; the untheorizable, therefore, is effectively banished from concern. But this is a mistake, and it is one that has severely constricted the discipline's field of meaningful inquiry and imaginative expression' (ibid.).

For Toulmin and Freeman, then, our extrication from the tyranny of theory and modernist rationalism will entail a closer association with the humanities – a move away from the scientific and the empirical, and, concomitantly, towards the artistic, the poetic and the hermeneutic. Rather than a wholesale rejection of theory as a failed symptom of a technocratic modernity, for Freeman there is a strong case for reanimating our notion of theory by reconnecting with its deeply human roots in the Greek notion of *theoria*, where it draws upon meanings both secular and ritual.

There are clear echoes here of the later Heidegger's embracing of the poetic and Merleau-Ponty's later consideration of the mysterious. Taking this impulse forwards in the present day, Clark (2008) has recently written passionately and insightfully of how poetry can illuminate therapeutic concerns and touch levels that our habitual propositional, theory-driven therapy approaches somehow necessarily miss. Many colleagues have told her how often clients bring poems to their sessions, for example (ibid.: 13); and in the following excerpt from her own published poem, 'Threshold', she speaks directly to the concerns of this chapter:

> ...It is my way
> to reach below the threshold
> of my conscious knowing
> and discover
> hidden words and images
> releasing meaning
> into life.
>   (ibid.)

Clark later refers to poetry as 'a "third thing" which enabled a deeper connection' between her and her clients – for 'poetry is a different linguistic form, which breaks the stranglehold which verbal prose places on our language of origin'; and (citing J. Morton-Smith), 'The language of poetry, the language of metaphor, is not limited or constrained by our habitual defences' (ibid.: 13, 14). Put another way, perhaps poetry (or whatever the transformative process for which it acts as a vehicle) has (or is) a way of revealing levels of 'truth' that rational, conscious attempts at articulation rarely if ever enable us to be open to. As Wittgenstein writes in the *Philosophical Investigations*, 'What is most difficult here is to put this indefiniteness, correctly and unfalsified, into words' (quoted in Heaton 2000: 44). There are also parallel echoes in all this of Wittgenstein's concern, even lament, that in modernity, people routinely no longer imagine that poets, artists and musicians can be the source of teaching and revelation about the world (quoted in Cooper 2002: 345). The psychologist Freeman, too, speaks of 'the turn to the poetic', suggesting that 'exploration of the "concrete details of practical experience" lends itself far more readily to poetics than to theoretics, and that the movement beyond theory may better attune us to the ethical – even ethico-religious – dimensions of inquiry into the human realm' (2000: 74). And even more presciently, poetry 'allows us to think about difficult issues such as "reality", "knowledge" and, especially, "truth" in a different, and perhaps more adequate, way than theoretical discourse ordinarily allows' (ibid.: 75).

J. KRISHNAMURTI AND DAVID BOHM ON
THEORY AND THOUGHT

Some of the great spiritual teachers also have penetrating things to say about these issues. As already alluded to, the great Indian sage J. Krishnamurti (or 'K') will be briefly mentioned. K has left a massive archive of speeches and books which throw a great deal of light on issues as diverse as perception, observation, theory, truth, relationship, love, conflict and so on, and at least some writers have recognised the relevance of his teachings to psychology (e.g. Butcher 1986). K certainly has much to say that is relevant to the positions taken in this chapter, being a lifelong scourge of theory and thought/thinking. He would have agreed wholeheartedly with Wittgenstein that 'One of the most dangerous ideas for a philosopher is… that we think with our heads or in our heads' (quoted in Heaton 2000: 45). K repeatedly and relentlessly confronts the question of Cartesianism, claiming that 'the observer' *is* 'the observed', and that it is possible experientially to dissolve this particularly tenacious dualism of the modern mind (though he also steadfastly refused – entirely consistently – to give any technique for so doing).

In his famous dialogues with the renowned sub-atomic physicist David Bohm, for example, these themes recur repeatedly (Krishnamurti and Bohm 1988; see also Bohm 1994), Thus, in their third dialogue, entitled 'Why has man given supreme importance to thought?', we read, 'K: [T]heory prevents the observation of what is actually taking place…. I have no theories…. I start at the schoolboy level by saying, "Look, don't accept theories, conclusions, don't cling to your prejudices. That is the starting point' (Krishnamurti and Bohm 1988: 55, 54). (One is reminded of the wonderful fairy tale of the Emperor's New Clothes.) And here is Bohm: 'inwardly, psychologically, [theories] are in the way, they are no use at all' (ibid.: 56). These dialogues, as with so many other of K's writings and talks, repay close attention to anyone interested in the kinds of existential and perennial spiritual questions that are surely a core concern of 'non-technicist' psychotherapy; and K's writings have indeed been criminally neglected by the psychotherapy field and a somewhat snobbish academic world – not least, perhaps, because to think about or embrace his ideas would be to expose the radical incoherence and philosophical unsustainability of much of psychotherapy and academic activity, as currently practised.

Krishnamurti also has much of prescience to say about education that is relevant to the therapy experience. In the teacher–pupil relationship, for example, we find the quintessentially postmodern view that such a relationship cannot be created 'by following a method' (quoted in Hunter 1988: 99). For K, 'the very institutions which claim to educate are in fact doing the opposite: *by overemphasising the intellect* they are preventing the awakening of true intelligence' (ibid.: 114, italics added). Along similar lines, Quinney (1988) argues that thought by itself is not only incapable of arriving at truth, but is actually 'a *source* of our incapacity to know' (ibid.: 101, emphases added). On this view, knowledge, theory and interpretation are all conditioned by the limitations of Western rationalism.

THE QUESTION OF PSYCHOTHERAPY TRAINING

From the 'post-existential', 'trans-modern' perspective adopted in this chapter and book, the increasing emphasis being accorded to academic (often heavily theoretical) work on therapy training courses is, at the very least, highly questionable. Moreover, the academicisation of training is arguably an inevitable accompaniment of the attempt to make the therapy field into a 'Profession' (House and Totton 1997/2011): for as Mowbray (1995: 29) points out, the knowledge base of the professions in general is typically highly theoretical and academic, with access usually depending on the possession of an academic degree. Mowbray goes as far as suggesting that 'The over-intellectual focus... may actually be counterproductive as a prerequisite for working in this area' (ibid.: 117). In this sense, then, the professionalisation of therapy work is as much a creature of modernity and its accompanying worldview as is the wrong-headed (!) preoccupation with theory-mindedness (House 2003a).

The radical implication is that the psychotherapy field's whole approach to the place of theory needs to be quite fundamentally revised and recast in ways more consonant with 'post-existential', or 'New Paradigm' thinking (House, 2008a) – and, concomitantly, away from the increasingly discredited, philosophically incoherent and profoundly damaging world-view of modernity (Polkinghorne 1990; Barratt 1993; House 2003a).

Just one potentially helpful way of responding to this malaise is for those studying and practising therapy (including trainers and trainees) to foreground the deconstructive study of therapy practice within both modern culture and also within the broader evolution of ideas that are manifestations of the evolution of human consciousness (for an admirable example, see Cushman 1995; cf. Tarnas 1991), embracing the kind of 'post-existential' sensibility very provisionally sketched out in this chapter. Anything less would be not only to risk practitioner complacency and complicity with the prevailing cultural ideologies, but to risk merely reinforcing a kind of modernist 'status quo theory' (Harvey 1973) which can only reproduce rather than help to transcend the degenerating modernist *Zeitgeist*.

CONCLUSION: TOWARDS A SPIRITUALISED POST-EXISTENTIAL PHENOMENOLOGY?

[T]he psychotherapist has not the faintest notion of what he is dealing with nor of how very simplistic even the most complex of psychological theories are because of the failure to recognize the reality of the spiritual world.
(Sardello 1990: 13)

It can be argued from a number of trans-modern perspectives that those aspects of 'relational' human experience which are most important in, for example, teaching, learning and therapy, are inherently and in principle unquantifiable (Rudolf Steiner called these 'imponderables' or 'intangibles'). Within the field of education, for example, the phenomenologically inspired work of Max van Manen is quite seminal, with a number of deeply insightful books on what might be called 'pedagogical subtlety' (e.g. van Manen 1991) – referring to the kind of subtleties which are notably absent, or at best neglected, in modern(ist) educational thinking and practice, with its mechanistic positivism and programmatic utilitarianism (House 2007a).

For educationalist van Manen as for the polymath seer Rudolf Steiner, then, the journey to becoming an authentic and appropriately sensitive teacher – or psychotherapist – necessitates a profound process of personal, even spiritual growth, and also the development of a reflective thoughtfulness. For van Manen, at their richest and most enabling, teaching and learning entail *an improvisational thoughtfulness* in which the very being of the person is necessarily involved, requiring in turn an acute attention and active sensitivity toward the other's subjectivity. In his book *The Essentials of Education* and in similarly phenomenological vein, Steiner writes that:

We must acquire a vision, a soul vision, to perceive the delicate, fleeting elements that play from soul to soul, and possibly we only come to understand the individual in himself when we are able to understand these intimate, spiritual currents playing between human beings.

– a quotation, I would argue, that is equally applicable to psychotherapy practice.

What Steiner, van Manen, Polanyi (e.g. 1966) and others have in common is their trenchant defence and advocacy of the subtle, and of the intangible and the inherently qualitative in human experience, against the bludgeoning juggernaut of 'modernity' and crass materialism in all its hegemonic manifestations. To the extent that the prevailing modernist *Zeitgeist* and its associated methodologies are preoccupied with quantification and measurability, and mechanistic conceptions of the person more generally, it can be argued that those methodologies will quite possibly yield results, lead to policy prescriptions and feed ideologies whose values fundamentally contradict the profoundly human mores and praxis to which psychotherapy and education at their best surely aspire. And writers like Cooper (2002) are beginning to engage with the later Merleau-Ponty in a way that gives serious consideration to, without being driven by the modernist desire to eradicate, 'the mysterious' in human experience.

The question remains, can we do, live or be without theory? Writers such as Slife and Williams (1995: 9), for example, claim that 'we cannot escape theory'. What we have found in this chapter is that some of the greatest philosophers of the previous century – Heidegger, Merleau-Ponty, Wittgenstein – seem to be agreeing with some of humankind's greatest sages and spiritual teachers, like Goethe, J. Krishnamurti and Steiner. It comes as no surprise, then, to discover, for example, that Heidegger explicitly referred to how Zen Buddhism expresses ideas that he himself tried to convey in his philosophy (May 1996); or that Steiner, like Husserl and Freud, studied in Vienna under Franz Brentano, and personally knew the phenomenologist Scheler, to whom he dedicated one of his many books (Schuller, n.d.).

Clues to the kind of direction that a viable 'post-existentialism' might profitably take are well illustrated by writers like Cooper (2002) and Keller and Daniell (2002), with the latter's leading-edge anthology showing how both the analytic and continental philosophical paradigms are breaking down, with new hybrids emerging in which, for example, cosmological-spiritual postmodernisms find ways of finding common philosophical cause with the process post-structural postmodernism of Alfred Whitehead. And Schuller (n.d.) has even referred to 'the spiritualization of phenomenology', where Western and Eastern traditions can perhaps meet and share common ground. In the field of psychoanalysis itself, too, we see recent incursions into and engagements with the realms of the paranormal (Totton 2003).

Yet there also remains what Freeman (2000: 74) refers to as 'a kind of gravitational pull backward, toward the rational, the scientific, the *theorizable*' (original emphasis) – and this caught-upness in the ideology of modernity is something that we need to make sense of – perhaps psychodynamically (Craib 1987), existentially, or even in terms of the evolution of human consciousness (e.g. Neumann 1954; Steiner 1966; Crook 1980) – a fascinating question which is, alas, well beyond the scope of this chapter but is waiting for others to pursue. The chapter appropriately ends with a quotation and a poem excerpt from Jean Clark, which I hope will speak for themselves:

I may write poetry when I am in a state of confusion or change, knowing that it will eventually bring me to a new way of seeing, to enter into a liminal state, that place between, where we do not know who or what we may meet.... [I]t opens up the possibility of surprise... it sometimes allows us to say the unsayable.

(Clark 2008: 14, 15)

Wait,
be still
hold the silence
within your heart
and maybe something
new and unexpected
will emerge and grow.
The creative thought
which is hidden
beyond chaos.

(from the poem 'Beyond Chaos' – Clark 2007)

CHAPTER 12

Towards a New Spiritual Psychology?
Integrating Carl Jung and Rudolf Steiner:
A review essay

> ...we can seek for [the path] in love and peace only if we forego the
> bold assumption that we alone have found it and possess it.
>> (From St Augustine's *Contra Epistulam Manichaei*, quoted on
>> p. 260)

INTRODUCTION

One of the great enigmas of Rudolf Steiner's wide-ranging influence on
modern culture is just why his work has had so little influence upon the
West's burgeoning field of psychotherapy and counselling. This might be
due, at least in part, to Steiner's trenchant early criticisms of the then-nascent
discipline and practice of Freudian psychoanalysis, which almost certainly
would have alienated him from that emerging field during the second decade
of the last century when he delivered his critical lectures (Steiner 1990). Yet
there are almost certainly far deeper, culture-wide reasons for the ignoring
of Steiner's therapy-relevant work (along with a similar lack of response in
other mainstream fields to which he contributed), and about which many
an academically inclined anthroposophist has attempted, often speculatively,

---

I was delighted when, in 2002, there appeared an English translation of the
book originally written over a decade earlier by Gerhard Wehr, *Jung and Steiner:
The Birth of a New Psychology*, and with a substantial accompanying introduction
by the excellent Robert Sardello. I have always been strongly drawn to Jung's
work and worldview; and I discovered the extraordinary work of Rudolf Steiner
when I started training as a Waldorf teacher in the mid–1990s. I have no doubt
(a dangerous confession for a postmodernist to make!) that Steiner is one of the
most extraordinary individuals and Masters that has ever lived. His work spans
so many diverse fields across the arts, the humanites and the sciences that it is
difficult to fathom how someone with such wide–ranging insights, and collected
works that total a staggering 360 volumes, can have been so neglected in modern
thought. Wehr's book goes some distance to righting this lacuna for the field of
psychology and the psychological therapies, as I hope this review essay will
amply demonstrate.

to propose explanations. The present book under review, being a translation of the German original from 1990, is a greatly welcome addition to the English-speaking literature for those of us who hold the strong belief that Steiner's cosmology has a far greater relevance to the therapy *Zeitgeist* than has to date been recognised or acknowledged.

My 'credentials' for reviewing this book are varied: I have read Steiner's works fairly widely and selectively, but by no means comprehensively (difficult, with collected works of around 360 volumes, many in German), though I have yet to embark in any systematic way upon Steiner's meditative programme and initiation schooling path; and I am a trained Waldorf Class teacher and Kindergarten teacher, having worked as an early-years teacher for some years in Norwich Steiner School. I also have a strong interest in Jung's work, though I have not done a specifically Jungian training. This, then, is the perspective from which I attempt to review this book – and my review will of course be constrained by my own limitations, and by the extent of my knowledge and understanding of the contributions of these two great figures of modern human culture.

In what follows I will focus less on the actual content of Wehr's rich text, and more on the implications which it has for qualitatively new approaches to psychology and psychological therapy – with particular reference to the 'Spiritual Psychology' of Robert Sardello, who has written extensively in this field, and who contributes a lengthy and challenging Foreword to the book. But more of this later. (It should be recalled that the subtitle of the book is, in fact, 'The Birth of a New Psychology'.)

It is certainly a remarkable fact that Carl Jung and Rudolf Steiner were earthly contemporaries for many years (i.e. between 1875 and 1925) and lived in close geographical proximity to one another – and yet seemingly never met, developing their respective cosmologies with very little reference to the work of the other. This is the starting point for Wehr's study – as he writes, 'Steiner... never spoke [of Jung the scientist] in the thorough and detailed manner that would have been desirable... [and] one gets the impression that the circumspect depth psychologist Jung ignored the essence and significance of [Steiner's] Anthroposophy' (p. 38). Wehr responds to this situation by attempting what he terms 'a factual dialogue' (ibid.) between Anthroposophy and Jungian psychology. We should not underestimate just what is at stake in this comparative study: Wehr's text is certainly far more than a mechanistic academic essay of 'Compare and contrast...'; and, quoting Jean Gebser, it perhaps presages, and constitutes a necessary preparatory ground-clearing for, 'a spiritual dimension that is not in opposition to psyche or physical body, but rather constitutes a new form of consciousness for which humankind seems to prepare itself' (quoted on p. 42).

THE LECTURES OF HANS ERHARD LAUER

The book is 'topped and tailed' with two distinct and substantial contributions – Robert Sardello's lengthy, contextualising Foreword (23 pp, which I examine later) and Hans Erhard Lauer's three-lecture appendix (55 pp) – contributions which, together, have the combined effect of transforming an excellent book into an outstanding one. Lauer's lectures, first published in 1960 and reproduced here in English for the first time, are an extremely valuable contribution from an anthroposophist who clearly has sympathies with Jungian depth psychology. Lauer starts by considering in two separate lectures 'the riddles of the soul' in the light of depth psychology and Anthroposophy respectively, and in Lecture 3 he then focuses more specifically on the differences between the two approaches.

Any reader who is relatively unfamiliar with Jung's work might find it useful to read Lauer's first lecture (pp. 263–79) first, before subsequently embarking upon Wehr's text proper. Moreover, such a reader might also benefit from reading both Sardello's provocative Foreword and Lauer's Lectures 2 and 3 *after* they have read the main text. Indeed, this order of reading seems to me significantly more fitting to all but those who are fairly well versed in both Jung and Steiner: that is, starting with Lauer's Lecture 1, the Wehr's main text, followed by Lauer's Lectures 2 and 3, and finishing with Sardello's Foreword.

THE BODY OF WEHR'S TEXT

Wehr is all too aware of the urgency of the human situation that forms a backdrop to his text – for writing around 1990 when the original German text was first published, he speaks graphically of 'a tortured humanity… experiencing turmoil and apocalypse as never before' (even more prescient some 20 years later, perhaps); and that 'there is a need for a synoptic effort toward wisdom and knowledge' (p. 47). And a bit earlier, we read that

> Humankind… urgently needs a 'community of spirit' in the form of a newly practiced humanity…. We need a concentration of spiritual forces that can help self-knowledge and world-transformation, even though they come from such divergent streams as Jung's analytical psychology and Steiner's Anthroposophy.
>
> (p. 43)

The scale of concern underpinning and motivating this comparative study can therefore hardly be overemphasised.

Following a wide-ranging introductory chapter, there follow some eleven major chapters, followed by five briefer appendices on a range of pertinent themes. The sequential chapter themes, which are chosen to allow Wehr to set the respective cosmologies of Jung and Steiner alongside one another, are as follows: their respective biographies; Jung and Steiner on 'the unconscious' and (early) psychoanalysis respectively; their spiritual backgrounds; their images of the human being; Steiner's 'second self' and the unconscious; their natural-scientific 'starting point'; initiation (Steiner) and individuation (Jung); the East/West question; and the question of gnosticism. The briefer appendices consider mental health through spiritual discipline; evil; androgyny; soul and spirit research; and *Unus Mundus* and the Cosmic Christ.

It would be quite impossible to do justice in a single chapter to Wehr's 225 pages of detailed comparative description and insightful analysis. I will focus here instead on just two of his chapters which particularly touched me in my own reading. First, psychoanalysis and 'the unconscious', and initiation and individuation. In Steiner's series of lectures on the then nascent field of psychoanalysis, the only work of Jung's that Steiner commented upon at length was the former's *The Psychology of the Unconscious*. Jung was at pains to emphasise how this book was very much 'preliminary work'; and Wehr is careful to do justice to both Steiner and Jung in emphasising that Steiner's 'much-cited lectures' on psychoanalysis should be seen as no more than 'documents of the time, not as a sufficient characterization or basis for critique' (p. 80 – which is not to deny that Steiner's lectures *do* contain still-relevant insights, as Sardello among others has pointed out). For it is clear that *Jung's work only began to reach its full flowering well after Steiner's death in 1925*. By the time that Steiner was encountering Jung, the latter had already distanced himself from Freud's overly materialistic sexual theory and the theory of the so-called 'neuroses', and Steiner does indeed acknowledge this. Yet there is in Steiner's general and wide-ranging critique of psychoanalysis perhaps less differentiation of Jung from Freud than would have been fair to the former.

Steiner criticised the way in which psychoanalysis studied 'psychic facts' – with, as he said, 'half-truths, under certain circumstances, [being] more harmful than complete errors' (quoted on p. 81). In sum, Steiner considered Jung's discovery of the Psychological Types to be a mere theory, though he did also (grudgingly?) concede it to be 'ingenious and brilliant' (ibid.).

Wehr is at pains to point out the 'far-reaching mutuality of interests between the spiritual scientist and the psychiatrist', while acknowledging their differing focus of interest – respectively, the question of the underlying spiritual reality, and the alleviation of psychological suffering (p. 83). Wehr concludes by speculating about the destiny factor at work in the Jung/Steiner relationship (p. 84), maintaining that Steiner's 1917 verdict on Jung – not least that 'psychoanalysis approaches the world of spiritual science... spiritually blindfolded' (p. 204) – 'can in no way be justly taken for an overall judgment about Jung's later work' (p. 84).

Wehr's book points out very clearly and comprehensively the differences between Jung's and Steiner's varying approaches to 'the unconscious', and to their respective paths of *individuation* through Jungian psychotherapy, and *initiation* through anthroposophical schooling practices. What I wish to highlight here is the degree of spontaneity and discipline which each approach entails and requires. Certainly, both Jung and Steiner place great emphasis on the importance of *direct personal experience*, but there is a key divergence in the nature of the methods employed. For Jung, his therapeutic method is that of *free association*, whereby the client/patient is encouraged to articulate, without censorship, whatever comes into her or his mind, with the analyst then interpreting and structuring whatever is expressed, according to the analyst's cosmology or chosen theoretical system. In this procedure, there is a trust that 'the truth of the soul and the spirit' will out, and that self-healing will occur as a by-product of the process – albeit in the face of personal resistances which will need to be challenged, 'owned' and worked through. By contrast, Steiner's initiation method is far more prescribed and disciplined from the outset; and while the experiential *results* of the schooling path will of course be unique for each person, the framework of exercises is the same for all.

I believe that different people will be temperamentally more suited to one or other of these approaches. The sanguine-temperament 'free spirit' who balks at anything imposed or handed down from an external source will perhaps tend towards the free association path (though they might not like the interpretations offered!); whereas those who are happier with adopting a prescribed framework of explanation or meditation (more suited to a melancholic temperament, perhaps?) may find the anthroposophical schooling path more congenial. It is crucial to emphasise that neither is right or wrong: rather, and as Wehr and Lauer both point out, at least part of the difference between free association and initiation is due to their different aims – namely, that the former has a primarily therapeutic, healing function, whereas the latter is about the acquisition of objective spiritual knowledge and understanding. Historically, then, the agendas and *raisons-d'être* of therapy and initiation have been very different – which may explain, at least in part, just why the work of Jung and Steiner has remained so distinct and apparently uninfluenced by the other.

Just how precarious the legitimacy of psychotherapy can be – and how potentially ideological – can be illustrated by the example of dream interpretation. In my own book *Therapy Beyond Modernity* (2003a), I argue that professionalised therapy routinely creates a self-serving 'regime of truth', whose commonly tacit assumptions create a self-justifying rationale, outside the discourse of which it becomes difficult or impossible for clients or therapists even to think. The very form that therapy takes will, then, be substantially influenced – even *determined* – by what the therapist and the therapist/client dyad assume to exist from the outset. Thus, in his Foreword to *Jung and Steiner*, Robert Sardello points out that, for Steiner, different kinds of consciousness are not states but *beings*; and that as a consequence, 'Psychological symptoms that appear seemingly out of nowhere… are sometimes due to the living presence of the dead who have not been remembered' (p. 14). It should be clear that a therapy which makes such an 'ontological' assumption about consciousness will look very different from one which assumes, for example, that the 'unconscious' is nothing more than the repository of repressed intra-psychic *this-life* material along with the baser 'instincts'.

With specific regard to dreams and their meaning, for example, it is clear that the way in which 'the unconscious' is conceptualised and understood will, in a very real sense, determine the nature of the interpretation made of a given dream. If, for example, the unconscious is seen merely as the repository of soul contents (a common assumption in much of psychotherapy), then clearly a given dream manifestation will be understood in a very different way compared with a view of the unconscious which sees it as a manifestation of Jung's 'collective unconscious' and archetypal forces, or, as in the anthroposophical view, as not a state but an expression of spiritual beings. What this strongly implies is that *client subjectivity itself* can actually be created, or at the very least influenced, by the assumptive base from which the 'expert' therapist is working. One response to this difficulty is that therapists should quite determinedly and self-awarely remain non-dogmatic in their theoretical models and clinical practices, if the obvious dangers of an imposed 'regime of truth' are to be avoided. (Compare, in this regard, the epigraph from St Augustine at the beginning of this chapter.)

Moving on now to my other chosen focus, my own interest in the philosophy of science drew me strongly to Wehr's Chapter 7 on Jung and Steiner's respective approaches to 'natural science'. In this arena as in most others, Wehr's thorough comparative analysis yields both commonalities and important differences between Jung and Steiner. On the similarity side: both regarded themselves as natural scientists and recognised the value of precise scientific investigation, yet with neither being satisfied with what could be empirically 'measured, counted, and weighed' (p. 119). Certainly, both Jung and Steiner were both acutely aware of the culturally ascendant totem of natural science, and both were determined that their respective cosmologies should fall within its broad culturally legitimate definition (pp. 119–20). Yet Jung seems slightly more wedded to the canons of modern natural science than Steiner, for while Jung repeatedly insisted that he was an 'empiricist' and not a philosopher, using a strictly inductive method of knowledge acquisition (p. 119), Steiner dares to take natural science into the realms of the spirit – for as Steiner himself said,

> To act in the spirit of natural science would be to study the spiritual evolution of humanity impartially, as the natural scientist observes the sense-world... [leading] to higher methodological principles, *which would certainly not be identical with those of natural science.*
> (quoted on p. 120, from his *Christianity as Mystical Fact*, my emphasis)

As Wehr points out, for Steiner there was no unbridgeable gap between material nature and spirit – and his method actually 'contributes a metamorphosis of scientific thought' (p.121).

Both Jung and Steiner relied upon personal experience rather than theoretical deduction or speculation in their discoveries, and both seemed to agree that traditional notions of reality had become obsolete, with, as Jung put it, 'Restriction to material reality... [remaining] a fragment [of the whole] only' (quoted on p. 122). For both men, they found that beyond a certain threshold, there was a need for a different way of thinking and knowing – with 'the phenomena themselves [demanding] a transcendental approach' (p. 122).

Steiner would no doubt have agreed with Jung in the latter's view that purely rational thinking led to a dangerous one-sidedness, and that abstract thinking is of little use for truly understanding life, soul and spirit (p. 125). Here is Jung himself: '[The intellect] shies away from taking the step beyond its limitation and from surrendering its universal supremacy.... The intellect, having its only purpose in hard science, cuts itself off from the source of life' (quoted on pp. 125–6). In this sense, we should surely recognise both Jung and Steiner as being two of the earliest and most incisive critics of a superficial technocratic positivism, the inadequacies of which mainstream philosophical thinking only succeeded in laying bare many decades later.

In sum, both men were struggling to discover the means of expression that would be acceptable to the culturally ascendant proponents of natural-scientific philosophy and practice, while at the same time grappling with phenomena which that very science considered to lie beyond its legitimate bounds. Here is Steiner on this very point: 'Our language today… makes it hard for us to adequately describe things that don't belong to the sense world but to the supersensible realm' (quoted on p. 127, from a 1919 lecture). Steiner's response was to seek 'a flexible thinking that will not press the definition and the exact words…' (ibid.). For Wehr, then, there is perhaps less of a misunderstanding between Anthroposophy and analytical psychology on the nature of thinking than is commonly believed (p. 128). In his description of Jung's approach to thinking, Wehr could equally be describing Steiner's view: 'Jung, much like Goethe, developed a thinking that forced open the rational straightjacket and shed the hulls of abstract concepts…. For Jung, "life" is not something abstract to be defined, but something concrete that can be characterized' (pp. 131–2). And as Steiner said in a 1918 lecture, 'Once can apply Goethe's way of seeing the world to the life of the soul itself' (quoted on p. 133). Wehr himself claims that 'The similarity between Jung's and Goethe's mental attitudes is often astounding' (p. 132) – and this despite the fact that Jung, though studying Goethe's works extensively, did not seem to have been consciously influenced or impressed by the latter's theory of knowledge in the way that Steiner most certainly was (p. 128; see Steiner 1988a).

Last but by no means least of their similarities in this realm is the fact that 'Both Steiner and Jung have described their subjective experiences in *objective, systematic terms*' (p. 135, Wehr's emphasis) – and that 'their teachings were not to be taken on authority' (ibid.).

Much more could be added to this commentary on the 'scientificity' of Jung's and Steiner's works – not least in the way in which Goethe's 'way of science' is relevant to both (Wehr has a great deal to say on this). Space unfortunately precludes any further elaboration of Wehr's wide-ranging comparative commentaries, but I hope to have conveyed a flavour of the mature authority and wide-ranging knowledge which Wehr brings to his subject, and the thoroughness and subtlety which informs his comparative study of these two great figures.

TOWARDS A NEW SPIRITUALISED THERAPY?

The method of spiritual psychology is a new form of therapeutic work that takes therapy away from concentration on the personal, which easily becomes ego-centered, and yet strengthens the soul and spirit forces that are… central to any therapeutic healing.

(Robert Sardello, Foreword, p. 25)

Some readers will probably be familiar with Robert Sardello's important contributions through such books as *Facing the World with Soul* and *Love and the World* (e.g. Sardello 1999, 2001, 2004). He has worked as a 'psychotherapist' for over two decades, founding the Dallas Institute of Humanities and Culture and the School of Spiritual Psychology – though some years ago now he publicly disowned the term 'psychotherapist' and now calls his work 'adult education into soul wisdom' and 'spiritual psychology'.

It is, again, impossible to do justice to Sardello's profound and provocative Foreword in the short space available here, but I can say that, for me, it offers a critical but sympathetic perspective which only deepens one's experience of reading Wehr's book, in the process drawing out perspectives that are imminent but never quite explicitly articulated in Wehr's text. Not least, Sardello emphasises how we need to transcend a simplistic approach that mechanistically 'compares and contrasts' Jung and Steiner with an unhelpful competitive either/or mentality that seeks to 'prove' one or the other to be superior. Rather, Sardello invokes the Grail myth (important to both Jung and Steiner, incidentally) to honour the quest of both figures – one pursing the inward soul dimension (Jung) and the other, the outward spiritual path (Steiner); and to emphasise, too, how important it is to hold the polarity that Jung's and Steiner's cosmologies constitute in tension, *without seeking to resolve it*, such that something qualitatively new can emerge from the creative interplay between the two (p. 11). (In passing, Sardello makes the provocative claim here that perhaps Dante was a greater psychologist than either Jung or Steiner – certainly, Steiner himself referred to Dante as 'the greatest man' – p. 11).

One crucial but often neglected phenomenon which yearns for attention, if we are to resist the premature resolution of this creative tension, is that of *desire*. Perhaps neither Jung nor Steiner needed to give much attention to desire in their respective cosmologies because, as Sardello puts it, their personal transformations 'ensured… that the desires they followed were free of personal traits' (p. 10). Unfortunately, however, at least some (and possibly many) of their followers have, according to Sardello, selectively embraced their mentor's spiritual path while 'foolishly ignoring the factor of desire in themselves, and the necessity of working with this *before all else*' (ibid., my emphasis). This line of argument is all too familiar to me as a therapist who has been embarked upon a personal development path for over 20 years – for one repeatedly comes across the phenomenon of self-delusion (both in oneself and in others): that is, I am referring here to just how ingenious the human psyche can be in creating the convenient delusion that we are free of our own unconscious psychic 'material' that distorts or even sabotages a true path to the spirit.

Steiner was all too aware of this challenge: 'When you look into your own inner self, you find things that you would rather not talk about' (quoted on p. 243). Sardello is by no means uncritical of anthroposophists here, in referring to their propensity (as he sees it) to confuse Steiner's 'I' with their own egotism 'because they often lack a sense of soul' (p. 17). Similarly, and just as challengingly, we read later how, according to Sardello, 'Without Jung,... Anthroposophy becomes the dogmatic application of the ideas of a remarkable individual without inner understanding' (pp. 20–1 – where the phrase 'without inner understanding' clearly refers to Anthroposophy and *not* to Steiner himself).

For Sardello, then, Jung's thorough-going, painstaking engagement with inner soul experience is an *essential prerequisite* of, and necessary foundation for, the spiritual-scientific schooling path of Rudolf Steiner; and without Jung's 'soul wisdom', Anthroposophy can fall prey to 'the imposition of [its] ideas onto others' (p. 21). (Note here, again, that Sardello is talking about some followers of Anthroposophy, *not* of Rudolf Steiner himself.) Later, Sardello reinforces this point when emphasising how the huge cultural split between the individual and the collective is such that 'it is dangerous... to do spiritual practices without accompanying soul work' (p. 26). It is hardly surprising, then, that Sardello disagrees with a common anthroposophical view that 'because of Steiner we have absolutely no need for psychology' (p. 21). To repeat, for Sardello the erstwhile and greatly experienced 'psychotherapist', Jung's detailed mastery of the interior of the soul is an essential complement to Steiner's initiation path.

Another way of looking at this crucial question is to think in terms of depth psychology's notion of 'psychological *defences*'. As my therapist-colleague Jill Hall once said to a group she was facilitating, '*Anything* can be used as a defence' – including (and perhaps even *especially*!) the self-conscious seeking of a personal or spiritual developmental path.... Sardello puts it thus: 'Much of ego life is not conscious.... Our ordinary ego is filled with pride, self-aggrandizement, anger, envy, and much besides.... Ego defends itself *but in wholly unconscious ways*' (p. 27, my emphasis). On this issue Sardello is uncompromisingly blunt: he is concerned that 'anthroposophical training goes on without any guidance in inner soul work, with no recognition of the importance of depth psychology' (p. ibid.) – and this is where, for Sardello, Jung can make an indispensable contribution, with 'inner soul work as a necessary preliminary to any kind of spiritual work' (p. 28).

As a transpersonally inclined therapist, I have met many people over the years who appear to me to have attempted to embrace 'the spiritual' without seeming to have done any serious individual soul-work (not least, perhaps, because the spiritual can commonly be used as an ingenious unconscious defence against fully engaging with one's egotism or narcissistic woundedness); and I must say that I find myself in full agreement with Sardello's passionate and challenging strictures on this question. Not least, having completed two Waldorf teacher training courses myself, I agree wholeheartedly with Sardello that 'Spiritual psychology as a practice... needs to be part of every Waldorf training program, every anthroposophical medical training program, and all other anthroposophical endeavors' (ibid.).

These, then, are sober and humbling cautionary remarks for all of us ongoingly to hold in mind during our individual and collective quests for the spirit – and I think this is what Sardello is alluding to in his challenging commentary.

So what qualitatively new phenomenon does emerge when the Jung–Steiner polarity is held in creative, unresolved tension? It is something which is notably (and tellingly?) lacking in Wehr's own text – namely, *love*: for 'the inherent reason for such tension is that... this is the only way that love enters, a love that is greater than any of our desires' (p. 11); and 'The purifying power of love enters through the opening, the soul space created by holding impossible contradictions' (ibid.). For Sardello, this is the new soul-space into which a new spiritual psychology can become manifest – with spiritual psychology being 'an active practice that develops embodied, conscious soul life to make that life more open and receptive to the spiritual realms. This is done as an act of love toward ourselves, others, and the world' (p. 10). This new psychology offers the promise of a quite new kind of 'psychotherapy', transcending by far the soulless and spiritless mainstream professionalised therapy of which myself and others are increasingly critical in the mainstream therapy literature (cf. House 2003a).

As Sardello puts it, this new 'spiritualised therapy', as I am calling it, will 'not be confined to the therapy office but is rather the work of living a conscious soul life' (p. 8). And later, we read that 'following Steiner's lead, spiritual psychology *refuses to literalize therapy* but sees individual meditative work as inherently therapeutic' (p. 25, my emphasis). The new spiritual psychology also requires a new myth to replace the core myth of modernity – the technological myth of materialism. For Sardello, then, we can (and should) work with soul and spirit at the same time (p. 13), or what he calls 'a dual consciousness of the future' (ibid.) – a consciousness which has been made possible 'because of the initiation experiences of these two individuals [Jung and Steiner]' (ibid.). For 'we need Jung's psychology in order to remain imaginal; [and] we need Steiner's spiritual science in order to apply this imagination to the forming of the world' (ibid.). Sardello also usefully shows how we must change our very ontology about human consciousness

('ontology' referring to our beliefs about what we assume to exist) if we are
to make spiritual-evolutionary progress. Thus, he writes that (and contrary
to Wehr's own apparent assumption), 'Soul is not a container of contents
but the inherent capacity for perceiving spiritual realities. We are soul and
spiritual beings, not beings with a soul and with a spirit' (p. 15). Similarly,
the modernist obsession with control-fixated *definition* is also quite
fundamentally challenged, with Sardello writing that the attempt to define
soul and spirit 'goes nowhere because it shifts something known and felt to
the level of the ordinary intellect, where is cannot be answered' (p. 16).
Steiner himself was all too aware of this difficulty: in 1919, he said, 'our
language today… makes it hard for us to adequately describe things… that
belong to the supersensible realm'. And in his *The Fall of the Spirits of
Darkness*, we read further that 'Reality doesn't exist in templates, reality
lives in constant metamorphosis…. One only can see the essence of things
by seeing the world in a spiritual way' (quoted on p. 127). And above all,
'Nothing is accomplished by definitions. Usually one doesn't see the
inadequacy of each definition' (ibid.); and 'Definitions are always one-sided'
(quoted on p. 328n).

Wehr also recognises the problem when he writes of the difficulty that
our intellectual conceptual language routinely 'seeks to express supersensible
reality in a language that is really only suited to describe observable facts
and the abstract thinking process" (p. 146).

For Sardello, then, Jung and Steiner need each other: for

> Taken alone, Jung seals soul off from the world and unwittingly
> promotes self-absorption; [while] taken alone, Steiner's perspective
> leads to a literalizing, unimaginative… working to bring practical
> endeavors of a spiritual nature into the world. When we hold both
> the spirit and the soul perspectives together, we have spiritual
> psychology.
> (p. 17)

– in which we develop the capacity to allow the spiritual to work through
us and into the world, in a conscious way.

It should be clear by now that Sardello is by no means uncritical of the
anthroposophical path pursued by anthroposophists – though he is clearly
a great admirer of, and is very conversant with, Steiner's work. He makes it
clear that depth psychology also has a lot to learn from Anthroposophy –
not least because Anthroposophy is oriented towards the future, with the
soul's immersion in destiny being shaped from the future. In this sense,
'depth psychology has a lot to learn from Anthroposophy, [for] it is as if half

of psychology has been neglected because of the discipline's bias toward explanations in terms of the past' (p. 23). Indeed, a great deal of psychotherapy as a healing practice has had this 'past-fixation'; and it is surely no coincidence in terms of therapy's evolutionary path that such a fixation is increasingly being challenged, even increasingly within the mainstream therapy literature of the present day.

CLOSING REMARKS

Wehr's impressive book can surely form one important harbinger of new evolving kinds of psychotherapy and counselling practice which explicitly embrace soul, spirit and the transpersonal. An evolutionary principle applies to the psychotherapy field as it does to any other human endeavour; and the pitched battle of ideas currently raging throughout modern culture between a one-sided materialistic modernity, on the one hand, and a 'new paradigm', transpersonal vision on the other, is playing itself out at least as much within the psychotherapy world as in any other field. I believe that the evolutionary principle is inexorably taking the therapy field towards an explicitly transpersonal, spiritual orientation, as the threadbare, soulless nature of much of modern therapy's mechanistic project becomes increasingly exposed. We only have to mention Jungian analytic psychology, anthroposophically inspired Biographical Counselling, Assagioli's Psychosynthesis therapy, the Spiritual Psychology of Robert Sardello and Alice Morawitz-Cadio and the later work of the founder of Person-Centred Therapy, Carl Rogers, to see how much potential there is for a convergence of these many, often quite independent tendencies to develop into a truly coherent and widely relevant *spiritualised psychology and therapy*, which is both a healing practice *and* a vehicle for deepening human knowledge of the spiritual dimension.

With a few notable exceptions (e.g. the work of Fraser Watts and Robert Sardello), Rudolf Steiner's work has had a surprisingly limited – and often non-existent – influence on modern psychotherapeutic theory and practice. I am delighted at the appearance of this excellent translation of Gerhard Wehr's path-breaking study, not least because it makes Steiner's psychology-relevant insights widely available to the English-speaking world – and hopefully serving in the process to encourage other writers and theorists thoroughly to work out the full implications of Steiner's work in so far as it can inform and underpin a new spiritualised psychotherapy. For it is becoming increasingly clear that, in its current form, modern 'professionalised' therapy is typically incapable of responding to the deep spiritual malaise of late modernity – a malaise which provides a great opportunity for Steiner's work to begin to influence a field which is crying out for the insights that his cosmology offers to those who are sufficiently open and ready to hear them.

If I am right in predicting that therapy will increasingly evolve in a spiritual direction, then as this process unfolds, the commonality between Jung and Steiner will become progressively clearer and more obvious – not least because the 'transpersonalising' of therapy as a healing practice will tend to bring it progressively closer to the kind of initiation path that Anthroposophy entails.

It would be churlish of me to re-enact the formulaic book reviewer's style of highlighting the 'rightness' or 'wrongness' of this book's contents (though it would have been nice to have an index!): for to do so would be entirely to miss the point – namely, that, as Robert Sardello points out, it is the dynamic tension arising from this richest of feasts that is crucial – together with what the reader him- or herself makes of it, of course, from their own unique perspective. It is also quite unavoidable that I have barely even scanned the terrain of the multitude of issues raised in and stimulated by *Jung and Steiner*. Like all really important books, this is one that will repay many readings, so subtle and complex are the questions it attempts to embrace.

Certainly, for anyone remotely interested in the fields of psychology, psychotherapy and counselling in so far as these healing practices relate to the transpersonal and the spiritual, and for anthroposophists and students of Rudolf Steiner open to deepening their engagement with the soul/spirit polarity, Wehr's book is quite simply indispensable reading.

PART III

Direct Challenges to the Professionalisation of Counselling and Psychotherapy

CHAPTER 13

Mowbray Distilled: A summary of Richard Mowbray's *The Case Against Psychotherapy Registration: A Conservation Issue for the Human Potential Movement*

INTRODUCTION

Great books stand the test of time, it is often said. The arguments so thoroughly and incisively set out in this remarkable book (referred to hereafter as *The Case*) have not been remotely responded to by those who still insist that the statutory regulation of psychotherapy and counselling would somehow be a beneficent process both for clients and for the field as a whole. Some years ago, an edition of BBC Radio 4's 'You and Yours' programme debated the regulation question, and the ensuing discussion illustrated just how inadequate the level of debate still is in this hotly contested area. First, there was the unchallenged assumption made in the programme that psychotherapy is a medical-model, '*health care*' issue. As *The Case* amply demonstrates, this is, to say the least, a highly contestable assumption which still seems to hold sway in the field outside of the Independent Practitioners Network and the more radical tendencies within the humanistic field. Indeed, the recent (2009) recommendations of the Health Professions Council's Professional Liaison Group for the state regulation of the psychological

---

As described in Chapter 1, Richard Mowbray's seminal text has become something of a bible for those within the psy field (not least, the Alliance for Counselling and Psychotherapy) who have grave concerns about the state and statutory regulation of the psychological therapies in Britain. Since I wrote this condensed verbatim summary of the book in the summer of 1995, I have received consistently positive feedback from practitioners wishing to be acquainted with the issues about regulation through a relatively easy-to-read summary of the central arguments. Because, as I write (July 2010), proposed psy regulation via the Health Health Professions Council is such a live issue in the UK, and because the arguments adduced in *The Case* are just as relevant today as they were 15 years ago, I've decided to reproduce 'Mowbray Distilled' in this book. The entire book is also downloadable free of charge at: www.transmarginalpress.co.uk as a pdf file. Finally, Richard Mowbray has given his kind permission for the verbatim text from his book to be reprinted here.

therapies in Britain (House 2009; Postle and House 2009) show conclusively that the medical-model view on therapeutic help is still very much alive and pre-eminent amongst the field's 'leaders'.

We were also told that 'The potential for abuse and incompetence [in this field] is enormous', and that 'the public remain unprotected'. Yet as many of us have consistently maintained, there is arguably not only no more potential for abuse in the therapy field than there is in many other spheres of activity, but the 'potential for abuse' seems to be expediently exaggerated by those pursuing statutory regulation (House 2009). As Mowbray himself argues, people/clients are far more resilient, and able to look after themselves, than the infantilising attitude of the pro-regulators give them credit for (Mowbray 1997). And it is indeed arguable that the institutional cementation in place of a state-sanctioned therapeutic orthodoxy might actually be far *more* abusive to clients than is the behaviour of the odd rogue unethical practitioner. At the very least, these questions need thorough and engaged debate from those who seem intent on state or statutory regulation.

Next, the field was repeatedly and quite uncritically referred to as 'the profession' – thereby assuming precisely that which has never been convincingly demonstrated in any of the field's burgeoning literature (cf. the many arguments in House and Totton 1997/2011).

The naïvely simplistic calculus seems to amount to the following assertion: 'There is damage done by/in therapy, *ergo* regulation will prevent it'. Yet as *The Case* convincingly shows, there is no clear reason whatsoever why state regulation will necessarily prevent damage or abuse in the peculiarly unique field of therapy and counselling. Indeed, there are compelling arguments suggesting that it could well actually *increase* the net level of abuse; and there has certainly been no attempt by the pro-regulators to argue through the logic and rationality of their dubious abuse-reduction assertion, despite repeated invitations to them to do so by myself and others over many years within the field's various professional journals.

We then heard the hoary old argument about the 'scandal' of anyone being able to call themselves a therapist: 'So are you saying that anyone should be allowed to call themselves a psychotherapist?', Denis Postle was asked. In practice, of course (which, after all, is all that surely matters), this simply hardly ever happens; and in those very rare cases where it *does* occur, it might be that the person is actually a very effective helper of others, notwithstanding (or even *because of?*) their limited therapy training; or if the person is indeed an inadequate or abusive practitioner, they simply won't get clients to any significant extent (not least because by far the majority of private-practice referrals surely come via word of mouth and/or personal recommendation – a far more effective regulator of good practice than the blunt bludgeon of state regulation).

Finally, there was no reference whatsoever in the programme to the demonstrable malaise that exists in the therapy field reported from the tightly state-regulated United States. For as a number of prominent and concerned authorities over there have argued (Professors Dan Hogan, Arnie Lazarus, Art Bohart…), the *net* harm that is done to the field as a whole by state regulation by far outweighs any limited and narrow benefits that might accrue from the 'outlawing' (and public 'naming and shaming' for good measure, *à la* BACP) of the odd rogue practitioner. At the very least, those favouring regulation have a responsibility adequately to demonstrate what the 'general equilibrium' effects of regulation would be on the field as a whole. And as Richard Mowbray and Juliana Brown themselves resoundingly conclude in *The Case*, 'Where there is a genuine need for [accountability] structures, we should develop structures that foster our values rather than betray them'.

In conclusion, I commend this book as strongly and passionately as when I first reviewed it in the mid-1990s. Certainly, many of the institutional shenanigans that have unfolded within and between the therapy bureaucracies over the past decade-and-a-half were entirely predictable from the analysis of power outlined in *The Case*. There could hardly be a greater tribute to Mowbray's book than the fact that its many and lucidly articulated arguments are just as relevant today as they were 15 years ago ago when the book was originally published.

ORIGINAL INTRODUCTION (FROM AUGUST 1995)

In 1995 Richard Mowbray published a book which was on merit of considerable importance in current debates on trends towards professionalisation within the counselling and psychotherapy fields in Britain. There had for some years been a substantial level of dissent within the humanistic psychology field, with profound uneasiness being expressed at the seemingly uncritical acceptance of, and acquiescence to, the drive towards registration and accreditation, yet such oppositional views had until then been somewhat disparate and diffuse.

In this book Richard Mowbray has drawn together and fully articulated the central arguments against registration in the psychotherapy and related fields; and with the publication of *The Case Against Psychotherapy Registration*, those with profound misgivings about the momentum of current developments were provided with a focus for their unease, and having at their disposal a comprehensive source of coherent, carefully thought-through and convincing arguments that call into severe question the very *raison d'être* of registration and professionalisation.

In August 1995 I attempted to distil the book's central arguments, using direct verbatim quotations from the text, and organised under a series of indicative headings. While I hope that this summary captures the essence of Mowbray's case against registration, it cannot substitute for a complete reading of this thoroughly documented monograph, the publication of which marked a pivotal moment in the development of the human potential movement in Britain.

****

MOWBRAY DISTILLED

Raison d' être

...calls for statutory registration to curb the 'menace' posed by 'unqualified' psychotherapists and suchlike practitioners have become more strident in the UK.... So far, the UK government has not been persuaded to introduce legislation to endorse any of [the proposed] registers.... However, such is the general lack of awareness of the arguments against such a move that governmental compliance might eventually be forthcoming. This book is an attempt to forestall that situation by raising the level of awareness of the issues involved and presenting the case against such statutory validation. (pp. 1–2).... Richard Mowbray explains why a conventional licensing system would be inappropriate, ineffective and actually harmful to the public interest. (flier)

A major concern of this book is to present a case for the maintenance of a clear boundary and appropriate terminological differentiation between human potential practice and psychotherapy with a view to the conservation of a broadly based and thriving human potential movement. (p. 4)

Inappropriate professionalization

...members of professions generally act as agents for their clients, carrying out for them tasks that they would not have the knowledge base to perform. I think that equating psychotherapy and even more so human potential practice with such professions is very misleading. Whilst the acquisition of an elaborate body of professional knowledge may be fundamental to competence in the typical profession, there is little reason to suppose that basic competence in psychotherapy or human potential work is founded on a similar basis. (p. 12)

I do not think it is appropriate to conceive of psychotherapy, counselling or personal growth work as 'professions' characterized by an elaborate body of knowledge inaccessible to their clients nor as activities in which the practitioners act as 'agents' in the sense of doing things for their clients which the clients are not capable of doing for themselves. (p. 79)

The European bogeyman

...the position in the European Community/Union regarding the regulation of psychotherapy (as of February 1995) is that there is no pressure from the Community institutions to introduce statutory regulation of psychotherapy in Member States.... It seems more likely that the supposed 'European pressure' has been a stalking horse for pressure from interested parties within the UK.... Increasingly this appears to me to be a classic case of a purported 'external threat' used to bolster domestic political objectives by harnessing the fear so engendered. (pp. 25–6)

...the main impetus [towards registration] seems to have been coming from a rather small nucleus of people within the movement (many with a vested interest in training) rather than from actual threats of regulation from outside. (p. 20)

United Kingdom Council for Psychotherapy (UKCP)

...the historical run-up to UKCP is... characterized more by fear, competition and rivalry than by altruism. (p. 52)

...[As of the mid-1990s – RH] approximately 90 per cent of [UKCP organizational members] are training and/or accrediting organizations. Training organizations have a particular vested interest in participating in regulation schemes like UKCP's, especially when a bandwagon has begun to roll. In a climate of uncertainty about the future right to practise and misinformation about the actual risks, prospective trainees may avoid organizations which are not 'approved'. Thus both training organizations and prospective trainees are under pressure to board the bandwagon whatever its merits.... The more established UKCP becomes and the more it is perceived as presaging some form of statutory control, the harder it may become to start up a new training organization, since potential trainees cannot be guaranteed eventual access to the register unless the organization is a UKCP member and the organization cannot become a member unless it has been running long enough and has enough graduates or trainees. This vicious circle for new organizations could effectively 'freeze' training in the hands of the established members and thereby stifle innovation. (pp. 55–6) UKCP is essentially an exclusive club for psychotherapy trainers – a political lobby for the psychotherapy training business. (p. 57)

...trainers are not... required to participate in any form of self and peer assessment. (p. 164) There is no representation of the public interest on the Boards of UKCP. There are no votes for consumer groups with an interest in the area.... Clients/patients (past, present or future) do not have any representation.... The non-training practitioner is barely represented in UKCP.... The Registration Board is the exclusive province of training and accrediting bodies. In sum, there is little involvement of the public interest, the consumer interest, the client interest, the trainee interest or the non-trainer practitioner interest in the core institutions of UKCP. (p. 57)

[UKCP] clearly intends to try to make its register a statutory one involving restriction of the use of the term 'psychotherapy' to those on its register. (p. 64) If [the register] becomes statutory..., it is likely to draw upon [the] public reflex of equating 'qualified', 'registered' practitioner with competence even though in this field, as we shall see, the equation does not hold. (p. 65)

Purported benefits of licensing

...the US context, where licensing is rampant, is ideal for studying what the effects of licensing actually are. (p. 78) Studies of disciplinary enforcement in professions in the USA have revealed that disciplinary action is extremely ineffective as a means of protecting the public. (p. 81) A recent investigation of the General Medical Council indicates that low levels of disciplinary enforcement are also the case in the UK.... Once established, professions are unlikely to take steps to actively expose [malpractice] in their midst. (p. 83) [There is a] poor track record of systems based on professional codes of ethics and conduct and self-disciplinary action as a means of protecting the public. (p. 84)

[Quoting J. Pfeffer]: It must be concluded that the outcomes of regulation and licensing are frequently not in the interests of the consumers or the general public. It is difficult to find a single empirical study of regulatory effects that does not arrive at essentially this conclusion. (p. 85)

Harmful side-effects of licensing

[Daniel B. Hogan] cites licensing laws as a significant factor in: (1) unnecessarily restricting the supply of practitioners [by introducing monopolistic factors into the market];... (2) inflating the cost of services;... (3) stifling innovation in the education and training of practitioners and in the organization and utilization of services; (4) discriminating against minorities... [by raising entry requirements in terms of time, cost and academic prerequisites]. (p. 86)

[Quoting Peter Breggin]: Overall, licensure laws enable groups of professionals to monopolize the psychotherapy market by locking out unlicensed competitors while guaranteeing a steady flow of clients and high fees for themselves (p. 142)

Pre-conditions for licensing not demonstrable

[Daniel B.] Hogan comes to the conclusion that laws that restrict a person's right to pursue an occupation... should not be enacted unless the following pre-conditions for licensing are met:

(a) *The profession or occupation being regulated must be mature and well established.* (p. 89) Psychotherapy does not meet these pre-conditions. It is not 'mature' and does not have a clearly defined area of practice which is capable of legal definition. (pp. 92–3)

(b) *The profession being regulated must have a clearly defined field of practice adequately differentiated from other professions.* (p. 90) Psychotherapy is not a unified field. There is not a consensus as to the values, goals and means amongst the activities that are referred to by this label. There are instead different underlying models, with different goals and values, vying for predominance. (p. 96–7) It is noteworthy that UKCP has established itself without apparently offering a public definition of psychotherapy, the activity which it seeks to oversee. (p. 52) [Quoting R. Leifer]: 'How can a professional group regulate an activity it is unable to define...? The answer, obviously, is that it cannot' (p. 97)

(c) *The benefits of licensing must outweigh the negative side effects.* (p. 90) [Quoting Hogan]: '...the harmful side-effects of licensing laws usually outweigh their supposed benefits'. (p. 86) ...the case against psychotherapy registration is that the effects of it would, on balance, actually be negative and represent a deterioration of the existing situation. This 'treatment' would be worse than the 'disease'. (p. 214) [See also earlier text under 'Purported benefits...' and 'Harmful side-effects...' – RH]

(d) *Simpler and less restrictive methods that would accomplish the same purposes must be unavailable (for example existing laws).* (p. 90) The existing situation regarding psychotherapy does not in general warrant any legislative changes other than what can usefully be effected as part of a general improvement in consumer legislation by legislative encouragement of the truthful, full disclosure of information relevant to any service, product or undertaking being offered for a reward. Such a general improvement in consumer legislation... would provide a cost-effective way of improving the existing situation regarding psychotherapy without the negative side-effects of creating a statutory monopoly. (pp. 215–16)

Laws that are applicable in this area as elsewhere include those concerning contracts, deception, truth in advertising (trade description), assault and breach of confidence (the creation of a legal obligation regarding confidentiality is not dependent upon professionalization). (p. 205)

(e) *The potential for significant harm from incompetent or unethical practitioners must exist and be extremely well documented.* (p. 90) Safeguarding the public from harm is the key argument upon which any claim for the legitimacy of a licensing system must rest. (p. 100) [Quoting Hogan]: 'The seemingly simple task of defining what constitutes an adverse result is in fact very difficult'. What constitutes... deterioration depends on how psychotherapy is conceived. (p. 101) ...[in Stanislav Grof's view] the intensity of what are regarded as symptoms under the medical model is actually an indication that a healing and transformative process is at work.... Most outcome studies of psychotherapy do seem to assume a medical model involving the diagnosis and treatment of psychopathology. (p. 103)

...even though the bias of research is liable to favour a medical model..., the evidence available does not appear to indicate that psychotherapy and personal growth work pose a particularly significant threat of harm to the public. Those who seek to justify the licensing of psychotherapy on this basis need to prove their case. (p. 106) [Quoting Michael Trebilcock and Jeffrey Shaul]:... 'if ignorance about what is a good or bad outcome, or what is good or bad procedure, is... pervasive..., then... no settled bench marks can be identified upon which to base any regulatory strategy directed to promoting service quality.' (p. 148)

(f) *Practitioner incompetence must be shown to be the source of harm.* (p. 91) ...rather than a simple Newtonian 'billiard ball' model of cause and effect which implies that the client is a passive recipient of the 'effects' of the psychotherapist, a more appropriate paradigm for looking at psychotherapy is that of 'Chaos Theory', in the light of which psychotherapy may be conceptualized as a non-linear system of mutually cueing feedback loops. ...Unfortunately one cannot do a 'double-blind' trial on a particular individual's life for the purposes of a control study. Reincarnation aside, we only have one shot. (pp. 106–7)

...it is by no means inevitable that an unequal balance of power and potential for abuse lies in the practitioner's favour. Such a view assumes that the situation is seen through the lens of a medical model..., whereas so much depends on the type of work and the type of client. (p. 111) [Quoting Hogan]: '...the lack of consensus as to what causes danger and how to measure it should prevent the enactment of laws restricting a person's right to practise... factors quite apart from the practitioner, such as the initial level of a patient's mental health, may account for a large share of the harm that occurs in therapy'. (p. 108)

(g) *The purpose of licensing laws must be the prevention of harm.* (p. 91) UKCP is promoting an increased academic content and higher academic prerequisites for training.... There is little if any evidence that the possession of academic qualifications by psychotherapists relates to basic competence or protects the public in any way. (p. 116) ...There is no clear evidence that professionally trained psychotherapists are in general more effective than paraprofessionals.

Privileging those with a background in medicine or psychology, lengthening the courses, increasing the academic prerequisites and content do not favour the most important variables that relate to basic competence in this area.... The personal qualities that are prerequisites of competence in this sort of activity cannot be 'trained in'.... (p. 118) ...Factors which UKCP is promoting, such as extending the duration of training, raising both the academic content and academic prerequisites for training courses, and fostering links with universities, will not produce more competent practitioners. (p. 124)

Does licensing necessarily prevent harm to clients?
[Quoting Hogan]: '...a similar array of horror stories could easily be assembled about highly credentialed psychiatrists and psychologists, all of them licensed'. (p. 105) ...Practitioner–client sex occurs in professions that are already licensed and have specific sanctions against it.... There is no clear evidence to [*sic*] that its incidence differs between licensed and unlicensed settings. (p. 112)

...The cases of abuse in therapy referred to by Masson... mainly involved practitioners who were already licensed professionals (i.e. medical doctors, clinical psychologists) and their resulting status in the community if anything made it harder to challenge their abuses. [Quoting Carl Rogers]: 'There are as many certified charlatans and exploiters of people as their are uncertified'. (p. 113) If protection of the public from harm has not been a proven consequence of such [licensing] systems in general, there is little prospect that such a system would protect the public in a field as indefinite as this one. (p. 114)

Fundamentals of practitioner competence

...The effectiveness of psychotherapy does not appear to depend upon any of the following: (1) The practitioner holding academic qualifications. (2) The length of training of the practitioner. (3) The school to which the therapist belongs. (4) The practitioner having had a training analysis. (p. 122)

[Quoting David Smail]: 'Empathy is of course important, but arises between people, and is not a quality (or "skill") possessed by individuals in some finite amount.' ...Perceptiveness (intuition?), talent and wisdom are also important factors. Jerome Frank believes that the therapist's personal qualities are the most significant factors and that techniques merely provide the ritual by which the personal changes are mediated. (p. 123) Some of the best practitioners may not be applying a 'developed body of psychological theory'.... Do good mothers mother on the basis of a 'developed body of mothering theory'? (p. 140)

Client choice of practitioner with and without licensing

...Establishing entry requirements [to the profession] that are not highly correlated with effectiveness restricts the size of the pool of people from whom the prospective client can choose an appropriate practitioner for themselves. The chances of finding someone with the appropriate personal characteristics are correspondingly reduced. (p. 124) [In choosing a practitioner to work with] there are no easily applied external qualifications that you can trust. (p. 127)

...Given access to appropriate information..., clients are the best judges of who are the competent practitioners for them, and on the basis of their personal responses to practitioners (and the approaches that they offer) rather than on the basis of misleading criteria such as those that UKCP promotes. (p. 124) Supporting the potential client's existing autonomy, whatever degree of 'adult' they already have, by empowering them with information and relevant questions to help them make the judgements that only they can make, is more appropriate than enhancing the official status of the practitioner with the accompanying assumption that competence has been assured. (p. 131)

With regard to safe selection of a therapist, discouraging transference and concomitant regression and encouraging what adult functioning and autonomy the person already has is the more appropriate stance.... The accreditation route fostered by UKCP promotes the myth that the public can be protected from the difficulties of choice in this area..., [which] actually increases the potential risk of harm to the public.... (p. 129) Potential clients can become lulled into a false sense of security and suspension of judgement by such a system. It encourages them to defer to the authority of... the institutions backed by the state that give [the practitioner] credibility... in a way that fosters dependency and a letting down of appropriate self-protective guards. (p. 130) ...It is attribution of a status of 'expert' to the practitioner that is likely to raise the client's suggestibility, and make them more vulnerable to errors [like 'false memory syndrome'] ...Vulnerability... is proportional to the power that the prospective client gives away to the practitioner. Official recognition based on unconfirmed criteria begets vulnerability. (p. 131)

Training, vested interests and monopolization

[Quoting Mark Aveline]: '...the correlation between training and effectiveness as a therapist is low'. (p. 132)

I am doubtful about the quality of personal work that can be effected as a course requirement. If it is being done in order to 'qualify' it is no longer really 'personal'. The pace and rhythm is no longer determined by personal growth factors alone and instead is subject to career ambition and compliance with outer pressures. (p. 133) [Quoting Guy Gladstone]: '...Becoming a therapist is a personally transmitted craft for which no amount of academic course work can substitute'. The apprenticeship model..., which involves working alongside a more experienced 'craftsperson'..., is in many ways more appropriate (particularly for humanistic work) than training programmes modelled after traditional professional disciplines.... (p. 135)

[Quoting Nick Totton]: 'Within psychotherapy people have been jockeying for position, putting their training courses and accreditation procedures in place, inventing hurdles for the next generation – hurdles they themselves will never have to jump!' Trainers... have the overwhelming say in UKCP compared with non-professional practitioners. (p. 132) Given sufficient acknowledgement by state and private health care funding systems, even without statutory registration, professional organizations may come to exercise a degree of power over access to employment and fee reimbursement that amounts to a form of indirect, *de facto* regulation – at least of psychotherapy or counselling offered as treatment.... A tie-in with insurance companies may occur whereby employers may require prospective employees to carry professional indemnity insurance and yet insurers only recognize members of the professional organizations as being eligible or the employing agency's insurance may require membership of, say, UKCP or BAC[P] by employees as a prerequisite for cover.... The unlicensed are in effect 'starved out'. (p. 147)

Standardized practice, professional indemnity and 'defensive psychotherapy'

...[A rigidified code of practice as a] means of addressing the problem of the morally deficient practitioner has the effect of requiring a standardization of practice..., [which] is akin to throwing the baby out with the bathwater.... (p. 150) ...As with the global ecosystem, 'species diversity' (pejoratively referred to as 'fragmentation' in this area) provides a greater prospect of long term health for the system than a 'monocrop'. (p.214) [This] is a system that encourages a legitimized mediocrity. (p. 154) Codes of ethics and practice are no substitute for inner integrity on the part of the practitioner. Clients should not be encouraged to believe otherwise.... (p. 150) What is fostered by such circumstances is not a fertile and innovative field but conformity of practice based not so much on true standards... as on practitioner self-protection – the practice of 'defensive psychotherapy'. Practitioners will do or not do things in order to avoid disciplinary action, malpractice suits and/or the invalidating of their insurance cover, rather than solely on the basis of whether or not the client would benefit.... In litigation-happy USA,... the effect [of the widespread practice of 'defensive medicine'] on the quality and availability of care has been 'disastrous' [quoting Jeremy Holmes and Richard Lindley]. (pp. 150–1) ...The practice of defensive psychotherapy tends towards passivity and a retreat into an interaction that is, at best, verbal....

So far, in the UK the likelihood of being sued, never mind successfully sued, for professional negligence as a psychotherapist has been almost zero.... (p. 153) So, members of UKCP are required to insure themselves against a risk that is virtually non-existent at the present time.... (p. 154) What appears to be on offer in such registration schemes is a sort of bogus insurance policy representing a collusion with regressive urges for a risk-free existence where responsibility for key life decisions is lifted from the individual by benevolent 'experts'.... Taking out the policy increases the risk! (p. 214) ...The prevalence of professional indemnity insurance makes a suit worth pursuing. (p. 151)

Seeking redress of a financial or punitive nature via the legal and insurance systems is rarely appropriate for an activity whose stock in trade is 'unfinished business' of an emotional nature. Encouraging a settlement on the level at which the problem exists – the emotional, the relational – perhaps with the aid of a facilitator or mediator, is usually more relevant than fostering an escalation to the level of litigation and insurance claims. (p. 154)

Distinguishing between human potential work and psychotherapy
...Activities of the human potential movement do not readily fit into the pre-existing social categories... and really deserve a category of their own.... I propose a terminological clarification to prevent human potential work becoming inappropriately subsumed, to reduce a source of client confusion, and also to attempt to distance clients involved in human potential work from the stigmatization of the 'patient' that so frequently accompanies remedial mental health treatments. (p. 159)

...Humanistic organizations and practitioners... have increasingly gravitated towards use of the term 'psychotherapy'. (p. 161) ...in pursuit of professional status,... humanistic organizations have gone along with all the non-humanistic features of UKCP, such as academic bias, the aim of a post-graduate profession, the medicalized thinking and terminology, the lack of representation and the absence of any humanistic form of accreditation such as true self and peer assessment.... The medical model and the model of a profession akin to medicine has been allowed to creep into humanistic psychology. (p. 166)

...The term ['psychotherapy'] was devised during the early years of scientific medicine.... 'Psychotherapy' is a nineteenth-century medical model word (p. 168) ...that has also been used indiscriminately to describe approaches that do not assume a medical model. (p. 188) The term 'psychotherapy' illustrates the 'linear', cause-and-effect, Newtonian-Cartesian basis for the medical model that held sway at the time of its coining. (p. 189) ...The choice of labels with which you ally yourself becomes a matter of crucial importance.... (p. 169) Labels are particularly important in this area because they shape people's expectations. They can be likened to verbal 'buttons' or 'triggers' that activate underlying models or metaphors and expectations appropriate to the model that is 'engaged'. (p. 187) Human potential practitioners have not fostered sufficient public awareness of an unambiguous distinguishing label for their work.... (p. 169) ...Self-realization processes and processes concerned with 'adjustment' and remedial restoration to 'normality' should not be addressed by the same terminology. (p. 187)

...Not least [because of] the risk that UKCP may attempt to go beyond the title protection of the term 'psychotherapy', I feel that its attempt to legally restrict the use of this term should, from a human potential movement point of view, be resisted even if one does not wish to use it. (p. 171)

[Quoting Juliana Brown and himself]: 'The key thing for us is that the Human Potential Movement is a manifestation of a different model, a holistic growth model'. (p. 172) The human potential practitioner is often under sustained pressure from clients and the wider society to revert from the human potential model to the dominant cultural model of 'therapeutic treatment'. (p. 175) [There has been a] gravitation of many human potential practitioners towards the world of conventional psychotherapy.... (p. 176) [In contrast to the psychotherapeutic medical model approach] human potential work is... focused on self-actualization. ...The approach is non-clinical and the orientation is towards growth... rather than deficiency... (p. 181) – fulfilling more of the potential of who you really are, rather than narrowly focusing on the cure of a 'disorder', the relief of symptoms or the resolving of a problem. It is concerned... with the emergence of authentic being..., [with] the meaning [of psychological and emotional phenomena] for the person [being] explored rather than efforts made to cure, suppress or eliminate them. (p. 182) ...In human potential work the practitioner does not apply treatments to the client, instead the client is seen as the 'expert' – on himself. (p. 183) The practitioner's role is to facilitate, to 'be with', to sit alongside.... The basis for relationship is one of 'informed agreement to explore' rather than 'informed consent to treatment'.... (p. 184)

Preserving a counter-cultural space

Because it addresses the 'normal', the movement that carries that process must stay on the margin and not be 'absorbed', not be tempted by the carrots of recognition, respectability and financial security into reverting to the mainstream but rather remain – on the 'fringe' – as a source that stimulates, challenges convention and 'draws out' the unrealized potential for 'being' in the members of that society. (pp. 198–9) A society needs a healthy fringe – a finge that is on the edge but not split-off in cult-like isolation. It is the seedbed from which much of what is novel will spring. It is where ideas that are ahead of their time will germinate and grow, later to be adopted by the mainstream. In order to remain a fertile seedbed the fringe needs to be legitimate rather than driven underground or 'criminalized' – which would stifle it, but also it must not be absorbed into the mainstream – which would stultify it with 'establishment' thinking and respectability. (p. 199)

    ...The rise of the 'therapy bureaucracies' and the possibility of their statutory endorsement poses a threat to the vitality of the 'fringe' – a threat which, in my view, those who value human potential work would be well advised to resist. (p. 200)

Viable alternatives to statutory licensing

(a) *Education*: ...in the interests of an informed consumer choice, the public could be better educated as to the criteria which are most pertinent to consider when undertaking psychotherapy, including what to look for in selecting a practitioner.... Information could also be made available about the potential pitfalls of the work, and what is best avoided or approached with caution on the basis of the evidence available.... Promoting a better understanding of the nature of transference in general and its pervasiveness both inside and outside the therapy situation should be an important educational goal. (p. 204) Rather than waste public funds in the inefficiencies of a licensing system, it would be more appropriate and effective to finance endeavours to educate the public as to the relevant factors to look for in a practitioner and what to expect from different types of work. (p .205)

(b) *The application of existing laws*: [see 'Pre-conditions for licensing...', and (d)]

(c) *Full disclosure provisions*: Full disclosure provisions are concerned with empowering the public to make informed decisions in their choice of practitioner by allowing them access to full relevant information. (p. 205) [Quoting Will Schutz]: 'All persons offering services aimed at enhancing the human condition [in whatever way] would be required to provide potential customers with a full disclosure of all information relevant to the competence of the professional. Such information would include the practitioner's education, training, philosophy, fees, membership in professional organizations, awards, and anything else the professional feels is relevant.' The role of the law in a full disclosure system would be to determine the veracity and completeness of the information, and to police lying and deceit, rather than to decide who is or who is not competent and thereby usurping the consumer's choice. So, rather than the client having someone else decide who is competent as with a licensing system, this decision would remain theirs but on the basis of full and accurate information. (p. 206) Full disclosure is a system that can support a pluralism that reflects the variety in this area rather than the standardization and conservatism that tends to emerge from licensing systems.

(d) *Non-credentialed registration*: Hogan... recommends a system of regulation in which the would-be practitioner registers with a state board of control for a nominal fee and without having to meet any educational, experiential or other prerequisites before being granted the right to practise.... Under a non-credentialed system, full disclosure of all relevant information would be required as part of the registration. In addition, practitioners would be required to inform clients as to how, if dissatisfied, they can file complaints with the state registration board (or an 'ombudsman' perhaps). Practitioners would be required to distribute evaluation forms to clients at the end of the working relationship. A sufficient number of negative responses would trigger the attention of a disciplinary board – a board whose composition would reflect a balanced representation of interests, including members of the public, clients and government officials along with practitioners, but it would not be dominated by members of the profession.... (p. 209) Such a system avoids the drawbacks of restricting entry to the occupation on the basis of qualifications that may not be related to competence or performance whilst allowing a means of halting those who do prove for whatever reason to be harmful. ...A levy could be made on practitioners, the money to be used to finance research and fund the education of the public.... (p. 210)

(e) *Self and peer assessment and accreditation*: IDHP [The Institute for the Development of Human Potential] has been using self and peer assessment and accreditation... since the mid-1970s and has refined these processes to a high degree.... Another forum in which alternative forms of accreditation have been explored was that provided by 'the Cambridge Conferences' [on accreditation] organized by the Norwich Collective [in 1991 and 1992].... ...Recently Nick Totton proposed the creation of a self and peer accredited network, a concept conceived in conjunction with Em Edmonson.... The ensuing organization, the 'Independent Therapists Network', is intended to be free from hierarchy and low on bureaucracy and to '...offer an alternative model of accountability and validation to that of the UK Council for Psychotherapy....' (p. 240) The basis of the Network is a linking of small groups of therapists who vet and accredit the members of their own group.... Each group would also have cross-linkages with other groups.... The Network does not seek to distinguish between different types of work, '...since we see a richly pluralistic and multi-skilled ecology as the ideal' [quoting the ITN publicity leaflet]. Rather than a central code of practice, each peer group can create one appropriate to its activities. This sort of practitioner validation through membership of a small group of peers is amongst the most flexible, practical and least detrimental arrangements for monitoring 'bad work'.... The proposed Network would go beyond this through the notion of cross linking with other groups for the purposes of support, 'oversight' and as part of the complaints procedure. (p. 241)

CODA

A thorough investigation of the case for a 'protected' profession reveals a tale of flimsy historical underpinnings, professional and political shenanigans and vested interests. [book flier] UKCP has acquired a bureaucratic momentum and a 'bandwagon' has begun to roll, driven I think more by fear and fatalism than by wisdom.... ...The establishment of what is merely a voluntary register by UKCP has already had a deadening effect on practice, training and innovation. (p. 3) If legislative restrictions such as those sought by UKCP et al. are to be introduced in Britain, the onus should be upon those who favour this change to prove the necessity and to substantiate their position that the restrictions they seek would be beneficial. I am of the opinion that the case for statutory registration in this field does not stand up to scrutiny. ...The balance of available evidence indicates that in all probability [statutory registration] would do more harm than good. (p.4) [Quoting Schutz]: 'Licensing does not protect the public. Licensing does not exclude incompetents. Licensing does not encourage innovation. It stultifies....' (p. 213) [Quoting Juliana Brown and himself] 'Where there is a genuine need for structures, we should develop structures that foster our values rather than betray them'. (p. 225)

CHAPTER 14

Ahead of His Time:
Carl Rogers on 'Professionalism', 1973

> Perhaps the safety, the prestige, the vestments of traditionalism that
> can be earned through certification and licensure may not be worth
> the cost. I have wondered aloud if we would dare to rest our
> confidence in the quality and competence we have as persons, rather
> than the certificates we can frame on our walls.
>
> (Carl Rogers, from 'Some new challenges to the helping
> professions', p. 374)

In this tribute to Carl Rogers, I want to offer a retrospective on his
outstanding and inspirational article 'Some new challenges to the helping
professions', published almost 40 years ago. On re-reading this seminal
article, what strikes me most is its freshness and telling prescience for anyone
concerned with the present state and future development of the 'psy' field
in Britain. 'Ahead of its time', 'definitive' and 'seminal' are not descriptors
to be thrown around lightly; but if I had to pick an article from the literature
which for me offers *the* most convincing argument against the institutional
regulation of therapy, it would be too close to call between John Heron's
brilliant paper 'The politics of transference' (orig. 1990, and reproduced as
Chapter 1 in the *Implausible Professions* anthology, 1997/2011); and Carl
Rogers' masterly article, the latter being published some years before Dan
Hogan's exhaustive 4-volume *tour de force, The Regulation of Psychotherapists*
(1979), and over twenty years before Richard Mowbray's formidable anti-
regulation treatise, *The Case Against Psychotherapy Registration* (1995; see
Chapter 13, this volume).

It is fascinating that the founder of person-centred therapy, Carl R. Rogers, was
expressing very similar concerns about the pernicious nature of
professionalisation in the psy field some 40 years ago. I was asked to write the
following piece for a commemorative issue of *Ipnosis* magazine to mark the
centenary anniversary of Rogers' birth. The towering historical figures of our
field commonly expressed a perennial wisdom that is eminently transferable
between generations; and in his extraordinary 1973 article - which is, if anything,
more relevant to our current plight than when he wrote it in the American context
- Rogers reveals himself to be one of those giants on whose shoulders we
falteringly attempt to stand.

In what follows I will highlight the relevance of Rogers' 'helping professions' article for illuminating the arguments about statutory registration that are (thankfully, and at long last) beginning to spread throughout the institutions of therapy (most notably, the UKCP and the BACP). That Rogers' prophetically incisive arguments have stood the test of time across some nearly four decades is testimony both to the enduring universality of perennial wisdom, and to the quality of insight possessed by this remarkable man – some other examples of which will no doubt be recounted by other contributors to this *Ipnosis* centenary symposium (*Ipnosis* 2002).

Rogers' article (which, for ease of reference, is usefully reproduced in *The Carl Rogers Reader* – Kirschenbaum and Henderson 1989) would make compelling reading on any general 'Sociology of Professionalism' course. Rogers poses five distinct questions which focus on 'the challenges that are currently facing us, or will… face us in the near future' (1989: 358). He asks, first, whether the psychology profession dares to develop a new conception of science; second and relatedly, whether our current taken-for-granted notion of 'reality' is the only one; third, whether we dare to be designers of society rather than reactive 'fire-fighters'; and whether we dare allow ourselves to be whole human beings. In this short chapter, however, I will reluctantly confine myself to Rogers' third question, constituting one section of about four pages (pp. 363–7), and provocatively titled 'Dare we do away with professionalism?'.

In just four pages, Rogers succeeds in elegantly distilling a quite devastating indictment of 'the professionalising mentality'; and one of the more remarkable features of the current therapy landscape is that, to my knowledge, not one of the proponents of therapy's state or statutory regulation has even *acknowledged*, let alone engaged with, Rogers' anti-professionalisation arguments. In Nick Totton's parlance, it has essentially been 'ignored to death' by the nascent therapy 'profession'; and I hope the current chapter helps to re-awaken a richly deserved interest in this much-neglected paper.

Rogers began by referring to 'the radical possibility of sweeping away our procedures for professionalization' (p. 363) – and the 'terror' that such a possibility strikes in the heart of the psy professional. For Rogers, 'as soon as we set up criteria for certification…, the first and greatest effect is to freeze the profession in a past image' – an '*inevitable*' result, he maintains (p. 364). For Rogers, then, certification is always, and necessarily, rooted in the past, and inevitably defines the profession in those terms.

Secondly, Rogers starkly exposed the flakiness of the one argument consistently adduced to support regulation – 'protection of the public'– when he wrote:

> there are many with diplomas on their walls who are not fit to do therapy…. [T]here are as many *certified* charlatans and exploiters of people as there are uncertified…. Certification is *not* equivalent to competence…, [and] tight professional standards do not, to more than a minimal degree, shut out the exploiters and the charlatans.
>
> (pp. 364, 365, Rogers' emphases)

A pernicious and hyperactive 'surveillance culture' and 'low-trust ideology' have recently swamped our institutions without public debate, and with minimal public awareness (e.g. Power 1997; Clarke et al. 2000; Cooper 2001; House 2000, 2007a). The fashionable drive towards the state or statutory regulation of therapy is arguably yet another case of such uncritical 'control-freakery'; and it would surely be a tragedy if the field were unwittingly to collude with such damaging cultural forces. Any remaining semblance of creativity, innovation and child-centredness within the mainstream education field, for example, has been comprehensively decimated by this mentality and the soul-less aridity of 'modernity' (House 2000, 2007a). If Carl Rogers were alive now in the UK, he would surely be arguing that it would be a disaster for a therapy field that makes claims to openness, awareness and insight to embrace pernicious values and practices such as these.

Thirdly, Rogers indicts the tendency for professionalisation to 'build up a rigid bureaucracy' (p. 364). Issues of quality so easily come to be neglected, and 'The bureaucrat is beginning to dominate the scene in ways that are all too familiar, setting the professional back enormously' (p. 365).

Rogers goes on to argue not only that there are plenty of psy workers who are 'unqualified' by conventional standards but who are nonetheless 'both dedicated and competent' (ibid.; one immediately thinks of the enormous voluntary counselling sector here), but further, that 'If we were less arrogant, we might also learn much from the "uncertified" individual, who is sometimes unusually adept in the area of human relationships' (pp. 365–6). The important work of Peter Lomas and David Smail comes to mind, with their emphasis on the healing value of unaffected *ordinariness,* in contrast to the often precious professionalised mentality which can so easily come to dominate psychotherapeutic 'regimes of truth' (House 1999a, 2003a; see Chapter 6, this volume).

Rogers continues, 'If we certify or otherwise give… individuals superior status as helpers, their helpfulness declines. They then become "professionals", with all of the exclusiveness and territoriality that mark the professional' (pp. 366–7). I am reminded here of a personal communication I received from Professor Art Bohart (then of the Psychology Department at California State University, Dominguez Hills), commenting on the American situation in the mid-1990s: 'I'm sorry to hear about the fight over licensure in Great Britain.... The battle, of course, is lost over here, and we are busy becoming more and more medical-like, rapidly losing our human souls. But we are a "Profession" ' (quoted in House and Totton 1997: 336). It is somewhat of a cliché that what happens in the USA almost inevitably follows here some years later; yet surely if we listen to the dire warnings given by Professor Bohart and others, a responsible and mature field still has time to choose *not* to pursue the statutory regulation route (House 2001b), with all its unwanted and unpredictable side-effects – and to find a better way. Certainly, it is highly noteworthy that in his article, Rogers expressed deep regret at not himself having stood out against the formation of the American Board of Examiners in Professional Psychology in the late 1940s. And just as it is unknown for turkeys to vote for (an early) Christmas, so it is also quite unheard of for 'professions' to legislate themselves out of existence.... So let everyone who deeply cares about the future of the therapy and human potential field take note: *once the regulatory path is engaged with, there will almost certainly be no turning back;* and, like Rogers in the 1970s, we will almost certainly be left to repent at our leisure.

Rogers posed perhaps *the* crucial accountability question, when he wrote: 'Can psychology find a new and better way? Is there some more creative method of bringing together those who need help and those who are truly excellent in offering helping relationships?' (p. 366). Rogers did offer a positive (if little-fleshed-out) proposal for an alternative to soul-less professionalisation, when he wrote that

> we might set up the equivalent of a Consumer Protective Service.... If many complaints come in about an individual's services to the public, then his [sic] name should be made available to the public, with the suggestion 'Let the buyer beware'.
>
> (p. 367)

Both Mowbray (1995) and Hogan (e.g. 1999, 2003) have taken this kind of proposal further, and the most comprehensive alternative framework for accountability yet developed is that of Postle (2003). (Currently at the time of writing, July 2010, such a system is being developed and set up for therapy practitioners in the Bristol area – RH.) With these detailed proposals shortly to be out in the public sphere and drawn to the attention of government, *there is no longer the slightest justification for arguing that there is no viable alternative to statutory regulation.*

It is interesting that in his latter years, Carl Rogers moved more and more in a transpersonal, even mystical direction (Thorne 2002a). There have indeed been interesting parallel discussions and controversies about 'professionalism' within the pastoral field. Herrick and Mann (1998: 103) epigraphically quote Alistair Campbell (no relation!), who wrote, 'If we professionalise pastoral care, we will lose the spontaneity and simplicity which characterises love'. They interestingly point out that the term 'profession' originally referred to the public declaration of faith associated with *a life of religious devotion* (p. 104, quoting Campbell). Herrick and Mann also draw what is surely a crucial distinction for the therapy field – between 'being professional' (adjective) and 'being *A* professional' (noun). For them, Jesus himself was certainly not *a* 'professional' in the *modern* sense: rather, he was 'a maverick in splendid isolation!' (p. 108) (rather like the so-called 'wild analyst' – see House 1997b; Chapter 21, this volume) – 'neither detached... nor emotionally neutral' (p. 109). Further, 'Jesus was "untrained". His knowledge and expertise came in the form of a natural "gifting" in relating to people and a unique sensitivity to the prompting of the Holy Spirit' (p. 106). Jesus also *'reversed all the world's hierarchies* in his own nature.... The great challenge... is to learn how to de-egotize leadership' (Richard Holloway, quoted on p. 110, my emphasis). I think much of this is consonant with what Carl Rogers was saying in, or implying by, his seminal 1973 article.

Returning briefly to the more profane matters of modern 'professionalism': thankfully, the debate about therapy's regulation has recently been opened up within the UKCP (House 2001b); and in the counselling (recently renamed the 'counselling and psychotherapy') field (by the BAC*P*), several major figures have recently dared to address an issue which had erstwhile been studiously ignored. Coming as it does from the Chair of the UKRC executive, Ian Horton's recent paper (2002) is well worth reading; yet it is notable that in his discussion of 'Arguments against regulation' (pp. 59–60), he makes no attempt to refute those arguments. Rather, he simply invokes the *ex cathedra* technique of tacitly dismissing one's opponents by referring to their arguments as 'vitriolic' and 'polemical' (p. 59) – as if this were somehow of itself sufficient to refute those very arguments. Perhaps it is precisely because of this kind of attitude to the manifold arguments against professionalisation that its critics often feel driven to resort to polemic and passion! Moreover, there is simply no basis to assume, as Horton and other supporters of professionalisation commonly do, that 'professional bodies, *presumably reflecting the views of the majority of practitioners*, either accept the inevitability of some form of regulation or welcome it as an important milestone in the evolution of the profession' (ibid.: 50, my emphasis).

The recent intervention by Brian Thorne (2002b) is far closer to the critical dissenting tradition demonstrated in Rogers' article. For Thorne 'smell[s] the allurement of the "closed shop" and the not easily disguised smugness of the "expert" who can claim the power to exclude' (p. 4); and 'Behind much of the thinking and activity directed towards statutory registration, I detect not humility but scarcely veiled arrogance and power seeking....' (p. 5). Certainly, with such formidable cohorts as the late Carl Rogers and Professor Thorne challenging so convincingly the foundational rationale for statutory regulation, 'the profession' must surely think long and very hard before pursuing a path which may do untold – not to mention quite *unpredictable* – damage to all that is best in therapeutic practice.

In this short tribute commemorating Carl Rogers' centenary, it's only right that he should have the final word. In a statement that resounds across the decades, and whose recommendation this journal itself [*Ipnosis*] is doing so much to actualise, he wrote: 'If we did away with "the expert", "the certified professional", "the licensed psychologist", we might open our profession to a breeze of fresh air, a surge of creativity, such as it has not known for years' (p. 366).... Amen to that.

CHAPTER 15

Unconsciously Generating Inevitability? Workable accountability alternatives to the statutory regulation of the psychological therapies

Co-written with Denis Postle

It is our intention in this text to have it reflect the live dialogue of our joint conference presentation. We'll begin by outlining its scope. We start by saying something about why we are here, what brought us to contribute to this book (Parker and Revelli 2008), and following that we will catalogue the downside, as we see it, of current proposals for statutory regulation of the psychological therapies. We then move on at greater length to introduce the Independent Practitioners Network (IPN), a substantial innovative response to the culture of institutional professionalisation that has in recent years come to dominate the British psychopractice field. We end with a perspective on the likely next steps that will need to be considered if present plans for statutory regulation are to be successfully interrupted and undermined (and here, note, we refer to 'statutory regulation' as *an aspect of* the 'state regulation' which is the main concern of Parker and Revelli 2008).

WHY ARE WE CONTRIBUTING TO THIS BOOK?

We are two experienced therapy practitioners who come from a broadly humanistic, human-potential background (though we are deeply influenced by a range of therapeutic approaches and perspectives), and together we

A version of this chapter was first co-presented with my IPN colleague Denis Postle at a March/April 2006 conference on 'Psychoanalysis and State Regulation' held at the London School of Economics and organised by the Institute of Social Psychology and the College of Psychoanalysts – UK. The papers presented at the conference were subsequently published in the book *Psychoanalysis and State Regulation*, edited by Ian Parker and Simona Revelli (Karnac Books, 2008). It reads to me as one of the most convincingly expressed arguments against the statutory regulation of the psychological therapies that I've been involved in writing.

share approaching four decades of consistent therapy practice of diverse kinds and in a range of different settings. We have both published extensively in the literature on the professionalisation of psychotherapy and counselling (see, for example, Ipnosis, an Internet journal for the Independent Practitioners Network [IPN], and before that g.o.r.i.l.l.a., now an Internet archive of the many cogent attempts to confront the professionalisation of psychopractice in the last 20–25 years, during which time we have been at the forefront of the British challenge to the statutory regulation of the psychological therapies in this country).

The early stages of the professionalisation of counselling and psychotherapy looked and felt like colonisation, or turf wars between rival factions – one of which, the United Kingdom Council for Psychotherapy (UKCP), behaved variously like a trainers club and a trade association, speaking the rhetoric of 'client protection' whilst, seen up close, being driven by the need to capture and sustain the practitioner 'training industry' (Gladstone 1997). Denis Postle (DP) began taking the colonisation seriously when the then chair of the UKCP (Emmy van Deurzen) started talking about overgrown gardens and getting rid of the 'weeds' of which, according to her criteria, he was clearly one.

A second wake-up call was the bizarre episode of the Alderdice Psychotherapy Bill that sought to capture the high ground for the psychoanalytic community. A text in which everyone mentioned is male, and which didn't survive first contact with the British Association for Counselling and Psychotherapy (BACP), who were understandably furious to have been ignored in the Bill's development. Richard House (RH) had a lot to say about the damage wrought by professionalisation, including co-editing and extensively contributing to two books, and writing a third. The corrupting effects of the drive for professionalisation were soon confirmed by the extraordinary experience of a publisher turning down the RH/Totton co-edited text *Implausible Professions* (1997/2011) on the grounds that they didn't want to upset the UKCP, who also published with them.

DP's resistance took a different route, using family resources to build and maintain several web sites devoted to writing for and building archives of essential texts. (See the relevant web address at the end of this chapter – Postle nd.) Our experience overall has been that what there is to say about the damage that statutory regulation will cause has been said, much of it many times over. Our experience, as Nick Totton has remarked, has been of *Totsweigen*, or 'being ignored to death'. We have yet to find a substantial text that argues cogently, and with adequate evidence, in favour of statutory regulation.

Both of us were freshly energised by Richard Mowbray's eagerly-awaited and long trailed book, *The Case Against Psychotherapy Registration: A*

Conservation Issue for the Human Potential Movement (see Chapter 13, this volume), which proved to be well worth the wait when it eventually appeared in 1995. *The Case* (as it soon became colloquially christened) very quickly became the 'bible' for practitioners in the field who had severe doubts about the whole direction in which the British therapy field seemed to be headed. RH remembers with great clarity and pleasure the effect that *The Case* had on him when he first read it. Here, for the first time in Britain, was an immaculately documented and thoroughly compelling rationale for all the unease he and others had felt since the professionalisation/accreditation issue had come to prominence some years earlier. Certainly, for anyone wishing to acquaint themselves with the history and advisability of therapy regulation, Mowbray's *Case* is still the indispensable starting-point, and is as freshly relevant today as it was well over a decade ago.

For those sufficiently open to see it, there seemed to us to exist a growing undercurrent of deep unease about the form and direction of therapy professionalisation in Britain; and hot on the heals of *The Case*, a second book and natural kind of sequel, *Implausible Professions*, co-edited with Nick Totton (House and Totton 1997/2011), sought to give a coherent form to those previously disparate voices. In the succeeding years it was followed by *Ethically Challenged Professions* (co-edited with Yvonne Bates and RH), and RH's *Therapy Beyond Modernity: Deconstructing and Transcending Profession-Centred Therapy*. More recently, DP has published his collected writings from almost 20 years of scrutiny of professionalisation and statutory regulation, *Regulating the Psychological Therapies: From Taxonomy to Taxidermy* (Postle 2007).

A third element of concern for us has been the extent to which regulation proposals look to be another instance of the UK's 'surveillance culture' that sees regulation of psychotherapy and counselling in terms of targets, measurement and 'evidence-based' practice (King and Moutsou 2010). As if this 'audit culture' weren't only too obviously a form of attempted (but, we maintain, futile) domestication of the unavoidable unpredictability, wildness and uncertainties of working with the hurts, humiliations and unhelpful happenstances with which clients come into therapy (Cooper 2001). As with most overweening, control-fixated state interventions like this one, the unintended negative side-effects will almost certainly outweigh by far any benefits which might ensue from the regulatory regime. What is perhaps most disturbing of all is that no attempt seems to have been made either by Government or by the therapy institutions to research into such side-effects, and to make an informed decision about statutory regulation based on all the possible complex countervailing impacts – including looking in detail at the system-wide impact of introduced regulation in other countries (cf. Hogan

1979). That such an investigative process has apparently not even been considered strongly suggests that the regulatory process has far more to do with ideology ('Modernity') and economic self-interest than it does with either client protection in particular or rational argument more generally.

THE DOWNSIDE OF STATUTORY REGULATION

We have been diligent across our two decades of resistance to statutory regulation to point to the accumulated research and inquiry of other people who have broadly shared our concerns. Hogan (1979, 2003) and Mowbray (1995) show how statutory regulation will very likely: restrict the supply of practitioners; inflate costs of services; stifle innovation in education and training; discriminate unnecessarily; and lead to 'defensive' therapeutic practice. All the major psychopractice organisations have openly used fear of being left out, fear of not being able to work, the 'trance inductions' of the 'inevitability' of statutory regulation, together with the un-researched assertions of the need for 'client protection', as crass instruments with which to shepherd (or scare) their generally deferential flocks in the direction of signing up to whatever might be the current form of regulation.

And as problematic in its own way is the tolerance of (or ignorance about) substantial incongruence between 'power over', top-down 'command and control' in the accountability structures that administer statutory regulation, on the one hand, and 'power with' behaviour in the working alliance with clients, on the other. Does no one else see this as damaging to clients' interests? After all, as David Smail and others have argued (Smail 2001), do not many or even most clients bring issues to therapy that in some sense centre on questions of authority, deference, exploitation, victimisation and the abuse of power?

We have also become aware of the widely shared sense that statutory regulation rides on several fallacies that have been vigorously contradicted by a variety of critics. One of these is that advanced/extended training and further (often quasi-academic) education necessarily lead to (increased) therapeutic effectiveness (see Bohart and Tallman 1996). There are also compelling arguments and associated research evidence suggesting that newly qualified or lightly trained paraprofessionals in the field can do therapy work which is at least as effective as highly trained practitioners (RH has set out some plausible reasons to account for such an important counterintuitive finding – see House 2001b).

An equally important fallacy is the taken-for-granted assumption that the advent of statutory regulation will necessarily have a beneficial effect on the level of client safety. One way of viewing training schools' embracing of statutory regulation is to see it as a tacit admission that their trainings are in practice unable to provide adequate ongoing quality-control protocols in trainees. Curiously, this level of educational inadequacy is somehow regarded as acceptable, even inevitable.

The overriding rationale offered by both Government and therapy institutions alike for the introduction of statutory regulation is that of providing a means of protecting the public from practitioners who are deemed unfit to practise and who could cause harm to those who seek their services. Given that this is indeed the central *raison d'être* underpinning the drive to regulation, the first and most obvious question is: What is the evidence that statutory regulation, compared with a 'no regulation' counterfactual comparison or scenario, would actually succeed in protecting the public by reducing the net level of abuse in the system?

We take it, first, that those arguing for statutory regulation would need to demonstrate that there currently exists, in the unregulated field, a level of abuse that is significantly greater than the level that would plausibly obtain under a statutorily regulated therapy field. In turn, this requires detailed information about the level of abuse that currently exists in the field. Now of course no one would seriously deny that abuse exists – after all, it exists everywhere in life; the crucial issue here concerns the scale of existing levels of abuse. We estimate that there are at least 20 million contact hours annually in UK psychopractice, not counting supervision or Continuing Professional Development, yet nowhere have we or our colleagues seen any empirical evidence about the current level of abuse within the British occupational field. Has any serious systematic research been carried out into this issue, and if so, why have its findings not been made public? After all, we presume that if such evidence *did* indeed exist, then it would be in the interest of both Government and therapy institutions to shout it from the rooftops, in order to legitimate their position. But our repeated attempts to elicit empirical evidence on this key question from the British Department of Health have consistently met with vague anecdotal assertions that 'we know substantial abuse exists' – but nothing more.

Of course there are pressure groups representing 'users' and clients (some possibly with axes to grind) who are calling for regulation; but this of itself does not make anything approaching a sufficient case for the appropriateness of statutory regulation, without the accompanying research on the current scale of abuse and dissatisfaction having been carried out (and on the scale of unintended negative side-effects, mentioned earlier). In short, we maintain that in any rational world it is not justifiable that dramatic and wide-ranging changes be made to our occupational field (and potentially harmful ones at that – see below) simply on the basis of a comparatively small number of high-profile, emotionally charged and anecdotal complaints or representations by user-groups, without comprehensive independent research first having been carried out.

In the literature referred to earlier, there is lengthy 'chapter and verse' on just why the 'public protection' argument does not hold water (e.g. see House 2009 for a detailed argument) – or is at the very least highly questionable. As the American authority on psychotherapy regulation, Professor Daniel B. Hogan, has written, '...a similar array of horror stories could easily be assembled about highly credentialed psychiatrists and psychologists, all of them licensed' (quoted in Mowbray 1995: 105). In other words, client and patient abuse occurs in professions that are *already* licensed and have specific sanctions against abuse and malpractice; and there is no clear empirical evidence in the literature to suggest that its incidence differs significantly between licensed and unlicensed settings.

Moreover, and as Richard Mowbray has pointed out, the various cases of abuse discussed by Jeffrey Masson in his well-known book *Against Therapy* were mainly perpetrated by involved practitioners who were already licensed professionals (i.e. medical doctors, clinical psychologists etc.), and their registered professional status within the community if anything made it harder to challenge their abusive behaviour. As Mowbray (1995: 114) writes, 'If protection of the public from harm has not been a proven consequence of [licensing] systems in general, there is little prospect that such a system would protect the public in a field as indefinite as this one'.

Another compelling challenge to the 'public protection' rationale is that, as we all know, potentially abusive practitioners who are determined to abuse will simply find another way of doing it – e.g. either by calling themselves something else that isn't regulated, or else by finding another arena/forum in which they can perpetrate abuse relatively unhindered. So on this view, perhaps the most one can say is that the statutory regulation of psychotherapy and counselling might merely *redistribute* abuse within society as a whole rather than removing it – thus invalidating the 'abuse reduction' argument for statutorily regulating the occupational field.

It might be countered that it is public perception that matters most, and that it is important for the Government to be seen to be responding to concerns about abuse, whether those concerns have wide-ranging substance or not. In our view this would amount to expediency of the worst kind, where appearance ('spin') matters more than substance and authenticity. Many cultural critics (including ourselves) maintain that the increasingly routine triumph of appearance over substance constitutes one of the most harmful trends in modern cultural and political life, and one which it would be potentially disastrous for the therapy field uncritically and incongruously to embrace and collude with. It would also surely constitute dishonesty of the most damaging kind for either our occupational institutions, or for Government itself, wittingly to generate substantially exaggerated fears and anxieties about the dangers of abuse in our field in order to create a pretext for legislation, when in reality the empirical evidence which would be needed to substantiate a rational case for regulation simply does not exist.

SO WHAT IS TO BE DONE?

We believe, first, that there is an urgent necessity for the personal/institutional naturalisation of dominance that lies at the centre of institutional professionalisation to be challenged and transformed, and a more enlightened 'power with' approach to accountability be adopted which is more congruent with the widely accepted therapeutic aim of clients' responsible empowerment. Specifically, we envisage the building of accountability institutions at macro and micro levels that embody 'power *with*' rather than 'power *over*' principles of organisational and human relationship.

The Independent Practitioners Network (IPN; see Chapter 16, this volume), in which we have both been full participants for nearly 15 years, offers one approach to addressing these important questions of the building of mature and congruent accountability structures (*Self and Society* 2004). What might be plausible criteria for adequate client/service user accountability? Rather than regulation, we maintain that *accountability* is a better and more widely acceptable way of framing ethically sound client/ practitioner working alliances.

Well over a decade of IPN theory and practice has helped to identify several key elements of effective accountability: (1) Ongoing, long-term, face-to-face contact with a settled group of peers that demonstrates a practitioner's capacity to form working alliances based on respect, negotiation, mutuality and rapport; (2) Declaration by each participant to the peer group of their training, competencies, special area of expertise if any, the client population for whom they are competent, their client workload, their continuing personal/professional development commitment, and their supervision arrangements; (3) Mutual disclosure in the peer group of challenges, deficits, difficulties, achievements, and significant developments in their practitioner work, coupled with disclosure of any developments in their personal life that might affect their fitness to practise; (4) Agreement between the practitioner group members about how disputes with clients should be handled; and (5) Self and peer accreditation in such a group institutionalises practitioner/client accountability in a way that greatly increases the likelihood of client satisfaction, and, we maintain, reduces closer to zero, compared with any conceivable alternative, the chances of abusive or exploitative practitioner behaviour.

Some people have raised the standard and predictable objection that the close personal contact of this process invites collusion. In the IPN model, when such a group has formed, they contract with other similar groups to establish external validation of their accreditation/dispute resolution process and possible collusive agendas. There is also a vested interest carried by every group member that their group colleagues' practice is sound and ethical (not least because if it is not, then that will reflect unfavourably upon their own judgement and practice). Moreover, this approach to accountability also draws fully upon what is commonly a very well-developed intuitive and perceptive sense in therapists and counsellors, such that our 'peers-in-relationship' are best placed by far to 'pick up' concerns about any given practitioner's fitness to do this demanding work (Heron 1997; House 1997a).

As IPN demonstrates, such a framing of psychopractice accountability can be orchestrated in innumerably different ways (House 2007b). If a regulation process lacks this mix of autonomy and external validation, how can it avoid being perceived by practitioners as coercive and stressful, and an unwarranted imposition? Will it not prove to be lacking in credibility, resulting in low compliance, and ineffectiveness in protecting clients, should the latter indeed prove to be a significant, evidence-based requirement?

Incorporating the key elements of a self and peer accreditation approach into Department of Health policy recommendations (to be implemented in a variety of ways by all the diverse organisations presently in the field) could ensure that quality assurance of practitioner/client relationships would be intrinsic, i.e. eliminating abuse through continuous monitoring, not as the threatened Health Professions Council route seems to indicate, extrinsic, via the detection, investigation and adjudication of complaints (Postle and House 2009). In so far as quality assurance is intrinsic, state regulation of the psychological therapies would be redundant.

Next, we advocate the building of political alliances that bridge cultural divides – on the assumption that in the broad field of 'therapy' (i.e. psychoanalysis, psychotherapy, counselling, counselling psychology...), what unites us in regard to statutory regulation is greater than what divides us (House 2005a; note that this proposal was made several years before the founding of the *Alliance for Counselling and Psychotherapy – against State Regulation*). This very edited collection (Parker and Revelli 2008) has, to our knowledge, been the first time outside of the humanistic and human potential movement that major concerns about the state regulation of psychopractice have been raised in a systematic and concerted way. We are delighted that within the field of psychoanalysis, at least some practitioners are at last waking up to the realities of state regulation, and the deleterious effects it could well have on the freedom to practise in a way that is driven by the singularity and particularity of each unique helping relationship, rather than by power-infused institutional and bureaucratic imperatives.

A related, if apparently paradoxical, strategic imperative is, wherever possible, to contradict the desire on the part of organisations that favour statutory regulation to present UK psychopractice as united and homogeneous when this is manifestly not the case. This suggests one plausible perspective on the unconscious drift of the organisations that seems to be towards the formation of a spurious psychological monoculture that seeks to hide their shaky foundations behind endorsement by the power of the state.

Finally, there is the exciting possibility of developing a non-credentialed registration approach to accountability as currently bering pioneered in the Bristol area cf. Mowbray 1995; Hogan 1979, 2003; Postle 2007) – an attempt to think 'out of the box' around accountability, to create a way of institutionalising accountability that would be congruent with clients' needs and practitioner values. DP has drawn up a carefully specified alternative approach to regulation based on this approach – viz. his Practitioner Full Disclosure List proposal, which is a variant on the so-called 'Non-Credentialed Registration' (or NCR) approach to regulation expounded by Professor Daniel B. Hogan and others, and successfully implemented in several States in the USA (e.g. in Vermont).

This model avoids many of the worst features of conventional statutory regulation, with practitioners opting into a national practitioner database in which their listing is endorsed and dependent on the support of identified practitioners who are publicly prepared to stand by their fitness to practise, competence and ethical stance, and an outline of how they will resolve disputes. On the basis of such practitioner self-description, made available via the internet with local printed supplements, clients would be able to make a much better informed choice of whom to select to form a working alliance than are offered by current listings or registers of names and modalities. Such a public commitment to practitioner openness may of course be difficult for psychoanalytic practitioners for whom personal disclosure might be anathema because of the very nature of psychoanalytic practice; but leaving that aspect of the non-credentialed approach aside, assembling a group of colleagues who know you and your work well enough personally to publicly endorse it on an ongoing basis seems only reasonable. If, we would provocatively ask, a practitioner wasn't able or prepared, with effort, to do this, should they be working in this field at all?

The Full disclosure List, while not an instrument of state control, would ideally be state administered, in the sense that the financing and resourcing of the database, and management of the IT structure, would be contracted out from the Department of Health. Two examples of this non-credentialed approach to accountability have been in place for several years in the USA, in the States of Vermont and Colorado.

IN CONCLUSION

What has become clear as a result of the College of Psychoanalysts – UK conference, and also the edited collection arising from the conference, is that there exists an unexpected common interest and shared understanding between the position of the College of Psychoanalysts and that of the Independent Practitioners Network; and our strong hunch is that this commonality of purpose and perception in relation to regulation is shared by a large (but unknown) number of other therapy practitioners in the many other organisations and modalities. Evidence of this emerged through an initiative some months after the conference, which gathered support for a 'statement of opposition' to statutory regulation, that very quickly collected over 600 signatures (and, as of mid-2010, now numbering several thousand – RH); and there are several petitions to the Prime Minister in the same vein. There is surely ample scope for expanding the informal links between like minds that have already begun to be forged through this important initiative.

Along with a number of other committed colleagues, we continue to do all in our power to challenge and derail the regulatory juggernaut, and we welcome approaches from like minds interested in coalition-building or other approaches to protecting the integrity of the psychological therapies from what we believe both personal experience and research evidence show to be an unnecessary and harmful intrusion into the very heart of therapy work.

CHAPTER 16

An Unqualified Good:
The Independent Practitioners Network as
a path through and beyond professionalisation

Bob Mullan: What are your thoughts about the 'registration' process?

Peter Lomas: I am appalled by it.... I am not sure whether we wouldn't be better without it altogether.... I do not think that people realise how dangerous [a register] is and how careful one should be with it... one should be very careful about what is considered irresponsible... the control, the monitoring of the training of therapists is very destructive of creativity... the greatest threat to our creativity is the register.

(quoted in Mullan 1996: 87–8)

BACKGROUND

In this chapter I offer a selective autiobiograpical account of my own particular vocational development within the climate of creeping (or do I mean land-sliding?) professionalisation that has characterised the British therapy landscape of the past 15–20 years. This reflection on my journey as a developing counselling practitioner focuses on the professionalisation process in general, and on nearly a decade's involvement with the IPN in particular. The lineage of my particular journey is traceable back, at least in Britain, to a series of early radical anti-regulation/pro-pluralism articles, appearing predominantly in *Self and Society* (Heron's brilliant 1990 article is seminal; others include Brown and Mowbray 1990; Kalisch 1990, 1992;

The Independent Practitioners Network has been referred to a number of times in the book. As described in Chapter 1, I have been involved as a founder-member of and participant in the IPN since its founding at the Open Centre in November 1994. The following piece was an invited contribution to the *Self and Society* special issue on the IPN published in the Autumn of 2004 (*Self and Society* 2004). I hope that the following piece clearly conveys the value of the Network, and just why it is a superior form of practitioner accountability compared to the statist and institutionalised regulatory alternatives on offer, and which are heavily critiqued throughout much of the book.

Postle and Anderson 1990; House and Hall 1991; Totton 1992; Wasdell 1992); through the two National Conferences on the Dynamics of Accreditation in the early 1990s (Cannon and Hatfield 1992; House 1992) and the Norwich Group Process Group originally led by Robin Shohet (House and Hall 1991); to the founding of the Independent Therapists Network (now the IPN) in 1994 (Totton 1994, 1995); and thence to the publication of Richard Mowbray's seminal book *The Case Against Psychotherapy Registration* in 1995 (see Chapter 13, this volume), and of the anthology *Implausible Professions* (House and Totton 1997/2011). (See Chapter 1, this volume, for a fuller outline.)

My own experience of 'practitioner becoming' has been above all overwhelmingly *experiential* and *self-fashioned*. Along with a number of colleagues in Norwich, in the 1980s I entered upon a self-development journey, out of which, *almost as a by-product of the experience*, most of us 'graduated' into working with clients. This is a centrally humanistic, experiential approach to 'training' (cf. Blomfield 1997) which is in very real danger of becoming extinct in the low-trust days of didactic professionalisation, where people decide that they want to be 'career' therapists and then train to be one, rather than their practitionerhood emerging organically from a personal development path.

Gladstone (1995: 15) has similarly written about what he terms the 'apprenticeship model' of practitioner development, in which 'becoming a therapist is a personally transmitted craft for which no amount of academic course work can substitute' (see also Gladstone 1997). For me it is little short of a tragedy that therapy trainings have become increasingly 'academicised', with more purely experiential trainings having virtually died out altogether because of their lack of credibility with a therapy bureaucracy intent on imposing didactic standards and 'competencies' from without, rather than enabling and *trusting* emerging practitioners to 'self- and peer-accredit' and organically develop their own authenticity and integrity in the work.

But I will rein myself back from critiquing the professionalisation process any further in this chapter, for its central intent is to communicate the positive experience which I have had through my involvement in the Independent Practitioners Network since its founding at the Open Centre in 1994.

SOME RELEVANT PRE-IPN DEVELOPMENTS

At a time when my own disquiet with the then creeping 'accreditation-mindedness' was mounting, I was thankfully being nourished through my involvement with the Norwich Group Process Group (1990–2) and the two National Conferences on the Dynamics of Accreditation which the Process Group organised (Cannon and Hatfield 1992).

Around 1990 a proposal emerged from the Norwich Collective (a large and diverse grouping of broadly humanistic local practitioners) for an experiential group that might meet regularly to explore the dynamics of the accreditation process. This in turn seemed to be inspired by no little unease with the regulatory 'noises' emanating from the then UK Standing Conference for Psychotherapy, and moves within the Association of Humanistic Psychology Practitioners (AHPP) to sharpen up its 'professional' act.

Initially, the Group Process Group met every month or so, for a day at a time, and we engaged Robin Shohet, a friend and peer-colleague of Jill Hall's and consultant to the Norwich Collective, to facilitate the group. Before long Robin decided to become a peer member of the group (no doubt as we got deeper into teasing out the alienating dynamics of hierarchy, accreditation and its shadow, *dis*creditation). A prominent role was taken in the group by Jill Hall, also an active member of the Norwich Collective and regular contributor to *Self and Society*; and as I remember it now, the original intention was to devise an alternative 'humanistic' accreditation model for group facilitation and therapeutic practice which could in some sense be 'recognised' or validated by the Norwich Collective.

Some of the deliberations of the Group Process Group on humanistic approaches to accreditation were published in House and Hall (1991); and after meeting for well over a year, the group eventually decided to organise a national conference on the dynamics of accreditation. In fact, two conferences were held in successive years (1991 and 1992), and reports of these highly successful events (in which [soon to be Professor] Brian Thorne and group consultant David Wasdell played a leading design and facilitation role) were published in Cannon and Hatfield (1992) and House (1992). Around one hundred practitioners from all over Britain attended both events combined, and within a few years at least some of the faces at those pioneering conferences were to appear again, and to become familiar colleagues and friends with the inauguration of the Independent Therapists Network in 1994.

Certainly these were exciting, heady times for all of us – and personally, the Group Process Group was one of the most richly nourishing and challenging experiential learning environments that I could ever wish to experience.

THE FOUNDING AND GROWTH OF THE INDEPENDENT
THERAPISTS (LATER, *PRACTITIONERS*) NETWORK, 1994

When, in early 1994, I read an interesting letter in *Self and Society* written by Nick Totton (Totton 1994), little did I know that his tentative proposal for a 'Self- and Peer-Accredited Therapists Network' would, within a few years, have given birth to a thriving, pluralistic nationwide network of therapy practitioners. About sixty practitioners (myself included) attended the ITN's resultant inaugural conference at the Open Centre, London, on the 19th November 1994; and since then I have myself been a member of an IPN practitioner group, the 'Leonard Piper' group – a grouping of (currently) seven practitioners from across the south of England who meet for a day every 4–5 weeks to witness, validate and challenge each others' work as practitioners. Our group has implemented a rigorous self and peer assessment (SAPA) process, through which we have all 'graduated'. This has been by no means an easy or conflict-free process, as peer-to-peer challenge, both professional and personal, is built into the SAPA procedure itself; and so the view that is often heard mooted, that such a process is cosily collusive, could hardly be further from the truth. The Leonard Piper group's SAPA process has been written up in detail by two (now former) members of our group – Juliet Lamont and Annie Spencer (1997).

MY EXPERIENCE OF THE NETWORK AS A LIVING ORGANISM

I see the Network as a living and vibrant example of what John Heron has evocatively termed a 'self-generating practitioner community' (Heron 1997), in which the twin motifs of *freedom* and *responsibility-taking*, set within an overarching and enabling environment of *trust*, are, for me, paramount. What does this mean in practice? Just some of the features I would highlight are:

- An environment of sustained, ongoing peership and a profound intimacy of peer relationship, leading to a deep knowledge of self and other (both personal and professional) which springs from sustained collegiate encounter and relationship;

- An organically and experientially grounded environment of trust and mutual respect;

- A safe-enough space for responsible interpersonal challenge to occur and be received relatively non-defensively;

- An embodied and *owned* ethical responsibility;
- Support through career development and personal struggles – making sense of the work, and of our respective relationships to it through both 'local' and national IPN collegiality and community.

The Network has a group, *communitarian* ideology, rather than a 'privatised', self-centredly individualising focus which is becoming so endemic in modern culture (Lasch 1979; Wallach and Wallach 1983), and to which the practice of individual therapy itself can also unwittingly be subject. The Network is therefore a form of 'self-generating practitioner community' in which participatory ethics (Brown 1997; House 1997a) (requiring responsibility-taking by all involved) are privileged over didactic, responsibility-eschewing institutional Codes of Ethics (cf. Pattison 1999).

The Network's self-regulating participative system of validation and accountability has been quite explicitly fashioned so as to be consistent with the core values of pluralistic therapeutic practice. The overall Network structure is therefore horizontal rather than vertical or hierarchical – rendering it far more in tune with recent progressive developments in 'postmodern' organisation theory (e.g. Jackson and Carter 2006) than the conventional old-paradigm alternatives on offer in the therapy and counselling field.

The Network stands for an approach to difficulties or complaints which encourages the willingness to own mistakes in an atmosphere of non-defensive openness (Totton 1997a), and thereby seeks to transcend the regressive 'victimhood, blaming dynamics (Hall 1993) that dominate conventional punitive, shame-inducing and victimhood-reinforcing complaints procedures.

It is interesting to note that the values underpinning the IPN do seem to have much in common with the Person-Centred and community-building philosophy of Carl Rogers, as Gassner (1999) has very clearly articulated (Jean Clark, personal communication). Overall, the IPN is founded in the values of creative pluralism (House and Totton 1997/2011; Samuels 1997), an unambitious modesty, and the celebration of growth and human potential development, rather than in those of infantilising hoop-jumping, 'power-over' hierarchy, and a quasi medical-model preoccupation with 'psychopathology'.

I would personally like to see a significant client/user dimension to the Network, as it is currently still exclusively practitioner-driven; but as is the way of the Network, the responsibility for initiating such a development is left to those who wish to pursue it – if I/we have the energy and commitment to follow it through.

It would be wrong to imply that the Network's strugglings with the intricate and subtle dialectic between radical individualism and communitarian values has not been variously challenging, frustrating, and at times exhausting. Yet these 'birth pangs' are perhaps a *necessary* and unavoidable process with which *any* grouping of individuals struggling towards a mature, operational *social community ethic and praxis* must engage. The extraordinary subtlety and complexity of what is at stake in all this is beautifully summed up in Rudolf Steiner's 'Motto of the Social Ethic', given to Edith Maryon in 1920 (and cited in Lipsker 1990: 60):

> The healthy social life is found when in the mirror of each human soul the whole community finds its reflection, and when in the community the virtue of each one is living.

It is certainly no coincidence that there are many interesting philosophical and procedural commonalities between the IPN, and the worldwide Steiner (Waldorf) educational (Steiner 1926, 1988b) and Camphill Community movements, and also, indeed, the Quaker movement.

THE 'LEONARD PIPER' IPN PRACTITIONER GROUP

In the course of our own 'Leonard Piper' Group's Self and Peer Assessment (SAPA) Process, each group member has written a detailed self-assessment, freely interpreted and under the following broad headings:

- Working history
- Training history
- Practice
- Supervision and support
- Accessibility
- Contracting and beginnings
- Endings and finishing
- Failings, limitations and weaknesses
- Boundaries
- Unacceptable practice
- Professional self protection
- Monitoring
- Personal life and self care
- Motivation
- Gender, race and class;

- Definition of a client
- Experience of personal therapy
- Self reflections
- My philosophy of counselling/therapy

SAPA is an ongoing, living process rather than a once-and-for-all form-filling exercise. Thus, we periodically conduct a SAPA updating process, where we each write something about how our practice and general life circumstances have changed or evolved since the last SAPA or SAPA update process.

There follows an excerpt from a SAPA Update which I myself wrote in March 2001, to give the reader a flavour of what can be involved in this process:

Way of Working

...I have noticed a slight evolution in my way of working [since our last SAPA Update] – by no means a dramatic change, but just perceptible to me when I reflect on it. I now find myself increasingly and quite spontaneously working out of deconstructive/spiritual/Zen ways of thinking-being which (sometimes quite explicitly) recognise *uncertainty* and the 'mystery of life' as very much central existential realities, with the essence of 'freedom' and 'freedom from anxiety' residing, paradoxically, in a full taking-in of just how little ego-control we actually possess. Relatedly, I also work with an awareness of the possible unconscious influence of cultural and transpersonal forces on individual self-experience – which I am increasingly coming to see as an important, and sometimes crucial, influence upon individuals' subjectivity and self-experience. (Of course this kind of perspective has to be worked with with sensitivity and subtlety, as it could so easily be seized upon in a 'blaming' way to deny any of the self-responsibility that I believe we do all have in creating our realities.) For me the greatest challenge of the work is now about subtlety and paradox – how to make sense of human experience in which we are somehow both creators of our worlds and yet also profoundly affected by 'forces' of which we are unconscious, and the influence of which is also commonly not experienced consciously. Rudolf Steiner's painstaking work on, and indications for, consciously becoming more aware of 'supersensible' forces/realities of course becomes very relevant here – an area which I have yet to explore in any systematic way; but I feel I am certainly working towards it.

This subtle trend in my work has meant, concomitantly, less of an emphasis on encouraging an analytical-deterministic understanding of people's 'psychodynamic' histories and their (alleged!) causal influence on the present. This change in my work could also reflect a shift in how clients are coming to counselling (i.e. less past-focused), and not just a shift in my own philosophy – though of course it's very difficult to assess something like this in any 'objective' way. Overall I am very comfortable with this evolution in my work, as I feel it congruently matches my own development as a person; and I really am noticing how clients do seem genuinely 'lighter' when I do share these kinds of insights (which I do from time to time – but by no means frequently: of course I only do share these types of insights when it seems to fit with the living context of the emerging work)....

Our 'Leonard Piper' group has also adopted a procedure for writing and exploring personal *Time-Lines*. We have each written a detailed Time-Line of our lives from birth to date, which has undoubtedly greatly informed and expanded our experience of each other, deepening in the process the levels of sharing and intimacy in our group – which, I believe, can only enrich the quality of our group relating and the effectiveness of the group as a holding and an enabling of our work as practitioners.

My own experience is that involvement in an IPN Group requires openness, a willingness to be vulnerable with one's peers both personally and professionally, commitment and reliability, and above all a willingness to engage in a live, authentically real, ongoing face-to-face way with one's peers. I believe that my work as a practitioner has been supported and deepened in a way that it is hard to imagine occurring in any other kind of setting.

One common criticism is that peer groups such as this can be, or can become, routinely cosy and collusive. In response, I can only give my own experience of my own group (which I assume is not self-deluding) – that our IPN group has been a source of both support and challenge for all of us – that we have challenged each other on many many occasions, but non-punitively and non-attackingly. In short, in a way which has maximised the likelihood of us each looking relatively non-defensively at our 'material', in a setting that encourages openness, truthfulness and potential development, both personally and professionally. Our group has also proved to be an excellent forum and crucible for questioning quite fundamentally the very nature of therapy itself – an ongoing process of questioning and open-minded deconstruction which, as I have written elsewhere (House 1999a, 2003a), I see as being quite essential to effective and non-abusive practitionership in a postmodern world.

To repeat: it is difficult for me to imagine a setting in which these precious, rare processes could have occurred more successfully or effectively.

I'd like to finish by referring to a recent link-group meeting which, for me, threw into strong relief all that is best about the Network. My own IPN group met with one of our two link groups in what were quite challenging circumstances. We spent much of the day together and, drawing upon our many and diverse professional and personal resources, we found creative ways of shifting and facilitating our respective individual and group processes in a way that was at once energising, moving and inspiring – and in a way that surely only honest, relatively non-defensive face-to-face peer exchange can achieve. It is experiences like this which ongoingly reaffirm the unique benefits that the IPN peer process confers upon all who participate in it.

I hope that I have given readers at least a flavour of something very precious and uniquely empowering which they might wish to experience for themselves in their own particular and unique journeys towards mature practitionership. Certainly, if you like what you have read here, it is likely that you and your participation in co-creating and deepening our practitioner community would receive a warm, open-hearted welcome at any of our regular national or regional gatherings.

PART IV

Radical 'Trans-Modern' Perspectives on Training and Research

CHAPTER 17

The Future of Training:
Towards 'trans-modern' therapy training?

A fuller appreciation of the importance of the realm of meaning for understanding human beings will require a different kind of training for scholars in the human sciences.

(Polkinghorne 1988: 183)

INTRODUCTION: DECONSTRUCTION AND THE 'TRANS-MODERN' TURN

[S]taying within the modernist repertoire may render psychotherapy obsolete in the sense that its emphasis on cultural adjustment tends to preclude its potential to assist in the construction of new relational possibilities.

(Lowe 1999: 81)

As with so much else in modern Western social formations, the training of counselling and psychotherapy practitioners is arguably in crisis. Notwithstanding the relentless ascendancy of cognitive behaviour therapy within the British National Health Service (House and Loewenthal 2008a, b; Loewenthal and House 2010) and around the Western world, the influence of postmodern, narrative and constructionist ideas is beginning to take firmer root in the psy world (e.g. Polkinghorne 1990; Kvale 1992; Anderson 1997; Parker 1999a, b; Payne 2000; House 2003a; Hedges 2010). As this

This chapter is a much extended and developed version of a paper that first appeared in *Counselling Psychology Quarterly* in 2008. It begins from the premise that a therapy training experience should be as congruent as is practicable with the core values and assumptive worldview of therapeutic work, or else it risks producing practitioners who are 'authenticity challenged'. Detailed suggestions are developed as to how training and practitioner development can be rendered more consistent with the kinds of 'new paradigm', 'trans-modern' values that underpin the 'post-professional' human-condition work followed by a growing number of practitioners.

paradigmatic trend accelerates and the old certainties of modernity come under escalating critical scrutiny, fundamental questions will begin to be asked about the assumptions according to which therapy trainings currently function – and more specifically, whether the current configuration that trainings typically take are consistent with the emergent 'trans-modern' world-view to which I have ongoingly referred in this book.

I use the term 'trans-modern' as opposed to 'postmodern' quite deliberately. The arguments of the postmodern critique of modernity are now well rehearsed, and will not be repeated at length here (for abundant references see Parker 1999; Lowe 1999; House 2003a; and Chapter 7, this volume). Yet it is important to outline the parameters of this debate, as its understanding is crucial to the wider discussion on what we might call (with apologies to Will Hutton) 'the state of training we're in'.

The chameleon term 'postmodernism' often triggers strong emotional (not to mention intellectual!) reactions, and can commonly obscure far more than it reveals, with some authorities even suggesting that we replace the term with less emotive ones, like (to take one example) 'a generalized climate of problematization' (Lowe 1999: 73). Rorty claims that the term has become so overused that 'it is causing more trouble than it is worth' (1991: 1). Certainly, the so-called 'postmodern turn' in therapy and within psychology more generally (e.g. Messer et al. 1988; Faulconer and Williams 1990; Parker and Shotter 1990; Kvale 1992; Gergen 1994; Burman 1998; Hepburn 1999a, b; Holzman and Morss 2000; Burman 2007; Hook 2010) has been prompted by a profound epistemological and political disillusionment with the perceived modernist tendencies of those disciplines, with their accompanying beliefs in

> a referential-representational view of language; individual autonomy and rationality on the part of therapists or clients (knowers and the known); historical, scientific and disciplinary progress; the desirability of grand and unifying theories and singular forms of knowing; objective and disinterested knowledge and professional expertise; and autonomous spheres of society.
>
> (Lowe 1999: 75)

Deconstruction is often cited as the method-*which is-not-one* of the postmodern worldview. For Parker, 'Deconstruction is... a processual activity that defies definition.... [it] is not a thing, and cannot be summed up in a neat definition or be put to work as a discrete technique' (1999b 11), being 'a process of critical reading and unravelling of terms, loaded terms and tensions between terms that construct how we read our place in culture and in our families and in our relationships' (ibid.: 6–7). While modern(ist) 'scientific' psychology typically seeks 'essential', universal laws and therefore downplays difference, Derridean deconstruction (founded in French philosopher Jacques Derrida's ideas) maintains that the acknowledgement of difference entails that we abandon any essentialism or foundationalism; for, it is argued, language is constitutive of meanings not in terms of the essence of a phenomenon but in its difference from other phenomena. Paradoxes, contradictions and double binds that are inherent in discourses of power are therefore highlighted in deconstruction, with the intention of limiting the extent to which the other's difference is repressed or denied (Larner 1999: 39).

Paradox and contradiction are central to deconstruction – 'a postmodern quandary' in which 'the dilemma of power is how to take a position... when such positioning itself involves a "violence that founds or positions" ' (ibid.: 40, quoting Derrida). For Derrida, the paradox of power cannot be grasped via reason and language, and must be lived with (ibid.). For Derrida, deconstruction should never be reduced to a school of thought, or a theory or a method, for 'There is no such thing as a deconstructive enterprise – the idea of a project is incompatible with deconstruction' (Derrida, quoted in ibid.: p. 43). Another feature of the deconstructive mentality is its 'both– and' rather than 'either/or' logic, and its thinking of opposites – 'for example, meaning and non-meaning, power and non-power – together' (ibid.: 45). The adopting of a postmodern *position* can also easily repeat a kind of modernist 'violence'; for 'All positions are grounded in "a kind of violent exclusion that must efface its other and eliminate difference to preserve its purity"' (Nealon, quoted by Larner 1999: 50).

In the practice of what Parker terms 'deconstructing psychotherapy', people's difficulties are 'understood as narrative constructions rather than as properties of pathological personalities, and as embedded in discursive practices rather than flowing from developmental deficits' (Parker 1999b: 2). Parker goes on usefully to outline a number of key features of what he terms 'a deconstruct*ing* psychotherapy' (with the '...*ing*' being important, as it conveys the idea of an ongoing process):

- it is 'always in process, rather than something fixed, a movement of reflexive critique rather than a stable set of techniques' (ibid.)
- it is 'profoundly respectful' (ibid.: 3)
- it pays close attention to contradiction (ibid.)
- it is 'intensely critical..: [it] does not presuppose a self under the surface.... To be "critical"... means understanding how we come to stand where we are' (ibid.: 3–4).

Postmodernism, then, is not an 'ism', a thing, but rather, *a key transitional moment in the evolution of ideas and human consciousness*, a moment denoting both an important disillusionment with the Enlightenment project of modernity, and a liminal, Winnicottian potential space which presages a 'new' which is as yet undefined and unknown (and may, of course, remain intrinsically so, as 'knowing' and 'definition' themselves are increasingly problematised – see, for example, Hart et al. 1997; Clarke 2005).

Lowe also makes the highly pertinent point that postmodern critique is the easy part (1999: 77); whereas the *putting into operation* of a descriptive postmodern praxis (including the training of therapists, of course) is another matter altogether. We should also not underestimate the extent to which the modernist world-view is still extraordinarily powerful (House 1996d); for as Thomas Kuhn showed in his seminal *Structure of Scientific Revolutions*, paradigms that are on the verge of being transcended go to often desperate lengths to re-assert themselves, even while in their death throes; and it seems that 'New Paradigm' thinking must needs assert itself in a kind of 'ongoing revolution', while we are still routinely faced with a control-fixated modernity that continues to 'lay Nature to the rack' (Francis Bacon) and saturates our culture and institutions (e.g. Power 1997; House 2000, 2007a; *Parallax* 2004). As Parker points out, the 'perpetual illusion' that we have moved beyond the modern' is continually asserting itself (Parker 1998: 612; cf. House 1996b).

A postmodern deconstructivist mentality problematises not only the 'clinical' procedures of therapy, but also the professionalised institutional structure which it takes (House and Totton 1997/2011) and the individualised, privatised self-focus of the 'Professionalised Therapy Form' (House 2003a: Chapters 1 and 2). All therapists, argues Lowe, have 'an ethical obligation... to actively participate in the deconstruction of their own texts, rather than complying with an external mandate' (1999: 81). We must surely wonder what might be the implications of this kind of view for the design and functioning of counselling and psychotherapy trainings.

The widely and uncritically embraced duality of modernism/postmodernism is perhaps not only unhelpful and overly simplistic, but itself creates a polarised 'either/or' debate which ironically replicates the very worldview which postmodern thinking at its best has noble aspirations to transcend (cf. Goss and Mearns 1997). One response is to step out of the polarised modernity/postmodernity duality, and into a more pluralistic, 'both–and' way of being which can respect and work with difference and the in-between (cf. Goss and Mearns 1997; Samuels 1997). As Goss and Mearns (1997: 193) have it, 'Perhaps we need a new logic – one in which apparent "opposites" can co-exist within a pluralist perspective'.

We might then profitably seek an alternative term, like 'trans-modern', which speaks to an ongoing transcending *movement beyond*, rather than a polarised, adversary position, and which recognises 'modernity' as a necessary (albeit immature) stage in the evolution of consciousness. Thus, the transmodern will not reactively repudiate and condemn what went before it as some kind of 'mistake', but rather, it will organically assimilate and build upon all that has gone before, but healthily transcend it into a more highly evolved level of consciousness. The journey from modernity through 'transmodernity' to whatever lies beyond it will not be an easy or straightforward one; and not unreasonably, I believe we can expect the therapy field to take an active part in these momentous developments.

In this chapter, I am primarily concerned with the effects and implications of these kinds of radically destabilising views for the training, education and 'be-coming' of therapy practitioners. For if we accept the relatively uncontroversial argument that the core bases of therapy training should accurately reflect the fundamental assumptions of the worldview on which our approach to therapy is based, then clearly we must at least begin to think about what a coherent and viable 'trans-modern' therapy training might look like as we pass through what Barratt (1993: xi) terms the 'death throes of the master discourse of modernity'.

Having outlined what I mean by the terms post- and trans-modern, I now move on to explore the configuration that therapy training or practitioner preparation, initiation or be-coming (whichever term we might prefer to invoke) might plausibly take when technological rationality's positivistic certainties are dramatically undermined, and the path to becoming a therapy practitioner coheres more closely with a 'trans-modern' *Zeitgeist* – a worldview which both acknowledges the (one-sided) contributions of modernity, yet takes us well beyond the constraining confines of the modernist worldview. I will focus in particular on the place (if any) of theory in therapy training (cf. Chapter 11, this volume). I will conclude with some paths that a trans-modern approach to therapy training might profitably pursue in future.

TRAINING AS A GUARANTEE OF COMPETENCE?...

[B]ecoming a mature practitioner is an outcome of a series of apprenticeships to people worth learning from in a variety of settings, *an idiosyncratic process* that escapes the market-driven logic and production lines of the institutionalised therapy training industry now emerging.

(Gladstone 1997: 171, emphasis added)

In House 1996a, I quoted Mark Aveline as arguing that, 'Sadly, the correlation between training and effectiveness as a therapist is low' (quoted in Mowbray 1995: 132), and Robert Young as writing that 'A very good therapist does not get that way primarily by taking more courses or studying at a particular institution' (Young 1993: 84). The question naturally arises, has anything happened in the intervening period either to reinforce or to challenge these earlier observations?

Certainly, the changes that I observed to be occurring apace in therapy trainings in the mid-1990s – with lengthening courses, increasingly stringent course requirements, escalating academic content and moves towards the 'post-graduatisation' of the field – have continued apace since then. There still seems to be little if any evidence that the achievement and possession of academic qualifications correlates with basic practitioner competence. In a more recent article, Aveline (2005) has written at length about 'the person of the therapist', maintaining that 'The character of the therapist is a vital component in effective psychotherapy' (2005: 155). Aveline (ibid.: 160–1) goes on to list some of the 'desirable characteristics' of therapists, mentioning:

- a genial personality
- an interest in human stories and the ability to help clients tell them
- being open to what clients are feeling
- possessing 'a basic optimism about the human condition'
- 'wanting the best for the other and being sufficiently free of envy to allow it to happen.

Now to say the least, it is not all clear just how these various qualities can be 'trained in', if at all – and Aveline's more recent views are certainly consistent with Mowbray's argument that 'The personal qualities that are prerequisites of competence in this sort of activity cannot be "trained in"' (Mowbray 1995: 118). Aveline's argument certainly supports the anecdotal hunch that *intrinsic nature* does play a very important part in the capacity to do the work of counselling, psychotherapy and counselling psychology.

Note, however, that it is quite contrary to the co-creative intersubjectivity which a trans-modern worldview embraces to assume that it is somehow *therapist* qualities that make the decisive difference in therapeutic effectiveness. Thus, Bohart and Tallman (1996) have written very convincingly about the so-called 'active client'; and here is Jerome Frank: 'Therapeutic success or failure depends not primarily on therapeutic procedure *per se*, but on the personal qualities of the patient which determine responsiveness to the healing properties of the therapist's personality' (Frank 1989b: 106).

Mowbray's survey of the available evidence (ibid.: 122) did indeed indicate that the effectiveness of psychotherapy does not appear to depend upon any of the following characteristics:

- the practitioner holding academic qualifications;
- the length of training of the practitioner;
- the school to which the therapist belongs;
- the practitioner having had a training analysis.

Mowbray went on rhetorically to ask, 'Do good mothers mother on the basis of a "developed body of mothering theory"?' (ibid.: 140) – and indeed, there seems to be much anecdotal evidence that mothering and parenting manuals actually have the effect of *disabling* mothers by cutting them off from their instinctual, non-propositional parenting knowledge (cf. Illich 1977; House 2003c). By analogy, it is by no means far-fetched to suggest that *a preponderance of theory in a therapy training might well have precisely the opposite effect to that intended* – not only because theory can so easily get in the way of the natural human qualities that inform practitioner effectiveness, but also because it can also 'school' trainees into a pre-conceived 'regime of truth', into which theoretical straight-jacket practitioners – wittingly or otherwise – proceed to shoe-horn their clients (for a detailed discussion, see House 2003a: Chapter 2; see also Chapter 11, this volume). I return to both of these important issues in the next section.

As argued in House (1996a), then, it may well be an illusion (and, incidentally, a very lucrative one for trainers) that extensive and formalised training can in any sense either create or guarantee competent therapy practitioners – and especially when a programmatic training agenda can actually get in the way of the '*unpredictable* time needed for the foundational preliminary of in-depth personal work' involved in becoming a practitioner (Gladstone 1997: 172, emphasis added), and 'the route to competence as a therapist passes through vagaries and vicissitudes that cannot be legislated for' (ibid.: 173).

These arguments are also crucially consistent with the kinds of postmodern critiques of conventional 'modernist' therapy that were discussed in the previous section. For it is clearly a modernist conception of training that tacitly leads to the kinds of unwarranted assumptions about the efficacy of training that are routinely and uncritically made within the wider therapy training business. A post- or trans-modern view of practitionership will more likely see the practice of therapy as *an art of meaning-making hermeneutics* rather than a quasi medical-model, programmatic practitioner-science; and if this view is anything like right, then it surely follows that the training of practitioners should also be a fundamentally artistic process (Schön 1987), with close parallels to Steiner Waldorf teacher training programmes. And approaches to competency and practitioner be-coming which make a fetish of formal training, skills, technique and theory may well be doing a fundamental violence to the art of what good and effective practitionership really consists in.

From a trans-modern perspective, then, the idea that there is a direct and unproblematic linear-causal relationship between training and competence, with training being a process that makes a person into a competent practitioner, is open to considerable question, if not outright derision. Moreover, and as I argued in House (1996a), if we embrace the client-centred view that what matters more in terms of therapeutic efficacy is the way in which clients 'use' whatever help is available to them to effect their own healing (Bohart and Tallman 1996), then not only does the somewhat counter-intuitive finding that all therapeutic modalities yield very similar success rates make complete sense, but the very basis for the view that the training of practitioners is the key factor in successful outcome is decisively undermined.

I maintain that the anxiety-driven, modernist impulse to measure, assess, control and mechanise a process that is quintessentially hermeneutic, intersubjective, mysterious and quite possibly in principle beyond the ambit of rationalist scientific understanding is not only inappropriate, but actually violating of the essence of both the therapeutic healing process and of the practitioner training process. And to the extent that this is so, then a *de facto* scientific and predominantly rationalist mentality will entail an assumptive ideology that will very likely be severely limiting of, and constraining upon, the be-coming of effective practitioners.

THE TROUBLED PLACE OF THEORY IN THERAPY TRAINING AND PRACTITIONER EFFECTIVENESS

> Theories are not innocent, value-free constructs, but are often themselves defenses against, or attempts to get rid of, the very phenomena that is their subject matter.
> (Davis 1989: 274)

Earlier I mentioned the place of theory in therapy training, which in turn is closely linked with the ideology of modernity and old-paradigm ways of thinking about the world. Such empirical or positivist ways of knowing, rooted as they are in a naïvely untenable 'correspondence theory of truth'

(House 1997a), are, I believe, inherently limited and limiting, and are beginning to give way to far more holistic, participative, tacit-intuitive, and even spiritual-clairvoyant ways of knowing (discussed later), as illustrated, for example, in the recent upsurge of interest in Goethean science (e.g. Bortoft 1996; Naydler 1996).

There has been a quite passionate debate in the therapy field about the centrality or otherwise of what is termed the 'core theoretical model' (or CTM), particularly in relation to practitioner training (Feltham 1997; Wheeler 1998). As Corbett has it, 'it has been common for senior analysts to teach the kind of orthodoxy that is expected which essentially repeats the party line' (quoted in Feltham 1997: 122). With the exception of the growing number of trainings which have an explicitly 'Integrative' orientation, it seems that such parochial 'theoretical hegemony' is the rule rather than the exception within the therapy training field. This situation leads to an inevitable tension, if not radical incoherence, at the core of most therapy training, for the common aim of psychotherapy – some kind of (at least) relative autonomy – is belied by the reality of training institutes which demand conformity from trainees, and by a resultant therapy practice which either mystifies clients or subtly converts them to believe in the tenets of the particular approach (ibid.). It seems clear that such a theoretical authoritarianism is a largely inevitable consequence of an approach to therapy training and praxis which is modernist and technological-rationalist in nature.

If we also take account of the transference and deference dynamics triggered in any training milieu – whether intentionally, as in analytic training, or otherwise – it is very difficult to see how there can be much 'potential space' for thinking outside of the presuppositions that are conditioned into newly training practitioners being schooled into one of therapy's many 'local' regimes of truth. And it is authentic creativity and genuinely imaginative elaboration which are likely to be the first casualties of such a system – qualities which are arguably quite essential in the art of therapy practitionership (cf. Kernberg 1996).

The notion of 'schooling into a regime of truth', or the inculcation of an ideology, is strongly suggested when considering the rationale typically offered in favour of a CTM, and which is described thus by Feltham:

> Failure to embrace one model in depth results in practitioners who are confused, lacking in rigour, and whose knowledge base is thin. Trainees... must learn and hone the practical and clinical attitudes, skills and techniques associated with a particular approach if they are to become competent practitioners.... They cannot achieve...

maturity without first having had a thorough grounding in a coherent
model.... [P]ractitioners should hold strong theoretical positions.
(Feltham 1997: 118, emphasis added)

Within the world-view of modernity, theory is typically clung on to as
representing some kind of 'objective truth', promoting methods which are,
thereby, assumed to be pretty much infallible: as Burman (1997: 126) has
it, mainstream psychotherapy is – or pretends to be – a quintessentially
rational, modernist enterprise which 'rehearses the modern condition of
western split subjectivity wedded to singular truths and linear histories'.
From a critical post- or trans-modern stance, perhaps the field's seeming
determination to promulgate CTMs has more to do with colluding with
the anxiety-driven needs for control and certainty than it does a sober and
appropriate engagement with the uncomfortable reality of intersubjective
relationship and the intrinsic uncertainty of human (including therapeutic)
relationship. Feltham again:

> All therapeutic models are partly fictions.... Many of us cling to an
> ideological object, such as a particular... psychotherapy, which we
> cherish and can never let go of. Arguably, all such ideologies act as
> opiates and their true function is to infuse us with a reassuring but
> defensive sense of certainty and direction in an unpredictable and
> frightening world.
> (1997: 120, 123–4 passim)

It is sobering indeed that perhaps the psychodynamics (or emotional
drivenness) of 'theory' (Craib 1987) is at least as important in therapy's
preoccupation with theoretical models and rationales as is any pretension
to therapeutic 'objectivity' or 'scientificity'. I maintain that it can hardly
lead to very effective or authentic therapeutic practitionership to have what
is an emotionally driven security need so successfully obfuscated by a garb
of objectifying modernist rubric about which even practitioners themselves
are often unaware. This is one area, then, in which the trans-modern, New
Paradigm critique of the modernist world-view becomes absolutely critical
– uncomfortable as it may be for those unwilling to relinquish their
comforting 'ideological object', for those with a vested interest in
perpetuating the theoretical fictions that dominate contemporary
professionalised therapy, or for those who believe that 'a first training must
treat (adult) trainees as babies to be spoon-fed traditional material (however
stodgy or toxic)' (Feltham 1997: 125).

Following my earlier discussion, I tend to agree with Feltham (ibid.:

THE FUTURE OF TRAINING 239

121) that 'Individual clinical giftedness, so overlooked as a factor in therapy, may well be more significant than any pedagogic theory'. Feltham goes on to remark upon how untrained carers or minimally trained practitioners sometimes seem far more 'human and insightful' than some 'highly trained practitioners... steeped in one or another core theoretical model' (ibid.: 124). Feltham's view is certainly in tune with a great deal of research pointing to a conclusion that is deeply uncomfortable for the professional therapy 'expert' – namely, that lightly trained para-professionals appear to effect outcomes at least as effective as trained therapy practitioners (see Bohart and Tallman 1996; for possible explanations, see House 1996a, 2001b).

I maintain, then, that the field's whole approach to the place of theory will have to be quite fundamentally problematised and recast in ways far more consonant with trans-modern New Paradigm thinking, and, concomitantly, away from the increasingly discredited, philosophically incoherent and profoundly damaging worldview of modernity (Polkinghorne 1990; Barratt 1993; House 2003a).

Yet another aspect of the theory question is the way in which therapy trainings are becoming increasingly 'academicised' (House 2001a, 2005a; Parker 2001), with training now set firmly at post-graduate level (van Deurzen 1997: 3). From a trans-modern perspective, however, the increasing emphasis being accorded to academic (often heavily theoretical) work on training courses is, at the very least, highly questionable. Nor can the increase in the academic/theoretical component of trainings be explained away as some kind of random event that is unrelated to professionalisation. Rather, the academicisation of training is an inevitable accompaniment of the attempt to make the therapy field into a 'Profession': for as Mowbray (1995: 29) points out, the knowledge base of the professions in general is typically highly theoretical and academic, with access usually depending on the possession of an academic degree. Indeed, Mowbray goes as far as suggesting that 'The over-intellectual focus... may actually be counterproductive as a prerequisite for working in this area' (ibid.: 117).

Finally, Freeman (2000) has convincingly argued that there is a profound need for psychology as a discipline to move *beyond* theory, if it is to respond adequately to Theoretical Psychology's growing impulse to transcend the Cartesian modernist *Zeitgeist* (see Chapter 11, this volume – though Freeman also makes clear that much of theoretical psychology is still wedded to the Cartesian project of a technocratic modernity). Freeman draws upon the analysis of Stephen Toulmin in his book *Cosmopolis* (1990), in which Toulmin argues for the rehabilitation of the neglected *humanist* dimension of modernity, which is rooted in the ideas of Renaissance humanists like Michel Eyquem de Montaigne. Such a view advocates 'a reformed version [of

Modernity] which redeems philosophy and science, by reconnecting them to the humanist half of Modernity' (ibid.: 72).

Toulmin further argues for limiting 'the scope of even the best-framed theories, and fight[ing] the intellectual reductionism that became entrenched during the ascendancy of rationalism' (quoted in ibid.), and urging us 'to extricate ourselves from theory in its abstract rationalistic form' (ibid.: 73). This in turn will entail a closer association with the humanities – a move away from the scientific and the empirical, and, concomitantly, towards the artistic, the poetic and the hermeneutic. Freeman cites Bakhtin, Buber, Heidegger and Levinas to show how

> The displacement of emphasis from the *cogito* to the Other... requires the movement beyond theory, toward the poetic, where truth becomes less a matter of adequacy to the object than fidelity – phenomenological and ethical – to others... who call forth our responsiveness and care.
> (ibid.: 76)

And rather than a wholesale rejection of theory as a failed symptom of a technocratic modernity, for Freeman there is a strong case for *reanimating* our notion of theory (cf. Berman 1981) by reconnecting with its deeply human roots in the Greek notion of *theoria*, where it draws upon meanings both secular and ritual (cf. Steiner 1989).

It seems clear, then, that those studying and practising therapy (including trainers and trainees) have a deep ethical responsibility to locate the practice of therapy within both modern culture and also within the broader evolution of ideas that are manifestations of the evolution of human consciousness (for an admirable example, see Cushman 1995). Anything less would be not only to risk practitioner complacency and complicity with the prevailing ideological state apparatus (Althusser 1971), but to risk merely reinforcing a kind of 'status quo theory' (Harvey 1973) which can only reproduce rather than help to transcend the degenerating modernist *Zeitgeist*.

THE CURRENT STATE OF TRAINING WE'RE IN

> It is impossible to schematise such a [healing] process, and *to talk of training anyone else to achieve its results is absurd*, yet some approximation to a character of this sort is the only basis on which psycho-therapeutic power can be built.
> (Robb, quoted in Groddeck 1951: 15, my emphasis)

It is instructive to look at one of the most recently published and authoritative books on therapy training – namely, John Rowan's *The Future of Training in Psychotherapy and Counselling* (2005) – to assess the current state of therapy training in Britain. Now Rowan is a very prominent and widely published humanistic and transpersonal writer-practitioner, and one would surely hope that a writer such as him would be looking robustly to transcend current modernist approaches to therapy training. It is certainly encouraging that in his Chapter 1, Rowan begins by asking the crucial question as to whether we actually *need* training – citing the research evidence referred to earlier which suggests that therapy outcomes from relatively inexperienced practitioners can be equally as good – or even better – than those of highly trained therapists. I would have preferred the book to begin with a prior question, however – viz. looking deeply into *what training actually is and means* – for, for me, 'training' is certainly a notion that is ripe for some overdue and telling deconstruction: a radical deconstruction that I felt the book tantilisingly never quite managed to achieve, despite its considerable authority and prescience. There is certainly a lot more to be said about whether training *as currently conceived* is indeed appropriate within an increasingly trans-modern cosmology.

Rowan does show some awareness of the issues I am raising here. He writes, for example, that

> Historically [training] has been so narrow. Trainees have been indoctrinated with the teachings of a particular school and left with the conclusion that this is enough. It is not.... The days of the single approach, the single narrow training, are over....
> (2005: 41, 71)

I also really liked his explicit embracing of paradox (achieved via his 'dialectical interpolations' statements at the end of each chapter – e.g. 'We are and are not concerned with cure'; ibid.: 131). In other respects, however, the book falls well short of some of the concerns raised in this chapter. Thus, the book is significantly light on the 'postmodern' perspective (for example, Lacan and Levinas don't figure at all, and Derrida gets just one passing mention). Moreover, Rowan writes far more about the state of training *as is* (albeit with ways of thinking about and understanding training that are often quite new), rather than really risking some 'clear-blue sky' thinking about what (for example) a truly New Paradigm, trans- or postmodern therapy training might conceivably look like, with values and organisation that are faithfully congruent with its own radical world-view.

It's not as if there isn't plenty of radical, leading-edge material for anyone fashioning such a vision to get their teeth into – for example, the important pioneering work of the self-directed South West London College Counselling Training from the 1970s and early 1980s (from which a number of now prominent practitioners 'graduated' – see Blomfield 1997); the experience of the self-directed IDHP trainings (Eales 1997); proposals from Twemlow and others (e.g. Twemlow 2001) that therapy training might be profitably infused with attributes of Zen practices; Hocoy's recent argument (2005) that therapy training can be seen as a kind of ethnography; and the courses in my own department at Roehampton University, in which, led and pioneered by Professor Del Loewenthal, the structure of the courses strive to be as self-directing and experiential as it is possible to be within the constraints of an academic higher-educational assessment framework (cf. Davies 1997).

To illustrate the point of my critique, I will (somewhat mischievously) cite the compelling quotation from David Michael Levin (quoted on Rowan's page 107), but substituting the word 'training', thus: 'All conceptual constructions of the *training* process are defence mechanisms, to the extent that they solidify into patterns of response that obscure a clear perception of one's situation and block an appropriate, effective and spontaneous involvement'. Rowan might well be quite critical of the postmodern turn in therapy – on page 40, for example, he claims (quite unwarrantedly, I believe), in what is a highly dubious generalisation, that 'the postmodernists are more at home in academia than in the consulting room'! (see also Rowan 2004).

The book also has little to say about the *politics* of training – and not least, the controversies around professionalisation and statutory or state regulation. In my experience it is an issue that therapy trainees talk about all the time and are more or less preoccupied with, so the absence of any extensive exploration of the issues from the book is somewhat deafening.

Moreover, there are important questions about the impact that new imposed practices in the therapy world are having, and will have in the future (e.g. the effects of the new regimes of 'evidenced-based, empirically validated' treatments in the NHS – e.g. Bohart 2002; Bryceland and Stam 2005; Bohart and House 2008; House and Bohart 2008) – and the consequent knock-on effects of these trends on the integrity of therapy trainings. Certainly, the tangible demoralisation of training and trainees in the USA is well documented (e.g. Rouff 2000) – and the same could well be on the way in Britain in due course. There is also little if any consideration given to the wider cultural forces within which therapy training is embedded – with the ascendancy of the pernicious 'surveillance', audit and accountability culture (e.g. Power 1997; *Parallax* 2004) that is arguably doing untold damage throughout modern social formations.

Finally, little is said about *love* (just a couple of pages); and while I am aware that John Rowan has gone into print arguing that 'love is not enough...' in therapy practitionership (Rowan 1996), it is surely the most under-researched and under-theorised aspect of being a therapist; and we might have expected a bit more about the healing power of love from such a leading humanistic and transpersonal authority (see, for example, Chaplin 1993; House 1996b; Shamasundar 2001; Sayers 2003).

Perhaps it is for others, then, to pick up the baton and give us some really new ideas about what therapy training might look like in a trans-modern, New Paradigm world through and beyond late modernity.

CONCLUDING REFLECTIONS: TOWARDS TRANS-MODERN THERAPY TRAINING?

We need a polytheistic psychology if we are to do justice to what is now called a postmodern world.

(James Hillman, quoted in Rowan 2005: 14)

There exists a rapidly growing tranche of compelling literature in post-positivist, even spiritual ways of knowing (e.g. Heron 1996, 1998; Hart et al. 1997; Olthuis 1997; Clarke 2005; Wickett 2005) and existential-phenomenological (e.g. Morris 1966; Vandenberg 1971; Curtis and Mays 1978; van Manen 1991; Grieder 1999; Jarvis 2005) and postmodern approaches to education and learning (e.g. Blake et al. 1998; Bonnett 2002; Dhillon and Standish 2000; Peters 1998, 2002; Standish 2001, 2002; Thomson 2002; Trifonas and Peters 2004; Usher et al. 1997) with which the future trainers of therapy practitioners will surely need fully to engage if a spiritually mature, trans-modern psychotherapy and counselling is to begin to emerge in the coming years.

In this chapter I have tried to illustrate just why the 'late-modern' training status quo is inadequate, in the process highlighting current emerging intimations of a new, 'trans-modern' approach to training and practitioner development which promises to take us beyond the constraining limitations or a modernist worldview which is increasingly becoming a fetter upon, rather than an enabler of, the healthy evolution of human consciousness. It remains for others in their respective training-organisational and academic-institutional settings to take forward the sketch of possible things to come that I have suggestively outlined in this chapter. Certainly, in the Research Centre for Therapeutic Education at Roehampton University, the department is quite explicitly wrestling with these challenging ideas within the unavoidable constraints of a higher-educational setting (House 2005b), with the aim of taking forward our existing thinking and praxis about the training and education of counselling psychologists, counsellors and psychotherapists.

Over 30 years ago, the French Marxist philosopher Louis Althusser (1971) coined the useful term the 'ideological state apparatus', in showing how an education (or training) system will tacitly tend merely to reproduce and reinforce the prevailing values of the society of which it is a part – in other words, a kind of self-perpetuating *status-quo theory* (as Marxist geographer and theorist of postmodernity David Harvey termed it – Harvey 1973), in which the prevailing materialistic *Weltanschauung* will be relentlessly re-asserted throughout a given culture. Similarly, in his famous 1962 book *The Structure of Scientific Revolutions*, Thomas Kuhn also showed how desperately an existing paradigm will cling on to its ideological hegemony, despite great quantities of disconfirming evidence accumulating to undermine its assumptive base and associated worldview.

At the beginning of the twenty-first century, the dominant worldview is, of course, overwhelmingly still that of materialism, consumerism and corporate managerialism – values which increasingly saturate and define mainstream culture. Within mainstream education, for example, we are witnessing the uncritical ascendancy of a soulless utilitarianism, in which quantity prevails over quality, the academic over the artistic and craft-oriented pursuits, ends over means, goals and targets over process – in short, head over heart (House 2007a; House and Loewenthal 2009). Such developments are gravely threatening children's and teachers' capacity for *imaginative elaboration* in their everyday learning and be-coming experiences (cf. Block 1997; House 2000) – along with the forces of inspiration and intuition which accompany the creative imagination.

Parallel and equally pernicious developments are afoot in the therapy world. Thus, with the uncritical rise of the 'therapeutic technology' of cognitive behaviour therapy in the NHS (e.g. House and Loewenthal 2008a, b), the NHS's ironically named 'NICE' Guidelines and the spuriously 'scientific', so-called 'empirically validated treatments' which they champion (Bohart 2002; Bohart and House 2008), and the threat of a therapy-regulatory regime founded in the medical-model Health Professions Council (House 2005a) and the technocratic specification and measurement of practitioner 'competencies' (Barnett 1994; Postle 2006; House 2009 – *come back, NVQs – all is forgiven?!...*), we can see all too clearly and disturbingly how the ideology of modernity is threatening to do a fundamental 'soul violence' to the very essence of what is most subtle, artistic and effective in therapeutic help.

In stark contrast, a 'trans-modern' approach to training and practitioner development (see Chapter 1, this volume) privileges moving beyond the prevailing positivistic *Zeitgeist*, which it is surely humankind's urgent evolutionary imperative to transcend. A cocktail of one-sided materialism and subservience to soulless technology, allied with an associated chronic loss of meaning, arguably lies at the heart of our emotional, spiritual and ecological malaise. And an approach to the training of therapists and the administration of therapy which tacitly mimics these same values cannot but reinforce that malaise.

It is instructive to look at parallel issues within the realm of education. In his book *The Child's Changing Consciousness and Waldorf Education*, educationalist Rudolf Steiner (1988b) was a trenchant critic of modernity and its accompanying worldview. While always being careful to acknowledge the positive achievements of modern science (hence my carefully chosen term 'trans-modern' rather than *post*modern in this chapter), Steiner points out just how much its one-sidedness has alienated human beings from themselves. On materialism, his critique is devastating, arguing that materialistically inclined minds can grasp only human *thinking* – and that materialism is the one view of the world which has no understanding of what matter actually is. Steiner championed a truly *living, artistic* pedagogy – for him, life is full of living movement and of transformation, and 'partaking in the creativity of the world is the very thing our present culture is waiting for' (ibid.).

Steiner saw the antidote to these pernicious forces consisting in the *qualities of heart* and pedagogical love (cf. van Manen 1991). Thus he maintained that teachers need forces of the heart so that the heart can be truly alive in our pedagogy – which is just one reason why he was so opposed to the kind of centrally imposed and determined 'national curricula' which have now become the norm in mainstream Western education. In a lecture on education given on the 20 August 1918, Steiner said:

> The State will tell us how to teach and what results to aim for, and what the State prescribes will be bad. Its targets are the worst ones imaginable, yet it expects to get the best possible results. Today's politics work in the direction of regimentation, and it will go even further than this in its attempts to make people conform. Human beings will be treated like puppets on strings, and this will be treated as progress in the extreme. Institutions like schools will be organised in the most arrogant and unsuitable manner.

One can imagine from this why, were he alive today, Steiner would almost certainly have strongly opposed state technocratic intrusions into the psychotherapy and counselling world such as we are witnessing at the present time, for, for him, the therapies and education belong most appropriately within the free cultural sphere, not in the hands of the polity. Steiner even maintained that it is teachers (including, we might add at the risk of grandiosity, therapy trainers) who stand in the forefront of bringing new impulses into human civilisation.

The technocratic mentality of 'modernity' and its accompanying myth of materialism – together with their psychological manifestation, self-centred ego-consciousness – are deeply pervasive in modern culture. In the training of therapists and the be-coming of practitioners, I maintain that we should quite self-consciously be pursuing values and practices which strive to enable the mature evolution of human consciousness far beyond the one-sided materialism of the prevailing *Zeitgeist*.

According to Heron,

> An ethically questionable degree of control characterises the current dominant world order, [including]... the legitimation of professional practice by statutory regulation.... Such control is out of tune with the emerging values of what seems to be a new kind of civilisation, one that is essentially peer to peer.
> (Heron 2003: i)

I hope that this chapter will inspire readers to begin the challenging yet exciting task of fashioning an approach to therapy training that is enabling of the mature evolution of human consciousness, rather than being satisfied with the prevailing training status quo which acts as a crippling fetter upon it.

CHAPTER 18

Research in a New Key: Towards 'new paradigm' methodology: A review essay

With the recent and highly welcome resurgence of interest in Goethean science (Bortoft 1996; Naydler 1996; Scientific and Medical Network 1997), the idea of *participation* is becoming a central focus in any account of how we derive embodied values or construct valid knowledge about the world (Edelglass et al. 1997; House 1997a; Skolimowski 1994). One of the leading figures in this movement is John Heron, who first developed an account of the participatory world-view in his book *Feeling and Personhood* (1992). His latest book, *Co-operative Inquiry* (hereafter referred to as CI) will be warmly welcomed by those looking for epistemologically mature and sustainable alternatives to the positivist *Weltanschauung*.

CI is fundamentally concerned with research *with* people, not research *on* or about them. All those involved are *both* co-researchers doing the thinking that generates, manages and draws conclusions from the research, and also co-subjects involved in the experience and action that is the focus of the inquiry. The inquirers move through several cycles of reflection and action, taking account of a range of validity procedures in the process.

CI contains detailed discussions of the various types of inquiry, and the range of inquiry topics: the setting up and facilitating of an inquiry; the stages of the inquiry cycle; and types of outcome and the enhancement of research validity. Heron uses his wealth of practical experience with the CI methodology to fill out the text with fascinating illustrative vignettes of actual CIs. The

---

John Heron is one of the most important figures in the history of the British Human Potential movement (though he now resides in New Zealand), having published a number of books that span both the relatively mainstream and the more esoteric literature. A central figure in the legendary Institute for the Development of Human Potential, he has profoundly influenced several generations of human potential and therapy practitioners around the world. His brilliant and far-sighted critique of the regulation of the psy therapies, published in 1990, still makes for seminal reading. When his book on Co-operative Inquiry came out in 1996, I wrote two review articles on the book, the longer of which I have, alas, been unable to trace for this volume. The shorter of these review essays follows, as it provides an effective portal into a fundamental consideration of the nature of research in the psy field.

dangers of collusion in the CI research process are explicitly addressed, with detailed procedures outlined to minimise its effects (pp. 146–8).

COMMENTARY

Within a CI, 'the primacy of the practical is privileged' (pp. 34–5) over and above the so-called propositional outcomes of over-intellectualised academic discourse and culture. Practical knowledge, then, 'takes the knowledge quest beyond justification, beyond the concern for validity and truth values, into the celebration of being values....' (which will be defined below – p.34; see his Chapter 9), In such a knowledge hierarchy, intellectual knowledge is *not* (as it is in positivist discourse) at the pinnacle, controlling everything below it; rather, in what Heron calls 'a dynamic up-hierarchy' (p.34), practical knowledge is afforded privilege over intellectual, propositional knowledge, and the latter is only of value to the extent that it can facilitate and inform practical being-values, For Heron, the central issue is whether the outcomes of the inquiry enable the inquirers to act in a coherent and concerted way within the inquiry domain.

CI fundamentally and refreshingly challenges 'the current mould still upheld by the majority of researchers today, that only the expert elite know how to acquire real knowledge, and how to apply it' (p. 100), For Heron, CI is 'the collaborative accomplishment of lived inquiry as an art-form' (ibid.). There are echoes here of the Goethean view of science to which Heron himself refers (pp. 91,174): for Goethe, science should be concerned with the phenomenological experiencing of the 'authentic wholeness' of nature, and with communicating such experience through artistic media, rather than atomising and reductionist approaches that necessarily do a violence to the indissoluble holism of nature by creating a fetish of split-off analytical ways of knowing. The CI methodology is as relevant to the natural or 'hard' sciences as it is to the social sciences; and the CI procedure promises the 're-enchantment of nature' (Berman 1981) for which new-paradigm scientists like David Bohm, Frijof Capra and Rupert Sheldrake have long been calling.

With his 'participative paradigm', Heron skilfully negotiates a sustainable path between the anti-science, 'anything-goes' anarchistic, post-structuralist epistemology of a Paul Feyerabend (1975; see Chapter 20, this volume), and the soul-less mechanistic positivism that currently dominates much of Western science. For Heron, 'it is clearly not the case that any old articulation will do' (p. 143), and he therefore calls for 'critical, rigorous and disciplined subjectivity' (ibid.). While he recognises the inherent limitations of propositional, conceptual ways of knowing, Heron carefully avoids the anti-intellectual, anti-conceptual positions sometimes embraced by the so-called 'New Age' movement.

In Chapter 9, Heron describes in detail the procedures by which validity within a CI is secured. For him, research can easily become 'a kind of pathological acting out of [researchers'] own repressive denial of the truth about themselves' (p. 150) – and indeed, 'the whole scientific enterprise can be seen as a defensive collusion' (ibid.). Thus, so-called 'objective' empirical research procedures routinely ignore the role of *anxiety* in distorting both the methodology and the findings of the research process (cf. Devereux 1967). In CI, by contrast, the effects of anxiety and other potentially 'acted-out' emotions are directly and experientially addressed in the research procedure itself. Trust-building will clearly be crucial in such an emotionally demanding process (pp. 155–6).

In the CI research process, 'outcomes... are valid if they are well grounded in the forms of knowing – practical, propositional, presentational, experiential – which supports them' (p. 158). Furthermore, and following Goethe again, 'Valid outcomes alone are not enough They need to be self-transcending, and metamorphose into exuberant outcomes. Beyond epistemological validity is the joy of human life' (p. 168). In this process, then, *passion and knowledge* become holistically reunited, and the artificial positivist splitting of reason from emotion can potentially be healed.

Heron's notion of 'being-value' is central to his CI philosophy, and one which surely has enormous potential. Being-value refers to that which is 'intrinsically worthwhile as a state of being' (p. 172). It seems to me that it is one's *'being-stance'* (p. 172) that must lie at the heart of CI: for in CI, being-orientation is just as important as doing-orientation; openness, iterative reflexivity and process monitoring are explicitly privileged over premature closure; and uncertainty, ambiguity and chaos are accepted as a natural aspect of the unfolding inquiry, rather than as unwelcome irritants to an allegedly 'objective' research process.

Heron's CI epistemology, then, moves beyond the conventional philosophical 'theories of truth' (correspondence, coherence) to offer what he calls an integrated, or 'congruence' theory of truth (p. 168), which notion broadens the meaning of truth to embrace *all* forms of knowing, and echoes Skolimowski's 'participatory truth (Skolimowski 1994; cf. House 1997b).

It will no doubt be very tempting to scour Heron's book for a recipe or template with which to implement a CI. It cannot be sufficiently emphasised, however, that, as Heron writes, 'There cannot be in this field such a thing as the one and only right, proper or correct method. There can only be my, or your, or our view as to what is a good method' (p.49). The only true way holistically to learn about CI is to experience it for oneself.

Heron's Chapter 10, 'A Postconceptual World View', both summarises beautifully the limitations of prevailing worldviews, and also articulates the possibility of a far less alienated, more integral way of being in the world. My only slight disappointment is that Heron doesn't say more about the psychodynamics of our alienated ways of being, rooted as they most surely are in commonly repressed anxiety and pain. Anyone familiar with the likes of Professors Lewis Wolpert and Richard Dawkins – and the quite contemptuous disdain they show for any approach which doesn't conform to the worldview of positive science (House 1997e) – will be acutely aware of the desperate rigidity with which the scientistic mentality clings to its 'objective' certainties, and must rubbish, perhaps through unacknowledged anxiety, any alternative worldview.

Heron also convincingly demonstrates just why control trial methodology (or CTM) (in which there is random allocation of subjects to an experimental treatment group and a matched control group) is woefully inadequate from a scientific viewpoint – namely, because: (1) its statistical methodology hides, through the comparison of means, what actually happens to *individuals* in the trial – meaning, for example, that there may easily be some people in *both* groups who are worse off after treatment; (2) CTM therefore ignores the different responses of different individuals to the same treatment, so that, as Heron argues, '[CTM] cannot help with the everyday question, "What is the treatment of choice for this individual patient?"' (p. 198); (3) CTM ignores the powerful effect of mind on body and the latent phenomenon of self-healing; (4) In true naïvely causal-empiricist mode, CTM assumes the validity of its mechanistic univariate approach which separates out the single treatment variable from all other influences to assess its causal impact (as if real, lived life were like that!); (5) CTM objectifies suffering as a 'thingified' process, reifying 'external' causal influence and ignoring subjective illness categories experienced and made sense of by the patient/client, and ignoring the meaning or 'tacit intentionality' (Heron) of the illness; (6) and finally, CTM ignores the possibility that its so-called 'statements of fact' (including variable specification and measurement) must inevitably be theory- and value-laden, and can only be formulated *within a pre-existing (and self-fulfilling) set of theoretical assumptions* (p. 197).

The CTM researcher also assumes that patients/clients are essentially the same, whereas the best of *clinicians* strive to be open to client uniqueness, difference, and even destiny. Of course clinicians will make all manner of human perceptual errors, misattributions and the like (see House 2005c); but a far superior way to respond to such shortcomings is surely to strive ongoingly to loosen and deconstruct one's assumptions and associated practices, than it is to throw out the 'baby' of individualised treatment with the 'bathwater' of the occasional errors it makes – or far worse, replace it with the technocratic positivism of CTM-informed clinical practice.

It follows from this (to my mind) devastating critique of CTM (and Randomised Controlled Trials) that what is urgently needed is a paradigmatic meta-view that attempts to locate and account for our historically and culturally specific methodological procedures within the context of the evolution of human consciousness (Steiner 1966; Crook 1980), if we are to gain a reflexive purchase on those methods and, hopefully, deepen and widen them.

CONCLUSION

As the modernist and anxiety-driven craving for certainty, controllability, replicability, audit, cost-effectiveness and the like takes hold in our culture (e.g. Power 1997), so the dangers of an uncritical (and epistemologically naïve) embracing of positivist research procedures should be all too obvious. CI certainly provides a welcome antidote to the soul-less positivist *Zeitgeist*.

The Scientific and Medical Network has recently begun experientially to explore David Bohm's Dialogue form of large-group inquiry (Bohm 1996), and there is enormous potential here for a rich cross-fertilisation between Bohmian Dialogue and Heron's CI methodology. Certainly, *Co-operative Inquiry* will be essential reading for anyone dissatisfied with or troubled by conventional 'old paradigm' approaches to apprehending and understanding the world, and I unreservedly recommend it to researchers of every hue.

CHAPTER 19

'Empirically Supported/Validated Treatments' as Modernist Ideology: Alternative perspectives on research and practice

Co-written with Arthur C. Bohart

What is most tangible has the least meaning and it is perverse then to identify the tangible with the real.
(Michael Polanyi)

INTRODUCTION

In Bohart and House (2008), we looked in some depth at how cognitive behaviour therapy (CBT) is just a part of a wider paradigmatic worldview which we can (rather inadequately) term 'modernity' (e.g. Toulmin 1990). A strong theme that came out of that discussion is that *not* to attempt to locate therapeutic practices and their assumptive philosophies within the evolution of ideas and human consciousness is a major (and telling) omission. For if we fail to seek, and gain some kind of philosophical purchase on, just what is entailed in the assumptive worldviews and research practices to which we adhere, then this can at worst lead to a kind *paradigm-bound* '*acting-out*', which will tend to be self-reinforcing and 'status-quo preserving' – that is, generating an inherently conservative 'status quo theory', to use the term coined by theorist of post-modernity, David Harvey – Harvey

In the critical anthology *Against and For CBT* (House and Loewenthal 2008), I co-wrote two chapters with the American humanistic psychologist Professor Arthur C. Bohart of Saybrook Graduate School and Research Center. Drawing on Art Bohart's previous incisive writings on what he terms 'empirically violated treatments', the chapter reproduced here sets out in detail a paradigmatic critique of the kind of positivistically derived evidence which is alleged to show CBT's clinical superiority over other therapy modalities. The ensuing discussion raises fundamental questions about what might count as legitimate scientific evidence in researching the differential efficacy of the psy therapies.

1973). This is surely the very antithesis of the kind of critical, deconstructive thinking that is arguably the way in which human consciousness can and does healthily evolve (Tarnas 1991).

In this chapter we will look more closely at the kinds of phenomena that could be argued to be central in an alternative paradigmatic world-view and its associated research undertaking – paying especial attention to issues like subtlety, intuition, discernment, and 'the tacit' in human relational experience (Polanyi 1966) – *phenomenological* qualities *par excellence* that rarely, if ever, figure in the kinds of scientistic research that regrettably dominates our field.

THE ROLE OF SCIENCE

The realisation that therapy is the *practice* of a professional activity leads us to view the role of science in a different way. In a practice view of what therapists are doing in their work, the practice itself is not, nor can it ever be, mechanistically scientific. Artists and artisans use science inventively and unpredictably to solve real-life problems in ways that simply cannot be specified beforehand (e.g. Lawrence 2005); and any such knowledge is certainly not 'manualistically' applied.

It is interesting and illuminating to imagine a thought-experiment world in which an alternative paradigm such as the one we are advocating here were routinely accepted, and in which no one might even think of doing empirically supported/validated treatments' (or ESVTs). For a start, they would ask very different research questions – for example, they might want to know about the principles of change involved in helping, and how expert practitioners blend tacit and explicit knowledge to co-create ways of being with, or make productive decisions with, individual clients. Or they might inquire into whether there is any causal connection between the kinds of experiential practices undertaken by therapy trainees and their capacity for intuitive relating and tacit knowing. Alternatively again, they might be interested in questions concerning sensitivity to individual cases; or they might be interested in how practitioners learn from, and adjust to, ongoing feedback they receive in sessions. Such knowledge would certainly not then be manualised, because it would be understood that *practice knowledge* is different from (but includes) scientific knowledge (Schön 1983; Sundararajan 2002). This is the kind of research that would tend to be pursued, then, rather than writing theory-based treatment manuals and then engaging in ramdomised controlled trials (RCTs) to test these manuals for so-called 'standardised disorders'.

In short, research would tend to investigate *principles and processes of change*. What would be useful to practitioners, for example, might be to study the tacit-knowing processes used by successful practitioners to discover whether they can be explicitly improved upon or deepened; beginning attempts have already been attempted in this regard. We can say, for instance, with some degree of scientific backing, that therapists who (a) are adept at facilitating the formation of a good therapeutic alliance; (b) are adept at dialoguing with the client, empathically listening, and taking the client's frame of reference into account (Duncan et al. 1997); (c) who are adept at supporting client involvement (Bohart and Tallman 1999) and mobilising their hope and optimism (Duncan et al. 1997; Greenberg 1999; Snyder et al. 1999); (d) adept at fostering the developing of insight, development of new perspectives, and clarification of the problem (Grawe 1997); (e) who allow or foster problem actuation in the learning environment of therapy (ibid.); and (f) who provide the opportunity for mastery experiences (ibid.) will be more likely to be successful.

In this sense, practitioners who work with these kinds of experiences could legitimately be said to be practising therapy in an 'empirically supported' fashion, although they do not at all necessarily practise empirically supported *treatments*! If it turns out that these are indeed the kinds of qualities that are more important than are standardised treatment packages for specific 'disorders', then the whole modernist ESVT approach may well turn out to have been an unfortunate and highly wasteful distraction – a mystifying detour that has actually taken us further away from a 'scientific' understanding (broadly defined) of therapy and relational experience.

THE NATURE OF THE HUMAN RELATIONAL EXPERIENCE

At a deeper level still, our alternative paradigm is arguably far more compatible with a postmodern, non-deterministic, post-foundational view of the universe (House 2003a) than it is with nineteenth-century Newtonian mechanics. Postmodernism is in fact not an '-ism', or any kind of thing, but rather, a key transitional moment in the evolution of ideas and human consciousness – a moment denoting both an important disillusionment with the objectivist Enlightenment project of modernity, and a liminal potential space which presages something that is as yet unknown and undefined (and may, of course, remain intrinsically so, as 'knowing' and 'definition' themselves are increasingly problematised – see, for example, Clarke 2005; Hart et al. 1997). Not only, then, is there the question of the place of the transpersonal and the spiritual in forms of knowing (see, for example, Baruss 1996; Clarke 2005; and Hart et al. 1997, 2000), but even at the level of modernist science, there is a degree of indeterminacy in the universe, and reality will never be known with 100 per cent predictability – *not* because we simply don't possess the computational capacity to learn everything (a purely practical problem), but because of the very nature of knowing itself. Complete predictability is not even in principle possible.

Our alternative paradigmatic approach has some affinity with a systems view that is, in turn, compatible with Stiles et al.'s (1998) notion of responsiveness. The two complex intersubjective 'systems' that are therapist and client influence one another and psychically interpenetrate in a multitude of different and often unspecifiable ways: verbally, non-verbally, emotionally, cognitively, perceptually, behaviourally, and even, some might argue, spiritually or transpersonally. These multiple paths of influence cross and re-cross in dynamic, circular, non-linearly causal ways. On this kind of view, *a 'meeting of persons' is a complex, indissolubly holistic phenomenon which simply cannot be dismantled into component, linear-causal parts.* There are just far too many ways in which two individuals can 'meet' and psychically interpenetrate; and 'meeting' even within the 'system' of the same two individuals can vary from moment to moment, as these two systems themselves change, mutually influence one another, and evolve.

Talking about 'meeting' or encounter in this way may seem too 'ill-defined' and wishy-washy to ESVT advocates, but that is because its very nature is that of a complex, interlocking, shifting phenomenon, not reducible to easily specified behaviours or their combinations. What is easily forgotten is that the label of 'wishy-washiness' is nothing more than a paradigm-bound belief underpinned by a modernist ideological mentality that ontologically assumes (often in an unexamined way) that 'reality' is necessarily sharply and easily definable and capturable. As critics of logical positivism have relentlessly pointed out over many decades, it is also a move of faulty logic to assume that that which cannot be measured and accurately specified therefore doesn't exist. Thus, because of what we believe to be the mutual, ongoingly reciprocal influence of the dynamic system which constitutes a therapeutic meeting or encounter, we maintain that *an operationalisable 'independent variable' cannot sustainably exist in psychotherapy research.*

Again, manualisation may offer some kind of reassuring illusion that such a variable is validly specifiable, but within our paradigm this is merely an illusion. When complex systems interpenetrate, it is both in principle philosophically incoherent and impossible in practice to chart simple linear-causal relationships between input from one system to another system. Therapeutic interventions simply do not map in a one-to-one fashion into client effects, but rather set up perturbations in complex ecological systems where, at best, all we will ever be able to expect are partial, incomplete and therefore *quite possibly misleading* correlations between inputs and ultimate outputs. Predictability is sometimes possible, but it is inherently imperfect and probabilistic.

Further, and to add to the complexity, because of the systemic nature of the co-creating intersubjective meeting, along with the phenomenon of emergence, the very meaning of any intervention shifts and changes as an ongoing function of its place in that evolving complex system. Because we realise that we can never have perfect predictability, and that there is no necessary standard solution for a given problem, we need to just try things out, trusting our phenomenological experience and intuition, experimenting, self-correcting, and so on. This in turn leads us to operating *intelligently*; and it then becomes important, in practice and in research, to *consult* with the system being worked with (cf. Heron 1996). Thus, one works *with* the system, not *on* the system. The systems involved must therefore be viewed as self-correcting – both therapist and client. The process is inherently *discovery-orientated*, including creative generation of new solutions through processes of dialoguing with the challenge or problem, and then reflexively correcting in an ongoing way. Ultimately, each approach or solution will be unique to that system's intersubjective nature and unfolding, sometimes in very obvious ways, sometimes in relatively subtle ways. This also implies that there is no one solution to any given problem: many different solutions may 'fit' a given problem (equifinality) – if indeed we are even to speak the discourse of 'problems'.

Thus, this approach is much more based on metaphors of *responsiveness* and *resonance;* and responsiveness and resonance are primary, and not additions or bolt-ons to a standardised format. *The client is not a 'dependent variable' to be operated on by an 'independent variable'.*

TACIT KNOWLEDGE AND ROLE OF THE THERAPY PRACTITIONER

In Bohart and House (2008) we referred in passing to the issue of tacit knowledge. Effective practitioners do not practise by following manuals, but learn how to use their intuition to transcend rules. Internalised rules become increasingly irrelevant because, through practice, practitioners progressively acquire a much more subtle and differentiated *tacit knowledge* of the terrain of practice than can ever, *in principle*, be expressed in explicit procedural rules. Once again, therefore, we can see how a manualisation approach fundamentally misrepresents what *actually happens* in therapy practice. In reality, we should note in passing that it is also unlikely that actual therapy practice in any ESVT research project is actually guided by manualisation either. Rather, it is guided by the considerable tacit learning that has occurred through training, and then through ongoing supervision by experienced practitioners. One of us (ACB) has personally observed Leslie Greenberg train therapists for his manualised research studies, and it was clear that Greenberg was using considerable tacit, fine-grained understanding in training his therapists in subtleties that went well beyond the descriptions in the training manual.

On this view, then, manuals therefore merely give *an illusion* of the comforting specificity sought after by researchers, but are actually nothing more than 'pretend pseudo-science' – a grand scientific 'emperor' with no clothes on. It is also quite illusory to believe that the immense degree of tacit knowledge often mysteriously conveyed by experienced practitioners in their tutoring process will ever be able to be specified well enough in manuals to render practice as 'scientific' as those who advocate ESVTs seem to be pursuing (Schön 1983). Despite manualisation, it will be expected that effective practitioners will practise differently, as they do in all other professions. The same melody played by two different musicians, or conducted by two different conductors, is always different. It is the player him- or herself that really matters, and not the technical, procedural content of what is played, to anything like the same extent.

We therefore support the radical conclusion that in the real world of actual therapy practice, there is no standardised 'treatment' which is being applied *even in the case of manualised therapies*. In our paradigm, a starting assumption is that each practitioner–client pair will generate its own unique ways of working effectively. Different practitioners will embody practice principles in different ways; and in all cases of practice, the role of the practitioner is crucial. Put somewhat differently, one might say that *diversity* (House and Totton 1997/2011) rather than *standardisation* 'rules' – however much the attempt is made to shoe-horn the subtleties and complexities of therapeutic experiencing into a measurable, predictable metric. Or as Moen (1991: 6) evocatively puts it, 'Selective analysis of general properties is not a substitute for the aesthetic intuition of a concrete and particular presence'.

Subtlety, intuition and therapeutic experience
In the kind of alternative, 'trans-modern' paradigm we are exploring both here and in Bohart and House (2008), the phenomenon of *subtlety* and its experiential handmaiden, the virtue of *discernment*, can be seen as key aspects of a therapeutic experience that a modernist, ESVT- and CBT-orientated worldview would find exceedingly difficult if not impossible to encompass.

The *Concise Oxford Dictionary* defines 'subtle' thus: 'pervasive or elusive owing to tenuity; evasive, mysterious, hard to grasp or trace; making fine distinctions, having delicate perception; acute; ingenious, elaborate, clever; crafty, cunning'. This is a useful starting-point – though the very nature of subtlety perhaps renders any attempt at a dictionary definition less than satisfactory.

Subtlety, then, is a quality of a kind of human consciousness that is tragically absent from the technocratic *Zeitgeist* of 'modernity' that still dominates modern consciousness. It is a telling commentary on the prevailing paradigmatic *Zeitgeist* that the book *The Subtlety of Emotions* (Ben-Ze'ev 2000) is one of the very few books that seems to have been written which explicitly addresses the question of subtlety.

In his voluminous writings, educationalist and polymath Rudolf Steiner repeatedly emphasised how modern materialistic natural science is incapable of the kind of subtle insight with which an alternative paradigm for psychotherapy is explicitly concerned. In April 1924, for example, he said that '...the kind of intimate observation that reveals fine and delicate changes in man's soul or his bodily structure does not evolve out of scientific ideas' (1968: 28); and 'The interests of this materialistic conception of the world... have developed in the educationist a terrible indifference to the more intimate and delicate impulses in the soul of the human being who is to be educated' (1926: 18) – with the result that 'materialistic thought is unpractical when the need is to enter into life in a living way' (1938: 60).

The educationalist and phenomenologist Max van Manen also explicitly addresses what we might call, after Steiner, the 'intangibles' or 'imponderables' in his writings on pedagogy. Van Manen was Professor of Education at the University of Alberta when he wrote a number of deeply insightful books on 'pedagogical subtlety' – the kind of subtleties which are notably absent, or at best neglected, in mainstream education (see Brown 1992; van Manen 1986, 1991).

Founding editor of the journal *Phenomenological Pedagogy*, van Manen's contributions are deeply influenced by hermeneutical-phenomenological thinking (where 'hermeneutics' refers to 'the process of describing the "essence" of something' – Brown 1992: 47). His two major studies, *The Tone of Teaching* (1986) and *The Tact of Teaching* (1991), are veritable goldmines of wisdom and insight on the 'soul-subtleties' of teaching as practice and experience; and his seminal text *Researching Lived Experience: Human Science for an Action Sensitive Pedagogy* (1990) gives us a glimpse of what research might begin to look like within a 'post-foundationalist' alternative paradigm. Rather than setting out manipulatively to control the world (as the technocratic Objectivist does), the sensitive phenomenologist offers the possibility of in-touch contact with, and full participation in, the 'life-world'. In short, the approach privileges sensitivity, openness to existential experience, and a commitment to inquire into lived, revealed meaning and to illuminate 'contextualized humanity' (Brown op. cit.: 49–51 *passim*).

Van Manen's book *The Tone of Teaching* is full of wisdom about an attuned pedagogy's intangible subtleties. He writes, for example, that '"Atmosphere".... is a vaporlike sphere which envelops and affects everything.... *Mood is a way of knowing* and being in the world.... Atmosphere is a complex phenomenon... – the way human beings experience the world' (van Manen 1986: 31, 32, emphasis added). Van Manen also pays attention to the critical question of 'presence'. Within the field of counselling and psychotherapy, *presence* refers to the Buberian I–Thouness of the therapeutic relationship (e.g. Robbins 1997) – the capacity to relate in a relatively undefended, open, non-projecting way which encourages real human contact, intimacy and genuine encounter. Just as the teacher's presence with and for the children in her charge is a vital aspect of their pedagogical identity, so it can be argued that a *passionate presence* (Natiello 2001), or encountering the other at *relational depth* (Mearns and Cooper 2005), constitute core dimensions of what we might call 'trans-modern' therapy practice from the kind of paradigmatic stance we are attempting to articulate.

Here is van Manen on presence – with the words 'therapist' and 'client' substituted for his terms, 'teacher' and 'child' (with our apologies to Max):

> The most important aspect of our living hope is a way of being with clients. It is not what we say and do, first of all, but a way of being present to the client.... When a therapist fails to be what ostensibly he or she *does*, then the therapist is really an absence.... We may be physically present to clients while something essential is absent in our presence.
>
> (1986: 27, 43, his emphasis)

Sardello (2002: 118) is surely referring to something very similar when he writes of 'a letting-be-present of the soul-being of the other in radical proximity to our own soul-being'. Buber wrote similarly about what he called 'contact' (a term also used, incidentally, in Gestalt psychotherapy): 'through his mere existence, only he must be a really existing man and he must be really present to his pupils; *he educates through contact*' (Buber 1990/1967: 102), emphasis added).

Van Manen proceeds to make an even more subtle link between

atmosphere and presence – for 'atmosphere is also the way a teacher [therapist] is present to children [clients], and the way children [clients] are present to themselves and to the teacher [therapist]' (1986: 36). Certainly, 'Pedagogic thoughtfulness and tact are not simply a set of external skills to be acquired in a workshop' (ibid.: 50), and 'A professional can act first because his or her body has been readied by thoughtfulness' (ibid.: 53).

Van Manen also has a strongly non-instrumental approach to teacher competency that is very different from the current mainstream ideology:

> Methods or techniques of teaching cannot be adequately described by external knowledge.... Teacher competency has more to do with pedagogical tactfulness, having a sensitivity to what is best for each child [client], having a sense of each child's [client's] life and his or her deep preoccupation.
> (ibid.: 49, 46)

Van Manen is also not afraid to enter the political arena: he writes, '...the "administrative" and "technological" have so penetrated the very lifeblood of our existence that parents and teachers are in danger of forgetting a certain other type of understanding....' (ibid.: 29).

In sum, 'teaching [or doing therapy] is much more than the dutiful execution of technical acts' (Brown 1992: 56): it involves an improvisational thoughtfulness involving 'the corporeal being of the person; an active sensitivity toward the subjectivity of the other' (van Manen, quoted in ibid.).

TOWARDS THE INTUITIVE PRACTITIONER: BEYOND 'COMPETENCIES', TOWARDS BEING

> Generalizable knowledge about teaching and learning will never fully reflect or be reflected in the individual cognitive framework of practitioners.
> (Atkinson and Claxton 2000a: 4)

The role of intuition (however we might attempt to define what it consists in) within the professions – most notably in teaching – has recently been recognised in an important book, tellingly titled *The Intuitive Practitioner: On the Value of Not Always Knowing What One Is Doing* (Atkinson and Claxton 2000b). Though focusing primarily on education, we maintain that this edited collection also has great relevance to the work of psychotherapy and counselling. It starts from the observation that, for much of the time, experienced professionals are unable to account for and explain what they are doing, or, indeed, tell us what they 'know'. Yet within the pravailing 'audit-culture' values (Power 1997) of the crass positivistic specification of measurable so-called 'competencies', professional development and practice are routinely discussed as if conscious understanding and specification are of central relevance and importance. *The Intuitive Practitioner* addresses the relationship between rational or explicit ways of knowing and learning, on the one hand, and inarticulate, intuitive or implicit ones on the other – embracing what is a seeming paradox, and exploring the dynamic relationship that exists between reason and intuition within the realm of professional practice. The book's contributors delve deeply and revealingly into the much-neglected nature of intuition, and illustrate the crucial role that it plays in the exercising and development of professional decision-making and judgement.

The 'modernist' tendency to 'fetishise' the conscious and the declarative, and to interpret reflection solely in terms of conscious articulation, is fundamentally questioned, and the value of forms of reflection that are not necessarily articulatable is strongly asserted. We should note in passing that the book has considerable relevance to therapy training in its offering of diverse practical lessons for the initial training and continuing professional development of educators that takes full account of the import of the intuitive.

The chapter by Broadfoot (2000) is especially pertinent to our current concerns in this chapter. Broadfoot opens up the question of the effect of what we might term 'assessment-mindedness' on intuitive capacity. There are important parallels here with so-called 'evidence-based practice' (King and Moutsou 2010) and the associated near-obsession with the need for certain kinds of research in the therapy world. It is virtually unheard of for anyone to challenge *the very idea* of 'research' (as currently conceived of as hypothesis-testing quantification) in our field, but that is precisely what we are going to do here. First, we think it is important to be aware of the *emotional dynamics* that may well be driving, at least in part, the field's current obsession with research, accountability and 'evidence-based practice' (King and Moutsou 2010) – rooted in part, one of us (RH) suggests, in a culturally pervasive and essentially unprocessed anxiety to do with loss of control, a phantasy of powerlessness, and cultural and spiritual anomie. An anxiety, moreover, which therapy practitioners would normally be expected to be particularly aware of and able to contain, and certainly not to 'act out' from. Yet in the field's uncritical embracing of the 'audit culture', the New Managerialism and the New Public Management (Clarke 2000; House 2008a; Power 1997), the grave concern is that we are unawarely colluding with these pernicious cultural forces in our obsession with accountability, efficacy, and 'scientific evidence' cast in a positivistic mould.

It is important not to assume, of course, that merely because a process may be anxiety- and unconsciously driven, that this *de facto* renders it necessarily invalid; but it certainly does cast considerable doubt on the essentially uncritical way in which research- and efficacy-mindedness have been embraced by the field without any critical debate as to their relevance and appropriateness in our peculiar field. One might reasonably ask why it is that, to date, there has been comparatively little engagement with these crucial issues in the therapy world. Might it be that there is some kind of insidious process operating in modern culture such that we all end up *'thinking like a state'* (Scott 1999) – with all of the deadly limiting and distorting consequences of that surreptitious mentality? Broadfoot puts it thus:

> assessment is... so central to the discourse of contemporary culture that [quoting Wittgenstein] we find ourselves in a 'linguistic prison'; we have been 'bewitched' by the concepts of... assessment... to such an extent that even what we are able to think is constrained by the boundaries of that conceptual language.
>
> (2000: 207)

These are surely the kinds of questions that culturally, critically and *politically* engaged psychotherapeutic thinking at its most incisive is very best placed to engage in; and to the extent that we don't do it, the therapy field could be in for very big trouble indeed. After all, the 'audit culture' and its accompanying ideology are systematically saturating every aspect of public and, increasingly, private life, and therapy is by no means immune from these arguably toxic developments. With the current obsession with 'evidence-based practice' (King and Moutsou 2010), for example, the very notion of 'evidence' itself is routinely taken for granted and uncritically assumed to be unproblematic. There are at last some welcome signs that the audit culture and its control-obsessed managerialist ideology is beginning to fall apart at the seams – certainly in the post-Blair UK; yet should not the insight that a psychotherapeutic ethos and sensibility affords us have led to a forensically critical deconstructive spotlight being shone upon the way in which the audit culture has been infecting the therapy world in all manner of ways? – not least through the CBT/happiness agenda (Pilgrim 2008) and the extraordinarily naïve 'outcomes' claims that have been made for the superiority of CBT-type approaches over other modalities (see various chapters in House and Loewenthal 2008a, b; and Loewenthal and House 2010).

Just as there has been a kind of 'trance induction' involved in the seemingly inexorable move toward the state regulation of the psychological therapies in Britain, a similar kind of trance induction has arguably been active in the case of the audit culture within therapy (King and Moutsou 2010), with erstwhile critically minded practitioners seemingly taking the notion of 'evidence' and 'evidence-based practice', and the underlying dynamics driving these preoccupations, as unproblematic givens.

The other important point to make here is the impact of what, elsewhere, RH has called 'audit-mindedness' (House 1996e) on the very subtle practitioner qualities that we are discussing here. For if, as we strongly believe, qualities like subtlety, discernment and intuitive capacity are key common-factor 'ingredients' of effective practitonership, and if those very qualities are not only *not* amenable to the positivistic 'violence' that is 'variable specification' and all that goes with it, but are actually *adversely affected by* such an 'evidence-based' mentality, then it may well be that the very act of importing a 'politically correct' preoccupation with accountability into our work substantially compromises it – and even ends up with the grotesque outcome that our anxiety-driven need to somehow guarantee the efficacy of our work, and the armamentarium of procedures that we adopt to prove it, *actually do far more net damage to the quality of therapy work than any improvements brought about by the assessment and accountability regime itself.*

We also surely have enough experience by now to know that virtually all technocratic intrusions into human systems generate all manner of normally unconscious 'material' around power (e.g. Hart 2003; Guilfoyle 2008; Proctor 2008), and routinely precipitate quite unpredictable side-effects which commonly do more net harm than did the pre-existing shortcomings the interventions were supposed to address. Crassly positivistic and technocratic conceptions of service evaluation – what Kilroy et al. (2004: 1) refer to as 'the reduction of (qualitative) thought to (quantitative) product, (critical) education to (utilitarian) skill-set' – are surely singularly inappropriate means of evaluating efficacy in the peculiarly unique and idiosyncratic field of psychotherapeutic help. As Broadfoot has it, 'attempts to pretend that a human being's achievements, or even more, their potential, can be unambiguously measured, are doomed from the outset' (2000: 215). Again, within the field of education Fendler (1998: 57) develops the kind of critique that has been notably missing in the mainstream therapy world. Below, we reproduce an aspect of her incisive critique, substituting 'therapy' for 'education' terms (as precisely the same arguments apply in both fields):

> Now there is a reversal; the goals and outcomes are being stipulated at the outset, and the procedures are being developed post hoc. The 'nature' of the [client's experience] is stipulated in advance, based

on objective criteria, usually statistical analysis. Because the outcome drives the procedure (rather than vice versa), there is no longer the theoretical possibility of unexpected results; there is no longer the theoretical possibility of becoming unique in the process of becoming ['treated'].... In this new system, evaluation of [psychotherapeutic] policy reform is limited to an evaluation of the degree to which any given procedure yields the predetermined results....

What our field should surely be embracing is the most radical thinking in relevant and associated fields (e.g. Trifonas 2004), rather than uncritically mimicking the worst features of the 'surveillance culture' and the soulless technocracies of 'high modernity' (King and Moutsou 2010). The kinds of epistemological and methodological critiques that will be necessary are at last beginning to be made within the field (ibid.), but we find ourselves asking, where have they been all these years?... Might it be the case, for example, that some process commonly occurs in which we are all in some sense infantilised by the state, and haven't yet found a mature place to take up in relation to overweening state intrusion into human experience, and into life itself? – and might this be especially so in the post-9/11 cultural milieu of acute and often largely unprocessed anxiety, which may well have triggered off all manner of unconscious phantasies?

These are the kinds of questions to which analytic and psychotherapeutic thinking might have a significant contribution to make, if we are not to sleepwalk into a thorough-going 'surveillance society'. And to follow Samuels' important work in this realm (e.g. Samuels 2001), as the anxiety-saturated 'audit culture' proceeds to penetrate every aspect of public and private life (Power 1997; King and Moutsou 2010), these are also questions that will surely manifest in the consulting room itself, and with which politically committed and aware practitioners surely cannot fail to engage with their clients and patients. There are also interesting institutional questions about the extent to which a *radical countercultural space* can be preserved in a psychotherapy field which becomes increasingly professionalised and subject to the all-pervasive audit culture.

Over a decade ago now, Spinelli provocatively wrote that '[T]here exists precious little about therapy that we can say with any certainty... therapists really don't know what they're doing – even if they insist upon pretending ... they are "experts"' (Spinelli 1996: 56, 59). We strongly concur with this view, which paradoxically further entails that the more we are able to admit to our 'ignorance' – albeit in a 'disciplined' way, perhaps – then the more likely it will be that we will discover the requisite abilities and capacities really to help our clients in a sensitive and effective way.

DISCUSSION

At the risk of oversimplification, we can say that the main culprits in the ESVT paradigm ultimately reduce to two tendencies: first, the underlying mechanistic assumptions upon which the ESVT paradigm appears to be based, which erroneously presume that greater and greater specificity will lead to better and better predictability and control, based on the research model wherein an independent variable is manipulated to 'control' the dependent variable; and the misguided metaphorical identification of psychotherapy with a medical-model, drug/treatment/cure ideology (e.g. House 1996c; Stiles and Shapiro 1989). In regard to the former, the ESVT paradigm can be argued to be based upon a traditional Newtonian, billiard-ball view of the universe, in which it is in principle conceivable (if not actually possible) to know everything, so that one can, in turn, predict and control everything. From this paradigmatic vantage-point, science is only imperfect because we haven't yet discovered and identified everything – while in principle, complete predictability is assumed to be possible.

In contrast, we maintain that in a complex, systemic, non-linear view of the universe, more compatible with postmodern, New Paradigm thinking, one will never *even in principle* be able to know with any degree of certainty how 'A' affects 'B' (if that is the causal-deterministic way we presume to chop up the universe), certainly where complex systems are involved. In other words, even within in its own terms, the linear-deterministic approach is quite inadequate for producing the kind of knowledge to which it claims to aspire.

Thus, simple input–output models of research, while perhaps useful as 'rough cuts', are positively misleading in understanding the complex nature of the phenomena involved (or more accurately, perhaps, they *may well* be – and we have no way from within the positivist worldview to ascertain the degree of misleadingness). When two complex non-linear systems 'bump up' against one another, one can perhaps hope for research to show an increase in probability that an input 'A' may increase the probability of an effect 'B'; but the idea that one can successively dismantle and disaggregate the phenomenal 'whole' and move closer and closer to complete mechanistic predictability is unrealistic and ontologically unsustainable. In sum, then, we can say that pro-ESVT advocates live in a modernist universe, while those sceptical of the ESVT ideology, like the present authors, inhabit something more akin to a post- or trans-modern one – however we might attempt a definition-*which-is-not-one* of the philosophically challenging postmodern mentality.

The second culprit appears to be the medical-model drug metaphor. In medicine, when a new drug comes along, RCTs are carried out to test its effects. However, when a medical doctor encounters a patient with a problem, in practice she or he does not mechanistically apply the drug and simply do nothing else. The drug, which has been validated in a drug trial, is used as a *part* of treatment (and of course we are ignoring here the crucially important question of the placebo effect – Shepherd and Sartorius 1989; Snyder et al. 1999; Kirsch 2009: Chapters 5 and 6). Note that *the whole course* of treatment is not in itself manualised. In contrast, because the whole course of a psychotherapy experience (e.g. a treatment for a 'disorder') is made analogous to a drug, in the psychotherapy domain, those who want to adopt the drug metaphor make the quite unwarranted jump of *manualising the whole course of treatment.*

From the kind of paradigmatic perspective adopted in this chapter and in Bohart and House (2008), it is a form of scientific hegemony, and an epistemologically naïve and unsustainable position, to suggest that all research should be carried out within the ESVT paradigm – and anyone that claims that it should be is either uncritically caught up in the 'ideology of modernity' (cf. Woolfolk and Richardson 2008), or else caught up in parochial vested interests or configurations of institutional power (cf. Guilfoyle 2008, in relation to the 'politics' of CBT). It is equally hegemonous, and again a scientifically unsustainable position, to argue that practice should be based on therapies that meet ESVT criteria, or, by extension, to argue that it is unethical if one does not use an RCT-supported therapy where appropriate (e.g. Persons, in Persons and Silberschatz 1998; Bryceland and Stam 2008).

ESVTers would no doubt raise objections to what we have argued here. First, it might be objected that the 'ideal-typical' picture we have painted of contesting paradigms in psychotherapy is oversimplified to the point of caricature, and that as a consequence, our critiques have a 'straw-man' quality which bears little relation to what actually happens in the world of therapy practice. We would certainly be committing precisely the error which we attribute to the modernist mentality if we were to assert a dichotomous, mutually excluding categorisation of therapy approaches into 'modernist' and 'postmodernist' ones. Not least, we are *all* in some quite unavoidable sense creatures of 'modernity' (House 1996d), and it is arguably impossible to absent ourselves from modernity's culturally pervasive influences and effects.

However, we do maintain that the epistemological *tendencies* that we have identified and elaborated upon in this chapter and in Bohart and House (2008) do have a very real and demonstrably tangible presence in modern therapeutic practice, and we base this on our own personal experience of both practising as therapists and reflecting deeply upon this peculiar work we do. We maintain, further, that if any coherent sense is to be made of the efficacy controversies that currently beset our field, then a full engagement with the *level* and the *nature of argument* developed in this chapter is an essential necessary condition if any progress towards insight and understanding is to be made.

ESVTers might propose a head-to-head test of a manualised empirically supported treatment versus therapy carried out from within the alternative paradigm propounded here. But this simply won't do; for the troubling question would then be: which set of research criteria from which paradigm would be used to answer the question? – or in other words, how do we decide which paradigmatic criteria should be given precedence in order to give an 'objective' answer to the question? Of course, we are entering the thorny and highly contested philosophical field of relativism here, which is a discussion well beyond the scope of this chapter. Yet we can see the kinds of philosophical and epistemological arguments that need to be engaged with to address the efficacy question in the therapy field – and to date, ESVTers have, tellingly, shown no inclination to enter and engage with these difficult arguments.

It is highly likely that the framing of such a question in a way that would satisfy advocates of the ESVT approach would not satisfy advocates of the alternative, postmodern paradigm – and, of course, vice versa. Moreover, and based on what we know about therapy research, the most likely outcome would be the Dodo bird verdict. And even if one approach *could* somehow be shown to be superior to the other, advocates of which ever approach had 'lost' would argue that the test wasn't fair. Surely a far better way to proceed is for researchers from different paradigms to pursue their varying ends, and somewhere, down the road, the slow, steady accumulation of results will decide the issue – with a Kuhnian paradigm shift perhaps being the outcome (Kuhn 1962), should post- or trans-modernist approaches prevail in the broad sweep of the evolution of ideas and human consciousness (cf. Lees 2008). So – let us allow the rich diversity of therapy approaches to flourish, and let us dare to trust the paradigmatic outcome!

Finally, what are the implications of our arguments for CBT and its mounting hegemony in the therapy world, driven as it is by complex cultural and political-economic forces (e.g. Pilgrim 2008), and the overriding 'ideology of modernity' (cf. Woolfolk and Richardson 2008)? Briefly, we maintain – with no little irony – that the detailed arguments developed here and in Bohart and House (2008) cast considerable doubt on, if not constitute a devastating undermining of, the allegedly *scientific* legitimacy that is routinely and uncritically claimed for CBT by its proponents. We maintain that, at the very least, philosophers of CBT and its theorists urgently need to construct a viable and defensible *metaphysical underpinning* for its theory and practice – for it seems clear from the many critical arguments here and in House and

Loewenthal (2008a, b) that, as yet, no one in the field seems to have attempted to construct such a metatheory that is able to make a coherent and sustainable case against the kinds of epistemological arguments and paradigmatic critiques presented here. Until such time as such an attempt is made, it seems to us that at the very least, a far greater degree of modesty is called for from those who aspire to entrenching CBT as *the* therapy of choice across the therapeutic realm. As Woolfolk and Richardson (2008) articulated so clearly over a quarter century ago, what is at stake in all this is a veritable Kuhnian 'paradigm war' (Woodhouse 1996) between the forces of modernity and post- or trans-modernity; and we maintain that it is impossible to understand the precipitate rise of CBT without locating it within such a cultural and paradigmatic worldview (cf. Lees 2008).

CONCLUSION

The need to recoup the loss of depth and particularity is urgent if we are not to treat fellow human beings as abstract objects or lapse into anesthetic and destructive indifference to the natural environment.
(Marcia K. Moen 1991: 6)

A 'trans-modern' worldview calls forth the imperative to move far beyond therapy as *technology* and a medical-model 'diagnosis-and-treatment' model of care, as envisaged in world of cognitively biased CBT and positivistic evidence-based practice (King and Moutsou 2010), to embrace instead the often uncomfortable reality that therapy as a healing practice entails many practitioner qualities that are *in principle* beyond rational 'modernist' specification – as a number of writers in diverse fields well beyond therapy have argued (cf. Michael Polanyi's notion of 'tacit knowledge' and Donald Schön's 'reflective practitioner', for example). As Frank put it, '[P]sychotherapy transpires in the realm of meaning.... [I]n contrast to facts, meanings cannot be confirmed or disconfirmed by the objective criteria of the scientific method' (Frank 1989a: 144).

In their excellent anthology *The Intuitive Practitioner*, we find Atkinson and Claxton (2000) arguing that there is a great value in 'not always knowing what one is doing', and that *intuition* is often the key to effective and successful practitionership in the human caring vocations. Such radical counter-cultural perspectives on therapy in the twenty-first century clearly have major implications for the be-coming of therapy practitioners, for the kinds of training experiences that might be most effective and enabling – and of course for the practice of psychotherapy research itself.

CHAPTER 20

Research Beyond Modernity?
Deconstructing *the very idea* of 'research':
An extended review essay

The external conditions which are set for the scientist by the facts of experience do not permit him to let himself be too much restricted, in the construction of his conceptual world, by the adherence to an epistemological system.

(Albert Einstein)

'Research': noun – the systematic study of materials and sources in order to establish facts and reach new conclusions.

(Concise Oxford Dictionary)

...specialists and common people reduce the abundance that surrounds and confuses them.... I... emphasize the essential ambiguity of all concepts... without ambiguity, no change ever.... One of my motives [is]... to free people from the tyranny of philosophical obfuscators and abstract concepts such as 'truth', 'reality', or 'objectivity', which narrow people's vision and ways of being in the world.... The attempt... to discover the secrets of nature and of man, entails... the rejection of all universal standards and of all rigid traditions.

(Paul Feyerabend)

When asked to contribute to a symposium of papers on John Lees and Dawn Freshwater's important new book on practitioner-based research (2008), it proved to be the opportunity I had been waiting for to get a lot off my chest about conventional, positivistic approaches to research in the psy field. The following chapter is a greatly extended version of the paper that was eventually published in *Psychotherapy and Politics International* in 2010. As the reader will see, I eventually find myself questioning the *very idea* of 'research', in the sense that it is unavoidably a socially and culturally constructed term that entails all manner of ideologies, interests, power issues and (often tacit) metaphysical assumptions. By opening up these inconvenient counter-cultural issues for critical reflection, I hope to join Lees and Freshwater in encouraging a far deeper reflective engagement with the culturally and historically located meaning of 'research' as an activity of late modernity, and to challenge mainstream approaches to research that take it as axiomatically a beneficent and unproblematic activity in the psy field.

It perhaps goes without saying that how one 'constructs' this, or any other text in one's reading of it will have a decisive impact on one's experience of it – whether we are moved or impressed by it, how 'good' or 'bad' a book we believe it to be, and so on. On this kind of view (a view also strongly advocated in the book under consideration here), a reading is also, and inevitably, *a construction* – that is, I don't begin or wish to claim that my response to Lees and Freshwater's *Practitioner-based Research* (2008) is some kind of objective, truthful representation of what exists in the book independent of my unavoidably partial and unique constructive reading of it. This in turn has emotional consequences for me as writer: for on the one hand, I have a trace of anxiety in letting go of the orthodox conventions of the 'expert' book reviewer who, from a position of some kind of alleged authority, pronounces on the value of a book; yet on the other, it also releases me from what one of the co-editors, Dawn Freshwater, refers to as 'the seduction of expertise' (p. 213), so that I too, as reviewer, can engage in a process of 'reflexive pragmatism' in both sharing my experience of this book, and at the same time reflecting on what that experience might reveal about me, and perhaps about the nature of the very notion of 'research' itself, and its limits and vicissitudes.

CULTURAL BACKDROP TO THE BOOK

The rise of such modernist totems as 'outcome research', 'clinical audit', empirically supported/validated treatments, systematic reviews, randomised controlled trials, the hierarchy of evidence, the National Institute of Clinical Excellence (NICE) guidelines and 'evidence-based practice' has come to dominate much recent research in the psy field, certainly within National Health Service contexts (e.g. Bohart and House 2008; King and Moutsou 2010). With statutory regulation of the psy field via the Health Professions Council possibly on the horizon (though this development is by no means uncontested in the wider field), a new hegemonic language has come to create a new 'regime of "scientific" truth' in the field, preoccupied as it is with notions like 'standards', 'competencies', 'quality assurance', 'audit' and 'cost-effectiveness' – a language that practitioners increasingly simply *have* to use (or at least go through the motions and 'play the game'...), if they are to be taken seriously in the modern super-audited Health Service. For many if not most practitioners, these are quite alien, 'managerialist' concepts (Clarke 2000) that simply do not belong in anything approximating values-congruent practice. These developments represent a critical shift in the locus of power away from the professional autonomy of practitioners themselves, and towards managerial and administrative bureaucracy (King and Moutsou 2010).

It is within this rather disquieting context that this new book on practitioner-based research should be located, with the editors forcefully arguing that psy and healthcare practitioners should just as legitimately be viewed as researchers as are academics and service managers. Co-editors John Lees and Dawn Freshwater, then, follow a quasi-Feyerabendian line (Feyerabend 1975) that no one ('scientific') paradigm should be assumed to be dominant or more valid than a multiplicity of others that are available. They therefore advocate a more balanced approach to research 'in which the voice of the practitioner is accepted as having equal validity to that of the academic and bureaucrat' (advertising flyer). Their aim is to establish what they term an 'epistemology of practice' which, they hope, will help to redress a balance that has tipped far too much towards the kind of 'technical rationality' which drives the dominant positivistic paradigm.

Lees and Freshwater argue that there exists a largely unrecognised body of 'practitioner researchers' who ongoingly reflect upon their clinical practice in an informed and insightful way, and yet whose work and approach commonly fail to 'play the game' in relation to the system's prevailing managerialist positivism. Part of their impassioned call is for 'all researchers and practitioners to reflect vigorously on their profession and the knowledge systems underpinning it' (ibid.). *Practitioner-based Research* is therefore a welcome challenge to the ways in which the limiting epistemological and ontological axioms of the dominant audit-driven paradigm influence, or even construct, how practitioners conceive of their work within the prevailing 'regime of truth'.

Aiming to be highly relevant to everyday practice and Continuing Professional Development, the book has a transformational aim, at both individual-practitioner and wider-profession levels, as the co-editors believe that 'working on our experiences in order to transform them is an essential and ethical need in training and professional development' (ibid.). The book's contributors commonly adopt a rich, eclectic and sometimes surprising mixture of reflexive, narrative and critical methods.

The book also has a recurrent theme of society-level change to match and balance its often relentless introspective, almost 'confessional' focus (I return to this latter issue later in this chapter). It also foregrounds *ways of thinking* about research, and not merely the procedural minutiae of the research process – presaging, as the editors hope, what will become an increasingly prominent approach to understanding and interrogating professional life.

THE BOOK ITSELF

I will concentrate first on the first and final chapters by co-editors Lees and Freshwater, respectively, with subsequent reference to other contributors' chapters, as it is the arguments of research *principle* which I want to foreground in this essay. In their editorial introduction the editors highlight their concerns about the way in which the academy is 'increasingly influencing the way we think as clinicians', with an ever-greater reliance upon abstract methodology being in danger of displacing a concern with real, lived human experience (p. xi), and 'a research culture that adopts the thinking of the academic lifeworld rather than the thinking of the clinic' (p. 5).

I will begin with some contextualising key quotations, that particularly struck me from Lees' chapter:

- …the profession… was fostering a research community that was more concerned with the aims of conventional academic research, such as replication and generalization, than with transformation. (p. 5)

- …academic research has become too constraining when it is not sufficiently fructified by practitioner research, and… practitioner research can become too chaotic and personalized when it is not sufficiently fructified by academic research. (p. 5)

- …these [orthodox] methods currently constitute the dominant discourse in healthcare research, and… are… in danger of unbalancing healthcare research communities. (p. 6)

- [Lees advocates] 'research that emphasizes a flexible approach to methodology'. (p. 7)

- …autoethnographic approaches are 'treated with deep suspicion and hostility within the academy' (quoting Sparkes 2002). (p. 7)

- All methods are inadequate and it is more useful… to see the inadequacy in one's own method than to concentrate on that of others. (p. 8)

- …the book is anti-hegemonic in the sense that it challenges the power of the conventional intelligentsia. (p. 14)

- By emphasizing the value of the work of the organic intellectual or practitioner researcher, we want to develop a form of discourse that concentrates on fitting the principles of the academy into the clinic, rather than the principles of the clinic into the academy. (p. 15)

In his Chapter 1, 'A practitioner's view of academic life, emancipation, and transformation', far from being something that should be 'bracketed out' to avoid methodological bias, Lees sees *personal experience* in the research process as a necessary complement to more conventional research methods (p. 1). Yet the fact that positivistic influences in the academy and the 'limited ways of thinking in the academy' (p. 9) have been crowding out *personal experience* in the research process has meant that the evidence that practitioner researchers can offer has become less and less recognised (p. 2), with the unfortunate result that the degree of pluralism in the research field is inevitably compromised.

Less then goes on to introduce the notion of 'autoethnographic research' (discussed further, below), a heuristic approach to research which informs or even underpins many of the chapters in the book; in which 'the liminal and the contextual' are privileged, prioritising 'their experience over and above methodological structures' (p. 8), and the principle of researcher transparency obtains, whereby the book's contributors have made 'their preconceptions, beliefs and experience transparent' (p. 13). Lees describes how, in his own clinical training, he learnt to believe that direct experience, and reflecting on it, was the most useful way of undertaking research, to which he responded by privileging case histories and vignettes for many years. When facilitating a university-based practitioner training programme, however, he found that once students had to focus on a 'research question' rather than on their own direct experience, they routinely had to 'suppress their emotions rather than focus on them, to remove themselves from the research process rather than put themselves at the centre of it, and to distance themselves from their experience rather than examine it' (p. 4). Concomitantly, the emphasis was upon 'logic and rationality rather than their direct capacity for knowing and emotion' (ibid.).

Lees makes no secret of his own preference for a practitioner-based approach to research, rather than an academic one, but rather than polarising, he advocates 'healthcare communities in which the practitioners [are] able to move seamlessly between both lifeworlds and see the... purpose of both of them' (p. 5), and preventing himself from 'polarizing and criticizing other approaches' (p. 7). Indeed, Lees also finds the polarisation between practitioner and academic research distinctly unhelpful (p. 8). In the research process, he tries 'to avoid designing the methodological process in detail at the beginning', not elaborating upon any methodological ideas at the outset, but allowing them to become an emergent property of the developing research process (p. 7).

Lees then links the argument into the cosmology of Rudolf Steiner, who, amongst many important contributions, had a great deal of insight to say about different kinds of thinking, an approach which Lees sees as extremely relevant when we are reflecting upon different kinds and epistemologies of research. Drawing too on Erich Fromm, he argues that an imbalance towards the academic, and its associated limited thinking, entails the danger of 'evolving' towards a kind of 'automaton consciousness' (p. 9). It was the Enlightenment thinking of Descartes, Lees argues, which moved too far towards the rational and away from the superstitious medieval mind, concluding quite erroneously that 'the direct experience of human beings is too unreliable to have any value' (p. 9); a self-fulfilling situation, moreover, whereby it has now become increasingly difficult today to trust our own experience (ibid.; cf. Reed 1995).

But it gets worse; for

> due to our reliance on protocols, procedures, criteria, and mechanical ways of thinking, our lived experience will increasingly become an irrelevance and we will eventually become reliant on 'evidence-based experience'..., los[ing] touch with our natural faculties and capacity for tacit knowing, with the result that our actions will become programmed... .
>
> (p. 10)

In the book's Chapter 5, Boyd also draws our attention to Jung's typology of thinking into directed or logical thinking, on the one hand, and fantasy thinking on the other, which is close to the imaginative thinking in the play of young children (cf. Isaacs 1933: 425–7) – a non-directed thinking where 'thinking in verbal form ceases, image piles on image, feeling on feeling' (Jung 1956, quoted on p. 82). Even more poignantly, Jung believed that mainstream science's emphasis on logical thinking was to the detriment of fantasy thinking, which, he claimed, 'led to an imperviousness to new ideas' (Jung ibid., quoted on p. 83), though he also cautioned against unbalanced fantasy thinking (ibid.; cf. Chapter 12, this volume).

For Lees, then, it could be that our future consciousness itself, and our associated quality of thinking, may well be negatively affected by the over-emphasis on the academic and overly intellectual in research. Lees himself even admits to experiencing his own 'self-alienation and habitual programming tendencies' (ibid.) (he calls this 'thinking about his own narrative' – p. 11). Hence, the rationale for this book – that is, to balance this unfortunate trend with practitioner research.

The importance of reflecting upon one's own narrative cannot be over-emphasised, for

it enables me to become more conscious of the extent to which I am influenced by dominant discourses; the way in which the social systems and ways of thinking that permeate my environment create a sense of alienation and a tendency to become robotic and indulge in abstraction.
(ibid.)

Mesirow (1981) is quoted in post-structural, Foucauldian terms in referring to 'becoming critically aware of how and why the structure of psycho-cultural assumptions has come to constrain the way we see ourselves and our relationships' (cf. House 2003a); and this can lead quite naturally to 'politically informed action or "praxis"' (p. 12, quoting Freshwater and Rolfe 2001). The recurrent theme is, therefore, one of 'explor[ing] the process of emancipation from restraints and the limitations of various aspects of society...', including our professional socialization' (p. 13; cf. House 2003a). The much-neglected Gramsci is also evoked, when referring to the book's challenge to the power of the conventional intelligentsia (p. 14). Part of this process is to find a way of writing that is clear and accessible, for (Lees), 'academic writing does not have to be obscure and inaccessible' (p. 15). Recent developments in narrative, heuristic and autoethnographic research are also invoked as giving 'a much-needed and coherent alternative to the dominant paradigm', and contributing to a pluralistic healthcare research community (p. 16).

One can immediately see the key concerns and themes in the title of the book's final chapter by co-editor Dawn Freshwater, 'Multiple voices, multiple truths: creating reality through dialogue' – the importance of diversity, a non-objectivist notion of truth, a social constructionist view of how we *actively create* realities... – and in which Freshwater weaves into the discussion dialogue, 'reflexive pragmatism' and discourse, heralding an evolution towards what one might term 'praxis-congruent therapy research'. On this view, 'Accessing knowledge... demands dialogue at many different levels, interacting with multiple discourses, truths, and voices' (p. 215), and we begin to sense here a kind of research and knowledge generation that lies far beyond the kind of comparatively narrow positivism that has come to dominate much psychotherapy research.

First, though, some key, contextualising quotations from the chapter that particularly struck me:

• ...the function of inquiry is not to represent reality; rather, it enables the individual to act more effectively. (p. 211)

- Pragmatic epistemology and the formal–informal continuum of knowledge provide a dialogic space within which all ways of knowing can be integrated. (p. 212)

- …reflexivity is essentially a constructivist activity and in principle is a process of inquiry/research activity that originates in the desire for social action, agency, and change. (p. 216)

- As humans we are consistently inconsistent, rendering it nigh on impossible to secure validity and reliability in practice/research. (ibid.)

- The object of dialogue is not… to win an argument, or even to exchange opinions. Rather, it is to suspend your opinions and to look at the opinions – to listen to everybody's opinions, to suspend them, and to see what all that means. (p. 219)

Like Lees in Chapter 1, Freshwater clearly wishes to embrace a coherent post-foundational approach to research, that, she would argue, is far more faithful to the subject-matter of the psy field, wishing to provoke us 'into reflecting more consciously and deeply on the process of reading' in an epistemology of reflective practice, referring to 'the ways in which metaphor and allegory can open up previously striated spaces, and in so doing, stimulate dialogue' (p. 210). We are also encouraged to reflect on what the text has done to ourselves as readers, and to make our own connection (p. 211), reflecting on 'how these contrasting and competing discourses [in the book] collide and collude with your own personal discourse' (p. 213).

It is what she terms 'reflexive pragmatism' that takes a key place in Freshwater's discussion. Pragmatism is located within the philosophical movement that historically includes Peirce, William James and Dewey, and more recently, Donald Davidson, Hilary Putnam and Richard Rorty. Freshwater distinguishes between 'doing' and 'being' pragmatism, and between reformist and revolutionary pragmatism, with the latter claiming the collapse of foundationalism and correspondence theories of truth, and the end of epistemology altogether (p. 214). While she does not associate herself with the latter, Freshwater does see pragmatism as in some sense revolutionary in its own right, which has the potential for 'emancipation, revelation, and transformation' in which all kinds of knowing can potentially be integrated (p. 215). She sees reflexivity as an approach to research in its own right (p. 216), and for her, reflexive pragmatism:

- is concerned with questioning assumptions;
- focuses on the social rather than the individual;

- pays particular attention to the analysis of power relations; and
- is concerned with democracy. (pp. 216–17)

Mikhail Bakhtin's closely associated notion of *dialogue* is then woven into the discussion, with dialogue (in the thinking of radical physicist David Bohm 1996) entailing the suspension of one's own opinions and the open consideration of other views, to the opening up and challenging of the whole process of thinking (cf. Krishnamurti 1997; Bohm et al. 1998), and to the experience of multiple truths (p. 219); for the process of thinking 'determines how we interpret and create our lives and… how we interpret and create the evidence by which we create our lives' (ibid.). There could be important links to be forged here with the work of Hal Roth at Brown University and others on the rise of contemplative studies in higher education and research (e.g. Roth 2006; Sable 2007; Zajonc 2003, 2009).

The dialectical interplay between structure and freedom is also highlighted, with it creating 'the dynamic tension and creative ambiguity that make the dialogal (*sic?*) process so exciting' (p. 220). Freshwater is drawn to the methodology of discourse analysis, which

> challenges the authority of the expert writer and replaces it with the authority of the reader…, [focusing] on the meaning and structure of acts of communication in context, both hidden and overt…, [revealing] how institutions and individual subjects are formed, produced, given meaning, constructed, and represented through particular configurations of knowledge.
>
> (p. 221)

There is also an important political dimension to discourse analysis. Foucault (e.g. 1970) used the notion of discourse to challenge positivist truth claims to knowledge, and discourse analysis itself is 'deeply concerned with power, and the complex ways that power and ideology can permeate society and social practices…, exposing power imbalances, [with] a political and ethical intention [which] emphasizes social action' (p. 222). Emmanuel Levinas is also introduced to the discussion of qualitative methodology, with his argument that 'the very search for intelligibility that dominates western philosophy implies reducing difference and otherness to the same' (p. 223; cf. Chapter 9, this volume). Levinas's alternative ethic of responsibility to the radically unknowable other is invoked, with Levinas urging us to 'seek a new relationship between ethics and psychology' (ibid.). Freshwater is arguing that all of these post-positivist ideas must be factored into any articulation of a viable and engaged conception and approach to research in our field. Above all, she champions practitioner-based research (PBR) which is 'a discourse of openness, of participatory dialogue, multiple voices, and multiple truths' (p. 224), with PBR being 'transient and dynamic…, moveable, changing, and fluid, and [perceiving] data as a series of moments, fragments knitted together through narrative time and space' (p. 225).

OTHER CONTRIBUTIONS

The other nine chapters in *Practitioner-based Research* illustrate the diverse post-positivistic perspectives offered by Lees and Freshwater in the first and final chapters. In Chapter 2, **Tris Westwood** is very critical of the way in which researchers often feel the need to fit themselves into conventional, constraining ways of thinking: thus,

> Part of the psychologist's training is learning to hide among the constructs and theories and the turning around of difficult questions so they don't have to DO psychology themselves; …the actual most important skill is that of obediently mumbling names and dates and at all costs not upsetting the people funding the research. Researchers do, after all, find just what it is they are paid to find.
>
>   (pp. 22, 31)

We also read about the key issue of *not knowing*, the defensive methodological practices to which it gives rise, and its crucial place in authentic practitioner-based research:

> When [fear and dread of not knowing] occur, then all sorts of methods, recipes, laws, oaths, prayers, gods, come along to try to stem our deep insecurity…. There is nothing quite like the uncertainty of not knowing to make people spout out names, dates, theories, and any other type of quantifying data.
>
>   (pp. 26, 33)

In a clear exposition of what engaged practitioner-based researcher can look like, in Chapter 3, **Barbara Hunter and John Lees** describe the development of their tutor–student relationship on a Masters course in Therapeutic Counselling. What is fascinating in this description is what can happen, and how it can be creatively responded to, when the dominant (academic) discourse collides with a more creative, intuitive, post-positivistic discourse which the student brought to a teaching relationship that got stuck, and which the protagonists found a way of unsticking and taking forward. We see how the participants themselves can be transformed when an authentic dialogue can be allowed respectfully to emerge between two very different ways of thinking and being (pp. 54, 53).

In her Chapter 5 **Jeni Boyd** interestingly shows how Carl Jung's cosmology has a distinctive post-positivistic, postmodern dimension (cf. Hauke 2000; cf. Chapter 12, this volume). As early as 1929, Jung was writing that 'I think it is best to abandon the notion that we are today in anything like the position to make statements about the nature of the psyche that are "true" or "correct"' – going on to advocate a phenomenology that advocates 'detailed presentation of everything that is subjectively observed' (quoted on p. 75).

Referring to 'an imaginal world, an alternative dimension of knowing and being' (p. 85), we further read, quoting Jung (2001), 'Learn your theories as well as you can, but put them aside when you touch the miracle of the living soul' (p. 77); and citing Freshwater (2005) and Jung (1956), 'bias can never be fully known…; what is conscious… will always be only a partial view…. The emphasis, in science, on conscious, logical thinking to the detriment of fantasy thinking has… led to an imperviousness to new ideas' (p. 77). Jung explicitly engaged with not knowing in his statement that 'I see conclusiveness nowhere' (quoted on p. 89). We also read that 'without heart, without passion and interest, we are unlikely to survive the vicissitudes of practitioner research' (p. 74) – another strong imploring that we need to balance out the overly academic bias that exists in the research in the academy. Boyd also refers to Jung's emphasis on the importance of the imagination and imaginative thinking (see above), and its important role in 'supplementing rational intellect' (Jung 1964, quoted on p. 88). For Boyd, the use of the imagination also has a direct role in data analysis, a view which the heuristic researcher, for example, would share (Etherington 2004). This chapter also reinforced for me the view that the transpersonal and the postmodern can indeed benefit richly from a mutually respectful dialogue, one with the other (see, for example, Griffin 1988b; Ward 1997; Keller and Daniell 2002).

In Chapter 6, **Christine Crosbie** looks at hope and despair in the therapeutic relationship, an in-depth, sometimes hermeneutic narrative-analytic exploration of her own personal and professional struggle around her experiences and concerns about the possible intrinsic abusiveness of therapy. It comes out very clearly how a client can end up feeling abused by therapists who adopt an interpretative stance founded in a causal-deterministic ontology of the the person and of the therapeutic process (p. 101), and also how the research experience itself can be fundamentally transformative for the researcher (p. 106). Crosbie also takes on the issue of power in therapy (pp. 107–11), addressing just how to put the kind of 'deconstructing psychotherapy' discussed by Parker (1999a) into practice (pp. 109–10). Citing Heidegger and Lacan, Crosbie also touches tantalisingly on the issue of time, which linear-positivistic research typically takes for granted, and yet which phenomenological and transpersonal research perspectives might conceive of in a very different way. Thus, there is the view that we could be at least as influenced by the future 'coming towards us' as by the past, of 'the call of the future' (p. 110; cf. Rudolf Steiner's anthroposophical cosmology); and there is a Levinasian twist with the view that sees the therapeutic encounter as 'sacred and as "wonder"' (p. 111, quoting Larner 1999), as a non-violative relationship is sought after. For a 'power-over' therapy relationships is 'essentially violent, and can do nothing to change the wider culture of violence' (ibid.).

In Chapter 7, **Sabi Redwood** looks with a refreshing critically deconstructive eye at ethics and reflexivity in research. 'I wish to trouble…' he writes, 'the production of the reality effect through which [conventional] dominant interpretations [of research ethics] attempt to place themselves beyond challenge and negotiation' (p. 117). What a relief it was to this reader at last to find some sound sense about research ethics, challenging the often stultifying institutional shenanigans of research ethics boards and committees (for other radical views on ethics in therapy research, see House 1997a and Pattison 1999). Redwood certainly makes no bones about the radical aim of his research, and his deconstructive approach to ethics in therapy:

> I wish to breach the borders surrounding the territories of traditional scientific research and the ethics that govern its practice. Narratives that have been produced in relation to these territories and practices which are presented as 'natural'… have closed and sealed themselves off against an outside of the non-scientific, the anecdotal, the frivolous, the political, and the tainted….
>   (p. 117)

And in similarly critical vein, he continues:

> The borders… are becoming increasingly tightly drawn as regulatory policies prescribe language and words into the pens and mouths of researchers and ethics committee reviewers. These narratives are also taken for granted to such an extent that they have become invisible and have ceased to be the subject of critical analysis. This has

diminished the vocabulary with which to speak about research ethics, and has congealed researchers' imaginations to think otherwise.
(ibid.)

Both cause and effect of this conventional 'regime' of ethics is the picture of the researched as potentially vulnerable and open to abuse, from which the researcher needs to protect them – what Furedi (2004) and Ecclestone and Hayes (2007) would term a 'diminished view of the self' in which *the very assumption* of vulnerability so easily self-fulfillingly creates exactly what has been assumed in the first place (cf. Mowbray 1997). Thus we read that '…many service users/patients, as well as participants in research, tend to be construed as vulnerable and in need of protection. They are seen as vulnerable to exploitation and as limited in their ability to give or refuse their consent.' (p. 118) Yet as Redwood poignantly asks, 'who is it that is being given shelter by ethics?' (p. 118). Moreover, the presumption of risk also has the effect of actively creating an approach to research which is over-active and over-controlling, which very mentality can easily be antithetical to authentic, embodied understanding emerging and making itself manifest in the research experience.

The psychodynamics of conventional regimes of ethics also need to be considered, for it seems highly plausible that at least part of the reason why researchers seem so uncritically to collude with institutionally systematised ethics procedures has to do with the phantasy that such procedures somehow make ethics unproblematic and no longer thought-about and engaged with once the various institutional hoops have been obediently jumped through. I agree with Redwood's very different view (cf. House 1997a) that

> we are really much more on our own with our decisions in our practice and in our research than ethics would have us believe; that ethics' careful spelling out of our responsibility and obligation fails to guide us in the rampant uncertainty of life.
> (p. 116)

So where does this leave us in relation to ethics, for 'if research ethics cannot be reduced to a set of principles and guidelines that can be applied to a research protocol and followed in the event of a decision being required, what does it mean to practise research "ethically"'? (p. 125). A much more human(istic) approach to ethics would be to engage with them experientially and unpreciously as another form of lived life (cf. House 1997a): quoting Frank (2004),

> We do not act on principles that hold for all times. We act as best
> we can at a particular time, guided by certain stories that speak to
> that time, and other people's dialogical affirmation that we have
> chosen the right stories.
>
> (p. 132)

As Redwood implies, one problem is that the ethics that are 'institutionally
overdone' and rendered too watertight can so easily take the edge off research
praxis, without which research can become 'play-safe' and little more than
anodyne. (Hence the quoting of Foucault here, who resisted the temptation
'to tame the wild profusion of existing things' – Foucault 1970, quoted on
p. 117). Thus, the narrative of conventional ethics practice

> exists unaffected by its relation to the messy world of practice. The
> borders of this enclosure are becoming increasingly tightly drawn as
> regulatory policies prescribe language and put words into the pens
> and mouths of researchers and ethics committee reviewers. These
> narratives... have become invisible and have ceased to be the subject
> of critical analysis. This has diminished the vocabulary with which
> to speak about research ethics and has congealed researchers'
> imagination to think otherwise.
>
> (ibid.)

The clear implication seems to be that far more interesting and useful research
findings may well be generated if only we could just relax a bit around
institutional, fear-driven ethics and their institutional paraphernalia, and
instead look to a far more individual, sometimes risky, even more
idiosyncratic relationship with the ethical. So here we see the 'paradigm
war' between modernity and postmodernity manifesting again all too starkly.

Even more radically, we might even follow philosopher John Caputo
in actually arguing *against* ethics (Caputo 1993; see p. 116). Loewenthal
and Snell (2003) have suggested, in comparable postmodern, Levinasian
vein, that ethical codes might themselves be argued to be *un*ethical, to the
extent that they actually interfere with the deeply personal and unavoidably
subjective and intersubjective process of ethical being and becoming in the
research experience, perhaps even violently objectifying the other. For
Redwood also,

> Codes of ethics institutionalize the 'top-down' model of ethical
> decision-making... which [starts] with an abstract and universal
> principle and [derives] from it judgements for particular situations....

> Ethical problems are presumed to have correct solutions that can be deduced from general principles, independent of the person, and social and cultural factors that are relegated as irrelevant.
>
> (pp. 121–2)

And in quoting the compelling Foucauldian critique of Halse and Honey (2005), we read that 'The widespread infiltration of the positivist model of research ethics has worked to visibly and invisibly inscribe the management, surveillance, and control of research ethics in ways that appear natural, benign and eminently reasonable to any "rational subject" (quoted on p. 123). Thus, for example, we see a quintessentially modernist, patriarchal and typically unquestioned assumption of the relationship between the researcher and the researched as being one of 'a contractual arrangement between two rational, autonomous individuals guided by universal, context-free ethical rules which, if they are applied in a reasonable manner, will ensure that the researched are treated ethically' (p. 122).

Thus, a feminist approach to a *relational* ethics (e.g. Gartrell 1994; Brown 1997) would tend to privilege 'an ethic of care and responsibility in which concrete circumstances and relationships shape ethical decision-making', with 'concepts like receptivity, relatedness, and responsiveness being more important than rights, norms, rules, and ideals' (p. 130). A feminist critique would also maintain that

> Emotions in research continue to be constructed in opposition to rationality and professionalism, and have therefore been marginalized and avoided in research accounts, with the effect that novice researchers are unprepared for the level of emotional engagement that qualitative research requires.
>
> (p.132)

Yet why should emotionality *not* play a key role in the research process? (cf. p. 132); and might not we succeed in 'bringing ethics alive' (Gartrell 1994) far more effectively if we were to adopt a reflexive model of research ethics 'that works to continually examine ethical concerns *as they arise* in research relationships…'? (ibid.: emphasis added)

The important methodologies of ethnography and autoethnography are introduced by **Roddie McKenzie** in Chapter 8, whereby researchers reflexively 'write themselves into the research story', with ethnographers undergoing the experience they are striving to understand, and treating their own experience as research data (p. 151). Autoethnographical methodology is usually written in the first person, introspectively paying attention to physical feelings, thoughts and emotions (ibid.). I will have more to say about this aspect of the book below. *Revelation* and *salvation* are also invoked, the former being concerned with revealing that which is hidden and which ordinary approaches to knowledge cannot reveal (p. 158), and the latter entailing personal transformation that restores wholeness (p.159).

Then in Chapter 9, 'Jana Helena' (a pseudonym), maintaining that 'there is no position outside theory, theory itself is always restrictive' (p. 173; see House 2008c; and cf. Chapters 11 and 17, this volume), proceeds to offer a breathtakingly intense personal report on her own 'fear of psychological death' (p. 168), which at times arguably verges on the confessional. For this reader, the question arose quite strongly as to the degree to which such highly personal material can usefully be regarded as research whose sharing is in some sense intersubjectively useful or illuminating for the other (i.e. the reader) – and indeed, just how and where, in any objective sense, one is to draw the line between legitimate heuristic or autoethnographical research, on the one hand, and a kind of confessional narrative which has more to do with the dramatic unfolding of the writer's own process, on the other. This is an issue that Helena is all too aware of, referring to this kind of research being far from 'self-indulgent or narcissistic, as some critics would have us believe' (p. 180). She certainly speaks openly about the way in which she, and her professional/clinical self, were transformed through the process of the research (e.g. pp. 180–1), and again one has to ask whether it is legitimate for such self-transformation to be the *prime motivation* of what we term 'research'.

The line between necessary and appropriate personal connection to research motivation, and tipping over into a kind of self-indulgent, Plathian confessionalism, then, is perhaps often a very thin one, and in the book it is a line that I found at times to be skated very precariously – an issue which several contributors recognise and explicitly acknowledge. Thus, in the following and penultimate Chapter 10, we find **Ashwini Bhalla** writing that such *autoethnographic research* does indeed have 'to face the accusation of self-indulgence and "narcissistic preoccupation with the self"' (quoting D. Scott; p. 204; cf. Bochner and Ellis 2001). Bochner and Ellis, for example, present approaches which embrace autoethnography, personal narrative, ethnographic performance and the blending of social science and the arts, with participatory ways of knowing, embodiment, experiential understanding, sensuous engagement, and intimate encounter to the forefront. It is perhaps these kinds of innovative research literature with which psychotherapy researchers need to start engaging in order to find methodologies that are more faithful to the core values and nature of psy work.

This again, in turn, throws up the key question of how we define (or socially construct) the very notion of 'research' itself; and it also leads me, as reader, to inquire reflexively into what my own dis-ease might consist in, when reading highly personal, almost stream-of-consciousness narratives that are positioning themselves in a book on 'research', and so presumably claiming in some sense to constitute 'research'. Ultimately, I take it that we just have our own phenomenological experience to go on, and to inform where interesting 'self-process' research tips over into something akin to self-indulgence. On reading some of the material in this book, I realised that I am still in the process of learning about just where this distinguishing boundary falls for me. (For an interesting critical/philosophical discussion of autoethnographic approaches to research and its problems, see Smeyers et al. 2007: 57–66.)

Indeed, how *is* 'research' conventionally and intersubjectively defined in society in general, and in our own field of the psychological therapies in particular? What ideological presuppositions and material vested interests are bound up in the orthodox, taken-for-granted definitions? I would have liked to see more engagement with these questions in the book, but at least the fearless opening up of the terrain of practitioner-based research exemplified in *Practitioner-based Research* has made the consequent opening up of such a discussion far more possible; and I, for one, am very grateful to the editors and the contributors for taking forward that possibility.

Perhaps this issue is most clearly addressed, and the difficulties with it exposed, in the chapter by **Ashwini Bhalla**, 'Searching for a voice'. She states that 'self-knowledge was one of the original aims of this research' (p. 202); and that 'The research started with an overall aim to gain a confident *free* voice' (205: original emphasis). Yet if we define as 'research' any undertaking which has as its aim 'self-knowledge', then is not the danger that the net that the term 'research' casts is so wide that it catches pretty much anything to do with personal development, with the consequent danger then being that the term becomes so catch-all that it loses anything resembling specificity or focus? There is some analogy with the therapeutic relationship itself, of course, in that it can be argued, and sometimes is, that each and every session with a client/patient is one of co-created inquiry; but do we find it helpful to use the term 'research' to describe all client therapy sessions (as Freud was wont to do for psychoanalysis)? One argument might be that for research to 'qualify' as such, it needs to possess, at the very least, a substantial orientation towards seeking understanding that is beyond the personal or the intra-psychic.

Back in Chapter 9, Jana Helena certainly reveals her own refreshing 'post-positivistic' view regarding the place of the self in research, with its lack of a 'linear and clearly defined process' (p. 176): thus, 'ultimately it is through the exploration of the personal and the subjective that theories are developed and challenged', she argues (p. 176); and in quoting Reinhartz (1997) – 'we not only *bring* the self to the field… [we also] *create* the self in the field' (p. 175, original emphases), with self-reflexivity becoming the methodological vehicle for her study reported in this book (ibid.). Being aware of its extraordinary power in my own work as a Steiner Kindergarten teacher, I agree with Helena who, following Jerome Bruner, maintains that *story* and narrative ways of knowing offer 'something fundamentally different' (ibid.), that should be regarded as an (at least) 'equally valid' research vehicle compared with more conventional empirical and positivistic approaches. Thus, for Helena, 'it is only through stories that we can begin to understand people as they struggle and deal with the complexities of life' (p. 182), sometimes leading to the questioning of the very limits of language itself (p. 175), and, crucially, the researcher's subjectivity also 'provid[ing] a bridge between the personal and the social' (p. 176).

Helena actually makes an even stronger claim – namely, that: 'it is *only* through stories that we can begin to understand people as they struggle and deal with the complexities of life. As such, it almost seems absurd that counselling research should exclude this dimension' (p. 182, emphasis added; see also Alterio and McDrury 2003; but for a provocative and more critical view of narrative research, see Smeyers et al. 2007: Chapter 4).

The academy doesn't get off lightly, either: 'Academia, sadly, I have to conclude, suffers from its own degree of madness' (p. 182) – a sentiment with which, from personal experience, I can only agree (though such 'madness' might well be generalisable to *all* human-made institutions). And finally, a cry from the heart of any and every phenomenological researcher who is in touch with their vulnerability: 'can we begin to truly value our own experiences and observations and build from them? To have the courage to trust ourselves and our experiences?' (p. 183). A psychodynamic or post-existential perspective might even try to argue that it is precisely this inherent vulnerability and fragility of our selves that forms the unconscious ground in which a comforting and procedurally controllable positivism is able to sink its roots. Boyd (Chapter 5) would concur: 'There is no distanced impartial objectivity, yet much psychotherapeutic research is still conducted along the lines of classical science in the form of RCTs, as if independent from any subjective influence' (p. 76; cf. House 2005c; House and Loewenthal 2008a, b). One certainly wonders just how the value of unknowing, uncertainty, the numinous and the ineffable, Keatsian 'negativity capability' and Bion's 'freedom from memory and desire', emphasised or alluded to by several of the book's contributors, can be remotely compatible with the 'evidence-based' ideology that has regrettably come to dominate much of psychotherapy research in recent years e.g. (Bohart and House 2008; King and Moutsou 2010).

If it is so, as Gordon argues (quoted without a reference by Freshwater, p. 218 – this is unfortunately the case for a number of references in the final chapter), that 'language… is not mine. It belongs to, comes from and returns to the human community…. The dialogical principle insists that we are immediately and irretrievably social', then such a view has very profound implications for any approach to 'research' that assumes a naïvely intra-psychic, epistemologically unsustainable correspondence-theory view of language (and truth) (cf. House 1997b; Chapter 21, this volume). If a superficially positivistic research cosmology needed any more nails in its methodological coffin (which it surely doesn't), then such a view would certainly apply the final *coup de gras* – were we not still caught up in the paradigm-bound worldview of a technocratic 'late modernity' which, while under challenge in all manner of ways, still tenaciously clings on in the 'paradigm war' between modernity and postmodernity (Kuhn 1962; Woodhouse 1996; Clarke 1997), and not least in our own field, through all the uncritical paraphernalia of the NICE guidelines, so-called 'evidence-based practice' (King and Moutsou 2010), and the like (Bohart and House 2008).

It is also very important for counselling and psychotherapy research to start building alliances and bridges with a range of other important research traditions – not least, with the emerging sub-discipline of Critical Psychology (e.g. Parker 2004; Stainton-Rogers 2009), and with explicitly *relational* research (Loewenthal 2007), conceptual-analytic research (Dreher 2000), feminist research (e.g. Lather 1991; Fonow and Cook 1991), hermeneutic/phenomenological research (e.g. Gadamer 1989; Cohen et al. 2000; Spinelli 2005b; Langdridge 2007), transpersonal research and ways of knowing (Hart et al. 2000; Klein 2003; Margitics 2009), 'spiritual-scientific' research (e.g. Steiner, R. 1989), and last but by no means least, explicitly and unshamedly *radical* research (Schostak and Schostak 2008).

With dictionary and commonly accepted definitions of 'research' normally being along the lines of 'systematic inquiry or investigation into a subject in order to discover or revise facts, theories, applications, etc.' (quoted from the Online Dictionary), we need to ask whether we are happy with such definitions; or should each and every researcher have the ethically individualistic right to define what constitutes legitimate 'research' for themselves, in something more akin to a Feyerabandian, 'anything-goes' kind of way (Feyeraband 1996)? It does seem remarkable, and a grave omission, that the 'anti-method(ology)' writings of the late, controversial philosopher of science Paul Feyerabend have been virtually and criminally ignored by virtually all therapy researchers to date; for there are surely yawningly obvious links to be forged between Feyerabend's anarchistic thinking, and the more critical postmodern, feminist and transpersonal research cosmologies.

While the issue of power in/and research is occasionally addressed in the book (e.g. p. 107–11), it is perhaps surprising that 'power' isn't an indexing term in the book, especially as the term *is* included in the book's subtitle. Perhaps questions of power and the kind of explicitly radical research advocated by Schostak and Schostak (2008) can be drawn upon together in order to pursue what is an urgent and long-overdue task of challenging at root, rather than uncritically colluding with, what some might even view as the fetishised *ideology* of 'research' itself – from psychoanalytic, existential-phenomenological and post-structural/postmodern viewpoints; and this is a task that psychotherapeutic thinking and praxis are surely very well placed to pioneer. Thus, for example,

- *psychoanalytically:* for example, what are the (often unconscious) ph(f)antasies that underpin and drive the *desire* to conduct 'research': the phantasy of the perfectly measurable, predictable and controllable universe, perhaps, in which, for example, all uncertainty, being 'subject to', not knowing, fear of breakdown and uncontrollable desire (to give just a few psychodynamic examples) are extinguished?;

- *existential-phenomenologically:* for example, what role does 'research' play in helping us to distance ourselves from encountering the brute reality of human experience, in the process facilitating our comforting denial of the unthinkable existential givens of existence, and in which, in phantasy, uncontrollable existential anxiety and the abyss of nothingness would be no more?; and

- *post-structurally:* for example, what is the nature of the discursive 'regime of truth' in which 'research' as idea and practice is located and embedded; what Foucauldian power–knowledge interests does its existence and cultural legitimation serve; and what unarticulated paradigmatic cultural task does it self-fulfillingly pursue and deliver?

In short, perhaps we therefore urgently need a kind of **critical *anti*-research**, that, paradoxically, at least opens up the possibility of *researching itself into oblivion*, and seeks to forge, instead, new sensibilities and understandings about the world and our healthy place in it that, like Paul Feyerabend, seek to go beyond the late-modernist paradigmatic discourse of 'research'.

I am also sceptical of the extent to which qualitative research as often carried out on/within the psy field is either genuinely critical, or encouraging of the transcendence of status quo thinking (or what David Harvey has called 'status quo theory' – Harvey 1973). Thus, in many if not most psychotherapy research programmes, what tends to happen is that, following the routine ritual dismissal of positivism (with which I concur, of course!), students then tend to opt for one of a relatively small number of qualitative methodologies (heuristics, IPA, hermeneutics, grounded theory, theme analysis, rhetorical analysis, case study, ethnography, action research, discourse analysis…), and then often pretty slavishly follow the methodology as laid down in the existing literature. This kind of approach to research can be even more dangerously conservative than quantitative positivism, in that under the *pre-text* of radical methodological thinking, qualitative research then nonetheless follows the accepted paths, rather than take a more radical Feyerabendian-type position, actually devising *new* or novel methodologies, or even problematising and transcending the ideology of 'methodology' itself (for beginnings in this regard, see, for example, Fonow and Cook 1991; Alvesson and Skoldberg 1999; Hollway and Jefferson 2000; and Parker 2004). Thus, for Feyerabend (e.g. 1975), *the* 'scientific method' simply does not exist, and in real-world practice, scientists need to invent new methodologies on their way to any discovery.

CONCLUDING THOUGHTS

'Recipe-book research' and 'theorizing in a vacuum' should be replaced by reflective activities, where the collecting, processing and analysis of qualitative data is regarded as a misleading description of what goes on…. (Alvesson and Skoldberg 1999: 287, 288)

For a certain type of intellectual mediocrity characterised by enlightened rationalism, a scientific theory that simplifies matters is a very good means of defence because of the tremendous faith modern man has in anything that bears the label 'scientific'.
(C.G. Jung)

I suspect that the editors of and contributors to *Practitioner-based Research* would broadly agree with Alvesson and Skoldberg (1999), who coin the term 'reflexive interpretation' to describe their not dissimilar approach to research, in which research 'consistently admit[s] ambiguity' (p. 288), 'does not conform to any linear process or monolithic logic' (ibid.), and negotiates 'a precarious balance between accepting the existence of some sort of "reality" out there, and accepting the rhetorical and narrative nature of our knowledge of this reality' (p. 289). On this view, then, they adopt 'the view of research as a *provisionally* rational product, in which the kernel of rationality is a question of reflection rather than procedure' (p. 288), and in which "there is an unstable and wavering relation between reality and rhetoric, but also a dynamism of re-construction, generated by this very instability' (p. 289).

A good place to end in capturing the spirit of this important new book, perhaps, is this wonderful quotation from Ben Okri: 'The fact of possessing imagination means that everything can be redreamed. Each reality can have its alternative possibilities. Human beings are blessed with the necessity of transformation' (quoted on p. 98). And as Dawn Freshwater has it in her concluding chapter, 'While [practitioner-based research] is likely in reality to become another dominant discourse (this cannot be avoided), it could also potentially become a discourse of openness, of participatory dialogue, multiple voices, and multiple truths' (p. 225).

PART V

Making What We Want:
Towards practitionership in a post-therapy era

CHAPTER 21

Intimations Towards a 'Post-Professional' Era: The pioneering genius of Georg Groddeck, 1866–1934

People have described [Groddeck] as a physician who burst like a storm into the soul of men, penetrating into the depths where all life is one, all boundaries are broken down, and body and mind are fused together.

> (Boss, in Groddeck 1951: 23)

It is absurd to suppose that one can ever understand life, but luckily one does not need to understand in order to be able to live or help others who want to live.

> (Groddeck 1951: 84)

INTRODUCTION

When I first came across the writings of Georg Groddeck (1866–1934) several years ago, I was stunned, even transfixed by his ideas, which coincided so closely with my own evolving thinking about healing, holism and the nature of the therapeutic change process. I felt as if I'd found a philosophical soul-mate, or mentor; and I found it quite extraordinary that, having done some 4–5 years of training in counselling and psychotherapy, I had never even heard his name mentioned before I came across his seminal book *The Meaning of Illness* in the course of a literature search about illness and disease.

I first discovered Georg Groddeck in the mid-1990s in the course of doing a training in body-oriented psychotherapy, and reading around the psychoanalytic literature for more critical perspectives on orthodox psychoanalysis. Groddeck stood out for me as a towering figure who, in his worldview and practice, moved way beyond the narrow Freudian psychoanalytic mentality, and prefigured the kind of trans-modern, post-professional approach to therapy that I am championing in this book. It is for this reason that I include here this lengthy examination of the so-called 'wild analyst' Georg Groddeck and his worldview, as it offers us a rich launching-pad from which to savour just what a 'post-professional' ideology and praxis might look like.

And yet in our rationality- and intellectually-dominated age of scientific reasoning, empiricist epistemologies and mechanistic-technocratic ways of seeing the world, perhaps the criminal neglect of Groddeck's work should come as no surprise. For Groddeck,

> any sort of treatment, scientific or old wive's poltice, may turn out to be right for the patient, since the outcome of medical or other treatment is not determined by the means prescribed but by what the patient's It likes to make of the prescription.
>
>   (ibid.: 78–9)

Dr Morris Robb revealingly wrote in an obituary to Groddeck,

> he seemed to be a part of nature, and his writings as natural as buds and flowers. Maybe this is the reason why he is taking such slow root in our culture and civilisation which looks askance at anything not canned, labelled and patented.
>
>   (Groddeck 1951: 17)

Groddeck's philosophy quite fundamentally challenges the notions that it is valid and appropriate to medicalise ill-health or discomfort, that the human body is 'nothing but a machine assembled from many parts' (Kollerstrom, quoted in Groddeck 1951: 18), that it is somehow possible to 'treat' a person's body, or mind, or 'faulty' thinking (cognitive-behaviourists, take note) separately from the whole person.

GRODDECK'S APPROACH TO HEALING

Broadly speaking Groddeck's approach was 'the treatment of the whole organism irrespective of whether the symptoms appeared to be physical or not' (ibid.: 19). His philosophy, then, is the perfect antidote to the mechanistic, mind–body-split dualism of Descartes which has had such a profound and deleterious effect on Western thinking since the dawn of the Enlightenment. No doubt Groddeck would have been highly critical of modern-day cognitive behaviour approaches to counselling and therapy, because of their implicit anti-holistic ontology of the person, whereby, in its cruder versions, rationality and thinking are effectively split off and treated as relatively isolatable and autonomous from the rest of the person's being. Here is Groddeck: 'up till now every step forward in technique has been paid for in increasing blindness to human life' (1951: 205–6).

Thankfully it is even starting to be recognised within science itself that 'thinking' and 'the emotional' form an indissolubly interdependent unity (Damasio 1994; Goleman 1995), and that it is quite invalid to consider one level of human beingness while ignoring, or attempting to hold constant, the other. Even a few Western philosophers have managed to throw off the baggage of rationality-dominated analytic philosophy to reach much the same conclusion (Johnson 1987; Solomon 1976; Oakley 1992). Perhaps this is what Groddeck was alluding to when he wrote that 'we are dishonest and misuse language when we speak of "pure" thought' (1951: 104). On this view, then, our belief systems and ways of thinking are inextricably implicated and rooted in our emotional histories, and human experience is always and necessarily *embodied* (Johnson 1987; Damasio 1994). For Groddeck, 'thinking' is a concept far wider in scope than is typically assumed in our mechanistic materialist worldview: 'In the assumption that one thinks only with the brain is to be found the origin of a thousand and one absurdities' (1951: 76).

Groddeck's approach to healing greatly illuminates current debates about the relative efficacy of differing approaches or schools in counselling and psychotherapy. Here is Groddeck himself: 'having found that all roads lead to Rome I do not consider it vastly important which road one takes, so long as one is willing to go slowly and is not too eager for wealth or recognition' (ibid.: 85). It is highly revealing to apply this thinking to the efficacy debate, for Groddeck's argument here is entirely consistent with the oft-repeated research finding that all forms of counselling and psychotherapy tend to yield very similar success rates. Following Groddeck, it is also clear that perhaps most of the current efficacy debate is based upon the quite false premise that it is the nature of the particular approach or technique(s) used by the practitioner which determine outcome (cf. Chapter 19, this volume). Seen from Groddeck's perspective, such a view is grossly naïve and just plain wrong: rather, clients-patients will 'use' (in the Winnicottian sense) whatever form of help is available (from high-tech medicine at one extreme to Shamanistic and spiritual healing practices at the other) in order to secure their own healing (cf. Frank and Frank 1991). Incidentally, this argument also accounts for what is, to many, the surprising counter-intuitive finding that, to quote Richard Mowbray, 'there is no clear evidence that professionally trained psychotherapists are in general more effective than paraprofessionals – Mowbray 1995: 118; and that 'Sadly, the correlation between training and effectiveness as a therapist is low' – Aveline 1990: 321; see also Russell 1981; Bohart and Tallman 1996; House 2001b.)

As soon as we accept this Groddeckian view of change, then, our attention quite naturally shifts to the question of what are the barriers and blocks to clients' self-healing, rather than to the wild goose-chase of trying to determine in a so-called 'scientific' sense which treatment modalities are the most efficaceous when 'applied to' the client-patient (see Chapter 19, this volume). Once again, then, the genius of Groddeck's early insight effectively short-circuits, and makes redundant and largely irrelevant, a whole literature on efficacy in the field of counselling and psychotherapy. Psychodynamically speaking, that wrong-headed debate in the literature does, in fact, depict very clearly a dysfunctional preoccupation with ego, control and instrumentalist reasoning, the artificial splitting of object from subject via objectifying a process which is irreducibly (inter-)subjective, the splitting of quality from quantity, and so on – issues to which I will have cause to return later.

GEORG GRODDECK THE MAN

Groddeck was a German physician practising around the turn of the century, who shared his physician-father's scepticism about so-called 'medical science'. According to Groddeck's translator, V.M.E. Collins (in Groddeck 1951: 5–6), he became known in both Germany and England 'as a masterful physician who had astonishing success with patients suffering from chronic symptoms long since abandoned as non-curable by others'. He held the view that disease and ill-health were the result of 'the patient's whole manner of living and attitude to life', and he strongly maintained that it was the patient–doctor relationship that was more important than any other factor in the treatment of illness and disease (ibid.). To the person-centred, humanistic practitioner this may all sound very familiar, but such ideas were by no means common in Groddeck's time, and his form of 'patient-centred medicine' can now be seen to be decades ahead of its time – certainly as far as modern Western medicine is concerned.

It was with the discovery of Freud's psychoanalytic ideas and the growing discipline of psychoanalysis that Groddeck was able to find confirmation of his developing ideas between 1910 and 1918 about the influence of unconscious symbolism in producing illness and disease symptoms; and in 1917 he published a pamphlet called 'Mental Determination of Organic Disease' – again, prefiguring by many decades very recent advances in the science of psychoneuroimmunology (e.g. Lyon 1993) and related fields. Collins is very definite in maintaining that the course of Groddeck's theories about disease and healing would have been the same whether or not Freud and Freudian psychoanalysis had existed (Groddeck 1951: 9). Indeed, *as early as 1888* Groddeck was concerned with the role of unconscious forces in organic disease (ibid.: 26); and so it is no surprise that Groddeck is often regarded as the father of psychosomatic medicine. His concept of the unconscious was far wider than that of Freud, and he constantly tested his theory on its most difficult and challenging terrain, that of chronic and mainly organic disease – in a way that philosopher of science Karl Popper would doubtless have approved of.

It is fascinating to quote Collins on Groddeck's approach, written nearly 65 years ago now, as it could be taken word-for-word as a description of humanistic person-centred counselling:

> he learned to feel himself into the patient's situation and to look at life through his eyes. By this self-immolation, this submerging of himself in the mind of another, he was able... to touch some key to the forces of life, and to cure many who had been ill so long that they came to him in despair rather than in hope.... [He became] the great-hearted friend to his patients, the unjudging commentator, the ever-ready helper.
> (ibid.: 9–10)

Collins quotes Groddeck himself as saying (echoing many of the great spiritual Masters), 'If you really want to be my follower, look at life for yourself and tell the world honestly what you see' (ibid.: 10). And Robb also states that for Groddeck, moral judgements were absent (ibid.: 14).

Yet Groddeck also believed in the *psychodynamics* of healing, and he is quite explicit about this – which in my view makes him possibly the first theorist to show how a fundamentally humanistic approach to helping the distressed and the sick, combined with a psychodynamic understanding, can be a very effective key to effective healing (cf. House 1997c). Thus, Groddeck himself writes, 'Any sick person who needs help must come under the influence of the transference as part of the cure... he [the patient] will unconsciously act the child and put the doctor in the place of the father or mother' (1951: 189); and it is the handling of the resistance to the transference which constitutes 'the alpha and omega of the healing art, no matter what the disease' (ibid.: 191; cf. Stein 1985). And Groddeck prefigures Karl Menninger's views, expressed many years later (Menninger 1963: Chapter 15), on the role of faith (and other 'intangibles') in treatment: 'where it [faith] is lacking the doctor can be of little use, whatever resources may be at his disposal.... Perhaps one can express it... as a trustful or confiding nature' (1951: 266).

Keyserling, in his 1934 obituary, wrote: 'He [Groddeck] took the view that the doctor really knows nothing, and of himself can do nothing..., for

his very presence can provoke to action the patient's own powers of healing'
(ibid.: 12, my emphasis). Susie Orbach (1994: 5) has written that 'language
has for many of us a way of hiding our feelings from ourselves, and a way of
not disclosing them to others' (contra the belief that therapeutic change is a
predominantly verbal, conscious, cognitive process); and how fitting is such
an insight in illuminating Groddeck's extraordinary success as a healer – for
'the real essence of Groddeck's treatment was his silent presence. One could
be with him when he asked no questions at all, and be more responsive
than when under treatment by the cleverest of psycho-analysts' (ibid.: 12).
Here is Groddeck himself: 'Silence may be strangling of a word but it is
none the less expressive of meaning' (ibid.: 207).

I have argued elsewhere (House 1996b) that it is essentially (non-
possessive) love that facilitates the client's healing (a point made at different
times in different ways by, among others, Carl Rogers, Anthony Storr, Donald
Winnicott, Peter Lomas and Rueben Fine): so it should come as no surprise
that 'Groddeck was one of the few men who fittingly and inevitably called
forth love, friendship and reverence in all who were able to know him'
(Morris Robb, quoted in Groddeck 1951: 14). And according to his
translator, Collins, 'The fate of his patients concerned him far more than
that of his theories' (ibid.: 28). Groddeck himself put it thus: 'Without the
arrow of Eros no wound can heal, no operation succeed....' (ibid.: 189).
And as remarked earlier, Groddeck fully immersed himself in his patients'
worlds, rather than relying on mere intellectual awareness of 'the facts of
the case. And – those favouring state regulation and registration please note
– for Robb, 'it is impossible to schematise such a [healing] process, and *to
talk of training anyone else to achieve its results is absurd*, yet some
approximation to a character of this sort is *the only basis on which psychotherapeutic power can be built*' (ibid.: 15, my emphases).

Groddeck was also very much a 'wounded healer' (to use Jung's term):
his parents, play-mate sister and brothers all died when he was still young –
losses which 'by some strange alchemy... were transmuted into a fuller
understanding of life, death, and grief' (ibid.). Perhaps it was, at least in
part, because of his profound insight and 'knowing' about pain and suffering
that he became a threatening figure to many: to quote Kollerstrom, 'Some
are offended and hurry away lest he should reveal to them their own hidden
sores' (ibid.: 20).

Here, then, may reside another reason why Groddeck's extraordinary
contributions have been so wilfully ignored: for just as Otto Rank's views on
the trauma of birth were systematically frozen out in the 1920s (and since)
perhaps due to the unconscious terror that his theoretical breakthrough
represented (e.g. Wasdell 1989, 1990), just so, Groddeck's capacity to quite

spontaneously go straight to the core of the person's distress would have been extremely threatening, and even dangerous, for those as yet unable to contain the full reality of their own woundedness and the rawness of their primitive developmental histories. Furthermore, 'People were... so much absorbed in sorting out the emotions he evoked in them that for a long time they were not in a state to appreciate his words exactly' (ibid.). Collins wrote over 60 years ago that Groddeck's ideas 'were indeed so strange and unexpected, so contrary to the crass materialism of his own generation, that it may be years before his contribution to medical science is fully understood' (ibid.: 28) (one is also reminded here of Rudolf Steiner's many extraordinary insights across the sciences, for which he has yet scarcely been recognised in modern culture). Sadly, perhaps in this sense little has really changed in the past 65 years.

GRODDECK, OBJECT RELATIONS AND THE TRANSPERSONAL

Those who knew Groddeck personally, and those who write about him, testify to his quite natural affinity with the transpersonal dimension of human experience. There is a very Jungian – not to mention object-relational – flavour to his view that

> [E]verything contains its opposite within itself.... One cannot even begin to understand life unless one realises that all its phenomena are conditioned by their opposites, that love is impossible without hatred, contempt without respect, fear without hope, loyalty without treachery.
> (ibid.: 90)

Thus writes Boss (ibid.: 23): 'he was always conscious of being at the mercy of forces greater than the self he knew'; and Robb describes how, in his writing, Groddeck would surrender himself to becoming 'an impersonal instrument performing a task which is imperiously demanded of him, when he loses himself to find a greater self' (ibid.: 16). Groddeck himself writes of 'a union with Infinite nature, a being at one with the creative universe, a surrender and dissolution of the barriers of personality so that the part, the ego, becomes merged with the whole' (ibid.: 49).

   In fundamental respects, this remarkable man also prefigured by some years the articulation and development of psychoanalytic object relations theory, for he believed that 'man creates the world in his own image, that all his inventions and activities, his science, art, finance, literature, vocabulary, industries and philosophies are in a special sense symbolic of his own nature and primitive experience' (Collins, in ibid.: 25); and Groddeck himself wrote that 'human thought and action are the inevitable consequence of unconscious symbolisation, that mankind is animated by the symbol' (ibid.: 89). He further writes that

> in those first few hours... and weeks of life... the child is still accepting all that he sees as part of his own body, symbolising everything in terms of his own body.... We ourselves never wholly abandon [such symbolisation] either in our conscious or our unconscious minds.... Man's unconscious dependence upon symbolism in his everyday affairs... has hardly been guessed at as yet, still less explored.
> (ibid.: 92, 152; cf., for example, Segal 1985)

GRODDECK ON THE LIMITATIONS OF THE SCIENTIFIC MENTALITY

For Groddeck, there is something intrinsically unknowable about life and human-beingness – which view he formulated in his idea of 'the It' (which Freud himself in turn 'borrowed' from Groddeck in his coining of the term 'the id'). Groddeck held the view that by their very nature, the unconscious forces operating in human behaviour will remain obscure and uncapturable in scientific terminology (ibid.: 40); and here is Groddeck himself: 'The sum total of an individual human being, physical, mental, and spiritual... I conceive of as a self unknown and *for ever unknowable*, and I call this the It...' (ibid.: 73, my emphasis) (a view that will not sit easily with those who fetishise the rational and ego-consciousness).

Elsewhere, Groddeck refers to 'the tyranny of conscious thought' (ibid.: 103). For him, the tyranny of the thinking ego 'has left us without a faith in anything greater than ourselves, and is in large measure responsible for those troubles which are threatening our very existence today' (ibid.: 106; do I hear apologists for the manic 'audit culture' wincing?). Some 70 years later, we find psychotherapist Jill Hall writing that 'Rational thought is not the most fitting mode with which to know the universe in its richness and fullness, and thus not a fitting mode with which to know ourselves' (Hall 1993: 4). For Groddeck, then, it was not medical science and the application of objective, disembodied skills or techniques that helped people in distress or dis(-)ease, but rather, 'that place of utter sincerity and selflessness where to be human is enough' (Collins, in Groddeck 1951: 29).

According to Groddeck, and in a view again many decades ahead of its time, the fundamental error that the scientific enterprise makes is to assume that its practices are not subject to the same unconscious forces that are operating in all other domains of existence and experience. Groddeck strongly believed that 'the unconscious forces at work in human behaviour are too obscure – and *by their very nature will probably always remain so* – to be confined in strictly scientific terminology' (ibid.: 40, my emphasis). Thus, science was just another expression of fantasy that has no legitimate right to the pre-eminence that it so arrogantly claims. Here is the celebrated neurologist Antonio Damasio in his important book *Descartes' Error*:

> I am sceptical of science's presumption of objectivity and definitiveness.... Perhaps the complexity of the human mind is such that the solution to the problem can never be known because of our inherent limitations. Perhaps we should not even talk about a problem at all, and speak instead of a mystery....
>
> (1994: xviii)

As Collins so beautifully puts it, Groddeck never forgot 'picture, poem and song whist working for the relief of the sick and the sorrow-laden' (Groddeck 1951: 31).

Some 70 years after Groddeck in her important book, *The Reluctant Adult*, Hall writes that

> the time has come to go beyond causal thinking... .If material existence is far too intricate and subtle a phenomenon to be understood through a cause/effect mode of thought, then surely we must let go the attempt to approach the human psyche from such a standpoint. When we come to try to understand the psyche, causal thinking is not only inadequate but is even positively dangerous.
>
> (Hall 1993: 2, 7)

Yet in the early years of the last century, Groddeck was writing that 'because we live we are bound to believe that... there are such things as causes and effects..., whereas we really know nothing about the connection between one event and another' (Groddeck 1951: 77). In our ego-bound and control-oriented way, furthermore, we delude ourselves in believing that we are masters of nature and of ourselves – a view which 'is assuredly false', but which it is necessary in our day-to-day lives to assume to be true (ibid.). The essential quality of man, according to Groddeck, is 'his over-estimation of himself' (ibid.: 78) – otherwise we will experience ourselves as impotent (or 'victims', to use Hall's terminology). Yet at this stage in the evolution of human consciousness, the ego is enormously reluctant even to countenance the view that 'everything important happens outside our knowledge and control' (ibid.).

For Groddeck, then, the scientific approach to reality is fundamentally alienating from our true nature. Maguire (1995: 60) has written that 'Men develop a capacity for mastering the universe and a compulsive preoccupation with what can be predicted, possessed, piled up and counted in order to deny the strength of their early emotional link with the mother'. In similar vein, and some 70 years earlier, Groddeck wrote that 'the more [man] struggles after exactitude in charting the world outside himself, the more deeply does he sink into his bondage to the ego' (Groddeck 1951: 105; cf. Hall 1993). For Groddeck, language is necessarily 'cut off from its symbolic expression, and... we must [therefore] go to the unconscious for evidence that the symbol is still operative in the depth of human nature' (ibid.: 199). And 'Through psycho-analysis we have come to understand that the symbol is vital, that it is life itself' (ibid.: 267).

There can be little doubt that if Groddeck were alive today, he would have no truck whatsoever with the current fashion of cognitive behaviour approaches to counselling and psychotherapy (see House and Loewenthal 2008, a and b): for as well as his disparagingly referring to 'the tyranny of conscious thought', he writes a bit later that 'There is little doubt that we Europeans have had enough to do with thinking' (ibid.: 104); and 'Our brains are being over-taxed by the continual effort to suppress our real nature – primitive, purposeful... – in favour of what we take to be the real, the objective' (106). Yet we can never in principle fully know the real: Groddeck refers to 'the arrogance which refuses to recognise the inevitable limitations of human knowledge' (106); and (prefiguring Lacan, perhaps?), while 'presumably the Real exists,... never for one moment can we come into contact with it' (91).

GRODDECK ON PSYCHOSOMATIC MEDICINE AND HUMAN CONSCIOUSNESS

For Groddeck, there are no random events in human experience, but rather, a deep and normally unconscious meaning waiting to be discovered. Thus,

> [I]t is my custom to ask a patient who has slipped and broken his arm, 'What was your idea in breaking your arm?'.... I have never failed to get a useful reply to such questions... we can always find both an inward and an outward cause for any event in life.
> (ibid.: 81)

However, 'For the most part... these internal causes are not known to the conscious mind' (ibid.: 82). Because conventional medicine typically fetishises and objectifies 'outward causes' and ignores the deep subjectivities of 'inward causes', Groddeck sees no harm in selectively emphasising the latter as a counterweight to the mechanistic excesses of orthodox 'scientific', *bits-of-person* centred medicine: thus, 'man creates his own illnesses for definite purposes, using the outer world merely as an instrument, finding there an inexhaustible supply of material which he can use for this purpose (ibid.: 81) (echoes, here, of Rudolf Steiner's view that 'We get ill for our own development').

Some 75 years ago, Groddeck was writing about the psychological or mental determinants of cancer, thus again prefiguring recent developments in psycho-onchology (Holland and Rowland 1989):

> [I]t is a little surprising to find a disease so important to our age as cancer left almost entirely uninvestigated on the mental side. My own experience in cases of cancer leads me to associate it with the personal attitude of the sufferer towards motherhood.
> (ibid.: 160)

Indeed, Groddeck explicitly advocated psychotherapy for cancer patients (ibid.: 166). More generally, he viewed the experience of guilt, and associated self-punishment and the desire for a clean slate, as a major psychological determinant of disease (ibid.: 161). Again, such a view dovetails very neatly with Jill Hall's argument, controversial to many, that ultimately and at some very fundamental level, we all have responsibility for what happens to us – whether we actually experience such responsibility or not (Hall 1993; cf. Hillman 1996).

Recent developments in the study of human consciousness have begun to question the previously taken-for-granted view that consciousness is exclusively a product of post-natal human development and a function of the brain alone (see, for example, Wasdell 1990; Hall 1993), with some commentators beginning to talk in terms of so-called 'cellular consciousness'; yet once again, Groddeck got there many decades earlier:

> I go as far as to believe there is some sort of individual consciousness even in the embryo, yes, even in the fertilised ovule, and for that matter in the unfertilised one too... that every single separate cell has this consciousness of individuality.
> (Groddeck 1951: 83)

GRODDECK ON 'THE CHILD WITHIN'

Groddeck writes eloquently, and with great wisdom, about the importance of the child inside us. Thus, he writes that 'The essential life of any man depends upon the degree to which he has been able to remain childlike, infantile, in spite of the blunting influences of adult life' (ibid.: 203). This all sounds very similar to Donald Winnicott's notion of 'the capacity to play' (Winnicott 1971/1974), for whom playing was the basis for 'the whole of man's experiential existence' (1974: 75; cf. House 2002, 2008d, e). Later, Groddeck writes that 'his childish nature remains with man and rules him till the end of his life' (Groddeck 1951: 207), and that 'the child knows far better how to live than does the adult; he can still live in fullness of spirit because *he has not come under the domination of the ego which distorts life*' (ibid.: 208, my emphasis). And in a quite enchanting statement on power, he writes, 'The greatest monarch in the world is the infant. Whoever desires power – and which of us does not? – should go to little children and let himself be trained by them' (ibid.: 218–19).

On individuation too, Groddeck prefigures many who have written on the subject since his time: 'life may indeed be regarded as one long process of getting free from the mother, beginning at the moment of conception' (ibid.: 214).

CONCLUSION: BEYOND THE MECHANISTIC *ZEITGEIST*

In these disquieting days of high-tech medicine (curing the patient rather than assisting the client to heal), registration-mindedness and credentialisation, preoccupation with audit, so-called 'scientific' evaluation and cost-effectiveness, and pressures towards ever-more short-term rationality-dominated cognitive behaviour therapeutic approaches, we would do well to pause and consider the profound wisdom and deep learning that can be gained from assimilating the quintessentially human(e)(istic) philosophy of Georg Groddeck. His writings are at once inspired, breathtakingly brilliant and creative, sometimes bewildering – like the best poetry, sometimes capturing in his soulful prose that which is normally impossible to articulate in human language. Here is Robb again: his writings 'are so much a part of himself, free, spontaneous.... They carry something of the man himself, who has breathed his very spirit into the written word. They make a long moment of inspiration' (Groddeck 1951: 16). And here again is Groddeck's translator, Collins: 'he was pre-eminently the artist rather than the scientist... [he] has the artist's vision which penetrates the veils we call reality, and the deep truths that he reveals are often only to be expressed in paradox' (ibid.: 28, 29). Again, Donald Winnicott would surely have heartily approved!

This chapter has inevitably been highly selective, and has concentrated predominantly upon Groddeck's book *The World of Man* (1934). Yet the other four books of his writings (listed in full below) are at the very least equally rich in insight and laced with the wisdom of this masterful healer-physician-psychoanalyst and extraordinary human being. That the brilliantly insightful, thought-provoking and challenging 'proto-postmodern' ideas of Groddeck have been so neglected is surely a telling testimony to the mechanistic *Zeitgeist* which is still in the ascendency some 85 years after Groddeck, despite increasing signs that the modernist technocratic world-view is everywhere falling apart – from the level of quantum physics, the physical environment, through the human psyche and consciousness and forms of human social organisation, and into the realms of astro-physics. When the current modernist, scientistic paradigm is eventually transcended, which it most surely will be, it is only then, perhaps, that the work of great seers like Georg Groddeck and Rudolf Steiner will receive the central recognition which their thought so richly deserves.

For those of us who profoundly believe that good and effective therapeutic practice is 95 per cent inspiration and intuition, and 5 per cent theoretical perspiration, Georg Groddeck is a criminally neglected figure in the history of healing and psychoanalysis. Humanistic-dynamic and transpersonal therapists could do much worse than return to Groddeck for their inspiration and affirmation of their values and practice – and I hope that this chapter has given readers a taste of the feast of wisdom and the goldmine of insight that awaits anyone who takes the step into Groddeck's inspirational world.

THE PUBLISHED WORKS OF GEORG GRODDECK

The Book of the It, Vision, London, 1950 (orig. 1927)

The Unknown Self, Vision, London, 1951 (orig. 1930)

Exploring the Unconscious, Vision, London, 1949 (orig. 1933)

The World of Man, Vision, London, 1951 (orig. 1934)

The Meaning of Illness: Selected Psychoanalytic Writings (incl. his correspondence with Freud), Hogarth Press, London, 1977

CHAPTER 22

From Professionalisation Towards a Post-Therapy Era

> Truth is a pathless Land.... Truth cannot be organised; nor should any organisation be formed to lead or coerce people along any particular path.... A belief is purely an individual matter, and you cannot and must not organise it. If you do, it becomes dead, crystallised; it becomes *a creed... to be imposed on others.*
> (Jiddu Krishnamurti, *Talks*, 1929 & 1974, emphasis added)

If the former Chair of the United Kingdom Council for Psychotherapy were to describe a newly published book as 'articulate', 'incisive' and one which will become 'an indispensable element of good training in the field', one might expect it to be predominantly favourable towards the professionalisation of the therapy field. The book in question, however, is Alex Howard's *Challenges to Counselling and Psychotherapy*, published (as I write, in late 1996) this very week by Macmillan; and the former Chair of the UKCP is Emmy van Deurzen-Smith, who has written the Foreword to the book. Yet far from Alex Howard being approving of current professionalising developments, the very opposite is the case – here are some choice selective quotations from this important book:

> There is no evidence that training, supervision or experience make a person less likely to abuse a client.... Nor, it seems, do accreditation and training schemes detect the likelihood of an individual abusing a client (p. 22). Can essential counsellor virtues be detected, taught and accredited within selection and training programmes? There is absolutely no evidence, or reason, to believe that they can. Why,

---

I first started using the term 'post-therapy era' in the mid-1990s, and I used the term in the title of this article which appeared in *Self and Society* in 1997. I reproduce the article here because I think some 15 years after the initial writing, it pretty much stands the test of time, and shows the way towards what I have since come to call principled 'post-professional' practice. Any reader who has read the book in full up to this point will be able to see how the thinking in this piece coheres with the trans-modern worldview that underpins the whole book.

then, should we regard counselling and therapy as professional activities if the human qualities they depend upon cannot be reliably delivered by due professional process? (p. 23). ...[accreditation]... certainly reveals a great deal about the understandable search for power, status and a secure income (p. 32).... Nor... can ordinary human virtues such as love, warmth, compassion and empathy, be professionally organised....

Let us be wary of any group that accredits itself as being able to provide love, or a substitute, and which siphons off ordinary humanity and sells it back for a fee.

(p. 159)

FROM PROFESSIONALISATION...

Rather than rehearse here the plethora of arguments that have been made against what might be called 'didactic professionalisation', I believe that a formidable case against registration *as a general principle* (whether statutory or voluntary) can convincingly be made in a few paragraphs. In a recent article in *Human Potential* (Autumn 1996), Tricia Scott provides the following rationale for registration: 'The important question is how best to organise the profession to ensure that the best job is done in the public interest', given that 'the people who come to us are vulnerable...'.

However, the public-interest argument in favour of registration simply doesn't stand up to scrutiny. There are two strands to the argument: first, can didactic accreditation and registration procedures be shown to create and guarantee practitioners who are more competent and less likely to harm clients than in a non-registration environment?; and secondly, if such a guarantee of competence can't be demonstrated or sustained, then the only remaining rationale favouring registration is that of 'weeding out' and disqualifying abusive or incompetent practitioners.

On the first point, Alex Howard's comments are very pertinent: 'I have found no relationship between the qualifications of a counsellor and the quality of his or her work', and Highly trained counsellors succumb at least as much as less skilled colleagues [to abusing their clients]'. He goes on to cite an unpublished paper presented to the British Psychological Society in 1991 by Carol Sherrard, which reviewed some 41 empirical studies comparing the effectiveness of professional and non-professional workers, *only one of which concluded that the professional group was more effective.* This somewhat counter-intuitive finding is entirely consistent with that of Roberta Russell, who in her exhaustive review of the literature concluded that

'Paraprofessionals consistently achieve outcomes equal to or better than professional outcomes', and 'therapists who have undergone traditional training are no more effective than those who have not'.

If, then, there is no evidence that registered or accredited practitioners are more effective or less abusive than the unregistered, the only remaining rationale for registration is that in the real world of therapeutic practice, registration and its associated disciplinary regime will be used to bring incompetent or abusive practitioners to heel. Such a justification turns on the following crucial issues: first, in reality, will the mechanisms and procedures set in place actually be used on the ground, and to any significant extent, against abusive or incompetent practitioners?; secondly, assuming for a moment that registration *will* bring about a real and significant weeding out of abusive practitioners, will any benefits that this brings to the client/ public interest in terms of enhanced safety more than outweigh any harmful side-effects that registration brings in its wake?; and thirdly, is registration the only means of achieving enhanced client safety? – for if there exist alternative and equally effective means of enhancing client safety and practitioner accountability, but without the accompanying negative side-effects of didactic registration, then clearly it would make far more sense to go for the former than the latter.

Indeed, as David Kalisch has recently pointed out to me in a personal communication (1996), even if it could be shown empirically that a system of registration would positively benefit client safety, this would be an argument in favour of a totally inclusive register rather than for the exclusive variety proposed by UKCP and BAC/COSCA. For it hasn't been demonstrated empirically that so-called 'competence' criteria of the kind enthusiastically embraced by the register-builders have any predictive value whatsoever in relation to practitioners' ethical behaviour – which is of course the real issue as far as client safety is concerned. Such an inclusive register would be essentially the same as the system of Non-Credentialed Registration mentioned by Mowbray (see also Postle 2003), and might best operate at local authority level in a manner that's very different from the high-status, high-profile exclusive registers currently being promoted by the training-accrediting lobbies – and which, effective as they are in terms of career-building for those on the registers, have never been shown to be effective in protecting clients from the 'professionals'.

First, to what extent will disciplinary procedures actually be used? According to Daniel Hogan (quoted in Richard Mowbray's *Case Against Psychotherapy Registration*, 1995), 'In the mental health professions [in the USA], data from the field of psychology support the proposition that board discipline is virtually non-existent'. Mowbray himself maintains that 'Given the poor track record of systems based on professional codes of ethics and conduct and self-disciplinary action as a means of protecting the public, what reason do we have to be confident that such a system would be any more effective in producing its purported benefits for the public?' And finally, the very nature of the therapy field suggests that abused clients will very often feel unable or be unwilling to make official complaints anyway (not least because of the experienced shame involved) – no matter how confident they might be about the outcome. So once again, registration will no doubt be very good at conveying *an illusion* of effective policing of the field – while abusive and incompetent practitionership continues apace.

Yet even if it *could* be shown that disciplinary procedures under a licensing system would be effective, a wealth of empirical and logical evidence has been accumulated by a number of sceptical commentators which strongly suggests that the harmful side-effects of registration by far outweigh any conceivable benefits that it would confer upon the field (e.g. Hogan 1979).

Finally, is registration the only way to secure practitioner accountability? One of Daniel B. Hogan's list of pre-conditions for licensing is that 'simpler and less restrictive methods that would accomplish the same purposes must be unavailable' (for example, existing laws). Mowbray (1995) sets out in detail a whole host of existing and comparatively easily implemented procedures which would, at the very least, effect the same purported benefits as licensing, but without the many negative side-effects – including education of the public, the application of existing laws, full disclosure provisions, non-credentialed registration, and self and peer accreditation.

In sum, it seems clear that the case for didactic registration falls at a whole host of hurdles – *any one of which would alone* be sufficient to conclude that registration is an inappropriate direction for our field to move in.

...VIA THE STATUTORY/VOLUNTARY SLEIGHT OF HAND...

There is also an important question to address regarding the alleged and, to date, little discussed distinction between statutory and voluntary registration. There has recently been a discernible shift within the humanistic movement towards embracing voluntary registration as a more palatable and apparently more 'humanistic' fall-back position, as the anti-statutory arguments have gained increasing currency in the field. Yet in practice and in the longer term, there may actually be very little effective difference between statutory and voluntary registration. There must be many unregistered practitioners who are increasingly experiencing a fall-off in their practice, as training organisations stipulate that trainees must only work with registered practitioners (I, with many others, could relate some horror stories about this), as the public services increasingly demand registration or accreditation for all their employees, and as referrers increasingly refer only to registered/ accredited workers. What this amounts to, then, is a form of *de facto* statutory regulation; indeed, the term 'voluntary register' is in fact a logically incoherent notion – for a register surely loses its very *raison d'être* if people are allowed not to be on it (whoever heard of a 'voluntary' school register, for example!)....

What this amounts to, then, is a sleight of hand, such that, (a) 'voluntary registration' sounds far less unhumanistic than statutory registration; (b) approximately the same degree of regulation of the field can be brought about by pursuing the 'voluntary' path as could be effected by statutory regulation; so (c) we'll support 'voluntary' registration, sound much more reasonable and humanistic, and yet still get precisely what we want, i.e. a *de facto*, effectively statutorily regulated field in all but name – and one which could, of course, be 'topped up' at any time in the future with further restrictive legislation.

It follows from this that the anti-regulation arguments set out above apply with just as much force to the so-called 'voluntary' position as they do to statutory registration.

...TOWARDS A POST-THERAPY ERA

The tide may well be beginning to turn against the professionalising mentality, as a steadily increasing number of practitioners begin to question many of the unsubstantiated assertions of the professionalisers. More generally, surely the very *energy* of professionalisation (not least its desire to tighten, control and above all somehow guarantee the safety of the therapeutic process) is quite fundamentally dissonant with the energy of personal growth, human potential development and transformation. We would do well to listen closely to that eminently wise sage Jiddu Krishnamurti, who vehemently criticised all institutions and man's urge to institutionalise – not least because it is surely naïvely unrealistic to expect more institutionalisation and systematisation to lead to healthy change when those very processes invariably aggravate rather than alleviate societal ills.

If we agree with Brian Thorne that counselling and therapy are essentially *subversive* activities, then as soon as the therapeutic mentality becomes a cultural norm and part of an Establishment (medical or state) orthodoxy, then perhaps that is, by definition, the time to challenge the very idea of 'therapy' and 'psychopathology', and to transform and transcend what are rapidly becoming ideologies that have outlived their usefulness as ways of comprehending and engaging with the world. Krishnamurti again: 'if one is only concerned with helping the individual to conform to the existing social pattern..., is one not maintaining the very causes that make for frustration, misery and destruction?' Indeed, for Krishnamurti, any kind of 'adjustment therapy' to a psycho-social norm inevitably infringes and prevents true freedom.

Perhaps, then, recently published books like those by Alex Howard (1996), Richard Mowbray (1995), Ian Parker et al. (1995) and David Smail (1996) (not to mention Jeffrey Masson, of course) are but the harbingers of a new *post-therapy era* which questions quite fundamentally the individualising, ideological assumptions of the psychotherapeutic mentality. Profound disquiet about the existing paradigm is even beginning to emerge from within psychoanalytic orthodoxy. Here, for example, are some recent thoughts of Joyce McDougall (1995):

> The question of a paradigm shift with regard to our metapsychology merits a full exploration.... There is the ever-present risk that our... analysands may employ much of their analytic process in an attempt to confirm their analyst's theoretical expectations!.... Our standard psychiatric and psychoanalytic classifications... are equally questionable.... It would be presumptuous to imagine that it is our theories that bring about psychic change and symptomatic cure!... Is not our leading perversion... the belief that we hold the key to the truth?
>
> (234–6 *passim*)

Krishnamurti would agree: 'You will always experience what you believe and nothing else. And this invalidates your experience.... *Belief conditions its own supposed proof.*'

One thing seems clear: registration or no registration, the human potential movement, in both its humanistic and transpersonal forms, will most surely take a leading role in this r/evolutionary process as the evidence relentlessly accumulates that the old paradigm and its associated *Weltanschauung* is no longer remotely adequate to meet the urgent needs and challenges of our deeply troubled times.

CHAPTER 23

Transforming Commodified Supervision
into Peer Support

INTRODUCTORY NOTE

This chapter was originally written in late 1995 and then revised in May 1996, being inspired at the time by Richard Mowbray's then recently published and now seminal book, *The Case Against Psychotherapy Registration* (Mowbray 1995; see Chapter 13, this volume). Mowbray convincingly argued that current trends towards bureaucratic professionalisation (hereafter, 'BP') in the fields of psychotherapy (via the UKCP) and counselling (via the then BAC) would inevitably end up with a 'profession' typified by, *inter alia*, the monopolised practices and prohibitive market-entry requirements for both trainers and trainee-practitioners, and a general resultant market-wide hike in the level of fees charged to clients.

There were, and still are, many humanistically inclined practitioners working in the broad field of personal development and human potential who are quite unable to accept the modernist ideology and 'control freak' values of BP – not to mention the deleterious consequences for clients that may well ensue if the logic of current developments prevails: for as Pfeffer has written, 'the outcomes of regulation and licensing are frequently not in the interests of the consumers or the general public. It is difficult to find a single empirical study of regulatory effects that does not arrive at essentially this conclusion' (quoted in Mowbray 1995: 85).

I include this piece, originally written in 1995, as an illustration of just one way in which the 'commodity form' taken by professionalised therapy might be creatively transformed into something less alienating and formal. My strong hunch is that non-marketised arrangements such as these probably exist right across the field; and whilst practitioners in the humanistic field were formerly happy to speak about them quite openly, with the spectre of state regulation and the New Surveillance stalking the land, perhaps practitioners are now more inclined to keep such eminently sensible arrangements for enhancing the quality of their work to themselves. I myself have a non-marketised peer 'inter-visory' relationship with a long-standing colleague from Norwich Collective days (see Chapter 1), and it enables me to charge fees to clients that are deliberately well below the going market rate for therapy services.

I believe there exist attractive, viable and rigorous alternatives to the bureaucratic model, which are more effective in terms of protecting the client interest; which build structures far more in keeping with the values of an emancipatory humanistic psychology than current professionalising developments; and which will help to reverse the trend towards the 'gentrification' of psychotherapy and counselling by making therapeutic and personal-developmental help available to a significantly wider spectrum of clients than is the case under the 'high-fees economy' that accompanies the bureaucratic 'psychotherapy (training) business' (ibid.: 57)

The Independent Practitioners Network (IPN), of course, forms a crucial aspect of such an alternative structure; and the following contribution aims to flesh out just what such a structure might look like which runs alongside and complements the outstanding group-level 'initiative for pluralism' that the IPN represents.

I lightly edited the article for inclusion in *Ipnosis* magazine in 2001, but in its essentials it is pretty much identical to the version that I revised about five years ago.

> The basic notion of available sources of feedback, confrontation and support is one thing. However, if a requirement for supervision goes beyond that to specifying the *form* it should take,... motivation for such a requirement may stem from the drive for professionalization and the business aspects of supervision... since significant income potential is involved.
> (Mowbray 1995: 248, original emphasis)

> Supervision is a difficult word to hear clearly. It stimulates emotional responses laden with superego affects. The word implies superior status, and a measure of control exercised over another.
> (Alonso and Shapiro 1993: 327)

> The supervisory orientation which I have found most effective and realistic is predominantly a lateral, rather than a vertical or hierarchical, orientation....
> (Searles 1965: 585)

INTRODUCTION

In this contribution I will focus on one particular aspect of the case against bureaucratic or what I call 'didactic' professionalisation: namely, the inflation of the cost of psychotherapy services consequent upon the kind of professionalising changes which are currently occurring in the field. What I will call the 'gentrification' of psychotherapy is the logical consequence of a professionalisation process which is predicated upon ever more stringent training 'standards' and, concomitantly, ever higher training costs for new practitioners, who in turn are forced to recoup their massive training outlays by charging higher fees to clients than they would otherwise have had to charge. In turn, access to services becomes the preserve of a diminishing number of economically well-off clients – and to make matters worse, this is happening at a time when NHS psychotherapy departments are being closed all over the country, as the accountancy audit-mentality of 'cost-effectiveness' spreads like a bush-fire throughout the NHS. Thus, the availability of public-service, long-term psychological support and help is being systematically sacrificed on the altar of 'cost-effectiveness' and 'audit-mindedness' (Fahy and Wessely 1993; for a critique see House 1996e).

Hogan (1979) has written of 'a significant increase in the cost of professional services' consequent upon the advent of licensing in the psychotherapy field (quoted in Mowbray 1995: 87). And for Trebilcock and Shaul (also quoted in Mowbray, p. 86), 'a general licensure regime [for mental health services] seems highly undesirable. Social costs in terms [e.g.] of higher fees for services... are likely to be substantial'. The radical psychiatrist Peter Breggin is even more blunt: for him, 'licensure laws enable groups of professionals to monopolize the psychotherapy market by locking out unlicensed competitors while guaranteeing a steady flow of clients and high fees for themselves' (quoted in Mowbray, p. 142).

The thorough-going incursion of market relations and the ideology of commodity exchange into the field of human potential development is deeply disturbing to many practitioners, and, I would argue, deeply antithetical to the foundational values on which humanistic theory and practice are based. The bureaucratic professionalisation of the field, and the associated adoption of immersion in the values of market exchange, are indicative of our field becoming swamped and swallowed up by the current socio-economic and cultural *Zeitgeist* of narcissistic materialism that is sweeping the globe at this point in human history (Lasch 1979; Steiner 1987).

Back in 1991, House and Hall wrote that 'any system of accreditation should as far as possible be consistent with the philosophy on which our approach to personal development is based' (p. 36). It follows that for those who find deeply disquieting the alienation, materialism and narcissism which full-blown market relations represent, there will exist a strong wish to seek other operational arrangements which subvert the commodity form, while retaining the rigour and thoroughness that personal development work necessitates. This chapter addresses one important area in which such a counter-cultural challenge can effectively be mounted – namely, in the field of one-to-one supervision.

'SUPERVISION' OR 'PEER SUPPORT'?

Juliana Brown and Richard Mowbray (personal communication) have argued that the very term 'supervision' is a hierarchy-laden concept: it implies a superiority on the part of the supervisor, and concomitantly lesser status on the part of supervisee. Yet as Fanning et al. (1994) have written, 'In other professions it is recognised that any practitioner needs to seek the opinion of another practitioner about some cases – not necessarily difficult ones, *nor must the help be sought from a more senior practitioner*' (quoted in Mowbray 1995: 247, my emphasis). Thus, for Mowbray, '"supervision" is usually supposed to indicate a *non-hierarchical* relationship with a "benevolent experienced other"' (ibid.: my emphasis). In view of this, there are very strong arguments for replacing the term 'supervision', as its more common everyday usage typically implies a hierarchical relationship.

I therefore propose to use the alternative term 'Peer Support' (or 'PS') in this chapter, which seems to me to be far more accurately descriptive of what actually happens when fellow professionals regularly meet to discuss and explore the practice of at least one of them. On this view, the term 'supervision' should perhaps be confined to those supervisorial relationships in which there *does* exist a hierarchical aspect – i.e. in the case of a newly qualified practitioner or a trainee who seeks the support of a more experienced worker as part of her/his apprenticeship in the field.

HOW BUREAUCRATICALLY PROFESSIONALISED PSYCHOTHERAPY BECOMES 'GENTRIFIED'

When costs of entry (through training, supervision, etc.) into the field are so exorbitantly high, then clearly something has to give: *either* new practitioners will have to charge higher client fees in order to recoup the very high costs of rendering themselves registrable with the UKCP, thereby taking psychotherapy and counselling even further out of the financial reach of the majority than it already is; *or* it will only be new practitioners from comparatively high income backgrounds who will be able to afford to render themselves registerable… – a sort of *embourgeoisissement* of the psychotherapy field. The result will be a psychotherapy 'profession' which becomes ever-more dominated by those (clients *and* practitioners) who are fortunate enough to be able to afford the high-cost services on offer in the market-place.

One possible response to these disturbing developments is to challenge the form taken by commodification at its root – that is, and in the case of PS, to devise a system whereby fellow practitioners exchange Peer Support (PS) services with each other, and in which no (or very little) actual exchange of money occurs. It is only through developments such as this (comparable to local LETS exchange relations, perhaps) that the prevailing cultural norms can be problematised and challenged.

PERSONAL PROFESSIONALISING EXPERIENCE

I can offer my own experience as a very real and highly pertinent example. Having trained as a counsellor between 1987 and 1990, and having been practising for some six years, I have recently completed a further three-year non-UKCP-recognised psychotherapy training [this written in 1995]. My route to UKCP registerability would therefore have been through Association for Humanistic Psychology Practitioner (AHPP) membership, necessitating two years of post-training weekly 'supervision'/PS (approximate cost: £2,600 before tax). Assuming this amounts to approaching £2,000 after tax, this sum is equivalent to about eighty sessions of therapy at local prevailing market rates. In other words, I would in some form (either by adopting very low rates for a few clients, or a slightly lower fee spread across all clients) be able to offer that value of growth work/therapy/counselling to clients over a two-year period without any loss of income, if I were involved in a PS network where practitioners exchange PS services outside of the market-exchange system.

My own experience in the field suggests that there already exists an informal and marked 'two nation' split in the field between those practitioners who are committed to hierarchically professionalised status, high fees and the ideology of market exchange relations; and those who are committed to self- and peer-affirmed status, lower levels of fees, and subverting approaches to market relations. In this contribution, I am proposing that the latter practitioners formalise their practices with greater rigour in the field of PS; and this is particularly important in the light of Rowan's essentially speculative but potentially damaging assertion (Rowan 1995) that what he calls 'Activity One' *psychotherapists* receive regular supervision, whereas 'Activity Two' *human growth practitioners* are 'probably not supervised' (p. 43). (For refutations of Rowan's attempted distinction between Activity One and Activity Two types of practice, see Mowbray 1996; Postle 1996). I set out below the kind of plausible structure that could very successfully replace the market-driven model of professional 'supervision'.

It should be noted that the Independent Practitioners Network has already gone a considerable distance in addressing these questions in its structure of relatively (but not wholly) autonomous peer groups (Mowbray 1995: 240–1; Totton 1995). What I am proposing here is intended to complement the existing IPN structure, in that what I describe below is intended to fulfil the need for *individual,* one-to-one PS. While the IPN peer group structure does include a vital PS function, it also has a wider focus than that of PS members' client practice alone.

THE 'PEER SUPPORT NETWORK' (PSN) CONCEPT

A PSN system could take several forms. The simplest one, described here, is a 'daisy chain' system, whereby in a group of three, A would give peer support to B, B to C, and C to A (at whatever frequency was agreed between PS pairings, but perhaps not less than three-weekly). An optimal PSN size might be five or six practitioners, who would also meet as a group periodically to share and explore matters of concern around PS practice and theory, and could thereby function as an ongoing PS 'continuing development group'.

Clearly, once a group of (say) six practitioners had formed, there would have to be a group-negotiated choice as to the specific PS relationships that were set up at the outset, and this might well be by no means a smooth and conflict-free process! But the open and successful negotiation of this process would most certainly bode well for the future cohesion and 'communality' of the PSN group.

The PSN group would also have an important *consultancy function,* whereby if there developed difficulties in any PS relationship within the network, both participants in the conflict could 'call in' at least one other network member as a process consultant to facilitate and work through the difficulty.

It might also be appropriate for each 'peer-supportee' to pay a small fee for each of their PS sessions (e.g. £2), which would then go into a PSN fund, which could be used for further group ongoing development in PS-related issues (workshops, conferences, buying in group consultancy services, etc.).

Each group could also undertake to supervise a recently or newly qualified practitioner, with the supervisor's fee perhaps being paid partly by the supervisee, and partly out of the group fund based on the small contributions just referred to. The new practitioner would take full part in the ongoing whole-group activities; and when the group felt confident that s/he was able competently to take the role of peer-supporter her/himself, s/he would be admitted into the group as full member, and at such a time the existing pattern of intra-network PS relationships could be reviewed and re-negotiated. In this way, peer support would not be the exclusive preserve of an already experienced and practising practitioner-elite, for there would be an institutionalised space for newly qualified practitioners receiving supervision at a reasonable cost. Such a system would also be very much in keeping with the 'apprenticeship' model of training advocated by Guy Gladstone, which is based on the premise that 'becoming a therapist is a personally transmitted craft for which no amount of academic course work can substitute' (quoted in Mowbray 1995: 135).

When one network member felt a strong wish or need to change her or his peer-supporter, this would have to be taken to the whole network and negotiated, hopefully with the minimum of disruption to the existing PS relationship pattern.

In the case of Norwich (where I work), the adoption of such a system would mean that after tax, each group member would be between £300 and £1,000 a year better off (depending on their pre-existing frequency of market-rate supervision), which for all six members together represents something between £1,800 and £6,000 a year. Practitioners would thereby be enabled to reduce their fees accordingly, or see more low-fee clients, or some combination of the two. At prevailing market rates in Norwich, *these savings represent between 72 and 240 extra client sessions per year per six-person group that could be offered to clients – sessions which would not* (ceteris paribus) *have been available under the pre-existing market exchange system of supervision* where practitioners each paid full market rates for individual supervision.

In this way, then, it is clear that personal growth work, psychotherapy and counselling would be made available to clients at the margin who would otherwise not be able to afford it – a necessary condition for being able to respond to the need for 'therapy for the world' talked about by Andrew Samuels (1993).

CONCLUSION

My strong hunch is that there probably already exist a number of similar informal, creative arrangements for PS in different parts of the country. One possible advantage of the system proposed here is that it can be seen to be rigorous and responsible in the public domain. Yet as Mowbray so clearly points out in his *Case*, standardisation of practice so easily leads to a *deadening* of practice, a stifling of creativity. And anyway, 'what evidence has been accumulated as to the contribution of a formal 1:1 supervisory relationship to enhanced practitioner competence compared with other types of feedback and support?' (Mowbray 1996). The model discussed here should be seen, therefore, as just one approach amidst a plurality of possible means of practitioner support.

In conclusion, I believe that the PSN system described above makes for an eminently viable and attractive alternative to current forms of commodified supervision. Such a networking system, if widely adopted, could sit very comfortably alongside other extant counter-cultural forms like the peer groups of the Independent Practitioners Network, which, taken as a whole, offer a principled and viable alternative to the 'psychotherapy training business' ethos of the UKCP and the BAC(P).

Note
I would like to thank Juliana Brown, Lindsay (now Grace Lindsay) Cooke, Richard Mowbray and Denis Postle for their insightful comments on an earlier draft of this article, which led to my making significant improvements to it.

CHAPTER 24

Towards Post-Professional Practice: Principled non-compliant practitionership in a post-regulation era

CULTURAL CONTEXTS

Over a decade ago now, I wrote an article for *Self and Society* titled 'From professionalisation towards a post-therapy era' (see Chapter 22, this volume), in which I partly advocated and partly predicted the dawning of a new era in human-potential, therapeutic practice which I labelled 'post-professional', and which I believed to be fully in keeping with the core humanistic values which I and other readers of that journal strive to uphold in our work. Part of this process, I hoped-cum-predicted, would be the gradual 'paradigmatic' movement beyond quasi-medical-model 'psychotherapy-mindedness', and towards a form of helping which was, following Ivan Illich, 'post-professional' in the sense developed at length in my subsequent book *Therapy Beyond Modernity* (2003a). Little did I know at the time of writing that article that

---

In this, the final main chapter of the book, this recently written piece combines an article published in the humanistic journal *Self and Society* (2008) with a paper prepared for the Alliance for Counselling and Psychotherapy (2010), making the case for what I call 'Principled Non-compliance' (or PNC) in a post-regulated psy world. As I write (August 2010), it is still far from clear whether the long-trailored Health Professions Council state regulation of Britain's psychological therapies will go ahead. Not least, a Judicial Review has recently been launched, and this is just one of a number of fronts on which the Alliance for Counselling and Psychotherapy Against State Regulation (of which I am a founder-member) is challenging HPC state regulation of the psy field (see also Postle and House 2009). In some circles, PNC has now morphed into Alternative Professional Accountability (or APA); but whatever we call it, the strong argument in favour of APA/PNC is that it advocates and supports accountability processes that will be far more effective than HPC regulation at maximising practitioner accountability whilst minimising the collateral unintended side-effects of regulation, as set out earlier in the book (see in particular Chapter 13). This struggle against the state regulation of the psy therapies in Britain is just one aspect of the wider 'paradigm war' between modernist and postmodernist forces which lies at the centre of this book, and the local outcome of which in the psy world may well have a major influence on the quality and nature of therapeutic help for many years to come.

the forces of 'modernity' would re-assert themselves in quite such devastating fashion under New Labour's political reign, with the accompanying super-saturation of modern culture by managerialist, 'audit culture' values (Power 1997; House 2007a, 2010; King and Moutsou 2010). Some commentators had indeed predicted that the thrashing around of modernity's tail during its death throes would be very marked – but few of us realised just how fierce it would be; a theme to which I return below.

Now, over ten years later, the form that therapy professionalisation has taken has continued to evolve – or should that be degenerate, depending on your viewpoint. All of my colleagues who have campaigned assiduously against the state and statutory regulation of the psychological therapies, and now at least some of those who have erstwhile (and often equally assiduously) campaigned for regulation, have been disturbed if not appalled by the prospect of our field being state regulated under the auspices of the Health Professions Council. And our angst is merely compounded by the extraordinary news that broadly defined humanistic work seems to be under severe threat in the incongruously termed 'NICE' new age of CBT-cultivated 'happiness' (House and Loewenthal 2008a, b). A central question therefore becomes what humanistic and allied practitioners are to do in the face of these oft-seeming inexorable cultural forces to which we seem to be subject.

Perhaps I should say a bit more about my own take on those forces, before suggesting what a principled, specifically humanistic response to them might look like. First, there is the way in which how things appear now dominates over substance and authenticity in modern public life – surely one of the most pernicious cultural developments in recent times, and one which is doing untold damage in all manner of ways. Then there is the not unrelated 'audit culture' and the associated 'low-trust' society (King and Moutsou 2010), together with a pervasive post-9/11 cultural anxiety which is presumably a major factor in these developments. The managerialist 'audit culture', and its accompanying disciplining and infantilising procedures, is saturating every aspect of public life and, increasingly, the private sphere as well; and the field of therapy and counselling is by no means immune from these developments. In the current fashionable and largely uncritical obsession with 'evidence-based practice' (see Chapter 19) and research (see Chapter 20), for example, what should be most in question – i.e. the culturally constructed and historically specific notion of 'research' and its accompanying dynamics, and questions about what might legitimately or meaningfully count as 'evidence' – is simply taken for granted and assumed to be unproblematic.

Since the late 1990s, I and others have been pursuing a relentless campaign against the audit culture in both the education and therapy worlds, drawing on the kinds of penetrating critiques set out in Mick Power's seminal 1990s texts (e.g. 1997). Although at long last there are welcome harbingers of the audit culture and its control-obsessed ideology beginning to come apart at the seams (with mounting numbers of press reports discovering that it is routinely bringing about the very opposite of its professed intention), all that is best in pluralistic human potential praxis is still under grave threat of submergence by the backwash generated by the thrashing about of modernity's audit culture in its terminal death throes.

Moreover, I find it both surprising and concerning that a forensically critical deconstructive sensibility has not systematically examined the manifold ways in which the audit mentality, with its crass modernist assumptions, has been infecting the therapy world in all kinds of insidious ways (House 2008b) – not least through the CBT/happiness agenda (House and Loewenthal 2008a, b) and the highly contestable 'outcomes' claims that have been made for the superiority of CBT-type approaches over other modalities (see Chapter 19, this volume). My IPN colleague Denis Postle has written eloquently about a kind of 'trance induction' involved in the seemingly inexorable move towards the state regulation of the psychological therapies; and a similar kind of volition-emasculating process has arguably been active in the case of the audit culture within the therapy world, with practitioners who are eminently critically minded in other contexts seemingly taking the notions of 'research' and 'evidence-based practice' as unproblematic givens (King and Moutsou 2010).

My central point is that this pernicious *Zeitgeist* is one which is quite antithetical to the core values of therapeutic human potential work at its best. In the therapy field, issues of accreditation, state regulation and 'professionalisation' have played an ever-more prominent role since the early 1990s. My colleagues and I (not least in the IPN and in the Alliance for Counselling and Psychotherapy) are beginning the task of outlining just what a progressive 'post-professional' human-potential ('therapy') practice entails and might look like; and at least some of the virtues it would surely embody include those of innovation, diversity, pluralism and responsible self-regulation. These are questions that are intensely and unavoidably political in nature, and which deserve urgent and concerted attention from all of us: staying neutral and disinterested in the face of the managerialist colonisation of the consulting room is no longer an option – for, as the old cliché goes, not to take up a position on this is to take up a position.

I believe that the audit culture, and its accompanying mentality and practices, inevitably have a quite deadly effect upon the delicate, subtle soul-qualities which give therapy practice at its best its uniquely distinctive characteristics – features that a materialistic 'modernity' with its regulation-

and credential-mindedness is placing under great threat, as an 'over-professionalised' psychotherapy and counselling practice seems destined uncritically to embrace these toxic cultural forces.

One pressing task, which has already been started by people like Mick Power, Andrew Cooper, Denis Postle and Guy Gladstone, is to tease out and name the insidious process in modern culture that leads us, quite unwittingly, to 'think like a state' (following James Scott's work – Scott 1999) – with all of the deadly sequelae stemming from that mentality. Might it be the case, for example, that we are all in some sense infantilised by the state, and haven't yet found a mature place to take up in relation to overweening state-driven intrusion into human experience? And might this be especially so in the post-9/11 milieu of acute, unprocessed anxiety, which may well have triggered off all manner of unconscious phantasies? Such a process would certainly account for the kind of paralysing 'trance induction' referred to earlier, such that we have been unwittingly drawn into unconsciously relinquishing our capacity for self-efficacy and self-determination to a polity only too eager to project its own disowned anxieties on to us, and then step in with an inevitably ill-fated attempt to assuage them.

These are surely the kinds of questions that critically and politically engaged therapeutic thinking is best placed to engage in; and to the extent that we don't do it individually and collectively, failing to take a stance – and stand – of principled and informed resistance and non-co-operation in relation to these forces, the therapy field is most surely in for very big trouble indeed – and we will surely deserve all we get.

We assuredly know by now that virtually all technocratic intrusions into human systems generate all manner of typically unconscious dynamics around power, precipitating in turn quite unpredictable side-effects which commonly do more net harm than did the pre-existing shortcomings that the interventions were supposed to address (House 2007a)... – those intent on state-regulating the therapy world, please take note. And 'credentialisation', accreditation and the statutory regulation of an over-professionalised practice are merely further instances of this 'audit and control' mentality.

More specifically, crassly technocratic conceptions of evaluation are surely a singularly inappropriate means of evaluating efficacy in the peculiarly unique and idiosyncratic field of personal growth and therapeutic help. What critical humanistic practitioners and readers of *Self and Society* should surely be embracing is the most cutting-edge radical thinking in associated fields, rather than uncritically mimicking and colluding with the worst features of the toxic 'surveillance culture'.

As the anxiety-saturated audit culture proceeds to penetrate every aspect of public and private life, these are issues that will also surely manifest in the consulting room itself (Samuels 1993), and with which politically committed and aware practitioners surely cannot fail but to engage with their clients. Moreover, as Richard Mowbray foretellingly posed in the early 1990s, to what extent can we preserve a radical countercultural space in a psychotherapy field which becomes increasingly professionalised and subject to the audit culture's worst excesses? Some humanistically inclined 'institutionalisers' might wish to claim that it is possible to retain their original radicalism and the integrity of our bold humanistic vision within a state-institutionalised and professionalised therapy field; but I have always severely doubted this myself – and recent outrageous moves to marginalise humanistic therapy within the state's Brave New therapy regime only confirm that scepticism.

In the 1970s and 1980s, many counter-cultural radicals came into the therapy field because it offered a creative and fluid 'subversive space' in which our most fundamental presuppositions about society and human experience could be thought about and challenged. Over time, some of those radicals have now, Animal Farm like, become part of the New Therapy Establishment; whilst others, like that revered political icon of the Left, Tony Benn, become if anything even more radical, the older they get. Those of us in the latter category end up wondering just what more we can do to 'rattle and shake' the New Therapy Establishment out of the institutionalised complacency into which we believe it to have been seduced by the trappings of status and power (meticulously detailed in Postle 2007) – for example, by exposing their effective abandonment of the radical roots from which much innovative therapy and human potential activity has historically sprung.

How, then, might we appeal directly to the radical heart of human potential work in this era of acute cultural anxiety, with the primitive material it seems to plug into, and the reactionary 'acting out' it seems to precipitate? Or has the therapy field changed so much, and are the motivations of most practitioners now so different from the radical roots (careerism as opposed to human potential development), that seeking to change the trajectory of the humanistic therapy field is pretty much a waste of energy, and we'd be far better off just continuing to do what we do in an approach of (to coin a phrase) principled non-compliance; and if like-minded people discover and join us, all the better. These are the kinds of unavoidably political questions that radically minded humanistic and other practitioners are thankfully now asking themselves. We might also be witnessing the beginnings of a concerted engagement by radical humanists with a spiritually informed, 'trans-modern' or 'New Paradigm' politics, considering in the process the form(s) which the latter might take as we voyage through and beyond the death throes of late modernity.

PRINCIPLED NON-COMPLIANCE: BACKGROUND TO A NEW CULTURAL MOVEMENT

> Some actions may violate a law that itself may be invalid or unconstitutional, and those actions may be part of the effort to change that law.
>   (James Childress)

Principled Non-compliance (or 'PNC' for short) is a comparatively new cultural initiative led by prominent figures in the fields of psychotherapy, counselling and education, as a considered and mature response to the ethically dissonant position into which professionals and citizens are increasingly being placed by increasing incursions of central government into realms of human life that have not previously be subject to the regulatory gaze of what some call 'The New Surveillance State'. PNC sits comfortably alongside Conscientious Objection, with its long and distinguished cultural history, as the last refuge left available to those individuals upon whom demands are being made by state edict with which they fundamentally disagree, from an informed and rationally argued ethical standpoint. It is a term and a movement which is being thoughtfully embraced by the Alliance for Counselling and Psychotherapy and by many practitioners deeply concerned by the direction being taken by the mooted HPC regulation of the psychological therapies.

For this writer, PNC is the natural 'child' of what are deeply disturbing cultural conditions in which we are witnessing unprecedented curtailments of civil liberties and escalations in 'the audit culture' and society-wide 'surveillance', and a government which – seeing the world in the only way of which they are capable (Scott 1999) – is quite unable to comprehend, let alone respond appropriately, to the profound ethical challenges that are being made to their overweening behaviour.

The term 'principled non-compliance' was first coined at a meeting of the Psychotherapy and Counselling Reference Group on 29th March 2007, looking at the pending regulation of the psychological therapies, held at the British Psychological Society offices, and which I attended representing the Independent Practitioners Network. (For reports of that meeting, see: http://ipnosis.postle.net/pages/RHouseRefGroupMarch2907.htm.) At the

meeting I spoke in favour of what, at the time, I spontaneously termed
'Principled Non-Cooperation' (now known as PNC) with the government's
White Paper regulation proposals. Informing my argued position was (and
is) the view that it should be an ethical imperative for therapists, and their
representative institutions, to preserve a space for the reflective critique of
prevailing cultural values and practices – not least because it is precisely
such values and ideologies that have so often damaged the clients looking
for help and support. The mounting counter-cultural critique of the current
cultural obsession with risk (e.g. Gill 2007) and the manic attempt to
extinguish it, is also highly relevant to arguments around PNC and its
philosophical rationale.

The terms 'compliance' and 'non-compliance' themselves deserve some
closer consideration. Here are some prescient quotations from the great
psychoanalyst and paediatrician Donald Winnicott, the great theorist of
compliance, and the damage it can do to the development of what he termed
'the authentic self'. Winnicott variously wrote:

> The mother who is not good enough... substitutes her own gesture
> for that of the child, which is to be given sense by the compliance of
> the infant.... This compliance is the earliest stage of the false self
> and belongs to the mother's inability to sense her infant's needs [for
> 'mother', you can read 'father', or any authority figure – even the
> HPC.]

And later, he continues:

> Through this False Self, the infant builds up a false set of
> relationships, and even attains a show of being real, so that *the child
> may grow up to be just like... whoever dominates the scene....* So The False
> Self hides the True Self by its compliance with environmental
> demands.
>   (emphasis added)

Winnicott also makes the key point that non-compliance is bound up with
the child's/person's integral drive for personal development – so here, too, is
a rationale for the relevance of non-compliance to practitioner development.
In his 1965 paper 'Morals and education', he explicitly values 'those who do
not copy and comply, but who genuinely grow to a way of personal
expression' – to which we might well add professional expression, too.

For Winnicott, then, a key consequence of forced compliance is the
development of a 'false self' – and the parallels with the psychological

therapies are crucial here, with the obvious danger that practitioners may all too easily (and without being aware of it) develop inauthentic, false professional selves as a result of the proposals to HPC-regulate the psy field. And perhaps even more crucially, Winnicott shows how the true/false self system is intimately related to creativity – with, according to Winnicott, creativity being one of the very first casualties of the compliant 'false self configuration'. This is very bad news indeed for a state-regulated professional practice which, for many if not most practitioners, holds creativity to be absolutely central to the effective work of psychological therapists/ practitioners.

There is a whole host of convincing reasons as to why the pursuit or imposition of centralised regulation is highly problematic for psy practitioners, which have been developed at great length in the literature and in this book; but one major factor to mention here is that if we can show that HPC regulation will have a net negative impact on the psy field as a whole, will practitioners not then be breaking the Codes of Ethics that they are sworn to uphold through their professional associations? In many if not most cases, the answer to this will most certainly be 'yes' – in which case we have an intolerable situation of professional dissonance and inauthenticity, in which the state is effectively making it legally compulsory that we break our own institutional ethical codes as therapists – the absurdity of this situation is difficult to exaggerate. If we weave these concerns into the arguments cogently made by Childress (1985) in his paper 'Civil disobedience, conscientious objection, and evasive non-compliance: a framework for the analysis and assessment of illegal actions in health care', then we have a compelling rationale indeed for the development of a carefully articulated PNC response to the proposed HPC state-regulation of the psychological therapies.

There is also a fascinating and highly prescient literature on Conscientious Objection and Public Disobedience as cultural phenomena, which is of direct relevance to the issues surrounding PNC. Random internet surfing soon reveals some very interesting parallels with the PNC movement. For example, at http://hasbrouck.org/draft/choice.html, 'Making a Choice: Conscientious Objection or Draft Resistance', we read: 'If you register, people in the government will interpret your registration as a sign that you acknowledge their "right" to draft you'. So the very act of registering is an active, explicit and unavoidable sanctioning of the right of the state to regulate the activity of the psychological therapies, and in a way that is substantially, if not wholly, incompatible with how psy professionals conceive of and describe their own work. On this view, then, to sign up to (HPC) regulation is an inherently and unavoidably political act, and there is simply no gainsaying that. So on this view, to collude with registration and regulation is to take a very active political position.

On the same (American) website, under 'Why Refuse to Register?', we read the following:

> The government started draft registration in 1980 to 'test the water' and see whether young people would cooperate. Well over a million of us didn't: we resisted. Since 1980, many times more of us have refused to register than during the entire Vietnam War. Unless the vast majority of us cooperate with the Selective Service System, the draft won't work. And the high rate of non-registration has the government worried. Draft resistance is already preventing the draft!
> (my emphasis)

But 'What If I'm Caught?'... The website continues:

> Nobody has been indicted for non-registration since 1986. Even when the government indicted a token 20 non-registrants in 1982–1986, they were always given another chance to register before being prosecuted....You lose nothing by waiting; the government hasn't prosecuted anyone for late registration. Your initial unwillingness to register may even be evidence you can use to show the sincerity of your Conscientious Objection claim.... Deciding whether to register or to resist isn't easy. This may be the most difficult and important decision you have faced, and it's not a choice anybody else can make for you. Talk to a draft counsellor [!], your friends and family, and other people whom you respect. Get as much information as you can before you decide. Don't be pressured into making a hasty decision.... Whatever you do, you're not alone.
> (my emphasis)

There is, then, a long and proud history of people making grave ethical, principled decisions that are very carefully thought-through, and that challenge the overweening power and authority assumed by the central state, where the diktats of that state fundamentally contradict the ethically informed position of individual citizens, and when, at worst, those citizens sincerely believe that their compliance with the demands of the state will perpetrate harm on the very people whose well-being and flourishing they have sworn in their ethical codes to uphold and facilitate. PNC is a modern cultural phenomenon, being symptomatic of, and a telling commentary upon, recent, highly pernicious developments in the balance between overweening state power and the autonomy of individual citizens and professionals. The growing movement towards Principled Non-Compliance, both in the field of the psychological therapies and now more widely in modern culture, should very much be seen in this light.

TOWARDS PRINCIPLED NON-COMPLIANT PRACTITIONERSHIP

Those of us responsible for the literature challenging therapy professionalisation probably share the view that if rational argumentation were to have been given due weight in the debate, then the argument for the state regulation of the psychological therapies would have sunk without trace a long time ago. Something different is therefore needed in addition to rational argument – something akin, perhaps, to ideological and political critique, allied with a relentless exposing of the (power) dynamics driving the audit-driven professionalisation psychodrama.

How could anyone believe that a government that duplicitously misled its populace into an appalling war in (or, more accurately, against) the Middle East, and which is presiding over quite unprecedented curtailments of civil liberties and escalations in 'audit' and society-wide 'surveillance', is remotely capable of listening to, understanding, and finally responding maturely to rational arguments that the therapy institutions have, far too late in the day, been putting about how the Skills for Health agenda, the NHS 'NICE' guidelines and the HPC route to regulation entail values and assumptions that the vast swathe of the therapy modalities simply reject outright?

In my view, the role of the therapist, and her/his institutions, should be to preserve a space of critique of prevailing cultural values – for as David Smail and others have cogently pointed out, it is precisely such values and ideologies that have so often damaged the clients who seek help and support for that damage and its sequelae, when they come to us for assistance. Just how authentic can any help I might offer be to such clients, if I have colluded with pernicious cultural forces which it should surely be the place of critically minded psycho-cultural commentators and practitioners fearlessly to deconstruct and problematise?

Perhaps we urgently need, then, to re-affirm and re-found the enduring, perennial quality of human potential practice at its radical best, as so strongly urged by Richard Mowbray 15 years ago (Mowbray 1995). Practitioners can only surely claim to be offering such an authentic experience to clients if they quite explicitly and self-reflexively undertake to strive for a deep congruence between their face-to-face work with clients and/or groups, and the approach they take to, and the relationship they have with, the cultural *Zeitgeist* and all its psycho-social machinations and vicissitudes. Of course, as an Independent Practitioners Network (IPN) participant, I would argue that the IPN peer-group process is a most effective and progressive way to enable such a congruence; not that it can ever be guaranteed, of course, for to claim that would be merely to mimic the worst modernist excesses of didactic professionalisation. But explicitly to aspire to 'Authentic Human Potential Practice', and all that that striving entails, seems to me to be a useful starting-point for driving a clear taxonomic wedge between those practitioners who really take a congruent self–society dialectic seriously as a core aspect of their work, and those who play fast and loose with the politics of the profession – as if engaging in the black arts of 'spin', power-driven manipulation and political inauthenticity had no relation whatsoever with, and could be neatly separated off from, the actual coal-face work we do with our clients.

The policy-makers, state regulators and apologists for therapy institutionalisation seem quite unable to grasp the postmodern subtleties and nuances of our work – or else are determined wilfully to ignore them. There is certainly a pressing need for the therapy world to deconstruct and lay bear the erroneous assumptions of the 'roles and competencies' ideology (see Chapter 19), and how, again, its imposition upon therapy practice will do our work a peculiarly excruciating kind of violence. The same goes for the 'NICE' guidelines, and their ignorant and quite unwarranted promulgation of CBT as the favoured, 'empirically validated' treatment in so many realms (House and Loewenthal 2008a, b).

CONCLUDING THOUGHTS

The new, recently launched petition challenging state regulation has in just a few weeks attracted over a thousand signatories, including such notables as Professors Chris Beaumont, Bernard Burgoyne, David Ingleby, Darian Leader, Ian Parker, Andrew Samuels, Diana Shmukler, Martin Stanton and Brian Thorne, and Paul Atkinson, Dina Glouberman, Paul Gordon, Christopher Hauke, John Heaton, Martin Jelfs, Haya Oakley and John Rowan (see http://www.petitiononline.com/statereg/petition.html).

When the tentacles of the so-called 'Surveillance Society' (or SS) begin to reach into the 'mental health' realm and into the consulting room itself, we should all realise that we are in very big trouble indeed. I maintain that, notwithstanding the fashionable cynicism engulfing our anxiety-ridden culture, the kind of healthy diversity and innovative richness to which humanistic therapy and the human potential movement still hopefully aspire can only be safeguarded and advanced by a principled non-compliance with the audit culture's misguided attempts to colonise the consulting room. And it might well be in the signing of petitions, resigning from our institutional registering bodies and (for example) joining the IPN, and our continuing to practise as we have done in the face of whatever state legislation is enacted, that we will succeed in protecting the infinitely precious counter-cultural space whose thriving existence becomes all the more urgent in the face of forces which would arrogantly do away with it.

OTHER RESOURCES

Richard House interviewed by Denis Postle on PNC, see video at: http://ipnosis.postle.net/pages/HPC01.htm
Richard House, film of address to the 2nd Alliance for Counselling and Psychotherapy conference, 11 October 2009, at: http://www.allianceforcandp.org/pages/AllianceConference2.htm

CONCLUSION

Preparing the Ground for Cultivating a New Post-Therapy Culture

I epigraphed this book with a quotation from the German poet Hölderlin: 'We are a poem that cannot be read'; and I hope that by now, the reader who has ventured this far into the book will deeply understand the appositeness of this quotation to the theme that threads its way throughout the book. There are already far too many words in the book, so this Conclusion will be brief. Overall, *In, Against and Beyond Therapy* will have more than served a useful purpose if it encourages and facilitates some clearest of 'blue sky' reflection and incisive critical thinking about 'the psy state that we're in' in the early twenty-first century.

The theme of therapy's cultural and historic task of *preserving a critical counter-cultural space* is one that I seem to keep returning to, and so I will end with it. Historically, psychotherapy and counselling have been conducted in a private, confidential space, free of externally defined institutional agendas, in which clients can take matters of deep personal concern for discussion and reflection. This therapeutic space is one of society's last surviving bastions against, and refuges from, narrowly stultifying mechanistic thinking, and from the abusive compliance experiences that bring most clients to therapy in the first place. I maintain that state regulation constitutes a gross intrusion into this precious and subtlest of private spaces, and the government's control-fixated compliance-and-control agenda can only compromise the quality of that space.

A growing number of therapists – amounting to some thousands of practitioners – is starting to challenge and resist these developments, and there is an urgent need to protect the consulting room from this unwarranted government colonisation. Current regulatory developments and pretensions can only fuel suspicions that regulation of the 'psy' field is merely the latest symptom of a wider cultural movement towards a 'surveillance society', in which therapy becomes inappropriately annexed to a governmental social-engineering agenda. So in the face of all this, just what is to be done, and how are concerned practitioners to position themselves in relation to these pernicious forces?

Over fifteeen years ago Richard Mowbray was arguing for a clear distinction to be made between remedial 'medical-model' psychotherapy, on the one hand, and what he called 'human potential growth work' on the other. Here is what he wrote (I have put this composite quotation together from Mowbray's book (1995):

> ...[A]ctivities of the human potential movement do not readily fit into the pre-existing social categories... and really deserve a category of their own.... I propose a terminological clarification to prevent human potential work becoming inappropriately subsumed, to reduce a source of client confusion, and also to attempt to distance clients involved in human potential work from the stigmatization of the 'patient' that so frequently accompanies remedial mental health treatments. (p. 159) [P]sychotherapy' is a nineteenth-century medical model word. (p. 168) ...that has also been used indiscriminately to describe approaches that do not assume a medical model. (p. 188) The term 'psychotherapy' illustrates the 'linear', cause-and-effect, Newtonian–Cartesian basis for the medical model that held sway at the time of its coining. (p. 189).... [T]he choice of labels with which you ally yourself becomes a matter of crucial importance.... (p. 169). Human potential practitioners have not fostered sufficient public awareness of an unambiguous distinguishing label for their work.... (p. 169) [S]elf-realization processes and processes concerned with 'adjustment' and remedial restoration to 'normality' should not be addressed by the same terminology.
>
> (p. 187)

> [Quoting Juliana Brown and himself]: 'The key thing for us is that the Human Potential Movement is a manifestation of a different model, a holistic growth model.' (p. 172) [In contrast to the psychotherapeutic medical model approach] human potential work is... focused on self-actualization.... The approach is non-clinical and the orientation is towards growth... rather than deficiency.... (p. 181) – fulfilling more of the potential of who you really are, rather than narrowly focusing on the cure of a 'disorder', the relief of symptoms or the resolving of a problem. It is concerned... with the emergence of authentic being..., [with] the meaning [of psychological and emotional phenomena] for the person [being] explored rather than efforts made to cure, suppress or eliminate them. (p. 182) ...[I]n human potential work the practitioner does not apply treatments to the client; instead the client is seen as the 'expert' – on himself. (p. 183) The practitioner's role is to facilitate, to 'be with', to sit alongside.... The basis for relationship is one of

'informed agreement to explore' rather then 'informed consent to treatment'....

(p. 184)

[T]he movement that carries [this] process must stay on the margin and not be 'absorbed', not be tempted by the carrots of recognition, respectability and financial security into reverting to the mainstream, but rather remain – on the 'fringe' – as a source that stimulates, challenges convention and 'draws out' the unrealized potential for 'being' in the members of that society. (pp. 198–9) A society needs a healthy fringe... It is the seedbed from which much of what is novel will spring. It is where ideas that are ahead of their time will germinate and grow, later to be adopted by the mainstream. In order to remain a fertile seedbed, the fringe needs to be legitimate rather than driven underground or 'criminalized' – which would stifle it, but also it must not be absorbed into the mainstream – which would stultify it with 'establishment' thinking and respectability.

(p. 199)

If – and, as I write, it still *is* a substantial 'if' – the HPC or other state regulation of the psy therapies does go ahead in the near or middle term, then it seems to me that the fault-line that Mowbray so eloquently identified between 'psychotherapy' and 'Human Potential growth work' will become the most obvious and viable response, with a very considerable number of practitioners 'sloughing off' and joining the kind of post-therapy, post-professional movement that I have been advocating in this book. The kind of new-paradigm, trans-modern ontologies and epistemologies that I have highlighted throughout this book would sit very well in such a movement (*-which-is-not-one...* – in the sense that, in true postmodern style, there would be no centralised institutional pyscho-bureaucracy organising it with all the attendant empire-building and power-infused shenanigans that would ensue and inevitably contaminate it).

In many ways, I end this book with the hope that if I do write another 'therapy' book (on which, after this one, the jury is very much out!), it will be centrally about such a new 'post-professional', Human Potential movement that is rich in diversity, leading-age thinking and innovative healing practices.

REFERENCES

Albee, G.W. (1990) The futility of psychotherapy. *Journal of Mind and Behavior* 11 (3–4): 369–84

Alcoff, L.M. (1996) *Real Knowing: New Versions of the Coherence Theory.* Ithaca, NY: Cornell University Press

Alcoff, L. and Potter, E. (eds) (1988) *Feminist Epistemologies.* Bloomington, Ind.: Indiana University Press

Alexander, R. (1995) *Folie à Deux: An Experience of One-to-One Therapy.* London: Free Association Books

Alford, C. F. (2002) *Levinas, the Frankfurt School and Psychoanalysis.* London: Continuum

Alonso, A. and Shapiro, E.L. (1993) Supervising psychotherapy in the 1990s. In J.S. Rutan (ed.), *Psychotherapy for the 1990s* (pp. 315–37). New York: Guilford Press

Alterio, M. and McDrury, J. (2003) *Learning Through Storytelling in Higher Education: Using Reflection and Experience to Improve Learning.* London: Routledge

Althusser, L. (1971) Ideology and the ideological state apparatus. In his *Lenin and Philosophy* (pp. 123–73). London: New Left Books

Alvesson, M. and Skoldberg, K. (1999) *Reflexive Methodology: New Vistas for Qualitative Research.* London: Sage

American Psychiatric Association (APA) (1994) *Diagnostic and Statistical Manual of Mental Disorders*, 4th edition (DSM-IV). Washington, D.C.

Anderson, H. (1997) *Conversation, Language, and Possibilities: A Postmodern Approach to Therapy.* New York: Basic Books

Arden, M. (1998) *Midwifery of the Soul: A Holistic Perspective on Psychoanalysis.* London: Free Association Books

Arribas-Ayllon, M. and Walkerdine, V. (2008) Foucauldian discourse analysis. In C. Willig and W. Stainton-Rogers (eds), *SAGE Handbook of Qualitative Research in Psychology* (pp. 91–108). London: Sage

Askay, R. and Farquar, J. (2006) *Apprehending the Inaccessible: Freudian Psychoanalysis and Existential Phenomenology.* Evanston, Ill.: Northwestern University Press

Atkinson, T. and Claxton, G. (2000a) Introduction. In T. Atkinson and G. Claxton (eds), *The Intuitive Practitioner: On the Value of Not Always Knowing what One Is Doing* (pp. 1–11). Buckingham: Open University Press

Atkinson, T. and Claxton, G. (eds) (2000b) *The Intuitive Practitioner: On the Value of Not Always Knowing what One Is Doing.* Buckingham: Open University Press

Aveline, M. (1990) The training and supervision of individual therapists. In W. Dryden (ed.), *Individual Therapy: A Handbook* (pp. 313–39).Buckingham: Open University Press

Aveline, M. (2005) The person of the therapist. *Psychotherapy Research* 15 (3): 155–64

Bannister, D. (1985) The psychotic disguise. In W. Dryden (ed.), *Therapists' Dilemmas* (pp. 167–79). London: Harper and Row; 2nd edn, 1997

Barham, P. (1993) *Schizophrenia and Human Value: Chronic Schizophrenia, Science and Society.* London: Free Association Books

Barnett, R. (1994) *Limits of Competence: Knowledge, Higher Education and Society.* Buckingham: Open University Press

Barratt, B.B. (1993) *Psychoanalysis and the Postmodern Impulse: Knowing and Being since Freud's Psychology*. Baltimore: Johns Hopkins University Press

Baruss, I. (1996) *Authentic Knowing: Convergence of Science and Spiritual Aspiration*. West Lafayette, Ind.: Purdue University Press

Bates, Y. (ed.) (2006) *Shouldn't I be Feeling Better by Now? Client Views of Therapy*. Basingstoke: Palgrave Macmillan

Bates, Y. and House, R. (eds) (2003) *Ethically Challenged Professions: Enabling Innovation and Diversity in Psychotherapy and Counselling*. Ross-on-Wye: PCCS Books

Bell-Boule, A. (1999) Psychotherapy and the law. *International Journal of Psychotherapy* 4 (2): 193–202

Bellah, R.N., Madsen, R., Sullivan, W.M., Swidler, A. and Tipton, S.M. (1985) *Habits of the Heart: Individualism and Commitment in American Life*. Berkeley: University of California Press

Ben-Ze'ev, A. (2000) *The Subtlety of Emotions*. MIT Press: Bradford Books

Benatar, E.L. (2006) Cultural notions of psychopathology: An examination of understandings of cultural healing and affliction across cultures. *Praxis* 6 (Fall): 58–63

Benedict, R. (1934) Anthropology and the abnormal. *Journal of General Psychology* 10 (59): 59–80

Berman, M. (1981) *The Reenchantment of the World*. Ithaca, NY: Cornell University Press

Best, S. (1991) Chaos and entropy: metaphors in postmodern science and social theory. *Science as Culture* 11: 188–225

Bird, C. (1998) Review of Moline et al.'s *Documenting Psychotherapy*. *Counselling* (BAC) 9 (3): 235

Blake, N., Smeyers, P., Smith, R. and Standish, P. (1998) *Thinking Again: Education after Postmodernism*. Westport, Conn.: Bergin & Garvey

Block, A.A. (1997) *I'm Only Bleeding: Education as the Practice of Social Violence against Children*. New York: Peter Lang

Blomfield, V. (1997) Practitioner development through self-direction: the South West London College Counselling Courses. In R. House and N. Totton (eds), *Implausible Professions* (pp. 255–70). Ross-on-Wye: PCCS Books; 2nd edn, 2011

Blum, J.D. (1978) On changes in psychiatric diagnosis over time. *American Psychologist* 33: 1017–31

Bochner, A. and Ellis, C. (eds) (2001) *Ethnographically Speaking: Autoethnography, Literature and Aesthetics*. Walnut Creek, Calif.: Altamira

Bohart, A.C. (2002) A passionate critique of empirically supported treatments and the provision of an alternative paradigm. In J.C. Watson, R. N. Goldman and M. S. Warner (eds), *Client-centered and Experiential Psychotherapy in the 21st Century: Advances in Theory, Research, and Practice* (pp. 258–77). Ross-on-Wye: PCCS Books

Bohart, A.C. and House, R. (2008) Empirically supported/validated treatments as modernist ideology, I: Dodo, manualization, and the paradigm question. In R. House and D. Loewenthal (eds), *Against and For CBT: Towards a Constructive Dialogue?* (pp. 188–201). Ross-on-Wye: PCCS Books

Bohart, A.C. and Tallman, K. (1996) The active client: therapy as self-help. *Journal of Humanistic Psychology* 36(3): 7–30; reprinted as Chapter 27 in Y. Bates and R. House (eds), *Ethically Challenged Professions* (pp. 258–74). Ross-on-Wye: PCCS Books, 2003

Bohart, A. and Tallman, K. (1999) *How Clients Make Therapy Work: The Process of Active Self-healing*. Washington, D.C.: American Psychological Association

Bohm, D. (1994) *Thought as a System*. London: Routledge

Bohm, D. (1996) *On Dialogue*. London: Routledge

Bohm, D., Krishnamurti, J. and McCoy, R. (1998) *The Limits of Thought: Discussions Between J. Krishnamurti and David Bohm*. London: Routledge

Bonnett, M. (2002) Education as a form of poetics: a Heideggerian approach to learning and the teacher–pupil relationship. In M. Peters (ed.), *Heidegger, Modernity and Education* (pp. 229–44). Lanham, Maryland: Rowman & Littlefield

Bortoft, H. (1996) *The Wholeness of Nature: Goethe's Way of Science*. Edinburgh: Floris Books

Boyle, M. (1990) *Schizophrenia: A Scientific Delusion?* London: Routledge; 2nd edn, 2002

Boyle, M. (1996) Schizophrenia: the fallacy of diagnosis. *Changes* 14 (1): 5–13

Bracken, P. (2002) *Trauma: Culture, Meaning and Philosophy*. London: Whurr Publishers

Bracken, P. and Thomas, P. (1998) Limits to therapy. *Open Mind* 93: 17

Breggin, P. (1993) *Toxic Psychiatry: Drugs and Electroconvulsive Therapy – the Truth and the Better Alternatives*. London: HarperCollins (orig. 1991)

Broadfoot, P. (2000) Assessment and intuition. In T. Atkinson. and Claxton, G. (eds), *The Intuitive Practitioner: On the Value of Not Always Knowing What One Is Doing* (pp. 199–219). Buckingham: Open University Press

Brown, J. and Mowbray, R. (1990) Whither the human potential movement? *Self and Society* 18 (4): 32–5; reprinted as Appendix A in Mowbray 1995

Brown, L.S. (1994) Concrete boundaries and the problem of literal mindedness: a response to Lazarus. *Ethics and Behavior* 4 (3): 275–81

Brown, L.S. (1997) Ethics in psychology: *Cui Bono?* In D. Fox and I. Prilleltensky (eds), *Critical Psychology: An Introduction* (pp. 51–67). London: Sage

Brown, R. K. (1992) Max van Manen and pedagogical human science research. In W. F. Pinar and W. M. Reynolds (eds), *Understanding Curriculum as Phenomenological and Deconstructed Text* (pp. 44–63). New York: Teachers College Press, Columbia University Press

Bryceland, C. and Stam, H.J. (2005) Empirical validation and professional codes of ethics: description or prescription? *Journal of Constructivist Psychology* 18: 131–55

Bryceland, C. and Stam, H.J. (2008) CBT and empirically validated therapies: infiltrating codes of ethics. In R. House and D. Loewenthal (eds), *Against and For CBT: Towards a Constructive Dialogue?* (pp. 179–87). Ross-on-Wye: PCCS Books

Buber, M. (1990) *A Believing Humanism: My Testament, 1902–65*. New Jersey: Humanities Press Int. (orig. 1967)

Buck, L.A. (1990) Abnormality, normality and health. *Psychotherapy* 27 (2): 187–94

Buck, L.A. (1992a) The myth of normality: consequences for the diagnosis of abnormality and health. *Social Behavior and Personality* 20 (4): 251–62

Buck, L.A. (1992b) A proposed category for the DSM: Pervasive Labeling Disorder. *Journal of Humanistic Psychology* 32 (1): 121–5

Burman, E. (1997) False memories, true hopes and the angelic: revenge of the postmodern in therapy. *New Formations* 30: 122–4

Burman, E. (1998) *Deconstructing Feminist Psychology*. London: Sage

Burman, E. (2007) *Deconstructing Developmental Psychology*, 2nd edn. London: Routledge

Burr, V. and Butt, T. (1999) Psychological distress and postmodern thought. In D. Fee (ed.), *Pathology and the Postmodern: Mental Illness as Discourse and Experience* (pp. 186–206). London: Sage; reprinted in Y. Bates and R. House (eds), *Ethically Challenged Professions* (pp. 75–93). Ross-on-Wye: PCCS Books, 2003

Burston, D. (1996) *The Wing of Madness: Life and Work of R.D. Laing*. Cambridge, Mass.: Harvard University Press

Burston, D. (2000) *The Crucible of Experience: R.D.Laing and the Crisis of Psychotherapy*. Cambridge, Mass.: Harvard University Press

Butcher, P. (1986) The phenomenological psychology of J. Krishnamurti. *Journal of Transpersonal Psychology* 18 (1): 35–50

Campbell, A. and Groundwater-Smith, S. (eds) (2007) *An Ethical Approach to Practitioner Research: Dealing with Issues and Dilemmas in Action Research*. London: Routledge

Cannon, C. and Hatfield, S. (1992) Some thoughts after the 2nd National Conference on the Dynamics of Accreditation, Cambridge, June 1992. *Self and Society* 20 (4): 28–34

Caplan, P.J. (1995) *They Say You're Crazy: How the World's Most Powerful Psychiatrists Decide Who's Normal*. Reading, Mass.: Addison-Wesley

Caputo, J.D. (1993) *Against Ethics*. Bloomington, Ind.: Indiana University Press

Caputo, J.D. (1998) Heidegger. In S. Critchley and W.R. Schroeder (eds), *A Companion to Continental Philosophy* (pp. 223–33). Oxford: Blackwell

Chaplin, J. (1993) *Love in an Age of Uncertainty*. Dartford: Aquarian Press

Childress, J. (1985) Civil disobedience, conscientious objection, and evasive non-compliance: a framework for the analysis and assessment of illegal actions in health care. *Journal of Medicine and Philosophy* 10: 63–83.

Chubin, D. and Chu, E.W. (1989) *Science off the Pedestal: Social Perspectives on Science and Ideology*. Belmont, Calif.: Wadsworth

Clark, J. (2007) *Water from the Rock: Poems Flowing from a Lifetime*. Norwich: Watershed Publications; available from jeanlclark@aol.com

Clark, J. (2008) Why poetry matters. *Person-Centred Quarterly* February: 13–15

Clarke, C.J.S. (1996) *Reality through the Looking Glass: Science and Awareness in the Postmodern World*. Edinburgh: Floris Books

Clarke, C. J. S. (1997) Superstition or liberation: Heretical ideas and the physical sciences. Paper presented at the Scientific and Medical Science conference, 'Science, Heresy and the Challenge of Revolutionary Ideas', London, May

Clarke, C. (ed.) (2005) *Ways of Knowing: Science and Mysticism Today*. Exeter: Imprint Academic

Clarke, J. and others (2000) Guarding the public interest? Auditing public services. In J. Clarke and others (eds), *New Managerialism, New Welfare* (pp. 250–66). London: Sage

Clegg, J.W. and Slife, B.D. (2005) Epistemology and the hither side: A Levinasian account of relational knowing. *European Journal of Psychotherapy, Counselling and Health* 7 (1–2): 65–76

Cloud, D.L. (1998) *Control and Consolation in American Culture and Politics: The Rhetoric of Therapy*. Thousand Oaks, Calif.: Sage

Cohen, M.Z., Kahn, D.L. and Steeves, R.H. (2000) *Hermeneutic Phenomenological Research: A Practical Guide for Nurse Researchers*. London: Sage

Cohn, H.W. (2002) *Heidegger and the Roots of Existential Therapy*. London: Continuum

Cooper, A. (2001) The state of mind we're in: social anxiety, governance and the audit society. *Psychoanalytic Studies* 3 (3–4): 349–62

Cooper, D.E. (2002) *The Measure of Things: Humanism, Humility, and Mystery*. Oxford: Clarendon Press

Craib, I. (1987) The psychodynamics of theory. *Free Associations* 10: 32–56

Craib, I. (1992) Reply to Pilgrim. In W. Dryden and C. Feltham (eds), *Psychotherapy and Its Discontents* (pp. 243–9). Buckingham: Open University Press

Critical Methods Conferences (n.d.) www.criticalmethods.org/mains.htm

Crook, J. H. (1980) *The Evolution of Human Consciousness.* Oxford: Oxford University Press

Curt, B. (1994) Crafty dodges: the question and questioning of methods. In her *Textuality and Tectonics: Troubling Social and Psychological Science* (pp. 103–33). Buckingham: Open University Press

Curtis, B. and Mays, W. (eds) (1978) *Phenomenology and Education: Self-Consciousness and Its Development.* London: Methuen

Cushman, P. (1992) Psychotherapy to 1992: a historically situated interpretation. In D.K. Freedheim (ed.), *History of Psychotherapy: A Century of Change* (pp. 21–64). Washington, D.C.: American Psychological Association

Cushman, P. (1995) *Constructing the Self, Constructing America: A Cultural History of Psychotherapy.* Reading, Mass.: Addison-Wesley

Damasio, A.R. (1994) *Descartes' Error: Emotion, Reason, and the Human Brain.* New York: Avon Books

Davies, J. (1997) Assessment tension on a university-based counselling training course. In R. House and N. Totton (eds), *Implausible Professions* (pp. 281–6). Ross-on-Wye: PCCS Books; 2nd edn, 2011

Davis, W.A. (1989) *Inwardness and Existence: Subjectivity in/and Hegel, Heidegger, Marx and Freud.* Madison, Wisc.: University of Wisconsin Press

Denzin, N.K., Lincoln, Y.S. and Tuhiwai Smith, L. (eds) (2008) *Handbook of Critical and Indigenous Methodologies.* London: Sage

Devereux, G. (1967) *From Anxiety to Method in the Behavioral Sciences.* Atlantic Highlands, NJ: Humanities Press

Dhillon, P. and Standish, P. (eds) (2000) *Lyotard: Just Education.* London: Routledge

DiCarlo, R. E. (ed.) (1996) *Towards a New World View: Conversations at the Leading Edge.* Edinburgh: Floris Books

Dreher, A.U. (2000) *Foundations for Conceptual Research in Psychoanalysis.* London: Karnac Books

Dueck, A. and Parsons, T. (2007). Ethics, alterity, and psychotherapy: A Levinasian perspective. *Pastoral Psychology* 55: 271–82

Duncan, B. L., Hubble, M. A. and Miller, S. D. (1997) *Psychotherapy with 'Impossible' Cases: The Efficient Treatment of Therapy Veterans.* New York: Norton

Dupont, J. (ed.) (1995) *The Clinical Diary of Sandor Ferenczi.* Cambridge, Mass.: Harvard University Press

Eales, M. (1997) Experiences of self and peer accreditation: developing self-determination: the Institute for the Development of Human Potential. In R. House and N. Totton (eds), *Implausible Professions* (pp. 271–5). Ross-on-Wye: PCCS Books; 2nd edn, 2011

Ecclestone, K. and Hayes, D. (2007) *The Dangerous Rise of Therapeutic Education.* London Routledge

Edelglass, S. and others (1997) *The Marriage of Sense and Thought: Imaginative Participation in Science.* Hudson, NY: Lindisfarne Books

Edwards, G. (1992) Does psychotherapy need a soul? In W. Dryden and C. Feltham (eds), *Psychotherapy and Its Discontents* (pp. 194–224). Buckingham: Open University Press

Embleton Tudor, L. and Tudor, K. (1994) The personal and the political: power, authority and influence in psychotherapy. In P. Clarkson and M. Pokorny (eds), *The Handbook of Psychotherapy* (pp. 384–402). London: Routledge

Erwin, E. (1997) *Philosophy and Psychotherapy*. London: Sage

Etherington, K. (2004) *Becoming a Reflexive Researcher: Using Our Selves in Research*. London: Jessica Kingsley

Evans, R. (1996) Introduction to van den Brink (1996), pp. vii–xvi

Fahy, T. and Wessely, S. (1993) Should purchasers pay for psychotherapy? *British Medical Journal* 307 (4 September): 576–7

Farber, S. (1993) *Madness, Heresy, and the Rumor of Angels: The Revolt Against the Mental Health System*. Peru, Ill.: Open Court

Faulconer, J.E. (2005) Knowledge of the Other. *European Journal of Psychotherapy, Counselling and Health* 7 (1–2): 49–63

Faulconer, J.E. and Williams, R.N. (eds) (1990) *Reconsidering Psychology: Perspectives from Continental Philosophy*. Pittsburgh: Duquesne University Press

Feltham, C. (1997) Challenging the core theoretical model. *Counselling* 8 (2): 121–5; reprinted in R. House and N. Totton (eds), *Implausible Professions* (pp. 117–28). Ross-on-Wye: PCCS Books; 2nd edn, 2011

Fendler L. (1998) What is it impossible to think? A genealogy of the educated subject. In T. S. Popkewitz and M. Brennan (eds), *Foucault's Challenge: Discourse, Knowledge and Power in Education* (pp. 39–63). New York: Teachers College Press, Columbia University

Fenwick, P. (1999) Neuropsychiatric difficulties in explaining consciousness. In D. Lorimer and others (eds) *Wider Horizons: Explorations in Science and Human Experience* (pp. 202–8). Leven, Fife: Scientific and Medical Network

Feyerabend, P.K. (1975) *Against Method: Outline of an Anarchistic Theory of Knowledge*. London: New Left Books

Fonow, M.M. and Cook, J.A. (eds) (1991) *Beyond Methodology: Feminist Scholarship as Lived Research*. Bloomington, IN: Indiana University Press

Foucault, M. (1970) The archaeology of knowledge. *Social Science Information* 9 (1): 175–85

Fox, D. and Prilleltensky, I. (eds) (1997) *Critical Psychology: An Introduction*. London: Sage; 2nd edn with S. Austin, 2009

France, A. (1988) *Consuming Psychotherapy*. London: Free Association Books

Frank, J.D. (1989a) Discussion. In M. Shepherd and N. Sartorius (eds), *Non-Specific Aspects of Treatment* (pp.142–6). Toronto: Hans Huber Publishers

Frank, J.D. (1989b) Non-specific aspects of treatment: the view of a psychotherapist. In M. Shepherd and N. Sartorius (eds), *Non-Specific Aspects of Treatment* (pp. 95–114). Toronto: Hans Huber Publishers

Frank, J. D. and Frank, J. B. (1991) *Persuasion and Healing: A Comparative Study of Psychotherapy*, 3rd edn. Baltimore: Johns Hopkins University Press

Freeman, M. (2000) Theory beyond theory. *Theory and Psychology* 10 (1): 7–17

Freides, D. (1960) Toward the elimination of the concept of normality. *Journal of Consulting Psychology* 24: 128–33

Freshwater, D. and Rolfe, G. (2004) *Deconstructing Evidence-based Practice*. London: Routledge

Freud, S. (1913) On beginning the treatment... In *Standard Edition* (pp. 123–44). London: Hogarth Press

Friedson, E. (1984) Are professions really necessary? In T.L. Haskell (ed.), *The Authority of*

Experts: Studies in History and Theory (pp. 3–27). Bloomington: Indiana University Press

Frosh, S. (1987) *The Politics of Psychoanalysis: An Introduction to Freudian and Post-Freudian Theory.* New Haven: Yale University Press

Furedi, F. (2004) *Therapy Culture: Cultivating Vulnerability in an Uncertain Age.* London: Routledge

Gadamer, H.-G. (1989) *Truth and Method*, 2nd edn. New York: Crossroad

Gantt, E. E. (2000) Levinas, psychotherapy, and the ethics of suffering. *Journal of Humanistic Psychology* 40 (3): 9–28

Gartrell, N.K. (ed.) (1994) *Bringing Ethics Alive: Feminist Ethics in Psychotherapy Practice.* New York: Haworth

Gassner, J. (1999) The IPN and the Person-centred approach. Seminar held at the Norwich Centre for Personal and Professional Development, January (mimeo)

Gendlin, E. (1987) A philosophical critique of the concept of narcissism: the significance of the Awareness Movement. In D. M. Levin (ed.), *Pathologies of the Modern Self* (pp. 251–304). New York: New York University Press

Gergen, K. (1994) Exploring the Postmodern: Perils or Potentials? *American Psychologist* 49 (5): 412–16.

Gergen, K.J. and McNamee, S. (1997) Foreword. In E. Riikonen and G. M. Smith, *Re-Imagining Therapy: Living Conversations and Relational Knowing* (pp. vii–ix). London: Sage

Gergen, M. (2008) Qualitative methods in feminist psychology. In C. Willig and W. Stainton-Rogers (eds), *SAGE Handbook of Qualitative Research in Psychology* (pp. 280–95). London: Sage

Gill, T. (2007) *No Fear: Growing Up in a Risk Averse Society.* London: Calouste Gulbenkian Foundation

Gladstone, G. (1995) Conference afterthoughts. *Self and Society* 22(6): 11–17

Gladstone, G. (1997) The making of a therapist and the corruption of the training market. In R. House and N. Totton (eds), *Implausible Professions* (pp.171–85). Ross-on-Wye: PCCS Books, 2nd edn, 2011 (in press)

Glass, J.M. (1993) *Shattered Selves: Multiple Personality in a Postmodern World.* Ithaca, New York: Cornell University Press

Goleman, D. (1995) *Emotional Intelligence: Why It Can Matter More than IQ.* London: Bloomsbury

Goleman, D., Smith, H. and Ram Dass (1985) Truth and transformation in psychological and spiritual paths. *Journal of Transpersonal Psychology* 17 (2): 183–214

Goss, S. and Mearns, D. (1997) A call for a pluralist epistemological understanding in the assessment and evaluation of counselling. *British Journal of Guidance and Counselling* 25 (2): 189–98

Grawe, K. (1997) Research-informed psychotherapy. *Psychotherapy Research* 7: 1–20

Greenberg, R. P. (1999) Common psychosocial factors in psychiatric drug therapy. In M. A. Hubble, B. L. Duncan, and S. D. Miller (eds), *The Heart and Soul of Change: What works in therapy* (pp. 297–328). Washington, D.C.: American Psychological Association

Greyson, B. (1993) The physio-kundalini syndrome and mental illness. *Journal of Transpersonal Psychology* 25 (1): 43–58

Grieder, A. (1999) Phenomenology and psychotherapy. *Changes* 17 (3): 178–87

Griffin, D. R. (ed.) (1988a) *The Reenchantment of Science: Postmodern Proposals*. Albany, NY: University of New York Press

Griffin, D.R. (1988b) *God and Religion in the Postmodern World: Essays in Postmodern Theology*. Albany, NY: State University of New York Press

Groddeck, G. (1951) *The World of Man*. London: Vision (orig. 1934)

Grof, C. and Grof, S. (1990) *The Stormy Search for the Self: Understanding and Living with Spiritual Emergency*. Los Angeles: Jeremy P. Tarcher

Grof, S. (1987) Psychodynamic factors in depression and psychosis: observations from modern consciousness research. In D. M. Levin (ed.), *Pathologies of the Modern Self* (pp. 439–78). New York: New York University Press

Guggenbühl-Craig, A. (1971) *Power in the Helping Professions*. Dallas, Tex.: Spring Publications

Guignon, C. (2000) Authenticity and integrity: a Heideggerian perspective. In P. Young-Eisendrath and M.E. Miller (eds), *The Psychology of Mature Spirituality: Integrity, Wisdom, Transcendence* (pp. 62–74). London: Routledge

Guilfoyle, M. (2008) CBT's integration into societal networks of power. In R. House and D. Loewenthal (eds), *Against and For CBT: Towards a Constructive Dialogue?* (pp. 233–40). Ross-on-Wye: PCCS Books

Guillen, M. (1983) *Bridges to Infinity*. Los Angeles: Tarcher Publications

Habermas, J. (1978) *Communication and the Evolution of Society*. London: Heinemann

Habermas, J. (1982) *The Theory of Communicative Action*. London: Heinemann

Hall, J. (1993) *The Reluctant Adult: An Exploration of Choice*. Bridport: Prism Press

Halling, S. and Nill, J.D. (1989) Demystifying psychopathology: understanding disturbed persons. In R. S. Valle and S. Halling (eds), *Existential-Phenomenological Perspectives in Psychology: Exploring the Breadth of Human Experience* (pp. 179–92). New York: Plenum

Halse, C. and Honey, A. (2007) Rethinking ethics review as institutional discourse. *Qualitative Inquiry* 13 (3): 336–52

Harding. S. (1986) *The Science Question in Feminism*. Ithaca, NY: Cornell University Press

Harding, S. (1989) *Whose Science? Whose Knowledge?* Ithaca, NY: Cornell University Press

Harding, S. (ed.) (1998) *Feminism and Methodology: Social Science Issues*. Bloomington, Ind.: Indiana University Press

Hare-Mustin, R.T. (1994) Discourses in the mirrored room: a postmodern analysis of therapy. *Family Process* 33 (1): 19–35

Hart, N. (1998) Discourses of power within the therapeutic relationship. Paper presented at the British Association for Counselling Research Conference, Birmingham (mimeo)

Hart, N. (2003) The power of language in therapeutic relationships. In Y. Bates and R. House (eds), *Ethically Challenged Professions* (pp. 218–25). Ross-on-Wye: PCCS Books

Hart, T., Nelson, P. and Puhakka, K. (eds) (1997) *Spiritual Knowing: Alternative Epistemic Perspectives*. Carrollton, Ga.: State University of West Georgia, Studies in Social Sciences Vol. 34

Hart, T., Nelson, P. and Puhakka, K. (eds) (2000) *Transpersonal Knowing: Exploring the Horizon of Consciousness*. Albany: State University of New York Press

Harvey, D. (1973) *Social Justice and the City*. London: Edward Arnold (revised edn, 2009)

Harvey, D. (1989) *The Condition of Postmodernity: An Enquiry into the Origins of Cultural Change*. Chichester: Wiley–Blackwell

Harvey, I.E. (1987) Schizophrenia and metaphysics: analyzing the DSM-III. In D. M. Levin (ed.), *Pathologies of the Modern Self* (pp. 305–29). New York: New York University Press

Hauke, C. (ed.) (2000) *Jung and the Postmodern: The Interpretation of Realities*. London: Routledge

Heaton, J.M. (2000) *Wittgenstein and Psychoanalysis*. Cambridge: Icon Books

Hedges, F. (2010) *Reflexivity in Therapeutic Practice*. Palgrave Macmillan: Basingstoke

Heidegger, M. (2001) *Zollikon Seminars: Protocols, Conversations, Letters*, ed. M. Boss (trans. F. Mayr and R. Askay). Illinois: Northwestern University Press (German original, 1987)

Heinze, R.-I. (1999) Multiplicity in cross-cultural perspective. In J. Rowan and M. Cooper (eds), *The Plural Self* (pp. 151–67). London: Routledge

Hepburn, A. (1999a) Postmodernity and the politics of feminist psychology. *Radical Psychology* 1 (2); downloadable from http://www.radicalpsychology.org/vol1-2/hepburn.html

Hepburn, A. (1999b) Derrida and Psychology: deconstruction and its ab/uses in critical and discursive psychologies. *Theory and Psychology* 9 (5): 641–67

Herman, N. (1991) Prodromal states of suicide: thoughts on the death of Ann France. *Free Associations* 2 (2): 249–58

Hermans, H.J.M., Kempen, H.J.G. and van Loon, R.J.P. (1992) The dialogical self: beyond individualism and rationalism. *American Psychologist* 47 (1): 23–33

Heron, J. (1990) The politics of transference. *Self and Society* 18 (1): 17–23; reprinted in House and Totton (eds), *Implausible Professions* (pp. 11–18). Ross-on-Wye: PCCS Books; 2nd edn, 2011 (in press)

Heron, J. (1992) *Feeling and Personhood*. London: Sage

Heron, J. (1996) *Co-operative Inquiry: Research into the Human Condition*. London: Sage

Heron, J. (1997) A self-generating practitioner community. In R. House and N. Totton (eds), *Implausible Professions* (pp. 241–54). Ross-on-Wye: PCCS Books; 2nd edn, 2011 (in press)

Heron, J. (1998) *Sacred Science: Person-centred Inquiry into the Spiritual and the Subtle*. Ross-on-Wye: PCCS Books

Heron, J. (2003) Foreword. In Y. Bates and R. House (eds) *Ethically Challenged Professions: Enabling Innovation and Diversity in Psychotherapy and Counselling* (pp. i–ii). Ross-on-Wye: PCCS Books

Herrick, V. and Mann, I. (1998) *Jesus Wept: Reflections on Vulnerability in Leadership*. London: Darton, Longman & Todd

Hillman, J. (1997) *The Soul's Code: In Search of Character and Calling*. London: Bantam Books

Hinshelwood, R.D. (1985) Questions of training. *Free Associations* 2: 7–18

Hinshelwood, R.D. (1997) *Therapy or Coercion? Does Psychoanalysis Differ from Brainwashing?* London: Karnac Books

Hitter, G.T. (1997) *Freud's Innuendo and Jamshid's Cup: The Postmodern Quest for Self in the Shadow of the Newtonian World*. Las Vegas: PsyQuest Books

Hocoy, D. (2005) Ethnography as metaphor in psychotherapy training. *American Journal of Psychotherapy* 59 (2): 101–18

Hogan, D.B. (1979) *The Regulation of Psychotherapists*, 4 volumes. Cambridge, Mass.: Ballinger

Hogan, D.B. (1999) Protection, not control. In S. Greenberg (ed.), *Therapy on the Couch: A Shrinking Future* (pp. 70–5). London: Camden Press

Hogan, D.B. (2003) Professional regulation as facilitation, not control: implications for an open system of registration versus restrictive licensure. In Y. Bates and R. House (eds), *Ethically Challenged Professions: Enabling Innovation and Diversity in Psychotherapy and Counselling* (pp. 160–71). Ross-on-Wye: PCCS Books

Holland, J.C. and Rowland, J.H. (eds) (1989) *Handbook of Psychoonology: Psychological Care for the Patient with Cancer.* Oxford: Oxford University Press

Hollway, W. and Jefferson, T. (2000) *Doing Qualitative Research Differently: Free Association, Narrative and the Interview Method.* London: Sage

Holroyd, S. (1991) *Krishnamurti: The Man, The Mystery and the Message.* Shaftsbury: Element Books

Holzman, L. and Morss, J. (eds) (2000) *Postmodern Psychologies: Societal Practice and Political Life.* New York: Routledge

Hook, D. (2001) Therapeutic discourse, co-construction, interpellation, role-induction: psychotherapy as iatrogenic treatment modality? *International Journal of Psychotherapy* 6 (1): 47–66

Hook, D. (2002) The Power of Psychodynamic Psychotherapy. Unpublished Ph.D. thesis, Johannesburg: University of Witwatersrand

Hook, D. (2010) *Foucault, Psychology and the Analytics of Power.* Basingstoke: Palgrave Macmillan

Horton, I. (2002) Regulation, registration and accreditation: some issues. In J. Clark (ed.), *Freelance Counselling and Psychotherapy: Competition and Collaboration* (pp. 49–63). London: Routledge

House, R. (1992) A tale of two conferences: organisational form and accreditation ethos. *Self and Society* 20 (4): 35–7

House, R. (1996a) The professionalization of counselling: a coherent 'case against'? *Counselling Psychology Quarterly* 9 (4): 343–58

House, R. (1996b) Love, intimacy and therapeutic change. *Self and Society* 24 (1): 21–6

House, R. (1996c) General practice counselling: a plea for ideological engagement. *Counselling* (BAC) 7 (1): 40–4; reprinted and updated in P. Milner and S. Palmer (eds), *Counselling Volume 2: The BACP Counselling Reader* (pp. 158–66). London: Sage, 2001

House, R. (1996d) Conference review: Beyond the Brain, Cambridge, August 1995. *Self and Society* 23 (6): 30–1

House, R. (1996e) 'Audit-mindedness' in counselling: some underlying dynamics. *British Journal of Guidance and Counselling* 24 (2): 277–83

House, R. (1996/2004) Mowbray Distilled: A summary of his *The Case Against Psychotherapy Registration*, mimeo: Independent Practitioners Network; reprinted with a new introduction in *Ipnosis* magazine, 13 and 14, 2004, 4–7 and 27–9, respectively; and in this volume, Chapter 13

House, R. (1997a) Participatory ethics in a self-generating practitioner community. In R. House and N. Totton (eds), *Implausible Professions* (pp. 321–34). Ross-on-Wye: PCCS Books; 2nd edn, 2011 (in press)

House, R. (1997b) Therapy in New Paradigm perspective: the phenomenon of Georg Groddeck. In R. House and N. Totton (eds), *Implausible Professions* (pp. 225–40). Ross-on-Wye: PCCS Books; see chapter 21, this volume

House, R. (1997c) An approach to time-limited humanistic-dynamic counselling. *British Journal of Guidance and Counselling* 25 (2): 251–62

House, R. (1997d) Training: a guarantee of competence? In R. House and N. Totton (eds), *Implausible Professions* (pp. 99–108). Ross-on-Wye: PCCS Books; 2nd edn, 2011 (in press)

House, R. (1997e) Bleached skeletons and new science (Letter – Reply to Lewis Wolpert). *The Therapist* 4 (4): 47

House, R. (1998) Counselling: performance or quality of being? *Counselling* (BAC) 9 (3): 175

House, R. (1999a) 'Limits to counselling and therapy': deconstructing a professional ideology. *British Journal of Guidance and Counselling* 27 (3): 377–92; reprinted in Bates and House (eds), *Ethically Challenged Professions* (pp. 94–109). Ross-on-Wye: PCCS Books, 2003, and as Chapter 6, this volume

House, R. (1999b) Letter to the Editor. *International Journal of Psychotherapy* 4 (2): 263–4

House, R. (1999c) The place of psychotherapy and counselling in a healthy European social order: a commentary on Tantam and van Deurzen. *European Journal of Psychotherapy, Counselling and Health* 2 (2): 236–43; with an expanded version as Chapter 3, this volume

House, R. (1999d) Review Feature: C. New's *Agency, Health and Social Survival. European Journal of Psychotherapy, Counselling and Health* 2 (1): 103–17

House, R. (1999e) Review article: Holistic perspectives in science. *Steiner Education* 33 (1): 41–2

House, R. (2000) Stress, surveillance and modernity: the 'modernising' assault on our education system. *Education Now: News and Review*, 30 (Winter); Feature Supplement, 4 pp

House, R. (2001a) Psychotherapy professionalization: the post-graduate dimension and the legitimacy of statutory regulation. *British Journal of Psychotherapy*, 17 (3): 382–90; reprinted in *Ipnosis: An Independent Journal for Practitioners* 5, 2002: 28–9 and 7, 2002: 26–7

House, R. (2001b) The statutory regulation of psychotherapy: still time to think again. *The Psychotherapist* 17 (Autumn): 12–17; reprinted as Chapter 13 in Bates and House (eds), *Ethically Challenged Professions* (pp. 142–7). Ross-on-Wye: PCCS Books, 2003

House, R. (2002) The central place of play in early learning and development. *The Mother* magazine 2 (Summer): 44–6

House, R. (2003a) *Therapy Beyond Modernity: Deconstructing and Transcending Profession-centred Therapy.* London: Karnac Books

House, R. (2003b) Commentary: Difference, the 'profession', and transcending the ideologies of late modernity: a response to Oakley. *European Journal of Psychotherapy, Counselling and Health* 6 (4): 281–92; available at http://www.uea.ac.uk/~wp276/article.htm

House, R. (2003c) Beyond the Victimhood mentality: from guilt to healthy parental responsibility. *The Mother* magazine, 7 (Autumn): 44–5

House, R. (2004a) General practice counselling: nascent postmodern therapy? *Psychodynamic Practice* 10 (3): 394–9

House, R. (2004b) Review Article: Therapy and Postmodernist Thought. Part II: Existentialist-Phenomenology, Levinas, and Postmodernising Therapy's Postmodern Turn. *Ipnosis* magazine, 15 (Autumn): 23–5, 29

House, R. (2005a) The state regulation of counselling and psychotherapy: sometime, never…?. *Journal of Critical Psychology, Counselling and Psychotherapy* 5 (4): 176–89

House, R. (2005b) 'Audit culture', accreditation and the Academy: staying faithful to authentic educational quality. *New View* 36 (Summer): 59–64

House, R. (2005c) Review of *Science and Pseudoscience in Clinical Psychology* by Scott O.

Lilienfeld, Steven Jay Lynn and Jeffrey M. Lohr (eds). *Review of the Scientific and Medical Network* 88 (Summer): 54–6

House, R. (2006) Conclusion: Welcoming the client-voice movement. In Y. Bates (ed.), *Shouldn't I Be Feeling Better by Now? Client Views of Therapy* (pp. 184–8). Basingstoke: Palgrave Macmillan; reprinted as Chapter 5, this volume

House, R. (2007a) Schooling, the state and children's psychological well-being: a psychosocial critique. *Journal of Psychosocial Research* 2 (July–Dec): 49–62

House, R. (2007b) The be-coming of a therapist: experiential learning, self-education and the personal/professional nexus. *British Journal of Guidance and Counselling* 35 (4): 427–40; reprinted as Chapter 1, this volume

House, R. (2008a) Training and education for therapy practitionership: 'trans-modern' perspectives. *Counselling Psychology Quarterly* 21 (1): 1–10; see Chapter 17, this volume

House, R. (2008b) The dance of psychotherapy and politics. *Psychotherapy and Politics International*, 6 (2): 98–109

House, R. (2008c) Therapy's modernist 'regime of truth': from scientistic 'theory-mindedness' towards the subtle and the mysterious. *Philosophical Practice* 3 (3): 343–52; reprinted as Chapter 11, this volume

House, R. (2008d) Play and playfulness in therapeutic and educational perspectives. *European Journal of Psychotherapy and Counselling* 10 (2): 10–19

House R. (2008e) Let us play. *The Mother* magazine 26 (Jan/Feb): 32–3

House. R. (2008f) Towards post-professional practice: principled non-compliant practitionership in a post-regulation era. *Self and Society* 36 (2): 44–50

House, R. (2009a) The PLG's Proposals for the Statutory Regulation of Counselling and Psychotherapy: Submission of Evidence. In D. Postle and R. House (eds), *Compliance? Ambivalence? Rejection? – Nine Papers Challenging HPC Regulation* (pp. 93–123). London: Wentworth Learning Resources

House, R. (2010) 'Psy' research beyond late-modernity: towards praxis-congruent research. *Psychotherapy and Politics International* 8 (1): 13–20

House, R. and Bohart, A.C. (2008) Empirically supported/validated treatments as modernist ideology, II: Alternative perspectives on research and practice. In R. House and D. Loewenthal (eds), *Against and For CBT: Towards a Constructive Dialogue?* (pp. 202–17). Ross-on-Wye: PCCS Books

House, R. and Hall, J. (1991) 'Peer accreditation... within a humanistic framework?' *Self and Society* 19 (2): 33–6

House, R. and Loewenthal, D. (eds) (2008a) *Against and for CBT: Towards a Constructive Dialogue?* Ross-on-Wye: PCCS Books

House, R. and Loewenthal, D. (eds) (2008b) CBT in Question: Special issue of *European Journal of Psychotherapy and Counselling* 10 (3)

House, R. and Loewenthal, D. (eds) (2009) *Childhood, Well-being and a Therapeutic Ethos.* London: Karnac Books

House, R. and Totton, N. (eds) (1997) *Implausible Professions: Arguments for Pluralism and Autonomy in Psychotherapy and Counselling.* Ross-on-Wye: PCCS Books; 2nd edn, 2011 (in press)

Howard, A. (1996) *Challenges to Counselling and Psychotherapy.* Basingstoke: Macmillan

Howard, A. (2000) Martin Heidegger. In his *Philosophy for Counselling and Psychotherapy: Pythagoras to Postmodernism* (pp. 327–40). London: Macmillan

Howarth-Williams, M. (1977) *R.D. Laing: His Work and its Relevance for Sociology.* London: Routledge and Kegan Paul

Hugill, B. (1998) Analysts in trauma over identity crisis. *Observer* newspaper, 22nd March

Hunter, A. (1988) Seeds of Truth: J. Krishnamurti as Religious Teacher and Educator. University of Leeds: unpublished Ph.D. thesis

Illich, I. (1977a) Disabling professions. In I. Illich and others, *Disabling Professions* (pp. 11–39). London: Marion Boyars

Illich, I. (1977b) *Limits to Medicine*. Harmondsworth: Penguin

Ipnosis magazine (2002) Special centenary edition on Carl Rogers. Issue number 6

Isaacs, S. (1933) *Social Development in Young Children*. London: Routledge & Kegan Paul

Jackson, N. and Carter, P. (2006) *Rethinking Organisational Behaviour: A Post-Structuralist Framework*, 2nd edn. London: Financial Times/ Prentice Hall

Jarvis, P. (2005) Towards a philosophy of human learning: an existentialist perspective. In P. Jarvis and S. Parker (eds), *Human Learning: A Holistic Approach* (pp. 1–15). London: Routledge

Jenner, F.A., Monterio, A.C.D., Zagalo-Cardoso, J.A. and Cunha-Oliveira, J.A. (1993) *Schizophrenia: A Disease or Some Ways of Being Human?* Sheffield: Sheffield Academic Press

Johnson, M. (1987) *The Body in the Mind: The Bodily Basis of Meaning, Imagination, and Reason*. Chicago: University of Chicago Press

Johnstone, L. (1989) *Users and Abusers of Psychiatry: A Critical Look at Traditional Psychiatric Practice*. London: Routledge; 2nd edn, 2000

Kalisch, D. (1990) Professionalisation: a rebel view. *Self and Society* 18 (1): 24–9

Kalisch, D. (1992) The living tradition and the division of the spoils: professionalisation again. *Self and Society* 18 (4): 36–7

Kalisch, D. (1996) Registration: who is asking the right questions? *The Therapist* 3 (4): 46

Keat, R. and Urry, J. (1975) *Social Theory as Science*. London: Routledge & Kegan Paul

Keller, C. and Daniell, A. (eds) (2002) *Process and Difference: Between Cosmological and Poststructuralist Postmodernisms*. Albany, NY: State University of New York Press

Kendall, T. and Crossley, N. (1996) Governing love: on the tactical control of countertransference in the psychoanalytic community. *Economy and Society* 25 (2): 178–94

Kennard, D. and Small, N. (1997a) Living together in uncertain times. In D. Kennard and N. Small (eds), *Living Together* (pp. 202–20). London: Quartet Books

Kennard, D. and Small, N. (1997b) Commentary: Cold comfort. In D. Kennard and N. Small (eds), *Living Together* (pp. 160–3). London: Quartet Books

Kernberg, O.F. (1996) Thirty methods to destroy the creativity of psychoanalytic candidates. *International Journal of Psycho-analysis* 77: 1031–40

Kilroy, P., Bailey, R., and Chare, N. (2004) Editorial sounding: auditing culture. *Parallax* Issue 31, 10 (2): 1–2

King, L. and Moutsou, C. (eds) (2010) *Rethinking Audit Cultures: A Critical Look at Evidence-based Practice in Psychotherapy and Beyond*. Ross-on-Wye: PCCS Books

King, P. and Steiner, R. (eds) (1990) *The Freud–Klein Controversies, 1941–45*. London: Routledge

Kirsch, I. (2009) *The Emperor's New Drugs: Exploding the Antidepressant Myth*. London: The Bodley Head

Kirschenbaum, H. and Henderson, J. (eds) (1989) *The Carl Rogers Reader*. London: Constable

Kirton, M.J. (ed.) (1994) *Adaptors and Innovators: Styles of Creativity and Problem-solving*, 2nd edn. London: Thomson Publishing

Klein, J. (2003) *Jacob's Ladder: Essays on Experiences of the Ineffable in the Context of Contemporary Psychotherapy*. London: Karnac

Kleinman, A. (1988) *Rethinking Psychiatry: From Cultural Category to Personal Experience*. New York: Free Press

Kotowicz, Z. (1997) *R.D. Laing and the Paths of Anti-psychiatry*. London: Routledge

Kovel, J. (1976) *A Complete Guide to Therapy*. New York: Pantheon Books (Penguin edn quoted)

Krippner, S. and Welch, P. (1992) *Spiritual Dimensions of Healing: From Native Shamanism to Contemporary Health Care*. New York: Irvington Publishers

Krishna, G. (1971) *Kundalini: The Evolutionary Energy in Man*. Berkeley: Shambhala

Krishna, G. (1974) *Higher Consciousness: The Evolutionary Thrust of Kundalini*. New York: Julian

Krishnamurti, J. (1997) *On Mind and Thought*. HarperSanFransisco

Krishnamurti, J. and Bohm, D. (1988) *The Ending of Time: Thirteen Dialogues*. London: Gollancz

Kuhn, T. S. (1962) *The Structure of Scientific Revolutions*. Chicago: Chicago University Press

Kurtz, S. (1989) *The Art of Unknowing: Dimensions of Openness in Analytic Therapy*. Northvale, NJ: Jason Aronson

Kvale, S. (ed.) (1992) *Psychology and Postmodernism*. London: Sage

Lacan, J. (1965) *Écrits*. Paris: Seuil

Laing, R.D. (1967) *The Politics of Experience and the Bird of Paradise*. Harmondsworth: Penguin

Lamb, H. (ed.) (1979) *Alternatives to Acute Hospitalization*. San Francisco: Jossey-Bass

Lamont, J. and Spencer, A. (1997) Self and Peer Assessment: a personal story. In R. House and N. Totton (eds), *Implausible Professions* (pp. 295–303). Ross-on-Wye: PCCS Books; 2nd edn, 2011 (in press)

Langdridge, D. (2007) *Phenomenological Psychology: Theory, Research and Method*. Upper Saddle River, NJ: Prentice Hall

Laplanche, J. (1989) *New Foundations for Psychoanalysis*. Oxford: Blackwell

Large, M. (2010) *Common Wealth*. Stroud: Hawthorn Press

Lasch, C. (1979) *The Culture of Narcissism*. New York: Norton

Laszlo, E. (1996) *The Whispering Pond: A Personal Guide to the Emerging Vision of Science*. Shaftsbury: Element Books

Lather, P. (1991) *Getting Smart: Feminist Research and Pedagogy within/in the Postmodern*. London: Routledge

Lawrence, R. L. (2005) *Artistic Ways of Knowing: Expanded Opportunities for Teaching and Learning*. San Francisco: Jossey-Bass

Lazarus, A.A. (1994a) The illusion of the therapist's power and the patient's fragility: my rejoinder. *Ethics and Behavior* 4 (3): 299–306

Lazarus, A.A. (1994b) How certain boundaries and ethics diminish therapeutic effectiveness. *Ethics and Behavior* 4 (3): 255–61; reprinted as Chapter 1 in Y. Bates and R. House (eds), *Ethically Challenged Professions*. Ross-on-Wye: PCCS Books, 2003

Lees, J. (2008) Cognitive-behavioural therapy and evidence-based practice: past, present and future. In R. House and D. Loewenthal (eds), *Against and for CBT: Towards a Constructive Dialogue?* (pp. 77–85). Ross-on-Wye: PCCS Books

Lees, J. and Freshwater, D. (eds) (2008) *Practitioner-based Research: Power, Discourse and Transformation*. London: Karnac Books

Lethery, G. (2003) *Feminist Research in Theory and Practice*. Milton Keynes: Open University Press

Levin, D.M. (1987a) Psychopathology in the epoch of nihilism. In D.M. Levin (ed.), *Pathologies of the Modern Self* (pp. 21–83). New York: New York University Press

Levin, D.M. (1987b) Introduction. In D. M. Levin (ed.), *Pathologies of the Modern Self* (pp. 1–17). New York: New York University Press

Levin, D.M. (ed.) (1987c) *Pathologies of the Modern Self: Postmodern Studies on Narcissism, Schizophrenia, and Depression*. New York: New York University Press

Lievegoed, B. (1991) *Developing Communities*. Stroud: Hawthorn Press

Lipsedge, M. (1995) Religion and madness in history. In D. Bhugra (ed.), *Psychiatry and Religion* (pp. 23–47). London: Routledge

Lipsker, B. (1990) Three pillars. In C. M. Pietzner (ed.), *A Candle on the Hill: Images of Camphill Life* (pp. 59–60). Edinburgh: Floris Books

Lissau, R. (1996) *Rudolf Steiner's Social Intentions*. Canterbury: New Economy Publications

Loewenthal, D. (1998) Editorial: The attack on European thought. *European Journal of Psychotherapy, Counselling and Health* 1 (3): 347–51

Loewenthal, D. (2007) Relational research, ideology and the evolution of intersubjectivity in a post-existential culture. In D. Loewenthal (ed.), *Case Studies in Relational Research* (pp. 221–40). Basingstoke: Palgrave Macmillan

Loewenthal, D. (2008) Introducing post-existential practice. *Philosophical Practice*, 3 (3): 316–21

Loewenthal, D. (2011) *Post-existentialism for Psychological Therapists*. London: Karnac Books (in preparation)

Loewenthal, D. and House, R. (eds) (2010) *Critically Engaging CBT*. Maidenhead: Open University Press

Loewenthal, D. and Snell, R. (eds) (2003) *Post-modernism for Psychotherapists: A Critical Reader*. Hove: Brunner-Routledge

Lomas, P. (1981) *The Case for a Personal Psychotherapy*. Oxford: Oxford University Press

Longman, J. (1998) Editorial. *Counselling* (BAC) 9 (2): 82

Lorimer, D. (ed.) (1998) *The Spirit of Science: From Experiment to Experience*. Edinburgh: Floris Books

Lorimer, D. (ed.) (2001) *Thinking Beyond the Brain*. Edinburgh: Floris Books

Lorimer, D. and others (eds) (1999) *Wider Horizons: Explorations in Science and Human Experience*. Leven, Fife: Scientific and Medical Network

Lowe, R. (1999) Between the 'no longer' and the 'not yet': postmodernism as a context for critical therapeutic work. In I. Parker (ed.), *Deconstructing Psychotherapy* (pp. 71–85). London: Sage

Lowson, D. (1994) Understanding Professional Thought Disorder: a guide for service users and a challenge to professionals. *Asylum: Magazine for a Democratic Psychiatry* 8 (2): 29–30

Luepnitz, D.A. (1992) Nothing in common but their first names: the case of Foucault and White. *Journal of Family Therapy* 14: 281–4

Lukoff, D. (1985) The diagnosis of mystical experiences with psychotic features. *Journal of Transpersonal Psychology* 17 (2): 155–81

Lukoff, D. and Everest, H.L. (1985) The myths in mental illness. *Journal of Transpersonal Psychology* 17 (2): 123–53

Lukoff, D., Lu, F. and Turner, R. (1992) Toward a more culturally sensitive DSM-IV:

Psychoreligious and psychospiritual problems. *Journal of Nervous and Mental Disease* 180: 673–82

Lyon, M.L. (1993) Psychoneuroimmunology: the problem of the situatedness of illness and the conceptualization of healing. *Culture, Medicine and Society* 17 (1): 77–97

McDougall, J. (1995) *The Many Faces of Eros: A Psychoanalytic Exploration of Human Sexuality*. London: Free Association Books

MacIver, J. (1983) *The Glimpse*. Roslyn Heights, NJ: Libra Publishers

Macleod, C. and Bhatia, S. (2008) Postcolonialism and psychology. In C. Willig and W. Stainton-Rogers (eds), *SAGE Handbook of Qualitative Research in Psychology* (pp. 576–89). London: Sage

Maguire, M. (1995) *Men, Women, Passion and Power: Gender Issues in Psychotherapy*. London: Routledge

Mair, K. (1997) The myth of therapist expertise. In R. House and N. Totton (eds) *Implausible Professions: Arguments for Pluralism and Autonomy in Psychotherapy and Counselling* (pp. 87–98). Ross-on-Wye: PCCS Books; abridged from C. Feltham and W. Dryden (eds), *Psychotherapy and Its Discontents* (pp. 135–60). Buckingham: Open University Press, 1992

Margitics, F. (2009) *Handbook of New Spiritual Consciousness: Theory and Research*. Hauppauge, NY: Nova Science Publishers

Martin, B. (ed.) (1996) *Confronting the Experts*. Albany, NY: State University of New York Press

Masson, J. (1988) *Against Therapy*. Atheneum (London: Fontana/Collins, 1990)

Masson, J. (1992) The tyranny of psychotherapy. In W. Dryden and C. Feltham (eds) *Psychotherapy and Its Discontents* (pp. 7–29, 36–40). Buckingham: Open University Press

May, R. (1996) *Heidegger's Hidden Sources: East-Asian Influences on His Work*. London: Routledge

Mearns, D. and Cooper, M. (2005) *Working at Relational Depth in Counselling and Psychotherapy*. London: Sage

Meichenbaum, D. (1988) What happens when the 'brute data' of psychological inquiry are meanings: Nurturing a dialogue between hermeneutics and empiricism. In S.B. Messer, L.A. Sass and R.L. Woolfolk (eds), *Hermeneutics and Psychological Theory: Interpretive Perspectives on Personality, Psychotherapy, and Psychopathology* (pp. 116–30). New Brunswick, NJ: Rutgers University Press

Menninger, K. (1963) *The Vital Balance: The Life Process in Mental Health and Illness*. New York: Viking Press

Merleau-Ponty, M. (1968) *The Visible and the Invisible*. Evanston, Ill.: Northwestern University Press

Mesirow, J. (1981) A critical theory of adult learning and education. *Adult Education* 32 (1): 3–24

Messer, S.B., Sass, L.A. and Woolfolk, R.L. (eds) (1988) *Hermeneutics and Psychological Theory: Interpretive Perspectives on Personality, Psychotherapy, and Psychopathology*. New Brunswick: Rutgers University Press

Michel, P. (1995) *Krishnamurti: Love and Freedom - Approaching a Mystery*. Woodside, Calif.: Bluestar Communications

Mills, J. (2003) A phenomenology of becoming: reflections on authenticity. In R. Frie (ed.), *Understanding Experience: Psychotherapy and Postmodernism* (pp. 116–36). London: Routledge

Moen, M.K. (1991) Introduction. In B.den Ouden and M. Moen (eds), *The Presence of Feeling in Thought* (pp. 1–9). New York: Peter Lang

Morgan, G. (2006) *Images of Organization.* London: Sage

Morris, V.C. (1966) *Existentialism in Education.* New York: Harper & Row

Morrow, R.A. and Brown, D.D. (1994) *Critical Theory and Methodology: Interpretive Structuralism as a Research Program.* London: Sage

Morss, J.R. (1996) *Growing Critical: Alternatives to Developmental Psychology.* London: Routledge

Mosher, L.R. (1996) Soteria: a therapeutic community for psychotic persons. In P.R. Breggin and E.M. Stein (eds), *Psychosocial Approaches to Deeply Disturbed Persons* (pp. 43–58). New York: Haworth Press

Mourad, R.O. Jr (1997) *Postmodern Philosophical Critique and the Pursuit of Knowledge in Higher Education.* Westport, Conn.: Bergin & Garvey

Mowbray, R. (1995) *The Case Against Psychotherapy Registration: A Conservation Issue for the Human Potential Movement.* London: Trans Marginal Press; downloadable as a pdf file free of charge at: www.transmarginalpress.co.uk

Mowbray, R. (1996) SAFAA is safer. *Self and Society* 23 (6): 16–19

Mowbray, R. (1997) Too vulnerable to choose? In R. House and N. Totton (eds), *Implausible Professions* (pp. 33–44). Ross-on-Wye: PCCS Books; 2nd edn, 2011 (in press)

Mullan, B. (ed.) (1996) *Therapists on Therapy.* London: Free Association Books

Mullan, B. (1999) *R.D. Laing: A Personal View.* London: Duckworth

Naples, N.A. (2003) *Feminism and Method: Ethnography, Discourse and Activist Research.* London: Routledge

Natiello, P. (2001) *The Person-Centred Approach: A Passionate Presence.* Ross-on-Wye: PCCS Books

Naydler, J. (ed.) (1996) *Goethe on Science: An Anthology of Goethe's Scientific Writings.* Edinburgh: Floris Books

Nelson, J.E. (1994) *Healing the Split: Integrating Spirit into our Understanding of the Mentally Ill.* Albany: State University of New York Press

Neumann, E. (1954) *The Origins and History of Consciousness.* New York: Pantheon Books/ Random House (orig. 1949)

New, C. (1996) *Agency, Health and Social Survival: The Ecopolitics of Rival Psychologies.* London: Taylor and Francis

Newnes, C. and Holmes, G. (1999) The future of mental health services. In C. Newnes et al. (eds), *This Is Madness* (pp. 273–84). Ross-on-Wye: PCCS Books

Newnes, C., Holmes, G. and Dunn, C. (eds) (1999) *This Is Madness: A Critical Look at Psychiatry and the Future of Mental Health Services.* Ross-on-Wye: PCCS Books

Nolan, J. L. (1998) *The Therapeutic State: Justifying Government at Century's End.* New York: New York University Press

O'Callaghan, M. (1996) The far side of madness: visionary process and psychosis. An interview with John Perry. *IASP Journal* 4

Oakley, A. (2000) *Experiments in Knowing: Gender and Method in the Social Sciences.* Cambridge: Polity Press

Oakley, J. (1992) *Morality and the Emotions.* London: Routledge

Olthuis, J.H. (ed.) (1997) *Knowing Other-wise: Philosophy at the Threshold of Spirituality.* New York: Fordham University Press

Orbach, S. (1994) *What's Really Going on Here?* London: Virago

Palmer Barnes, F. (1998) *Complaints and Grievances in Psychotherapy: A Handbook of Ethical Practice*. London: Routledge

Papadopoulos, R.K. (2006) Jung's epistemology and methodology. In R.K. Papadopoulos (ed.), *The Handbook of Jungian Psychology* (pp. 7–53). London: Routledge

Parallax (2004) Special theme issue on 'Auditing Culture'. Issue 31, 10, 2 (April–June)

Parker, I. (1996) Postmodernism and its discontents: therapeutic discourse. *British Journal of Psychotherapy* 12 (4): 447–60

Parker, I. (1997a) *Psychoanalytic Culture: Psychoanalytic Discourse in Western Society*. London: Sage

Parker, I. (1997b) Discourse analysis and psychoanalysis. *British Journal of Social Psychology* 36: 479–96

Parker, I. (1998a) Constructing and deconstructing psychotherapeutic discourse. *European Journal of Psychotherapy, Counselling and Health* 1 (1): 65–78

Parker, I. (1998b) Paper presented to British Association for the Advancement of Science conference, Cardiff; reported in: Psychology a fake science that abuses public, says expert. *Daily Telegraph* 12th September: 14

Parker, I. (1998c) Against postmodernism: psychology in cultural context. *Theory and Psychology* 8 (5): 601–27

Parker I. (ed.) (1999a) *Deconstructing Psychotherapy*. London: Sage

Parker, I. (1999b) Deconstruction and psychotherapy. In I. Parker (ed.), *Deconstructing Psychotherapy* (pp. 1–18). London: Sage

Parker, I. (2001) What is wrong with the discourse of the university in psychotherapy training? *European Journal of Psychotherapy, Counselling and Health* 4 (1): 27–43

Parker, I. (2004) *Qualitative Psychology: Introducing Radical Research*. Milton Keynes: Open University Press

Parker, I. and Shotter, J. (eds) *Deconstructing Social Psychology*. London: Routledge

Parker, I., Georgaca, E., Harper, D., McLaughlin, T. and Stowell-Smith, M. (1995) *Deconstructing Psychopathology*. London: Sage

Pattison, S. (1999) Are professional codes ethical? *Counselling* (BAC), 10 (5): 374–80; repinted as Chapter 5 in Bates and House (eds), *Ethically Challenged Professions* (pp. 46–56). Ross-on-Wye: PCCS Books, 2003

Payne, M. (2000) *Narrative and Therapy: An Introduction for Counsellors*. London: Sage

Peck, M. S. (1993) Salvation and suffering: the ambiguity of pain and disease. *Human Potential* Summer: 15, 17, 24–6

Perry, J. (1974) *The Far Side of Madness*. Englewood Cliffs, NJ: Prentice-Hall

Persons, J. B. and Silberschatz, G. (1998) Are results of randomized controlled trials useful to psychotherapists? *Journal of Consulting and Clinical Psychology* 66: 126–35

Peters, M. (ed.) (1998) *Naming the Multiple: Post-structuralism and Education*. Westport, Conn.: Bergin & Garvey

Peters, M. (ed.) (2002) *Heidegger, Modernity and Education*. Lanham, Maryland: Rowman and Littlefield

Philosophical Practice (2008) Special issue on 'Post-existential Counseling', volume 3 (3)

Pilgrim, D. (1992) Psychotherapy and political evasions. In W. Dryden and C. Feltham (eds) *Psychotherapy and Its Discontents* (pp. 225–43, 249–53). Buckingham: Open University Press

Pilgrim, D. (1997) *Psychotherapy and Society*. London: Sage

Pilgrim, D. (2008) Reading 'happiness': CBT and the Layard thesis. In R. House and D. Loewenthal (eds), *Against and for CBT: Towards a Constructive Dialogue?* (pp. 256–

68). Ross-on-Wye: PCCS Books

Pokorny, M. (1998) Alchemy, day-dreams and fictions: psychotherapy in Britain today. *International Journal of Psychotherapy* 3 (2): 265–6

Polanyi, M. (1966) *The Tacit Dimension.* New York: Doubleday

Polkinghorne, D. E. (1988) *Narrative Knowing and the Human Sciences.* New York: State University of New York Press

Polkinghorne, D. (1990) Psychology after philosophy. In J.E. Faulconer and R.N. Williams (eds), *Reconsidering Psychology: Perspectives from Continental Philosophy* (pp. 92–115). Pittsbugh, Pa: Duquesne University Press

Postle, D. (1995) Glacier reaches edge of town. *Self and Society* 23 (6): 7–11

Postle, D. (1997) Counselling in the UK: jungle, garden or monoculture? In R. House and N. Totton (eds), *Implausible Professions* (pp. 151–8). Ross-on-Wye: PCCS Books; 2nd edn, 2011 (in press)

Postle, D. (1998) The alchemist's nightmare: gold into lead – the annexation of psychotherapy in the UK. *International Journal of Psychotherapy* 3 (1): 53–83

Postle, D. (2003) Psychopractice accountability: a practitioner 'full disclosure' list. In Y. Bates and R. House (eds), *Ethically Challenged Professions: Enabling Innovation and Diversity in Psychotherapy and Counselling* (pp.172–8). Ross-on-Wye: PCCS Books

Postle, D. (2006) Roles, competencies and complacency – mapping the territory of psychotherapy and counselling with the Department of Health. Available at: http://ipnosis.postle.net/pages/RoleCompetenciesEtc.htm.

Postle, D. (2007) *Regulating the Psychological Therapies – From Taxonomy to Taxidermy.* Ross-on-Wye: PCCS Books

Postle, D. (nd) 'Ipnosis' http://ipnosis.org

Postle, D. (nd) 'g.o.r.i.l.l.a.' Internet archive of statutory regulation texts: http://g.o.r.i.l.l.a.postle.net

Postle, D. and Anderson, J. (1990) Stealing the flame. *Self and Society* 18 (1): 13–15

Postle, D. and House, R. (eds) (2009) *Compliance? Ambivalence? Rejection? – Nine Papers Challenging HPC Regulation.* London: Wentworth Learning Resources

Power, M. (1997) *The Audit Society: Rituals of Verification.* Oxford: Oxford University Press

Prilleltensky, I., Prilleltensky, O. and Voorhees, C. (2009) Psychopolitical validity in counselling and therapy. In D. Fox, I. Prilleltensky and S. Austin (eds), *Critical Psychology: An Introduction,* 2nd edn (pp. 355–72). London: Sage

Proctor, G. (2008) CBT: the obscuring of power in the name of science. In R. House and D. Loewenthal (eds), *Against and For CBT: Towards a Constructive Dialogue?* (pp. 241–55). Ross-on-Wye: PCCS Books

Puhakka, K., Nelson, P.L. and Hart, T. (1997) *Spiritual Knowing: Alternative Epistemic Perspectives.* Carrollton: State University of West Georgia

Pylkkanen, P. (ed.) (1989) *The Search for Meaning: The New Spirit in Science and Philosophy.* Wellingborough: Crucible/Aquarian Press

Quinney, R. (1988) Beyond the interpretive: the way of awareness. *Sociological Inquiry* 58 (1): 101–16

Ramazanoglu, C. and Holland, J. (2002) *Feminist Methodology: Challenges and Choices.* London: Sage

Raschid, S. (ed.) (2005) *R.D. Laing: Contemporary Perspectives.* London: Free Association Books

Reed, E. (1996) *The Necessity of Experience.* New Haven: Yale University Press

Reinharz, S. and Davidman, L. (1992) *Feminist Methods in Social Research*. Oxford: Oxford University Press

Rieff, P. (1966) *The Triumph of the Therapeutic: Uses of Faith after Freud*. London: Chatto & Windus

Riikonen, E. and Smith, G. M. (1997) *Re-Imagining Therapy: Living Conversations and Relational Knowing*. London: Sage

Riikonen, E. and Vataja, S. (1999) Can (and should) we know how, where and when psychotherapy takes place? In I. Parker (ed.), *Deconstructing Psychotherapy* (pp. 175–87). London: Sage

Robbins, A. (1997) *Therapeutic Presence: Bridging Expression and Form*. London: Jessica Kingsley

Robbins, B.D. (2000) Putting ourselves out of business: Implications of Levinas for psychology. Presented at the 3rd Annual Conference on Counselling and Spirituality, Gannon University, Pa., September

Rogers, C. (1973) Some new challenges to the helping professions. *American Psychologist* 28 (5): 379–87; reprinted in H. Kirschenbaum and V.L. Henderson (eds), *The Carl Rogers Reader* (pp. 357–75). London: Constable, 1990

Rorty, R. (1991) Introduction: pragmatism and post-Nietzschean philosophy. In his *Essays of Heidegger and Others* (pp. 1–6). New York: Cambridge University Press

Rose, H. (1994) *Love, Power and Knowledge: Towards a Feminist Transformation of the Sciences*. Cambridge: Polity Press

Rose, N. (1989) *Governing the Soul: The Shaping of the Private Self*. London: Routledge

Rose, N. (1996) *Inventing Ourselves: Psychology, Power and Personhood*. Cambridge: Cambridge University Press

Rosenberg, M. (1984) A symbolic interactionist view of psychosis. *Journal of Health and Social Behavior* 25: 289–302

Roth, H.D. (2006) 'Contemplative Studies: prospects for a new field', *Teachers College Record* (online), available at: http://www.tcrecord.org/Content.asp?ContentId=12682 (downloaded March 2010)

Rouff, L.C. (2000) Clouds and silver linings: training experiences of psychodynamically oriented mental health trainees. *American Journal of Psychotherapy* 54 (4): 549–59

Rowan, J. (1988) Review of France (1988). *Self and Society* 26 (6): 275–7

Rowan, J. (1995) An Open Letter to Richard Mowbray. *Self and Society* 23 (4): 43–4

Rowan, J. (1996) Love is not enough (letter). *Counselling* (BAC) 7 (1): 12

Rowan, J. (1999) Review of Casement (ed.), *Post-Jungians Today*. *Self and Society* 27 (3): 50–1

Rowan, J. (2004) What is wrong with Lacan. *Journal of Critical Psychology, Counselling and Psychotherapy* 4 (1): 11–18

Rowan, J. (2005) *The Future of Training in Psychotherapy and Counselling: Instrumental, Relational and Transpersonal Perspectives*. London: Routledge

Rowe, D. (1990) Foreword. In J. Masson, *Against Therapy* (pp. 7–23). London: Fontana/ Collins

Russell, R. (1981) *Report on Effective Psychotherapy: Legislative Testimony*. New York: R.R. Latin Associates

Sable, D. (2007) The impact of contemplative practices on transformative learning. Albuquerque, NM: paper presented at the 7th international conference, Transformative Learning: Issues of Difference and Diversity, University of New Mexico, 24–26 October; retrievable at: http://transformativelearningbermuda.com/uploads/

2007_Transformative_Learning_Conference_Proceedings.pdf#page=299 (downloaded March 2010)

Samuels, A. (1992) Foreword. In W. Dryden and C. Feltham (eds), *Psychotherapy and Its Discontents* (pp. xi–xv).Buckingham: Open University Press

Samuels, A. (1993) *The Political Psyche*. London: Routledge

Samuels, A. (1997) Pluralism and psychotherapy: what is good training?. In R. House and N. Totton (eds), *Implausible Professions* (pp.199–214). Ross-on-Wye: PCCS Books; 2nd edn, 2011

Samuels, A. (2001) *Politics on the Couch: Citizenship and the Internal Life*. London: Karnac

Sands, A. (2000) *Falling for Therapy*. Palgrave Macmillan, London

Sannella, L. (1992) *The Kundalini Experience: Psychosis or Transcendence?* Lower Lake, Calif.: Integral Publishing

Sardello, R. (1990) Introduction. In R. Steiner (ed.), *Psychoanalysis and Spiritual Psychology: Five Lectures, 1912–21* (pp. 1–29). New York: Anthroposophic Press

Sardello, R. (1999) *Freeing the Soul from Fear*. USA: Riverhead Books (Penguin)

Sardello, R. (2001) *Love and the World: A Guide to Conscious Soul Practice*. West Stockbridge, Mass.: Lindisfarne Press

Sardello, R. (2002) *The Power of Soul: Living the Twelve Virtues*. Charlottesville, Va.: Hampton Roads Publ. Co.

Sardello, R. (2004) *Facing the World with Soul: The Reimagination of Modern Life*, 2nd edn. Edinburgh: Floris Books

Sass, L.A. (1988) Humanism, hermeneutics, and the concept of the human subject. In S.B. Messer, L.A. Sass and R.L. Woolfolk (eds), *Hermeneutics and Psychological Theory* (pp. 222–71). New Brunswick: Rutgers University Press

Sayers, J. (2003) *Divine Therapy: Love, Mysticism and Psychoanalysis*. Oxford: Oxford University Press

Sayre, G. (2005) Toward a therapy for the Other. *European Journal of Psychotherapy, Counselling and Health* 7 (1–2): 37–47

Schacht, L. (1977) Introduction. In G. Groddeck *The Meaning of Illness: Selected Psychoanalytic Writings* (pp. 1–30). London: Hogarth Press (Karnac Reprint, 1988)

Schaef, A.W. (1992) *Beyond Therapy, Beyond Science: A New Model for Healing the Whole Person*. New York: HarperSanFrancisco

Schön, D. A. (1983) *The Reflective Practitioner: How Professionals Think in Action*. New York: Basic Books

Schön, D.A. (1987) *Educating the Reflective Practitioner: Toward a New Design for Teaching and Learning*. London: Jossey-Bass/Wiley

Schostak, J. and J. (2007) *Radical Research: Designing, Developing and Writing Research to Make a Difference*. London: Routledge

Schuller, G. (n.d.) The relevance of phenomenology to Theosophy. Mimeo; retrieved at http://www.alpheus.org/html/articles/philosophy/phen&theos.htm, April 2008

Scientific and Medical Network: Gibliston Mill, Colinsburgh, Leven, Fife KY9 1JS, UK

Scott, J.C. (1999) *Seeing Like a State: How Certain Schemes to Improve the Human Condition Have Failed*. New Haven: Yale University Press

Scott, M. (1989) *Kundalini in the Physical World*. London: Penguin Arkana (orig. 1983)

Searles, H.F. (1965) Problems of psychoanalytic supervision. In his *Collected Papers on Schizophrenia and Related Subjects* (pp. 584–604). London: Hogarth

Segal, J. (1985) *Phantasy in Everyday Life: A Psychoanalytic Approach to Understanding Ourselves*. Harmondsworth: Penguin

Self and Society (2004) Issue 32 (4) – Special Theme issue on the Independent Practitioners Network

Shamasundar, C. (2001) Love, praxis, and desirable therapist qualities. *American Journal of Psychotherapy* 55 (2): 273–82

Shank, G. (1993) The extraordinary ordinary powers of abductive reasoning. Paper presented at I Conferencia Internacional Sobre Los Nuevos Paradigmas de la Ciencia, University of Guadalajara, Guadalajara, Mexico, November; downloadable at http://www.education.duq.edu/FacultyStaff/shank/pdf/PDFSemiotics/1993MexicoParadigm.pdf, retrieved June 2009; reprinted in *Theory and Psychology* 8 (6), 1998: 841–60

Shepherd, M. and Sartorius, N. (eds) (1989) *Non-Specific Aspects of Treatment.* Toronto: Hans Huber

Skolimowski, H. (1994) *The Participatory Mind: A New Theory of Knowledge and of the Universe.* London: Penguin/Arkana

Slife, B.D. and Williams, R.N. (1995) *What's Behind the Research?: Discovering Hidden Assumptions in the Behavioral Sciences.* Thousand Oaks, Calif.: Sage

Sloan, T. (ed.) (2000) *Critical Psychology: Voices for Change.* Basingstoke: Macmillan

Smail, D. (1983) Psychotherapy and psychology. In D. Pilgrim (ed.), *Psychology and Psychotherapy: Current Trends and Issues* (pp. 7–20). London: Routledge & Kegan Paul

Smail, D. (1987) Psychotherapy and 'change': some ethical considerations. In S. and G. Fairbairn (eds), *Psychology, Ethics and Change* (pp. 31–43). London: Routledge & Kegan Paul

Smail, D. (1996) *How To Survive Without Psychotherapy.* London: Constable

Smail, D. (2001) *The Nature of Unhappiness.* London: Robinson

Smeyers, P., Smith, R. and Standish, P. (2007) *The Therapy of Educaton: Philosophy, Happiness and Personal Growth.* Basingstoke: Palgrave Macmillan

Smith, H. (1976) *Forgotten Truth: The Primordial Tradition.* New York: Harper and Row

Smith M. (1996–7) Psychosis and ritual transformation: insights from shamanism and the analytical psychology of C.G. Jung. *IASP Journal* 5

Smith, M.B. (1994) Selfhood at risk: postmodern perils and the perils of postmodernism. *American Psychologist* 49 (5): 405–11

Snyder, C. R., Michael, S. T. and Cheavens, J. S. (1999) Hope as a psychotherapeutic foundation of common factors, placebos, and expectancies. In M. A. Hubble, B. L. Duncan and S. D. Miller (eds), *The Heart and Soul of Change: What Works in Therapy* (pp. 179–200). Washington, D.C.: American Psychological Association

Sokal, A. and Bricmont, J. (1998) *Intellectual Impostures.* London: Profile

Solomon, R.C. (1976) *The Passions: Emotions and the Meaning of Life.* Notre Dame, Ind.: University of Notre Dame Press

Soreff, S. (1985) Symposium on alternatives to hospitalization. In S. Soreff (ed.), *The Psychiatric Clinics of North America* 8 (3). Philadelphia: W.B. Saunders

Soyini Madison, D. (2005) *Critical Ethnography: Method, Ethics, and Performance.* London: Sage

Sparkes, A.C. (2001) Autoethnography: self-indulgence or something more? In A. Bochner and C. Ellis (eds), *Ethnographically Speaking: Autoethnography, Literature and Aesthetics* (pp. 209–32). Walnut Creek, Calif.: Altamira

Spears, R. (1996) Introduction. In T. Ibanez and L. Iniguez (eds), *Critical Social Psychology* (pp. 1–26). London: Sage

Spinelli, E. (1994/2006) *Demystifying Therapy.* London: Constable; republished 2006 by PCCS Books, Ross-on-Wye

Spinelli, E. (1996) Do therapists know what they're doing? In I. James and S. Palmer (eds), *Professional Therapeutic Titles: Myths and Realities* (pp. 55–61). Leicester: British Psychological Society, Div. Couns. Psychol., Occasional Paper 2

Spinelli, E. (2005a) *The Interpreted World: An Introduction to Phenomenological Psychology,* 2nd edn. London: Sage

Spinelli, E. (2005b) Phenomenological research. In his *The Interpreted World: An Introduction to Phenomenological Psychology,* 2nd edn (pp. 128–42). London: Sage

Spinelli, E. and Longman, J. (1998) Counselling and the abuse of power. *Counselling* (BAC) 9 (3): 181–4

Sprague, J. (2005) *Feminist Methodologies for Critical Researchers: Bridging Differences.* Lanham, Md.: AltaMira Press

Stainton Rogers, W. (2009) Research methodology. In D. Fox, I. Prilleltensky and S. Austin (eds), *Critical Psychology: An Introduction,* 2nd edn (pp. 335–54). London: Sage

Standish, P. (2001) Ethics before equality: moral education after Levinas. *Journal of Moral Education* 30 (4): 339–48

Standish, P. (2002) Essential Heidegger: poetics of the unsaid. In M. Peters (ed.), *Heidegger, Modernity and Education* (pp. 151–70). Lanham, Maryland: Rowman & Littlefield

Stein, H.S. (1985) *The Psychodynamics of Medical Practice: Unconscious Factors in Patient Care.* Berkeley: University of California Press

Steiner, G. (1978) Has truth a future? *The Listener* 12th January: 42–6

Steiner, G. (1989) *Real Presences.* London: Faber and Faber

Steiner, R. (1926) *The Essentials of Education: Five Lectures...* London: Anthroposophical Publ. Co.

Steiner, R. (1928; orig. 1921) On Anthroposophy and the threefold social order. *Anthroposophical Movement* 5 (29), 15 July: 225–7

Steiner, R. (1938) *The Education of the Child in the Light of Anthroposophy.* London: Rudolf Steiner Press; New York: Anthroposophic Press

Steiner, R. (1966) *The Evolution of Consciousness as Revealed through Initiation-knowledge,* 2nd edn. London: Rudolf Steiner Press (orig. 1926)

Steiner, R. (1968) *The Roots of Education.* London: Rudolf Steiner Press

Steiner, R. (1972; orig. 1919) *The Threefold Social Order.* Spring Valley, NY: Anthroposophic Press

Steiner, R. (1987) *Materialism and the Task of Anthroposophy.* Hudson, NY: Anthroposophic Press

Steiner, R. (1988a) *The Science of Knowing: Outline of an Epistemology Implicit in the Goethean World View with Particular Reference to Schiller.* New York: Mercury Press

Steiner, R. (1988b) *The Child's Changing Consciousness and Waldorf Education.* Hudson, NY, and London: Anthroposophic Press and Rudolf Steiner Press

Steiner, R. (1989) *Knowledge of the Higher Worlds, How is it Achieved?* London: Rudolf Steiner Press (orig. 1918)

Steiner, R. (1990) *Psychoanalysis and Spiritual Psychology: Five Lectures, 1912–21.* New York: Anthroposophic Press

Steiner, S. (1999) Why it's good to talk to a therapist. *The Times* 1st July

Stiles, W.B. and Shapiro, D.A. (1989) Abuse of the drug metaphor in psychotherapy process-outcome research. *Clinical Psychology Review* 9: 521–44

Stiles, W. B., Honos-Webb, L. and Surko, M. (1998) Responsiveness in psychotherapy. *Clinical Psychology: Science and Practice* 5: 439–58

Stronach, I. and Maclure, M. (1997) *Educational Research Undone: The Postmodern Embrace.* Buckingham: Open University Press

Sundararajan, L. (2002) Humanistic psychotherapy and the scientist-practitioner debate: an 'embodied' perspective. *Journal of Humanistic Psychology* 42 (2): 34–47

Tankha, H. (ed.) (1992) *The Krishnamurti Index. 1. Full Index: Audio and Video Recordings, 1965–86.* Brockwood Park, Hants: Krishnamurti Foundation Trust

Tantam, D. and van Deurzen, E. (1998a) Creating a European profession of psychotherapy: The European Certificate of Psychotherapy. *European Journal of Psychotherapy, Counselling and Health* 1 (1): 121–40

Tantam, D. and van Deurzen, E. (1998b) Letter to the Editor. *European Journal of Psychotherapy, Counselling and Health* 1 (3): 504–5

Tarnas, R. (1991) *The Passion of the Western Mind: Understanding the Ideas that Have Shaped Our World.* New York: Ballantine

Thorne, B. (2002a) *The Mystical Power of Person-Centred Therapy: Hope Beyond Despair.* London: Whurr

Thorne, B. (2002b) Regulation – a treacherous path? *Counselling and Psychotherapy Journal,* March: 4–5; reprinted in Y. Bates and R. House (eds), *Ethically Challenged Professions: Enabling Innovation and Diversity in Psychotherapy and Counselling* (pp. 148–50). Ross-on-Wye: PCCS Books

Totton, N. (1992) Therapists on the couch. *i to I*: July–Sept.

Totton, N. (1994) Letter to the editor. *Self and Society* 21 (6): 47

Totton, N. (1995) The Independent Therapists' Network. *Self and Society* 23 (3): 31–3

Totton, N. (1997a) Learning by mistake: client–practitioner conflict in a self-regulated network. In R. House and N.Totton (eds), *Implausible Professions* (pp. 315–20). Ross-on-Wye: PCCS Books; 2nd edn, 2001 (in press)

Totton, N. (1997b) Conclusion (with R. House). In R. House and N. Totton (eds) *Implausible Professions: Arguments for Pluralism and Autonomy in Psychotherapy and Counselling* (pp. 335–7). Ross-on-Wye: PCCS Books; 2nd edn, 2011 (in press)

Totton, N. (1997c) The Independent Practitioners Network: a new model of accountability. In R. House and N. Totton (eds), *Implausible Professions: Arguments for Pluralism and Autonomy in Psychotherapy and Counselling* (pp. 287–93). Ross-on-Wye: PCCS Books; 2nd edn, 2011 (in press)

Totton, N. (1997d) Not just a job: psychotherapy as a spiritual and political practice. In R. House and N. Totton (eds), *Implausible Professions: Arguments for Pluralism and Autonomy in Psychotherapy and Counselling* (pp. 129–40). Ross-on-Wye: PCCS Books; 2nd edn, 2011 (in press)

Totton, N. (ed.) (2003) *Psychoanalysis and the Paranormal: Lands of Darkness.* London: Karnac Books

Toulmin, S. (1990) *Cosmopolis: The Hidden Agenda of Modernity.* Chicago: University of Chicago Press

Trifonas, P. P. (2004) Auditing education: deconstruction and the archiving of knowledge as curriculum. *Parallax* Issue 31, 10 (2): 37–49

Twemlow, S.W. (2001) Training psychotherapists in attributes of 'mind' from Zen and psychoanalytic perspectives, Part 1: Core principles, emptiness, impermanence, and paradox. *American Journal of Psychotherapy* 55 (1): 1–21

Usher, R., Bryant, I. and Johnston, R. (1997) *Adult Education and the Postmodern Challenge:*

Learning beyond the Limits. London: Routledge

van den Brink, M. (1996) *More Precious than Light: How Dialogue Can Transform Relationships and Build Community.* Stroud: Hawthorn Press

van den Brink, M. (2004) *Transforming People and Organizations: The Seven Steps of Spiritual Development.* London: Temple Lodge

van Deurzen-Smith, E. (1996) The future of psychotherapy in Europe. *International Journal of Psychotherapy* 1 (1): 121–40

van Deurzen-Smith, E. (1997) Counselling: Registration – what it will mean to you the counsellor. Paper presented at the 5th St George's Counselling in Primary Care Conference, London

van Deurzen Smith, E. and Jones, D. (1995) An interview with Emmy. *Self and Society* 23 (4): 41–2

van Manen, M. (1986) *The Tone of Teaching*, Richmond Hill, Ontario: TAB Publishers

van Manen, M. (1990) *Researching Lived Experience: Human Science for an Action Sensitive Pedagogy.* Albany: SUNY Press

van Manen, M. (1991) *The Tact of Teaching: The Meaning of Pedagogical Thoughtfulness.* New York: SUNY Press

Vandenberg, D. (1971) *Being and Education: An Essay in Existential Phenomenology.* Englewood Cliffs, NJ: Prentice-Hall

von Eckartsberg, R. (1998) Introducing existential-phenomenological psychology. In R. Valle (ed.), *Phenomenological Inquiry in Psychology: Existential and Transpersonal Dimensions* (pp. 1–20). New York: Plenum Press

Wallach, M.A. and Wallach, L. (1983) *Psychology's Sanction for Selfishness: The Error of Egotism in Theory and Therapy.* San Francisco: W.H. Freeman

Walsh, R.D. (2005) Beyond therapy: Levinas and ethical therapeutics. *European Journal of Psychotherapy, Counselling and Health* 7 (1–2): 29–35

Walsh, R. and Vaughan, F. (1993) The art of transcendence: an introduction to common elements of transpersonal practices. *Journal of Transpersonal Psychology* 25 (1): 1–9

Ward, G. (ed.) (1997) *The Postmodern God: A Theological Reader.* Bognor Regis, Sussex: WileyBlackwell

Warren, J. (2005) Towards an ethical-hermeneutics. *European Journal of Psychotherapy, Counselling and Health* 7 (1–2): 17–28

Wasdell, D. (1989) Constraints encountered in the conduct of psychosocial analysis. London: Unit for Research into Changing Institutions

Wasdell, D. (1990) The roots of the common unconscious; Meridian Monographs 1. London: Unit for Research into Changing Institutions

Wasdell, D. (1992) In the shadow of accreditation. *Self and Society* 20 (1): 3–14; reprinted in R. House and N. Totton (eds), *Implausible Professions* (pp. 19–31). Ross-on-Wye: PCCS Books; 2nd edn, 2011 (in press)

Waterman, C. (1946) *The Three Spheres of Society.* London: Faber and Faber

Watts, M. (2001) *Heidegger: A Beginner's Guide.* London: Hodder and Stoughton

Wehr, G. (2002) *Jung and Steiner: The Birth of a New Psychology* (with 'The Riddles of the Soul: Depth Psychology and Anthroposophy' by Hans Erhard Lauer), trans. Magdalene Jaeckel. Great Barrington, Mass.: Anthroposophic Press (orig. 1990)

West, W. (1998) Therapy as a spiritual process. In C. Feltham (ed.), *Witness and Vision of the Therapists* (pp. 158–79). London: Sage

Wheeler, S. (1998) Challenging the core theoretical model: a reply to Colin Feltham.

Counselling 9 (2): 134–8

White, M. (1991) Deconstruction and psychotherapy. *Dulwich Centre Newsletter* 3: 21–40

White, M. and Epston, D. (1990) *Narrative Means to Therapeutic Ends*. Adelaide: Dulwich Centre Publications

Wickett, R.E.Y. (2005) The spiritual and human learning. In P. Jarvis and S. Parker (eds), *Human Learning: A Holistic Approach* (pp.157–67). London: Routledge

Wilber, K. (1998) *The Marriage of Sense and Soul: Integrating Science and Religion*. Dublin: Newleaf

Wilensky, H.L. (1964) The professionalization of everyone? *American Journal of Sociology* 70 (2): 137–58

Wilkinson, H. (1999) Editorial: Psychotherapy, fascism and constitutional history. *International Journal of Psychotherapy* 4 (2): 117–26

Williams, R.N. (2005) Self-betraying emotions and the psychology of heteronomy. *European Journal of Psychotherapy, Counselling and Health* 7 (1–2): 7–16

Willig, C. and Stainton-Rogers, W. (eds) (2008) *SAGE Handbook of Qualitative Research in Psychology*. London: Sage

Winnicott, D.W. (1965) Morals and education. In his *Maturational Processes and the Facilitating Environment: Studies in the Theory of Emotional Development*. New York: International Universities Press

Winnicott, D.W. (1971/1974) *Playing and Reality*. Harmondsworth: Tavistock/Penguin

Wodak, R. and Chilton, P.A. (eds) (2007) *A New Agenda in Critical Discourse Analysis: Theory, Methodology and Interdisciplinarity*. Amsterdam: John Benjamins Pub Co.

Woodhouse, M. B. (1996) *Paradigm Wars: Worldview for a New Age*. Berkeley, Calif.: Frog

Woolfolk, R.L. and Richardson, F. (2008) Behaviour therapy and the ideology of modernity – revisited. In R. House and D. Loewenthal (eds), *Against and For CBT: Towards a Constructive Dialogue?* (pp. 52–71). Ross-on-Wye: PCCS Books

Young, R.M. (1993) The profession of psychotherapy in Britain. *Free Associations* 29: 79–84

Zajonc, A.J. (2003) Spirituality in higher education: overcoming the divide. *Liberal Education* 89 (1): 50–8

Zajonc, A.J. (2009) Vision and work: shaping the future of further and higher education – the path ahead. London: Crossfields Institute seminar, Rudolf Steiner House, 24 June

INDEX

IN THE END

Do you really know, really know where I came from
and where I am going?

Isn't there still a mystery in your quest,
in our quest?

Isn't there still a big uncertainty about
many of the questions I bring with me?

In the end perhaps my quest is
the same as yours;
In the end perhaps all I need is to share
the mystery of who I strive to become,
with you.

In the end, it may not even be
what I become that is important,
but that you and I together accept
that we are mysteriously…
becoming.

Sylvie Hétu